Common Principles of Psychotherapy

Chris L. Kleinke
University of Alaska Anchorage

Brooks/Cole Publishing Company
Pacific Grove, California

I**T**P ™ The trademark ITP is used under license.

A CLAIREMONT BOOK

Brooks/Cole Publishing Company
A Division of Wadsworth, Inc.

Printed in the United States of America

10 9 8 7 6 5 4 3 2 1

Library of Congress Cataloging-in-Publication Data
Kleinke, Chris L.
    Common principles of psychotherapy / Chris L. Kleinke.
      p.   cm.
    Includes bibliographical references and index.
    ISBN 0-534-09998-4
    1. Psychotherapy. 2. Psychotherapy—Vocational guidance.
I. Title.
RC480.5.K54   1993
616.89'14—dc20   93-30265
                                                     CIP

Sponsoring Editor: *Claire Verduin*
Marketing Representative: *Tamy Stenquist*
Editorial Associate: *Gay C. Bond*
Production Editor: *Kirk Bomont*
Manuscript Editor: *Barbara Kimmel*
Permissions Editor: *May Clark*
Interior Design: *Roy R. Neuhaus*
Cover Design: *Karen Marquardt*
Art Coordinator: *Lisa Torri*
Typesetting: *Kachina Typesetting Inc.*
Cover Printing: *Color Dot Graphics, Inc.*
Printing and Binding: *Arcata Graphics/Fairfield*

To the memory of
Tom Besh

Preface

The "state of the art" in psychotherapy lies in defining commonalities among various schools of psychotherapy, and *Common Principles of Psychotherapy* is directed toward this goal. This book will be of interest to students and professionals who wish to learn what various theories and schools of thought have in common. The ideas in this book are based on the writings of influential psychotherapists from a wide range of backgrounds and on research findings published in major professional journals. An attempt is made to offer practical suggestions that psychotherapists can use in their work with clients.

Chapter 1 discusses shared therapeutic components that are defined by Jerome Frank; Judd Marmor; Nicholas Hobbs; Marvin Goldfried; John Paul Brady; Toksoz Karasu; Hans Strupp; Lisa Grencavage and John Norcross; and William Stiles, David Shapiro, and Robert Elliott. Common processes outlined in this chapter include paying a fee for a service, giving advice, helping clients expand their worldview, the client's recapitulation of generic conflicts, the corrective emotional experience, enhancing positive expectations, experiencing emotions, social influence, and practicing new skills.

Chapter 2 begins by discussing the following principles: (1) pathology is not necessary as an explanatory concept, (2) the goal of therapy is change rather than cure, and (3) clients are responsible for making changes in their lives. Common therapeutic goals are outlined, including overcoming demoralization and gaining hope, enhancing mastery and self-efficacy, overcoming avoidance, accepting life's realities, and achieving insight.

Chapter 3 focuses on psychotherapy skills. This chapter includes a discussion of desirable therapist characteristics, including such skills as responsiveness, verbal immediacy, verbal skills, speaking skills, the power of humor, communication skills (the language of metaphor and the language of paradox), helpful therapist behaviors, and avoidance of common mistakes in psychotherapy.

Chapter 4 is devoted to the therapeutic relationship. Attention is given to the power of empathy, the contrast between the therapeutic relationship and friendship, the distinction between content and process, the value of focusing on the here-and-now, the therapist's sensitivity to client frustrations, and client and therapist self-disclosure.

Chapter 5 focuses on suggestions for helping clients effect change. The chapter begins with a discussion of the following four principles: (1) clients must work at their own pace, (2) the client is the agent of change, (3) change requires action, and (4) change requires risks. Attention is given to the issue of resistance and strategies for managing resistance. Good moments in psychotherapy sessions are described, and suggestions are given for using paradoxical interventions and metaphors, for facilitating treatment adherence, and for maintaining therapeutic gains.

Chapter 6 discusses the satisfactions and challenges of psychotherapy as a career. Attention is given to impairments suffered by psychotherapists, suggestions are provided for coping with burnout, and strategies are offered for dealing with difficult clients. The chapter concludes with an introduction to the topic of multicultural competence.

Chapter 7 is devoted to a discussion of ethical principles for psychotherapists. These include competence, informed consent, dual relationships, confidentiality, professional relationships, record keeping, and public representation. Relevant legal issues are summarized, and suggestions are given for complying with legal and ethical obligations.

Chapter 8 explains how therapists can optimize their effectiveness with clients. The chapter begins with a description of how clients decide to come to therapy and with the challenge of clients who drop out of therapy prematurely. Guidelines are offered for assessing a client's likelihood of success and for preparing clients who decide to enter therapy. The importance of negotiating the client/therapist relationship is emphasized, and a number of useful psychotherapeutic strategies are presented. Time-limited therapy is discussed as a viable approach for many clients.

Chapter 9 outlines a coping-skills model of assessment, a developmental model of assessment, Arnold Lazarus' BASIC-ID, and the following five themes that often become the focus of psychotherapy: losses, interpersonal conflicts, symptoms, personality disorders, and cognitive and social development. Arguments are given about the values and disadvantages of clinical diagnoses, and biases in clinical judgment are described and discussed. This chapter also provides a list of useful questions to ask clients when completing an assessment.

Chapter 10 discusses two important processes in psychotherapy: goal setting and termination. An outline is presented regarding purposes of goals, selecting goals, and defining goals. The importance of appropriate termination with clients is emphasized. Consideration is given to setting termination goals, deciding when to terminate, initiating termination, and handling premature termination. The chapter also addresses how termination affects clients and therapists, presents a model for terminating therapy, and offers guidelines for successful termination.

Chapter 11 begins with a discussion of psychotherapists' values and the implications these values have for psychotherapy. Values suggested for consideration include autonomy, learned resourcefulness, sense of coherence, mindfulness, flexibility, taking a salutogenic approach, happiness, positive illusions, optimism, possible selves, social interest, and forgiveness. The chapter concludes by outlining the importance of finding meaning in life through purpose, value, efficacy, and self-worth.

Chris L. Kleinke

Contents

♦ Chapter 3

Psychotherapy Skills 51

♦ Chapter 4

The Therapeutic Relationship 81

♦ **Chapter 5**

Helping Clients Change   103

◆ Chapter 6

Professional Challenges   127

♦ Chapter 9

Assessment 195

♦ Chapter 10

Goal Setting and Termination 219

◆ Chapter 11

Some Philosophical Issues   241

CHAPTER 1

The Therapeutic Process

INTRODUCTION: A DEFINITION OF PSYCHOTHERAPY

The word *psycho* comes from the Greek *psyche*, meaning spirit, soul, or being (Breggin, 1991). The word *therapy* comes from the Greek *therapeutikos*, meaning attendant or one who takes care of another. Therefore, *psychotherapy* means to care for or attend to another person's spirit, soul, or being. Psychotherapists do this by listening to their clients, taking them seriously, offering understanding and respect, and responding in a way that will help clients find solutions to their problems. There are as many definitions of psychotherapy as there are books written about it, but Jerome Frank (1982) provides an excellent place to start:

> Psychotherapy is a planned, emotionally charged, confiding interaction between a trained socially sanctioned healer and a sufferer. During this interaction the healer seeks to relieve the sufferer's distress and disability through symbolic communications, primarily words but also sometimes bodily activities. The healer may or may not involve the patient's relatives and others in the healing rituals. Psychotherapy also often includes helping the patient to accept and endure suffering as an inevitable aspect of life that can be used as an opportunity for personal growth. (p. 10)

Some professionals dislike the term *psychotherapy* because they don't want to be identified with providing a treatment or cure. Although the term *counseling* doesn't carry the implication of treatment and cure, it is often identified with reassuring people and giving them advice. Thomas Szasz (1988) suggested the term *iatrologic*, which refers to provision of "healing words." Whereas iatrologic may provide the most accurate description of the profession described in

1

this book, it is not a familiar term to most people. Although I have chosen to use the terms *psychotherapy* and *psychotherapist*, I trust that professionals who call themselves by other names will be able to incorporate the principles described here into their work. Furthermore, I refer to the people who pay for the services provided by psychotherapists as *clients*, with the realization that other professionals prefer the term *patients.*

FINDING COMMONALITIES IN THERAPIES

In 1980, Herink published a book identifying more than 250 different therapies, and in the following year Corsini combined these into a handbook of 64 innovative psychotherapies (Corsini, 1981). Given the proliferation of theories, techniques, and approaches to psychotherapy and the desire of many therapists to be recognized, appreciated, admired, and exalted, it is not surprising that Colby (1964) would begin his chapter on psychotherapy processes for the *Annual Review of Psychology* with the words "Chaos prevails." In his address to the 1989 Convention of the American Psychological Association, Arnold Lazarus (1990a) updated Colby's characterization of the state of affairs in psychotherapy by adding the terms *confusion, derangement, turmoil,* and *bedlam.*

> Have you ever really listened to a debate between two or more therapists who are strongly committed to a particular orientation? Meaningful discourse and intelligent communication between and among them does not seem possible. It is like asking a fundamentalist who understands only English to debate a nuclear physicist who understands only Chinese. (Lazarus, 1990a, p. 355)

Others have also commented on the proliferation of psychotherapeutic schools. Omer and London (1988) described how social introductions used to begin with "What's your sign?" and introductions between psychotherapists began with "What's your school?" Albert Bandura (1969) urged therapists to dispense with the use of "brand names" for identifying their services, and Thomas Szasz (1985b) offered the following opinion:

> Our field is full of various sects: Freudians, Jungians, Rankians, Reichians, Frommians, transactionalist, rational-emotive, reality. The English language is not big enough to fill it. Now if this isn't what the therapists wanted, I don't think the patients, the clients, could themselves dream up these roles. [Therapists] want what parents want. They want to reproduce their own kind. Because as soon as a therapist becomes any good, the first thing he does is found a school and makes more of his own.

There has been a growing desire among therapists to identify commonalities in the psychotherapeutic process. Historical overviews of attempts to integrate various approaches to psychotherapy are provided by Goldfried and Newman (1986) and Arkowitz (1992). In 1982, Goldfried edited a book on this topic, and in 1986 the American Psychological Association devoted the February issue of the *American Psychologist* to the identification of common principles in psychotherapy. The *Handbook of Eclectic Psychotherapy* was also published in 1986 (Norcross, 1986a). Since that time, a significant number of psychotherapists have expressed an interest in tying together workable principles from various approaches to psychotherapy. Two journals presently devoted to this goal are the *Journal of Integrative and Eclectic Psychotherapy* and the *Journal of Psychotherapy Integration*.

Fortunately, our approach toward therapeutic processes can be constructive. There are two ways out of the morass. First, we can appreciate that there are as many innovative approaches to psychotherapy as there are psychotherapists; it is just that some therapists are more vocal than others. Second, we can search for things that therapists have in common. After all, even though therapists may differ in their personalities, temperaments, worldviews, and even in their theories about how people change, there are similarities in how they practice their craft. Marvin Goldfried advises that the best level of abstraction for seeking commonalities in psychotherapy lies in the area of *strategies* or *principles* of change (Goldfried, 1980a; Goldfried & Safran, 1986).

Goldfried (1980a) aptly set the stage for the endeavor to seek rapprochement among so-called competing schools of therapy with the following admonition:

> Clearly, we need to rewrite our textbooks on psychotherapy. In picking up the textbook of the future, we should see in the table of contents *not* a listing of School A, School B, and so on—perhaps ending with the author's attempt at integration—but an outline of the various agreed-upon intervention principles, a specification of varying techniques for implementing each principle, and an indication of the relative effectiveness of each of these techniques together with their interaction with varying presenting problems and individual differences among patients/clients and therapists. (pp. 997–998)

COMMON THERAPEUTIC STRATEGIES AND PRINCIPLES

The purpose of this book is to outline therapeutic principles that appear to be shared by all psychotherapists. A number of researchers have outlined common components in psychotherapy. In this section, the shared therapeutic components defined by nine representatives of this group are discussed. All the researchers listed here emphasize the areas of strategies or principles of change common in the therapeutic process.

Jerome Frank Frank (1982) identifies the following four therapeutic components shared by all forms of psychotherapy.

1. *An emotionally charged, confiding relationship with a helping person (or persons).* All therapists appreciate the importance of the therapeutic relationship, and they strive to use this relationship in the most constructive way possible.
2. *A healing setting.* The healing setting provides structure and formality to the therapy process and helps to distinguish therapy from friendship or casual conversation. The use of a healing setting (whether it be a hospital, clinic, or office) also enhances the client's expectation that a special kind of work is going to take place.
3. *A rationale, conceptual scheme, or myth.* The rationale provides a plausible explanation for the client's symptoms and prescribes a ritual or procedure for resolving them. The point here is that it doesn't matter so much what kind of therapeutic rationale is followed, as long as both the client and therapist agree about its use and have faith in it.
4. *A ritual.* The ritual requires active participation of both client and therapist and is believed by both to be the means of restoring the client's well-being.

Judd Marmor Marmor (1985) delineates the following commonalities in psychotherapeutic principles.

1. A *client/therapist relationship,* in which clients come seeking help from a person who is endowed with help-giving potential. Two significant components of the therapeutic relationship are *transference* and *countertransference.*
2. The ability of clients to *confide and express feelings* to a person whom they trust and count on as being supportive and understanding. This release of emotions takes place in an atmosphere of positive expectancy and hope.
3. A certain amount of *cognitive learning* that gives clients an intelligible and meaningful framework for understanding their problems.
4. *Operant conditioning* through which the therapist (explicitly or implicitly) expresses approval or disapproval of certain client behaviors.
5. A *corrective emotional experience* characterized by a new and different kind of response given by the therapist to the client.
6. *Modeling* through which clients incorporate the values and skills of the therapist.

7. *Suggestion and persuasion* by the therapist.
8. *Rehearsal and practice* of skills and new adaptive techniques that are learned by the client in therapy.
9. A *supportive atmosphere* in which the therapist is sufficiently nondirective to facilitate the client's autonomy.

Nicholas Hobbs   Hobbs (1962) has outlined five areas of change that occur in all forms of psychotherapy.

1. A therapeutic relationship is established in which it is possible for the client to be close to another person without getting hurt.
2. A process occurs through which other people, objects, events, or thoughts are divested of their anxiety-producing potential.
3. A transference relationship is created through which the client learns that certain neurotic stratagems are not effective.
4. Locus of control for the client's problem is transferred to the client.
5. The client is helped to develop an acceptable sense of meaning for life.

Marvin Goldfried   Goldfried (1980a) emphasizes these two areas of commonality in psychotherapy: a new, corrective experience and feedback.

1. *Corrective experience.* The notion of the corrective experience implies that the client will *do* things. The client takes risks and tries new ways of thinking and acting.
2. *Feedback.* Therapists arrange for clients to get feedback and to learn about themselves, to view themselves, and to understand their thoughts and actions from a different perspective. Feedback is offered directly by the therapist and is also achieved by teaching the client to engage in self-monitoring and self-observation.

John Paul Brady   Brady (Brady et al., 1980) lists the following six strategies and principles that all therapeutic orientations have in common.

1. Development of a therapist/client relationship characterized by trust, mutual respect, and positive emotional feelings.
2. Procedures and strategies that will increase the client's expectation of a positive outcome or a benefit from the treatment program.
3. Strategies and procedures that will increase the client's sense of self-worth, mastery of the environment, and general effectiveness.
4. Related to the above, tactics and strategies that will make the client more effective in handling certain situations and in overcoming maladaptive fears; to help the client act in a manner or engage in behaviors that, in the client's view and in that of others, make the client a worthwhile, effective person.

5. The client's new ways of behaving, thinking, and feeling in therapy, whether through simple discussion, role playing, or the like, need to be practiced in the natural environment to ensure their persistence and generalization, and details of these experiences should be brought back to the therapist.
6. The client should be encouraged to view his or her behavior, thoughts, and feelings as ultimately under his or her control; the client must assume responsibility for change in treatment.

Toksoz Karasu　Karasu (1986) suggests these three commonalities shared by psychotherapies: affective experiencing, cognitive mastery, and behavioral regulation.

1. *Affective experiencing.* Affective experiencing is a necessary by-product of the commitment to face unpleasant aspects of one's life and to take risks by attempting new coping responses. Affective experiencing also sets the emotional stage for receptivity to change. It prepares clients for new cognitive input.
2. *Cognitive mastery.* Cognitive mastery involves providing clients with a new way of thinking and a different perspective on life. This is accomplished by giving interpretations and information and by teaching clients to modify the way they interpret events in their lives.
3. *Behavioral regulation.* All therapies require that clients make changes in their behaviors. This is accomplished when clients make a commitment to practice new ways of responding in their everyday lives.

Hans Strupp　Two common processes in psychotherapy identified by Strupp (1986) are the creation of an interpersonal context and therapeutic learning.

1. *Creation of an interpersonal context.* This notion is similar to Frank's (1978) description of the therapeutic relationship and healing setting. The therapist seeks to create a climate or atmosphere in which the client can feel free to share personal problems, experience painful emotions, and take risks. The therapist works with the client to form a therapeutic alliance and a collaborative working relationship.
2. *Therapeutic learning.* This process includes unlearning old lessons that are not working in the client's favor and learning or relearning new ways of acting and thinking that are more adaptive. During this process, the client gains personal insight. The therapist's goal is to become a better teacher or mentor than significant figures in the client's past have been.

William Stiles, David Shapiro, and Robert Elliott   Stiles, Shapiro, and Elliott (1986) suggest three common cores of psychotherapy: therapist factors, client behavior, and the therapeutic alliance.

1. *Therapist factors.* Therapists offer empathy, acceptance, unconditional positive regard, and warmth to their clients. Therapists also provide clients with a new perspective on their problems and their life.
2. *Client behavior.* Clients actively participate in the therapeutic process by engaging in self-exploration and self-disclosure. Clients are also encouraged to have positive expectations and a belief that they can change and that therapy can be helpful.
3. *Therapeutic alliance.* All therapies rely on building a strong therapeutic alliance between the therapist and the client. The therapeutic alliance provides an emotional bond and a sense of trust, and it reinforces a feeling of shared responsibility. With a good therapeutic alliance, therapists and clients believe they are on the same track and are working toward mutual goals.

Lisa Grencavage and John Norcross   Grencavage and Norcross (1990) categorized published works by psychotherapists according to their common features. The following themes were identified: client characteristics, therapist qualities, change processes, treatment structure, and therapeutic relationship.

1. *Client characteristics* most commonly mentioned by psychotherapists as important were the client's positive expectation and hope and the process of clients who are distressed actively seeking help. The point here is that clients must believe that psychotherapy can benefit them.
2. *Therapist qualities* of greatest importance were having a personality suited to cultivating the client's positive expectation for change and the ability to motivate clients with warmth, acceptance, and empathic understanding.
3. *Change processes* included affording clients the opportunity to express their emotions, helping clients acquire and practice new behaviors, providing clients with a therapeutic rationale that makes sense to them, fostering insight and enhanced awareness, and promoting emotional and interpersonal learning.
4. *Treatment structure* was defined as helping clients define their problems in a way that enhances their sense of empowerment and self-acceptance. Psychotherapists also emphasized the importance of focusing on the client as an individual with particular emotions, values, and ways of looking at the world. Also important was the notion that therapists must develop a theory of behavior and change to guide them through their therapy sessions.

5. *Therapeutic relationship* was the most frequent commonality mentioned, and it was highlighted by the development of a good alliance and close working relationship. The therapeutic relationship involves the process of emotional engagement between therapist and client, which includes the concepts of transference and countertransference.

COMMON THERAPEUTIC PROCESSES

In addition to the components just listed, there are a number of important processes common in psychotherapies. Nine common therapeutic processes that will be discussed in the remainder of this chapter are (1) exchanging a fee for a service, (2) giving advice, (3) expanding the client's worldview, (4) helping the client recapitulate generic conflicts, (5) establishing the corrective emotional experience, (6) enhancing positive expectations, (7) allowing the experiencing of emotions, (8) exerting social influence, and (9) encouraging the practicing of new skills. The establishment of the therapeutic relationship, which is also an important therapeutic process, requires greater discussion and is the topic of Chapter 4.

Exchanging a Fee for a Service

Thomas Szasz (1985a) describes the process of clients' paying a fee for a service by saying "I sell something and I collect money, and no one comes to me who doesn't pay money." What clients are paying for in Szasz's view is a Socratic dialogue based on the philosophy that two heads are better than one (Szasz, 1985b). Arnold Lazarus (1985) explains the service provided by therapists as a pooling of the client's and therapist's resources to find a solution to the client's problems. The point is that clients pay therapists for a service, or what Szasz (1985a) calls "promises." It is therefore proper for this service to be negotiated and for the client to be informed about what he or she can and cannot expect. (Informed consent is an ethical issue that will be discussed further in Chapter 7.)

Giving Advice

Harry Truman's suggestion about advising children also applies to adults: "Find out what they want to do and advise them to do it." Donald Meichenbaum (1990) applies this idea to therapy by explaining:

> I am at my therapeutic best when the clients I see are one step ahead of me offering the advice that I would otherwise offer. And the artfulness of therapy is how to provide the conditions whereby they come up with it.

Why Therapists Avoid Giving Advice

There are three reasons psychotherapists avoid giving advice to their clients. First, there is the question of whether it is ethical for clinicians to presume that they know what is best for their clients. A second reason therapists avoid advice giving is because it encourages clients to be dependent on the expertise of the therapist rather than to think for themselves. This kind of client dependence is inconsistent with the collaborative relationship emphasizing client responsibility that the therapist is trying to establish. A third reason not to give advice to clients is because it usually doesn't work. For example, one study found that advice giving discouraged participants from focusing on their feelings (Ehrlich, D'Angelli, & Danish, 1979). A second study showed that college students essentially ignored advice given that was relevant to their vocational goals (Malett, Spokane, & Vance, 1978). In their extensive review of psychotherapy studies, Orlinsky and Howard (1986) concluded that "giving advice does not appear to be an aid in psychotherapy" (p. 328). Clients can get all the advice they want from acquaintances, friends, and family members. They hardly need to pay a therapist to tell them what to do. As Harry Stack Sullivan (1970) explains:

> When patients want my advice, I am usually given to some sort of feeble witticism such as, "Why pick on me? You can ask anybody, anywhere, for advice and get it. Now why in the world waste your time with a psychiatrist by asking for advice." If a psychiatrist advises on very adequate grounds, then he is often insulting the intelligence of the person advised. If he advises without grounds, then he is just talking for his own amusement. (p. 212)

Sullivan (1970) also gives the following warning about advice giving.

> The difficulty which psychiatrists get into by rash advice is often quite pathetic. There are few things that I think are so harrowing as the occasional psychiatrist who knows a great deal about right and wrong, how things should be done, what is good taste, and so on and so forth. Such a psychiatrist often feels a missionary spirit so that he wants to pass his own values on to his patients. Not only is this hard on the patient but it also makes things difficult for any other psychiatrist who wants to get something useful done. (p. 214)

When Therapists Might Give Advice

In spite of the pitfalls of advice giving, there are occasions when it might be appropriate. These occasions occur when a client and therapist have agreed upon a course of action and the client is willing to accept the therapist's suggestions. For example, a therapist might provide a client with various kinds of referrals or suggestions about how to accomplish a goal to which the client is committed. Sullivan refers to this as a prescription of action, to distinguish it from everyday advice giving (Wachtel, 1977, p. 68). As Thomas Szasz (1990b) puts it,

"If you do X, you can expect Y." A prescription of action is negotiated with clients to ensure their cooperation. Arnold Lazarus (1985) suggests saying something such as, "I can tell you something that worked for me. Let's see if we can tailor it for you."

Another occasion when a therapist might give advice is when a client is set on doing something that is bound to be harmful. The therapist can usually help clients in these situations by encouraging them to anticipate the consequences of their actions. By taking a problem-solving approach, the therapist can reinforce the clients' feelings of choice and responsibility.

Expanding the Client's Worldview

When clients come to therapy, they are typically "stuck." They don't know how to solve their problems and the solutions they are trying are not working for them. An important process in therapy is to help clients see their problems from a new perspective and become aware of coping responses they either hadn't considered or never thought were possible. As Jerome Frank (1987) explains, psychotherapy clients learn to give new meanings to events that are causing them problems.

> All psychotherapeutic endeavors, whatever their form, transpire entirely in the realm of meanings. All psychotherapies depend on the fact that human thinking, feeling, and behavior are guided largely by the person's assumptions about reality, that is, the meanings that he or she attributes to events and experiences, rather than their objective properties. (p. 293)

Frank (1961) refers to people's expectations about what is possible for themselves and what they can expect from others as their *assumptive world*. People's assumptive worlds influence their interpretations about the meaning of others' behaviors as well as their predictions about the effects (or lack of effect) of their own actions. One's assumptive world is therefore closely related to one's ability to cope, one's emotional states, and one's feelings of well-being. Frank (1961, p. 30) believes that a major process in therapy is to help clients feel and function better by enabling them to make appropriate modifications in their assumptive worlds. It is often difficult for people to modify their assumptive worlds by themselves because the styles of thinking, feeling, and acting they have developed elicit predictable reactions from others, which in turn reinforce their assumptive worlds. It requires a therapist, who is trained *not* to respond to a client's style in this predictable manner, to show the client other possibilities, other ways of perceiving the world.

A more specific way to understand people's assumptive worlds is by defining the schemas they create for themselves. People construct a *self-schema* to define their self-worth and their possibilities for getting what they want out of life (Markus, 1977). People also construct an *interpersonal schema* (Safran, 1990a; 1990b), or a *role-relationship model* (Horowitz, 1988), that dictates how they relate to others. An interpersonal schema provides the person with what Sullivan (1953) called a *security operation;* a set of action rules for interacting with others in a way that will help the person feel safe. Examples of interpersonal schemas are:

- Being suspicious and withdrawn (or aggressive) because other people are potentially harmful.
- Taking a cautious attitude toward others because of the need to be perfectly competent and to never make mistakes.
- Feeling that one will bore others unless one is constantly active, humorous, and entertaining.
- Being passive and placating out of fear that one will be devastated without constant approval from others.

Problems occur when people's schemas become rigid and prevent them from adapting flexibly to various kinds of situations. The goal in therapy is to allow clients to experience their schemas during the therapy session, to decide whether or not these schemas are in their best interest, and to experiment with alternative styles of perceiving oneself and of interacting with others.

Paul Watzlawick (1978) broaches the question of expanding the client's worldview by defining the difference between *first-order* and *second-order reality.* First-order reality refers to the objective world. Second-order reality refers to one's perceptions of the world, which are decidedly subjective. People are influenced not by the objective world but rather by their perceptions and interpretations of this world, which is a product of their assumptive world, or second-order reality. As the Greek philosopher Epictetus pointed out, "People feel disturbed not by things, but by the views they take of them" (cited in Ellis & Harper, 1975, p. 33); or, as William Shakespeare wrote, "There is nothing either good or bad, but thinking makes it so" (*Hamlet*, act II, scene 2).

The process of modifying a client's assumptive world, or second-order reality, is explained by Albert Ellis, whose goal is to help clients evaluate the rationality of their beliefs (Ellis, 1962; Ellis & Dryden, 1987). This is done by teaching clients to challenge their reasoning and by encouraging them to take risks and attempt new solutions. Victor Frankl (1963) describes how he helped a man whose wife had recently died to gain a new perspective on this painful event.

> Once an elderly general practitioner consulted me because of his severe depression. He could not overcome the loss of his wife who had died two years before and whom he had loved above all else. Now how could I help him? What should I tell him? Well, I refrained from telling him anything, but instead confronted him with the question, "What would have happened, Doctor, if you had died first, and your wife would have had to

survive you?" "Oh", he said, "for her this would have been terrible; how she would have suffered!" Whereupon I replied, "You see, Doctor, such a suffering has been spared her, and it is you who have spared her this suffering; but now, you have to pay for it by suffering and mourning her." He said no word but shook my hand and calmly left my office. (pp. 178-179)

Another way to understand the process of expanding the client's worldview is by considering the value of teaching clients to be flexible. Paulhus and Martin (1988) define the concept of *functional flexibility* as an important feature of personal adjustment. Functional flexibility contains the following two components.

1. *Having a wide range of coping responses in one's repertoire.* For example, the more ways you know how to respond to a person who is trying to take advantage of you, the more flexible are your options when this happens. As another example, having a range of skills for getting others to like you will increase your chances of matching the way you relate to a person to his or her idiosyncrasies.
2. *Being able to match the appropriate response to the situation.* A flexible person not only has a wide range of coping responses available but also knows how to choose the appropriate response in a given situation.

Gaining a new world perspective requires not only a change in attitude but also the development of personal coping skills. Although we typically view attitude change as preceding behavior change, often the case is that behavior change precedes attitude change (Kleinke, 1978; 1984). In other words, sometimes therapists can help clients modify their assumptive worlds, or second-order realities, by showing them new insights. However, what is also important is to recognize the possibility of helping clients see their world differently by encouraging them to risk new behaviors. By acting *as if* certain goals and possibilities were true, clients gain a new reality (Watzlawick, 1990b). Heinz von Foerster explains this process by saying, "If you desire to see, learn how to act" (cited in Watzlawick, 1978, p. 127).

Helping Clients Recapitulate Generic Conflicts

One of Freud's contributions to psychotherapy was his recognition of clients' tendency to transfer unresolved conflicts from childhood to the therapist. This process was called *transference* and was viewed as a crucial element of therapy. The therapist's task was to permit a *transference neurosis* to develop and to provide appropriate insights and interpretations. The reliving of the repressed past through the process of the transference neurosis (in the safety of the therapeutic relationship) was thought to provide the client with an opportunity to overcome neurotic defenses and resistances (Wachtel, 1977, p. 37). The concept of transference has been broadened by psychotherapists since

Freud's time to include the transfer of feelings and action patterns not only from one's childhood conflicts with parents but also from significant others throughout one's life.

While clients and therapists are focusing on the client's issues and problems, an interpersonal process occurs in which clients behave toward the therapist as they have learned to behave toward other significant people in their life. Clients who have a dependent style are dependent on the therapist. Clients who are challenging and demanding are challenging and demanding toward the therapist. Clients with low self-esteem seek approval and reassurance from the therapist. Clients who are obsessive behave obsessively with the therapist. The therapist's task is to avoid responding to clients in the predictable manner. As Wachtel (1977, p. 52) points out, the therapist does not wish to become an accomplice with other significant people in the client's life by reinforcing an interpersonal style that is not in the client's best interest. Rather than reinforcing dependence, the therapist's task is to help the dependent client behave independently. Instead of confronting the challenging and demanding client with anger, the therapist's task is to help the client act more diplomatically. The therapist does not succumb to the temptation to nurture and reassure the client who has low self-esteem, but rather the therapist teaches the client to recognize his or her own competencies. The therapist avoids obsessing with the obsessive client and makes it possible for the client to experience spontaneity.

Edward Teyber (1992) explains that the key point about therapy is that clients do not just talk with therapists about their problems in an abstract manner. Rather, they recreate and act out in their relationship with the therapist the same conflicts that have led them to seek help. To resolve their problems, clients must experience in their relationship with the therapist a new and more satisfying way of responding. Hans Strupp (1989) provides the following description of this process.

> Thus, in subtle, disguised, and convoluted ways, the patient relates to the therapist as a personification from the past. In turn, this has the effect of evoking certain affective reactions that "pull for" particular responses from the therapist. In short, the therapist is being recruited to play a complementary role in the drama of the patient's making that fundamentally constitutes his or her "illness." (p. 718)

> The great paradox of therapy is that by offering another person a benign and empathic relationship one simultaneously opens the door to becoming the target of his or her accumulated frustrations, wishes, conflicts, and fears. Thus, as a therapist, one cannot avoid becoming an unwitting coactor in the patient's interpersonal drama. The course and outcome of therapy is largely determined by the manner in which the therapist approaches and deals with these recurrent challenges. (p. 719)

In traditional psychoanalysis, in which the client lies on a couch and the therapist acts as a "blank screen," transference is thought to be a distortion that comes entirely from projections of the client. However, since most therapists work with clients by interacting with them, it is reasonable to assume that transference is a two-person affair (Basescu, 1990; Strupp, 1992). The therapist's responses to the client's behaviors—especially those that are challenging and provocative—are crucial elements in the process of therapy. Therapists acknowledge their participation in the therapeutic relationship by pointing out the transactional nature of the process that occurs in the therapy session. Therapists avoid making the following kinds of statements (Safran & Segal, 1990).

- "I feel as if you are trying to control this session."
- "You seem to have difficulty trusting me."
- "You are acting out your passive style right now."

Instead, therapists communicate their feedback with statements such as the following.

- "I feel as if I am in a struggle with you right now. What are you experiencing?"
- "I have a sense that we are not really connecting. How does it feel to you?"
- "My reaction to you right now is to protect you and tell you what to do, but this makes me feel uncomfortable. What is going on with you at this moment?"

Freud used the term *countertransference* to describe the subjective reactions of the therapist toward the client. Freud originally believed that countertransference was an impediment to therapy that therapists should overcome and avoid. However, it makes more sense for therapists who interact with clients and engage them in an interpersonal relationship to use their feelings and reactions toward the client as important information to be shared with the client in appropriate ways at appropriate times (Fisher, 1990; Strupp, 1992).

Strupp (1989) outlined the following steps for therapists to consider about the process of clients' recapitulating their conflicts with the therapist.

1. The therapist is keenly aware of his or her feelings about the client and reactions toward the client's behaviors.
2. The therapist attempts to understand the meaning of the client's behaviors and how these behaviors can be understood within the context of the client's life experiences and relationships with significant others.
3. The therapist avoids playing a complementary role in the client's life dilemmas.

4. The therapist helps the client gain insight into the effects of his or her behaviors on the therapist (and on others).

If the therapist can accomplish these steps, the client is obliged to alter his or her interpersonal behaviors and is therefore provided with a *corrective experience.* Teyber (1992) explains this process in the following way.

> Furthermore, the client's developmental conflicts are not just talked about abstractly in therapy—they are brought into the present by being reenacted in the therapeutic relationship. In order to change, the therapist and client must not recapitulate the client's conflict in their interpersonal process, as so commonly occurs. Instead, they must mutually work out a resolution to the client's conflict in their real-life relationship. If this *corrective emotional experience* occurs, the therapist will be able to help the client generalize this emotional relearning to other arenas in the client's life in which the same conflicts are being enacted. Conversely, if the therapist and client only talk about issues and dynamics, but their interpersonal process does not enact a resolution of the conflicts they are discussing, change will not occur. (p. 200)

Establishing the Corrective Emotional Experience

The concept of the *corrective emotional experience* was introduced by Alexander and French (1946) to explain a central goal in therapy: "to reexpose the patient, under more favorable circumstances, to emotional situations which he/she could not handle in the past" (p. 66). Alexander and French felt that insight alone often was not sufficient to help clients make substantial changes in their life. "Rather, it is the opportunity to experience the interaction with another person *without* the feared consequences, or with outcomes contradictory to those anticipated, that leads to change" (Budman & Gurman, 1988, p. 224). The process of the corrective experience involves the following ingredients.

1. *A safe therapeutic relationship.* For a client to risk and to be receptive to the therapist's feedback, the client must have a sense of safety and trust.
2. *Therapist empathy.* Heinz Kohut (1984) points out that the main component of the corrective emotional experience is empathy. Indeed, as Carl Rogers (1957) expressed in many of his writings, receiving empathy from another person is a corrective experience because it validates one's sense of being. Rogers also pointed out that because receiving empathy and acceptance (unconditional positive regard) from others is such an uncommon occurrence, it is a unique experience that can be provided in therapy.
3. *Reexperiencing in the here-and-now.* Merton Gill (1982) argues that because the client's difficulties were acquired experientially,

they must be modified experientially (Kahn, 1991, p. 55). This modification occurs in the here-and-now of the therapeutic relationship. Clients are taught to examine their reactions to the therapist, to identify self-defeating components of these patterns, and to develop an increasingly flexible and mature interaction with the therapist (Bauer & Mills, 1989). The therapist accomplishes this by "stopping the action" at appropriate places and looking at "what just went on" (Budman & Gurman, 1988, p. 227).

4. *Responding in a way that is different from what the client expects.* Clients come to expect particular responses to their styles of interacting with others. These expectations become self-fulfilling prophecies that reinforce the clients' self-defeating styles. The therapist's task is to disconfirm the client's expectations by providing a response that is new and different—that is, *corrective.*

Some examples of how therapists avoid allowing clients to enact their maladaptive styles in therapy were given earlier in this chapter. Here are some additional examples of therapists' attempts to provide clients with new and different types of interpersonal processes.

- Clients who expect to be blamed for their misdeeds are accepted by therapists as worthwhile people.
- Clients who expect the same advice or admonition they have received from others are approached by the therapist with an openness to look at all possibilities.
- Clients who expect to have their anger and suspicion met with hostility are given understanding.
- Clients who expect to be rejected because of their depression or passivity find a therapist who has faith in their potential.
- Clients who are used to gaining acceptance by meeting the needs of others find a therapist who is willing to value them for who they are.

A famous example of a corrective emotional experience is found in Victor Hugo's novel *Les Miserables* (1862/1938). Valjean, a lifelong criminal, receives acceptance and forgiveness from a Catholic bishop. The bishop does not chastise Valjean, who has been caught stealing from him. Instead of calling Valjean a thief and asking the police to take him to jail, the bishop protects him by telling the police he had given Valjean the goods that the police believed he had stolen. This kindness totally upsets Valjean's worldview.

> He felt instinctively that this priest's forgiveness was the greatest and most formidable assault by which he had yet been shaken; that his hardening would be permanent if he resisted this clemency; that if he yielded he must renounce that hatred with which the actions of other men had filled his soul during so many years, and which pleased him; that this time he must either conquer or be vanquished, and that the struggle, a colossal and

final struggle, had begun between his wickedness and that man's good-
ness. One thing which he did not suspect is certain, however, that he was
no longer the same man; all was changed in him, and it was no longer in
his power to get rid of the fact that the bishop had spoken to him and
taken his hand. (pp. 108–109)

Another illustration of a corrective emotional experience, which is
remarkably similar to Victor Hugo's description, is found in August
Aichorn's (1925/1943) book *Wayward Youth*. Aichorn was a pioneer
in the residential treatment of delinquent children in Vienna.
Although very much influenced by the psychoanalytical thinking of
Freud, Aichorn's method fits well into the integrative approach taken
in this chapter. Aichorn describes his work with a young man who was
stealing funds from the tobacco shop. Aichorn arranged for the man to
meet with him in his office to help him dust his books.

> The "drama" was played as follows. We began our work. I inquired how he
> was getting along and gradually we approached the topic of the tobacco
> shop. "How much do you take in each week?" He mentioned a certain sum.
> We continued to dust the books. After a pause, "Does the money always
> come out right?" A hesitating, "Yes" of which I took no further notice. After
> another pause, "When do you have the most trade?" "In the morning."
> Then still later, "I must look in on you some time to go over your cash
> drawer." The boy was getting more restless all the time, but I ignored it,
> went on working and kept coming back to the tobacco shop. When I felt
> that I had intensified his uneasiness sufficiently I suddenly brought the
> crisis to a head. "Well, when we get through here I'll go and take a look at
> your cash." We had been working together for about an hour and a quar-
> ter. He stood with his back to me, took a book from the shelf, and suddenly
> let it fall. Then I took cognizance of his excitement. "What's the matter?"
> "Nothing." "*What's wrong with your cash?*" His face became distorted with
> anxiety, and he stammered out the sum. Without saying a word I gave him
> this amount. He looked at me with an indescribable expression on his face
> and was about to speak. I would not let him talk because I felt that my
> action must have time to take effect and so I sent him away with a friendly
> gesture. About ten minutes later, he came back and laid the money on the
> table, saying, "Let them lock me up. I don't deserve your help—I'll only steal
> again." He was greatly excited and was sobbing bitterly. I let him sit down
> and I began to talk to him. I did not preach, but listened sympathetically to
> what he poured out, his thievery, his attitude toward his family and to life
> in general, and everything that troubled him. The emotion gradually re-
> ceded, relieved by the weeping and talking. Finally I gave the money back
> to him, saying that I did not believe he would steal again; that he was
> worth that much to me. I said, too, that it was not a present, that he could
> smoke less and pay it back gradually. (pp. 159–161)

Aichorn explained his therapeutic approach in the following way: "Reeducation, however, is not achieved through words, admonition,
scolding, or punishment, but through what the child actually *experiences*" (p. 162, emphasis added).

Some sixty years later, Donald Meichenbaum (1986) made a similar point when he explained that the goal of the therapist is to make the therapeutic process an *irreversible experience*.

Enhancing Positive Expectations

The fact that clients do better in therapy when they have positive expectations has been well documented in experimental research (Frank, 1978; Kirsch, 1990; Luborsky, 1984). A good example of the process of enhancing clients' positive expectations can be found in hypnotherapy. The hypnotic induction given by the therapist is designed to utilize the client's perceptions and experiences to make the hypnotic experience as real as possible. However, positive expectations are an important component of all psychotherapeutic approaches and enhancing the client's expectancies for success is a major therapeutic goal. A number of methods used by therapists to instill positive expectations in their clients are described next (Kirsch, 1990, ch. 7).

Reinforcing Clients' Seeking Therapy

The first way to enhance clients' positive expectancies is to reinforce them for having come to therapy in the first place. Clients may benefit from being told that the majority of troubled people do not seek help when they need it (Wills & DePaulo, 1991). Clients should be informed that making the effort to obtain therapy indicates that they care about themselves and believe that therapy can be helpful, and it is evidence that they are motivated to seek solutions to their problems.

Preparing Clients for Therapy

For therapy to be successful, therapists and clients have to "speak the same language." They must agree that the way they are going to work together is sensible and has a good chance of being effective. Clients often don't know what to expect when they come for therapy, and they need to be instructed about what they are going to do. They need to understand and accept their roles and responsibilities, as well as those of the therapist. The process of teaching the client about the therapeutic process is called *structuring*. Structuring is defined as communication between therapist and client with the purpose of arriving at similar perceptions and expectations about (1) the therapist's and client's roles, (2) the kind of activities that will take place during therapy, and (3) the goals toward which the therapist and client are committed (Cormier & Cormier, 1991, p. 51). Frank (1978) designed a study of a role induction interview, in which clients were carefully instructed about what would happen in therapy, how therapy could help them, what they were expected to do, and what the therapist would do. Clients who received the role induction interview subsequently had better success in therapy than a comparable group of clients who were not given this treatment.

An important component of structuring is taking into account the individual perceptions, beliefs, and worldview of the client. No matter how much research can be cited to document the effectiveness of a particular approach to a particular problem, the approach has to be accepted by the client. Therapists must take the time and effort to explain the therapeutic process in the client's language. Kirsch (1990) suggests that clients with a different belief system from that of the therapist can often be convinced that the therapist's approach is relevant to their belief system. What is generally more fruitful is not to argue with clients who see the world differently but instead to suggest doing an experiment together to test out the client's hypotheses about the world. A contract can be made to try a particular approach for a limited amount of time. If the approach is not working, the client and therapist can then agree to modify their approach or try something different.

Instilling Realistic Expectations

Because therapy is rarely 100% effective and clients are bound to experience setbacks, it is critical that clients approach therapy with realistic expectations. A good metaphor for therapy is a road map showing where the client is now and where the client would like to be. The road is by no means straight, and it is certainly not paved all the way. There are bumpy sections, steep hills, stoplights, stop signs, washed-out bridges, and many detours (Ludgate & Beck, 1990). Another way to represent the course of therapy is with a graph showing time on the horizontal axis and showing progress on the vertical axis. Improvement does not occur in a steady fashion. Although the slope of the graph is generally upward, there are many plateaus and even some "downturns." Clients who expect roadblocks and relapses in therapy will be more prepared to cope with them when they occur.

Emphasizing Client Responsibility

Clients must be instructed that successful therapy depends more on their efforts than on any particular expertise possessed by the therapist. This approach discourages clients from passively depending on the therapist. Instead, clients are encouraged to take an active and self-reliant approach toward solving their problems.

Providing Symptom Relief

Therapists often benefit from spending some time looking for ways of ameliorating a client's immediate pains or concerns. The experience even of temporary relief from pressing problems or uncomfortable emotions can assure clients about the promise of therapy and encourage them to stick with therapy long enough to make more definitive changes in their lives.

Developing a Positive Therapeutic Relationship

A positive relationship between therapist and client is crucial for instilling a belief on the part of clients that therapy can help them. Clients must believe that their therapist has the knowledge and commitment necessary for working with them to reach their goals.

Allowing the Experiencing of Emotions

It is difficult to imagine a psychotherapeutic process in which clients (and therapists) don't experience emotions. Therapy is not simply an intellectual exercise in which clients talk about and analyze their problems; they also *feel* them. To understand the process of experiencing emotions in psychotherapy, one should consider three categories of emotions (Greenberg & Safran, 1987).

Primary emotions are "authentic" feelings experienced in the here-and-now. These are emotions that clients "get in touch" with in therapy and are owned by the person "at the moment." Primary emotions are spontaneous experiences that facilitate problem-solving and goal-directed behaviors. For example, the immediate experience of anger, sadness, or fear during the therapy session will motivate clients to explore the causes of these feelings and ask themselves what they can do about them.

Secondary emotions are those emotions that are disruptive to problem solving. They are the nagging emotions such as anger, depression, and anxiety that clients come to therapy to eliminate. The point of arousing secondary emotions in therapy is not to motivate clients or to provide useful insights; however, clients can best analyze the events or cognitions that precipitate secondary emotions when they are actively experienced and aroused.

Instrumental emotions are used consciously or unconsciously to achieve personal gain. Instrumental emotions are explored during the therapy session as they are recapitulated in the therapeutic relationship.

The experiencing of emotions in therapy involves six processes: acknowledgment, creation of meaning, arousal, taking of responsibility, modification of dysfunctional affective responses, and expression of feelings in the therapeutic relationship (Greenberg & Safran, 1987).

Acknowledgment

Therapists encourage clients to acknowledge their feelings by communicating a sense of interest, acceptance, and trust. Therapists teach clients to focus on themselves at the moment and to become sensitive to what their bodies, images, and thinking patterns are telling them (Gendlin, 1981). Clients learn that it is acceptable to experience emotions and that there is something to be gained by sharing them with the therapist. Acknowledging emotions is the first step in motivating clients to search for appropriate coping responses.

Creation of Meaning

Acknowledging one's emotions creates a clearer sense of self-understanding. To truly know ourselves, we need to have more than an intellectual understanding of our wants, needs, and desires—we must also feel them.

Arousal

Clients cannot fully understand their emotions by talking about them in an abstract fashion. Clients are taught to feel their emotions during therapy with the use of imagery and various kinds of interactions and exercises.

Taking of Responsibility

Clients are taught to own their feelings and to take responsibility for them. They learn to express how they are feeling in an immediate manner. They also learn how their emotions are precipitated by environmental circumstances and are moderated by their behaviors and cognitions.

Modification of Dysfunctional Affective Responses

Secondary and instrumental emotions often do not serve the client's best interests. After acknowledging and taking responsibility for these emotions, clients are usually sufficiently motivated to learn techniques for making these emotional responses more adaptive.

Expression of Feelings in the Therapeutic Relationship

During therapy, clients learn the virtues of expressing themselves openly and honestly with people whom they can trust. Having one's feelings accepted and validated is a corrective experience, and learning to accept and validate others is a valuable social skill.

Exerting Social Influence

Most psychotherapists would acknowledge that it is impossible to be completely neutral toward clients and their problems (Marmor, 1985). Therapists are bound to have beliefs, values, and ways of understanding the world that influence how they work with people. Being aware of one's beliefs and values, as well as of one's personal needs, is an ethical responsibility for psychotherapists that is discussed further in Chapter 7. However, because the therapist's goal is to "help clients change" (Kanfer & Goldstein, 1991), one should not be surprised that therapists' interactions with clients include a certain amount of social influence. Jerome Frank (1961) and Larry Beutler (1990) describe psychotherapy as a process of "persuasion." Thomas Szasz (1988; see also Frank, 1987; Glaser, 1980) defines psychotherapy by its application of *rhetoric:* using words to influence attitudes and induce actions.

Operant Conditioning

Therapists "operantly condition" their clients by selectively ignoring, reinforcing, or challenging particular themes, behaviors, and topics of conversation (Marmor, 1985). An interesting example of operant conditioning in psychotherapy is seen in a study analyzing transcripts from a therapy session conducted by Carl Rogers (Truax, 1966). Rogers tended to communicate the most empathy and acceptance when the client was engaged in self-exploration and insight. On the other hand, Rogers was most directive and least empathetic and accepting when the client was ambiguous. This selective responding by Carl Rogers appeared to enhance the client's focus on self-exploration and insight and to decrease the amount of client ambiguity.

Modeling

The therapist's goal is to serve as a good model of reality and adult behavior (Strupp, 1986, p. 126). To be an effective model, the therapist must establish a relationship of trust and acceptance. Therapists will find behaving as a *coping* rather than as a *mastery* model advantageous (Rosenthal & Steffek, 1991). Instead of telling clients how to solve their problems, therapists work together with clients to define options and possible solutions. By serving as a good example, therapists can demonstrate effective coping skills and strategies for dealing with problems.

Encouraging the Practicing of New Skills

An important process in therapy involves providing clients with the opportunity to practice new skills (Brady et al., 1980). New ways of behaving, thinking, and feeling are practiced, first in therapy, and then in the client's life. Clients record their progress in practicing their new skills and then work with the therapist to overcome any problems they are having. A common method for setting up the practicing of new skills is through the use of *homework assignments.* Homework assignments provide continuity between therapy sessions. Homework assignments also help clients generalize what they have learned in therapy sessions to their everyday lives, and homework enables clients to test out alternative ways of responding to various challenges (Okum, 1990).

Meichenbaum and Turk (1987) compiled the following guidelines for administering homework assignments.

Devising Homework Assignments

Homework assignments should be devised with the client's input and cooperation. The goals of the assignment must be realistic and the client has to agree that the assignment is worthwhile. Homework assignments should be designed to ensure that clients attribute improvements to their own efforts.

Presenting Homework Assignments

After it is established that the client believes in the value of a homework assignment and agrees to carry it out, the assignment must be clearly explained. Clients need to know the following things.

1. *What to do.* The client first practices the assignment with the therapist to make certain that it is perfectly clear.
2. *How often to do it.* A contract is drawn up specifying exactly when the client will attempt the homework assignment.
3. *How to monitor one's progress.* A recording sheet is devised to help the client monitor his or her progress.
4. *How to obtain feedback.* The therapist and client agree that the client will bring the recording sheet to therapy at regular intervals to check on the client's progress.
5. *Contingencies for completing the assignment.* The therapist and client agree on how the client can reward herself or himself for completing assignments and on what steps can be taken when the client fails to complete an assignment.

Heading Off Problems

To ensure that the client will experience success with a homework assignment, the therapist should anticipate with the client any problems that might interfere with the assignment. The following questions can be addressed:

1. Is the homework assignment clear?
2. Does the client agree that it is worthwhile?
3. Does the client possess the skills necessary to carry it out?
4. What kinds of life events might prevent the client from completing the assignment?
5. Will other people in the client's life interfere with successful completion of the assignment?

Once potential sources of interference with the homework assignment have been identified, the possibility exists for the therapist and client to come up with contingency plans. The therapist's goal is to reinforce both the belief that the homework assignment is worthwhile and the expectation that the client will carry it out and experience success.

SUMMARY

There are hundreds of schools of psychotherapy and as many innovative approaches to therapy as there are therapists. Of interest in this chapter is what these therapeutic approaches have in common. A number of different clinicians have suggested procedures that are shared by all psychotherapists. Common therapeutic processes outlined in this chapter include: (1) exchanging a fee for a service, (2) giving advice, (3) expanding the client's worldview, (4) helping clients recapitulate generic conflicts, (5) establishing the corrective emotional experience, (6) enhancing positive expectations, (7) allowing the experiencing emotions, (8) exerting social influence, and (9) encouraging the practicing of new skills.

Therapists generally do not give advice because it may be unethical, it encourages clients to be passive, and it usually does not work. Therapists may advise clients with a prescription of action after clients have committed themselves to a goal.

Therapists help clients reevaluate their assumptive worlds and recognize the difference between their first-order and second-order realities. A goal of expanding a client's worldview is to strengthen his or her functional flexibility.

A predictable occurrence in therapy is the tendency of clients to recapitulate their maladaptive styles with the therapist. The therapist's goal is to avoid becoming an accomplice in the client's dilemma. Instead, the therapist responds in a different way than the client expects, thus providing a corrective emotional experience. Factors conducive to a corrective emotional experience are a safe therapeutic relationship, therapist empathy, clients' reexperiencing in the here-and-now, and therapists' responding in a way that is different from what the client expects.

Research has indicated that clients generally respond more favorably to therapy when they have positive expectations. Positive expectations are enhanced by reinforcing clients for seeking therapy, preparing clients for therapy, instilling realistic expectations, emphasizing client responsibility, providing symptom relief, and developing a positive therapeutic relationship.

In psychotherapy, clients as well as therapists experience emotions. The experiencing of emotions in therapy involves the following processes: acknowledgment, creation of meaning, arousal, taking of responsibility, modification of dysfunctional affective responses, and expression of feelings in the therapeutic relationship.

Therapists influence their clients by using operant conditioning and modeling. Homework assignments offer clients the opportunity to practice new behaviors and ways of thinking and feeling in their everyday lives.

SUGGESTIONS FOR FURTHER READING

Frank, J. D. (1961). *Persuasion and healing* (rev. ed.). Baltimore, MD: Johns Hopkins University Press.

Frank, J. D., Hoehn-Saric, R., Imber, S. D., Liberman, B. L., & Stone, A. R. (1978). *Effective ingredients of successful psychotherapy.* New York: Brunner/Mazel.

Kirsch, I. (1990). *Changing expectations: A key to effective psychotherapy.* Pacific Grove, CA: Brooks/Cole.

Teyber, E. (1992). *Interpersonal process in psychotherapy: A guide for clinical training.* Pacific Grove, CA: Brooks/Cole.

Wachtel, P. L. (1977). *Psychoanalysis and behavior therapy: An integration.* New York: Basic Books.

Watzlawick, P. (1978). *The language of change: Elements of therapeutic communication.* New York: Basic Books.

CHAPTER 2

Psychotherapy Goals

The orientation of this book is that psychotherapy is not a "treatment" that clients receive from therapists (Marlatt & Gordon, 1985). Rather it is a working relationship between therapists and clients to find solutions to clients' problems that are more advantageous than the solutions clients are using at the present time. As Irvin Yalom (1980) states, "The therapist must determine what role a particular patient plays in his or her own dilemma, and find ways to communicate this insight to the patient." (p. 231). Thomas Szasz (1973) offers a similar description.

> In most types of voluntary psychotherapy, the therapist tries to elucidate the unexplicit game rules by which the client conducts himself; and to help the client scrutinize the goals and values of the life games he plays. (p. 109)

Allen Ivey (1986) views psychotherapy as a means of assisting clients with their development. Ivey describes life as a journey that inevitably brings people back to experiences of the past. The goal of psychotherapy is to help clients view their process of development with a greater sense of awareness of where they have come from and where they are going. This involves becoming more flexible with behaviors, beliefs, expectations, and ways of coping.

The definition of psychotherapy as a working relationship between therapists and clients has three important implications: (1) pathology is not necessary as an explanatory construct, (2) the goal is change rather than cure, and (3) clients are responsible for making changes in their lives.

FROM PATHOLOGY TO COPING

Pathology is not necessary as an explanatory construct. People come to therapy because the solutions they are applying to their problems are not working. The job of the therapist is to assess where clients are stuck and to help them get unstuck by modifying their behaviors, attitudes, and ways of thinking. Because clients' problems reside in inadequate or faulty coping styles (Kleinke, 1991), the concept of pathology is not necessary for understanding the goals of psychotherapy (Fisch, 1990). Instead of asking *why* a client is stuck with a problem, the therapist asks, *what for* (Watzlawick, 1990b). In other words, what function does a client's problem serve at this time, and how can the client be persuaded to seek alternative solutions (see Beutler, 1990). Szasz (1973) reminds us of Freud's great discovery: "For the mental patient's family and society, mental illness is a 'problem'; for the patient himself it is a 'solution'" (p. 88).

CHANGE RATHER THAN CURE

When viewing clients' problems as "problems in living" (Szasz, 1988), one becomes aware that in psychotherapy the idea of "cure" is inconceivable (Budman & Gurman, 1988, p. 13). According to Strupp (1990), "The goal is not total cure (which may be impossible under virtually all circumstances) but a significant improvement of the patient's current interpersonal difficulties, including symptoms and maladaptive interpersonal behavior" (p. 66). To improve the current conditions of their life, clients must come to the point where they believe the following (Yalom, 1980, pp. 340–341):

1. Only I can change the world I have created.
2. There is no danger in change.
3. To get what I really want, I must change.
4. I have the power to change.

The therapist's objective is to help clients appreciate that change is a *possibility*. Yalom notes, instead of asking "Why should I change?", clients must be persuaded to ask, "Why not?" Therefore, a major goal of psychotherapy is to bring clients to the point where they can make a free choice about what they want to change in their lives (1980, pp. 243, 401).

THE CLIENT IS RESPONSIBLE

Thomas Szasz (1965) explains that a client's symptoms and problems are often an expression of a loss of control—the client's inability (or unwillingness) to control his or her life. The therapist's task is to discourage the client from speaking the language of excuses ("I can't," "I couldn't help it," "I had to") and to encourage the client to speak the language of responsibility ("I want to," "I decided," "I chose").

A useful framework for understanding the client's responsibility can be found in four models of responsibility proposed by Brickman and his associates (1982). These models apply to life events for which people are assumed to be either responsible or not responsible for: (1) the cause of the problem and (2) the solution for the problem (see Table 2.1).

Moral Model

In the moral model, clients are held responsible both for causing their problems and for solving them. The moral model applies to clients who have caused problems for themselves through negligent or harmful behaviors. The advantage of the moral model for therapy is that it requires the client to be an active participant in therapy. The disadvantage is that it can result in guilt and self-blame, which is generally not therapeutic.

Enlightenment Model

The enlightenment model holds clients responsible for causing their problems but not for solving them. The enlightenment model applies to clients who need support systems to help them solve problems beyond their control. The advantage of the enlightenment model is that it encourages clients to take advantage of professional assistance. However, it also can instill guilt and self-blame as well as limit feelings of self-esteem and internal control.

Compensatory Model

The compensatory model applies to clients who do not cause their problems, but are held responsible for solving them. Some examples include rehabilitation after injury, illness, or victimization and the learning of new skills. The compensatory model has the advantage of encouraging mastery and internal control while avoiding guilt and self-blame.

Medical Model

In the medical model, clients are not held responsible either for causing their problems or for solving them. The medical model is appropriate for people who suffer from medical illnesses or physical injuries that require professional care. The medical model is inconsistent with the orientation taken toward therapy in this book, because it implies cure and treatment, which are not assumed to be the focus of psychotherapy. It is true that psychotherapy clients may receive medica-

Table 2.1 Four Models of Responsibility

Responsibility for problem	Responsibility for solution	
	High	Low
High	Moral model	Enlightenment model
Low	Compensatory model	Medical model

Source: From "Models of Helping and Coping," by P. Brickman, V. C. Rabinowitz, J. Karuza, D. Coates, E. Cohn, and L. Kidder, 1982, *American Psychologist, 37*, pp. 368–384. Copyright 1982 by the American Psychological Association. Adapted with permission of the authors.

tion for certain kinds of problems; however, if it is only medication that is given for a client's problems, it is considered to be medical treatment and not psychotherapy. For psychotherapy to occur, the client must be expected to collaborate by agreeing with the usefulness of the medication and by taking the responsibility to adhere to the prescription. In addition to prescribing medication, the therapist must engage the client in a therapeutic relationship oriented toward the kinds of goals described in this chapter.

In psychotherapy, it is not as important to determine whether clients are held responsible for *causing* their problems as it is important for therapists to offer unconditional acceptance of clients as people (Ellis & Dryden, 1987; Rogers, 1951). It is also a necessary condition of successful psychotherapy that clients and therapists agree that clients must take responsibility for seeking *solutions.* Carl Rogers (1961) emphasizes the client's responsibility for change: "Whether one calls it a growth tendency, a drive toward self-actualization, or a forward-moving directional tendency, it is the mainspring of life, and is, in the last analysis, the tendency upon which all psychotherapy depends" (p. 35). Harcum (1989) defines the acceptance of responsibility as the client's *commitment to collaboration,* which assures that "both client and therapist intend to work as a team toward a common goal" (p. 200). Seltzer (1986) defines the client's responsibility by saying "*all* therapies can be perceived as endeavoring to assist clients in comprehending the voluntariness—and thus controllability—of behaviors that have come to appear nonvolitional" (p. 164).

RECOGNIZING HOW PEOPLE AVOID RESPONSIBILITY

Once one understands the virtues of the compensatory model and of holding clients accountable for seeking solutions to their problems, one is interested to realize how different kinds of symptoms and personality styles allow people to avoid exactly this kind of responsibility (Schlenker, Weigold, & Doherty, 1991).

- People who suffer from anxiety are "unable" to make speeches, take tests, meet social obligations, or even venture out of their house.
- People who adopt an aggressive or paranoid style, with their rebuking attitude, preclude others from making requests, expecting things from them, and from holding them accountable for their behaviors.
- Depressed people are viewed as "unable" to engage in activities that would be in their best interest. By taking on an apologetic and self-condemning style, depressed people prevent others from "expecting too much" of them.
- People often avoid being held accountable for behaviors that occurred while they were under the influence of alcohol and drugs.
- Histrionic people cannot be held responsible for their "temperamental nature." Their emotionality is "beyond their control."
- Schizophrenics are too "sick" to be held responsible for almost anything. (Although it is interesting that hospitalized schizophrenics are usually not too sick to understand rules that, if broken, would deprive them of privileges.)

The preceding examples of responsibility avoidance can be defined as *self-handicapping strategies* (Higgins, Snyder, & Berglas, 1990). People who are labeled or identified as "not responsible" because of certain symptoms or problems no longer have to make excuses—they have *become* the excuse (Higgins & Berglas, 1990; Snyder, 1990). Alfred Adler (quoted by Ansbacher & Ansbacher, 1967) describes this process in the following way.

> The patient declares that he is unable to solve his task "on account of the symptoms, and only on account of these." He expects from the others the solution of his problems, or the excuse from all demands, or, at least, the granting of "extenuating circumstances." When he has his extenuating alibi, he feels that his prestige is protected. His line of success, embedded into the life process, can remain uninterrupted—by paying the price. (p. 266)

The "price" to which Adler refers is a life compromised by the problem or symptom that clients must suffer. Since self-handicapping strategies protect the client from anxiety, they are difficult to give up. Although self-handicapping strategies can often be useful coping responses (Kleinke, 1991), they are problematic when they become part of a person's personality style (Berglas, 1989). People suffer when their personality styles lead them to respond to life challenges in fixed and rigid ways without taking the time to analyze the situation and engage in problem solving (Millon, 1981). Self-handicapping is reinforced by the notion of "mental illness" and the use of diagnostic labels.

Although diagnostic labels may seem to provide answers for why people behave the way they do, the label itself can become a self-fulfilling prophecy; people with these labels act as they are *expected* to act (Snyder, 1990).

The examples of responsibility avoidance just given are not meant to imply that clients take on problems intentionally or that they don't suffer from them. Being held responsible can cause anxiety, and to be expected to control aspects of our lives about which we have limited confidence is especially frightening (Brehm & Smith, 1986). However, holding people accountable for their behaviors is also a sign of respect. The therapeutic challenge is to help clients realize that they *can* solve their problems; that they are *able to respond*. This is not done by cajoling and prodding clients but by setting up therapeutic conditions in which clients experience collaboration in the learning process, seek solutions to their problems, and take risks to experiment with new coping styles.

FUNDAMENTAL THERAPEUTIC GOALS

The specific goals in psychotherapy depend on the particular problems and desires of the client. However, there are some goals that are relevant in almost all psychotherapeutic relationships. These include (1) helping clients overcome demoralization and gain hope, (2) enhancing clients' sense of mastery and self-efficacy, (3) encouraging clients to face their anxieties rather than avoiding them, (4) helping clients become aware of their misconceptions, (5) teaching clients to accept life's realities, and (6) helping clients achieve insight. Each of these goals will be discussed in the remainder of this chapter.

Overcoming Demoralization and Gaining Hope

Jerome Frank (1961; 1982) described the feelings of demoralization experienced by most psychotherapy clients. Clients' demoralization is characterized by feelings of incompetence, low self-esteem, alienation, and hopelessness. The most common manifestations of demoralization are anxiety, loneliness, and depression.

A major goal of psychotherapy is to help clients overcome their feelings of demoralization and gain a sense of hope. C. R. Snyder and his colleagues have identified two important components of hope (Snyder, 1989; Snyder, Irving, & Anderson, 1991). The first ingredient of hope is a sense of empowerment, energy, and determination to reach one's goals. The second ingredient of hope is a sense of confidence in one's skills and in one's ability to find a suitable pathway for reaching desired goals. Therapists work with clients to enhance both of these components of hope.

Empowerment, Energy, and Determination

Hopeful people who have a sense of empowerment, energy, and determination are able to answer "yes" to the following items from the Hope Scale (Snyder, 1989).

- I've been pretty successful in my life.
- My past experiences have prepared me well for the future.
- I meet the goals I set for myself.
- I energetically pursue my goals.

There are two major ways therapists help clients increase their feelings of agency, energy, and determination (Frank, 1982, p. 21). The first involves solidifying a therapeutic relationship in which the therapist communicates to the client a willingness to understand, accept, and take seriously the client's experiences, feelings, and issues. (The therapeutic relationship is so important that it is discussed as a separate chapter in this book; see Chapter 4). A second way therapists instill agency, energy, and determination is by inspiring and maintaining the client's expectation of help. Recall that the importance of a client's positive expectancy and faith in therapy was discussed in Chapter 1.

Pathways for Reaching Goals

Hopeful people who can see many pathways toward achieving their goals are able to answer "yes" to the following items from the Hope Scale.

- I can think of many ways to get out of a jam. Even when others get discouraged, I know I can find a way to solve the problem.
- There are lots of ways around any problem.
- I can think of many ways to get things in life that are important to me.

Therapists help clients increase their ability to find successful pathways for reaching their goals by teaching new skills and by helping clients gain a different perspective on their lives and see possibilities they had never appreciated before.

When therapists help clients increase their sense of hope, they are doing more than simply making clients "feel good." The goal is to teach clients to view their problems as challenges rather than as threats (Lazarus & Launier, 1978). People who view their problems as threats tend to respond with a fatalistic attitude that encourages wishful thinking and avoidance; they don't see any way out. On the other hand, people who view their problems as challenges are able to be flexible. They see themselves as capable of finding suitable pathways for solving their problems (McCrae, 1984; Snyder, Irving, & Anderson, 1991).

Psychotherapists also facilitate their clients' sense of hope by teaching them to set goals and take responsibility for their life. Viktor Frankl (1967b, p. 104) explains this as encouraging clients to undergo a so-called Copernican reversal, such that they no longer ask *what they can expect from life* but instead commit themselves to the belief that *life is awaiting something from them*. Nietzsche made this point when he said "He who knows a *why* for living, will surmount almost every *how*" (Frankl, 1967b, p. 103).

Enhancing Mastery and Self-Efficacy

Another major goal of psychotherapy is to enhance the client's sense of "can-ness" (Combs, 1989, p. 76). Thomas Szasz (1990) explains that the goal of therapy "can only be what is called empowerment. I prefer the idea of increased independence and mastery of oneself and of the world about one. And in that sense, in the best political and economic sense, freedom. Freedom to have options." Julius Heuscher (1980) makes a similar point: "The primary fundamental function of effective psychotherapy, regardless of the biases of any one particular school, is the progressive revelation, acceptance and exercise of human freedom" (p. 467).

Clients who are stuck and demoralized and who see "no way out" are transformed through the therapeutic process to the point at which they are able to say "I *can*; I *will*; I *shall*" (Zeig, 1985). Inspiring a sense of mastery in clients is a common goal of all therapies (Liberman, 1978). As noted by Hans Strupp (1970), "One of the chief purposes of psychotherapy, if not the primary purpose, is to promote the acquisition of self-control" (p. 393).

For Freud, insight into unconscious processes resulted in increased self-control ("Where the Id was, there shall Ego be"); he used the term *Bewaltigungstreib* (drive for mastery; Liberman, 1978, p. 37). Adler believed that clients should be brought

> through various devices to the point where they necessarily acquire faith in their own mental and physical powers. . . . One must put tasks in their way which they can accomplish and from the accomplishment of which they gain faith in themselves. (Ansbacher & Ansbacher, 1956, p. 400)

One of the most influential frameworks for integrating the concepts of mastery, empowerment, and "can-ness" is Albert Bandura's concept of *self-efficacy* (Bandura, 1977; 1982). Self-efficacy refers to the perception that one has the ability to execute particular behaviors that are necessary for mastering life challenges. The concept of *self-efficacy* is based on a long tradition of research and theorizing about the importance of people's expectancies that they can cope successfully with difficult situations (Kirsch, 1986; Maddux, 1991). Self-efficacy has an important influence on a person's cognitions, motivation, and moods (Bandura, 1989).

Cognitions   Self-efficacy inspires people to set meaningful goals because they have faith that they can reach them. People with feelings of self-efficacy perceive desirable outcomes in life as possibilities that can be achieved with planning, problem solving, and acquisition of necessary skills.

Motivation   Self-efficacy inspires persistence, perseverance, and patience. People with feelings of self-efficacy don't give up easily after failing. They seek alternative ways of reaching their goals.

Mood   Because people with high self-efficacy have confidence in their coping skills, they are less prone to react to life challenges with anxiety or depression.

People with high self-efficacy are aware of their strengths and limitations. They set realistic goals and they have reasonable expectations. Because they have faith in their coping skills, they don't avoid challenges that are difficult but that they know they can master. They also know how to recognize unreasonable and unrealistic desires that, if rigidly pursued, are bound to result in disappointment.

Three dimensions of self-efficacy are magnitude, strength, and generality (Bandura, 1977; 1982).

Magnitude of self-efficacy   Magnitude of self-efficacy refers to the difficulty of challenges a person is willing to take on. Some clients, for example, may be willing to practice a new skill with the therapist but not in their outside life. Clients may be willing to be assertive with their children but not with their co-workers or their boss. A client may feel confident about speaking to small groups of people but not about addressing a large convention.

Strength of self-efficacy   Strength of self-efficacy refers to a person's convictions that he or she can perform a behavior in question. It is the difference between thinking "I *might* be able to do it" and thinking "I *know* I can do it."

Generality of self-efficacy   Generality of self-efficacy refers to the extent to which a person feels confident about being able to perform specific behaviors in a wide variety of situations. After practicing a new skill with the support of a therapist, client's are taught to use this skill in their daily life.

According to the self-efficacy model, the following three conditions must be met for a person to be willing to expend the effort to reach a goal or face a challenge (Bandura, 1977).

1. The person believes that a particular goal is reachable. The person has the expectation that if he or she is willing to expend the effort, the goal can be achieved.
2. The person believes that she or he possesses the necessary skills to reach the goal.
3. The goal has enough value to be worth the effort.

How can therapists facilitate self-efficacy in their clients? The basic process for teaching self-efficacy is to provide clients with experiences of success. This process is similar to the process of the corrective emotional experience discussed in Chapter 1. It also follows the philosophy of taking a *mastery-oriented* rather than *performance-oriented* approach toward life challenges (Dweck & Leggett, 1988; Elliott & Dweck, 1988). People who are performance-oriented focus on judgments they receive from others. Since their primary concern is to avoid failure, they face challenges with anxiety and trepidation. They are cautious about setting goals that require taking risks. Performance-oriented people tend to say the following kinds of things to themselves.

• What will people think of me?
• There is nothing to be gained from failure.
• Making a good impression is more important than enjoying myself or improving my skills.
• It's better to set goals that are safe than to try new things and risk failure.

Mastery-oriented people, in contrast, focus their energies on turning challenges into useful learning experiences. Rather than being concerned about what others think of them, they are motivated by the opportunity to develop new skills and competencies. Mastery-oriented people tend to say the following kinds of things to themselves.

• How can I use this challenge to increase my skills?
• Even if I fail, it can be a useful learning experience.
• It's scary but also challenging to take risks and try new solutions.
• I'm more interested in proving something to myself than with earning the approval of others.

Clients are taught to achieve success in confronting new challenges through *guided mastery* (Wiedenfeld et al., 1990). The steps taken by therapists to help clients increase their sense of self-efficacy and personal control are outlined in Figure 2.1. After identifying the client's goals, the therapist and client determine whether these goals are reachable. This is an important step because people often underestimate their capacity to achieve their goals. The reason for this is that it is difficult to take a flexible approach toward a problem and see it from all angles. Clients often need to be taught to pay attention to how their behaviors can affect others and to recognize the possibilities they have for influencing events in their lives (Thompson, 1991). Of course, clients must also learn to identify things in the world that are beyond their control and to cope with these events by "flowing with them" or by seeking alternative outcomes.

The therapist and client next analyze what kinds of skills are necessary for coping with a particular problem. Clients who possess the necessary skills must first be aware of their abilities. Clients often sell themselves short and don't give themselves enough credit for what they can do. When this happens, the therapist teaches clients to make more accurate attributions about the abilities and skills they possess for controlling events in their life (Murdock & Altmaier, 1991). If the clients do not possess the necessary skills, the skills are practiced through guided mastery.

Sometimes the most helpful method is for the therapist to model the skills for the client. The client can practice the skills by role playing with the therapist and then applying them in the outside world. The client usually benefits best by mastering new skills in small steps and setting goals that can be assessed along the way. This not only provides useful corrective feedback but also serves as an opportunity for clients to reward themselves for progress (Bandura & Cervone, 1983; Bandura & Schunk, 1981). Along with mastering skills, clients can learn self-relaxation techniques to cope with the anxiety they are likely to experience in taking the risk of attempting new behaviors. Therapists also encourage clients to pay attention to their thoughts and teach clients to engage in adaptive self-talk. While working with clients to increase their feelings of self-efficacy, therapists actively involve the client in planning and decision making, and they encourage clients to take responsibility as well as credit for their progress (Thompson, 1991).

Kanfer and Schefft (1988, p. 108) suggest the following "think rules" for helping clients enhance their perceived self-efficacy.

1. Think behavior.
2. Think solution.
3. Think positive.
4. Think small steps.
5. Think flexible.
6. Think future.

Other suggestions for teaching self-efficacy are offered by Goldfried and Robbins (1982).

Teach clients to take pleasure in small accomplishments
Clients need to monitor their progress so that they can appreciate the improvements they are making. These improvements may not otherwise be apparent. Clients should be instructed about the pitfalls of

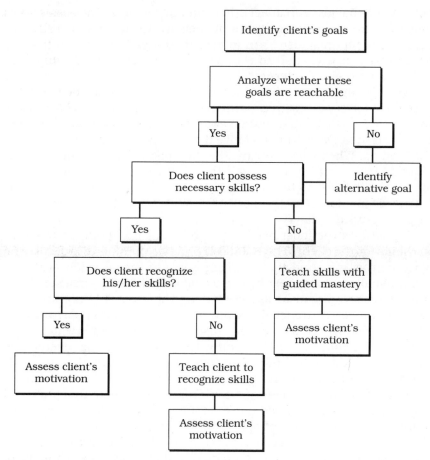

Figure 2.1   Steps in enhancing clients' self-efficacy.
Source: From S. C. Thompson, "Intervening to Enhance Perceptions of Control." In C. R. Snyder and D. R. Forsyth, *Handbook of Social and Clinical Psychology* (pp. 607–623). Copyright © 1991 by Simon and Schuster. Adapted with permission of the author.

judging their worth against the accomplishments of others. They need to take pride in their own progress and appreciate the fact that accomplishments are often small and obstructed by setbacks.

Teach clients to take credit for their accomplishments   A common goal of therapy is to encourage clients to attribute accomplishments to their own efforts rather than to external factors such as the therapist, other people, or luck.

Teach clients to see self-efficacy as part of their identity
Clients are taught to adopt coping as a life philosophy (Kleinke, 1991). They learn to look at their successful experiences in coping not as

isolated events but as part of their personal identity. Clients are often amazed to realize how strong and competent they are when a therapist helps them appreciate the number of times they have stood up to challenges in their lives.

Teach clients to have realistic expectations   Sometimes clients will handle a challenge with reasonable skill but then disappoint themselves by saying "I could have done better," or "I did OK, but I still felt anxious." Clients must learn to appreciate the distinction between acceptable coping responses and unpleasant moods and emotions that everyone experiences.

Overcoming Avoidance

A driving force behind many (if not most) of our problems is avoidance. We derive coping styles to protect ourselves from anxieties, fears, and unpleasant situations, which are often essential and inevitable conditions of life. Avoidance can be a useful strategy for coping with problems that don't have long-term consequences (Suls & Fletcher, 1985). There is often no point in suffering stress engendered by confronting problems that will resolve themselves. However, avoidance is not a good strategy for coping with problems that will not go away unless we do something about them. Because many problems are not successfully resolved by avoidance, they remain as potential sources of stress and anxiety. Soon people who avoid confronting their problems suffer more from their fear of facing the problem than from the problem itself.

Another disadvantage of avoidance as a coping style is that avoidance prevents the constructive use of personal feedback. A fact of life is that people receive both negative and positive feedback from others (Bednar, Wells, & Peterson, 1989). People who avoid negative feedback are not able to use this information (much of which is accurate) to make effective changes in their ways of thinking and acting. Avoiders also miss out on the benefits of positive feedback. Because they are so used to putting up a false front, they can't distinguish when another person's compliments are believable. As Bednar and his associates (1989) argue, "One of the quintessential qualities of abnormal behavior is a tendency to choose a type of reaction that represents an attempt to escape from psychological conflict to avoid the fear and anxiety associated with the conflict" (p. 76). They go on to assert:

> Avoidance is basically a form of denial and escape that requires distortions of thinking and perception. These processes virtually preclude the possibility of personal growth and development because of the inadequacies inherent in these responses. (p. 77)

> [But] the very act of successfully controlling patterns of avoidance is a major therapeutic achievement and constitutes a basic remedial improvement in the structure of the personality. (p. 217)

The ubiquity of anxiety in people's problems was recognized by Freud and is articulated in the following way by Seltzer (1986).

> For instance, proponents of all the major schools of therapy have advanced the position that the principal determinant of dysfunctional behavior is fear, and that various types of psychopathology can be understood as an individual's attempt (however poorly realized) to gain some measure of control over this fear. Dysfunctional behaviors, consequently, are perceived as essentially *avoidant* behaviors—that is, they are perceived as depicting the individual's anxious refusal to cope with fears directly. (p. 163)

A major goal of psychotherapy is to help clients overcome avoidance and face their problems squarely until they can find suitable solutions for them. As Seltzer (1986) explains:

> It has become almost mundane in the psychotherapy literature to observe that for most varieties of treatment to be effective clients must work *through*, rather than *around*, the pain or problem they have brought to therapy. Across theoretical persuasions it is commonly held that if clients are to cease being incapacitated by dysfunctional behavior, they must first agree to the disagreeable and willingly confront their internal demons. This fundamental similarity among different therapeutic schools may be disguised by artificially distinct lexicons, but the notion that successful treatment involves prompting clients to face fears they have routinely avoided is a pervasive theme in virtually all methods of therapy. (p. 181)

> In short, effective treatment must somehow succeed in empowering individuals to overcome, or "work through," their fears—so as to put them to rest once and for all. (p. 163)

One might expect that clients would be aware of their need to take risks and would be willing to follow a therapist's directives to do so. However, for several reasons, this is not the case. First people find it difficult to give up an avoidant coping style because it does offer short-term relief. If people are to change their style of coping, they must first gain a new perspective on the problem. Otherwise, the commonsense response when anxieties about a problem begin to rise is to use more of the same avoidant coping style they have adopted (Watzlawick, Weakland, & Fisch, 1974). A second reason it is difficult to stop avoiding is because people commonly learn that uncomfortable feelings are "bad" and they should be "gotten rid of" (Hayes & Melancon, 1989). The therapist's goal is to help clients make the distinction between themselves as people and the problems they wish to solve.

- Instead of saying "I am a depressed person," a client should learn to say "I am a person who feels depressed."

- The client who says "I am a procrastinator" should learn to say "I am a person who procrastinates."
- The client who says "I suffer from low self-esteem" should learn to say "I feel unworthy."
- The client who says "I am an anxious person who does not do well on tests" should learn to say "I feel anxious when taking tests."

These differences in self-statements may seem subtle, but they carry an important message. It is a mistake to equate a *label* for a problem with a disease or condition that actually exists (Watzlawick, Weakland, & Fisch, 1974, p. 8). In other words, feeling depressed is not the same thing as having an illness of depression. Feeling bad about oneself is not the same thing as suffering from a case of low self-esteem. Being anxious in social situations or when taking tests is not the same thing as being afflicted with shyness or test anxiety. As Thomas Szasz (1985a) has pointed out, the literalization of metaphors for people's problems causes trouble because it implies that the problem is an entity that must be fixed or cured (or avoided) rather than a fact of life with which one must learn to cope.

Because the emotions connected with problems are viewed as negative characteristics to be disposed of, clients have difficulty confronting their problems and finding solutions for them.

> It may be a useful simplification to postulate that whoever comes into therapy signals in one way or another: Anything except *that*. By this I mean that emotional suffering creates a willingness to do *anything* for its alleviation, except one and only one thing: and this "one thing" is exactly what causes his suffering. . . . (Watzlawick, 1978, p. 139)

The "one thing" Watzlawick is referring to is overcoming one's fear of fear (Hayes & Melancon, 1989, p. 185; Seltzer, 1986, p. 57). The therapist's goal is to help clients do "the very things they fear" (Frankl, 1967a, p. 146). This goal is accomplished through exposure, reframing, and benevolence.

Exposure   Psychotherapy is not simply an exercise in talking; clients are expected to *do*. Clients have new experiences; they take risks; they *confront* the very problems that are troubling them. Some of these experiences and risks occur within the therapy session; others occur in the client's daily life. By exposing themselves to the problems they fear, clients learn that they can tolerate, face, and find solutions for their problems.

Reframing   Clients overcome avoidance by learning to view their problems not as intolerable symptoms residing in themselves but as challenges to be solved. For example, clients learn that *feeling* as if one is a bad person is not the same thing as *being* a bad person. Feeling as if one is a failure is not equivalent to being a failure. Clients learn that, by avoiding their unpleasant emotions, they end up avoiding the search for effective solutions to the causes of these emotions (Hayes & Melancon, 1989). Clients are taught that the "intolerable" emotions they have avoided are indeed tolerable (albeit unpleasant; Ellis, 1962; Ellis & Dryden, 1987). Clients learn to stop struggling with unpleasant emotions as something to eliminate and learn to flow with their emotions, experience them, and learn where they are coming from. Clients are encouraged to explore the ways they might be contributing to their problems and experiment with more adaptive ways of thinking and behaving.

Benevolence   If clients feel forced to confront problems they wish to avoid, they will naturally resist (see Chapter 5). Therapists should not struggle with clients to make them stop avoiding. Instead, therapists should take a benevolent attitude in which choice and control are assumed to reside within the client (Haley, 1963).

Escaping the self   Another kind of avoidance, outlined by Roy Baumeister (1991), is escaping oneself. Self-escape can be harmful or beneficial, depending on the circumstances. Harmful self-escape occurs when the demands people place upon themselves become so extreme that they find it intolerable to face their shortcomings. This kind of self-escape results in an evasion of self-responsibility through behaviors that are passive, rigid, or impulsive. The desire to avoid looking at oneself can become so intense that people will resort to self-harm, substance abuse, and binge eating. Beneficial self-escape occurs when people put aside their self-focus and allow themselves to be creative and achieve pleasurable experiences. The goal of therapy is not to heighten clients' self-esteem to the point at which they will never feel the need for self-escape; this is not possible and, in the long run, may preclude clients from developing their creativity. Instead, therapists want to help their clients accomplish the following goals.

1. Setting realistic standards for themselves so they can achieve success without a chronic fear of failure.
2. Learning how to give themselves a break and take time out from self-focus in a way that is not harmful or maladaptive.
3. Learning how creative self-escape can enhance one's pleasures and sense of achievement.

Becoming Aware of One's Misconceptions

In his book, *Misunderstandings of the Self*, Victor Raimy (1975) describes how psychotherapists guide clients to reevaluate their perceptions and interpretations about what they want and what they are getting from life. The goal of this process is for clients to modify the beliefs or expectations about life that are not in their best interest. For example, Raimy lists the following observations: (1) depressed people are likely to have the following kinds of misconceptions:

- I am, have been, and will remain hopeless.
- I have nothing to look forward to in life and never will.
- I am rejected by most people because I have nothing to offer, and they don't like me.

(2) obsessive people are likely to have these kinds of misconceptions:

- I must be orderly, precise, and perfect in everything I do.
- I must depend on intellect and logic and ignore my feelings.
- Being right is more important than anything else.

(3) histrionic people often have these misconceptions:

- I am most effective when I am flirtatious, seductive, vivacious, and dramatic.
- I make things more interesting for others and gain more approval when I exaggerate and bend the truth.
- I cannot stand disappointments and frustrations.

and (4) people who are paranoid have misconceptions such as:

- I must be constantly on guard against people because they want to harm me.
- If I don't watch out for myself, nobody else will.
- This is a dangerous world, and I must be very careful about what I say or do.

These misconceptions are very similar to the kinds of *cognitive distortions* described by Aaron Beck (Beck, 1967, 1976; Beck, Freeman et al., 1990; Bedrosian & Beck, 1980) and the *irrational beliefs* outlined by Albert Ellis (Ellis, 1962; 1987; Ellis & Harper, 1975). Here are some examples of cognitive distortions.

1. *Selective abstraction* involves focusing on a disturbing problem out of context. For example, a person may become depressed over a single failure while neglecting many other successes. Or, a single unfriendly response from someone may override friendly responses that are received from others during the course of a day.
2. *Arbitrary inference* refers to conclusions based on incomplete or inadequate information. For example, another person's frown "proves" that he doesn't like you. Or, because the boss didn't say hello as she passed you in the hall, you can be certain that she is displeased with your performance.
3. *Overgeneralizations* are blanket judgments and inferences based on only one or two incidences. A single failure or rejection is taken

to mean "I am an inadequate person." A negative response from one person proves that "Nobody likes me."

4. *Personalization* is an inference that negative events are directed particularly toward oneself: "An impolite motorist in traffic is surely directing his aggression at me." "It is raining just to make my day miserable."

5. *Polarized thinking* is black-and-white thinking: "You are either on my side or you are my enemy." "If I don't get what I want I can't be happy."

6. *Magnification and exaggeration* is making minor displeasures into catastrophes: "You forgot the wine. Now the dinner is ruined." "I only got a "B" on the test. My academic career is shot."

7. *Assumption of excessive responsibility* is unrealistic self-blame: "My girlfriend wouldn't have broken up with me if I were (more athletic, more musical, more charming, and so on)." "My husband gets angry when I don't do things right. I have to learn to make fewer mistakes so he won't get so upset."

Some examples of irrational beliefs include:

• People who are important to me should always love me.
• People should never treat me badly, and they are bad people if they do.
• It's awful when things are not the way I want them to be.
• When things are uncertain, I have to keep worrying about them.
• I must achieve success at all times.

Albert Ellis explains that irrational beliefs or misconceptions can be recognized by their rigidity and common use of "shoulds" and "musts." Two other misconceptions described by Raimy (1975) include phrenophobia, and the notion that one is different or special.

Phrenophobia is defined by Raimy as the false belief that our problems are proof that there is something wrong with us and that we are in danger of going crazy. Clients may falsely convince themselves that their feelings of anxiety indicate impending insanity, that any memory gaps they experience are evidence that they are "losing their mind," and that their irritability is a sign of personal weakness and an impending mental breakdown. The *special-person* misconception is based on six faulty beliefs (Raimy, 1975):

1. I must control others.
2. I am superior to others.
3. I should not compromise.
4. I suffer more than others.
5. I must try to be perfect.
6. I cannot trust others.

Misconceptions about being a special person occur when we forget that all human beings are generally in the same boat and that we can benefit more by offering mutual support than by isolating ourselves and believing our problems are "different" or "special."

Reevaluating Misconceptions in Therapy

There are a number of ways therapists can help clients reevaluate their misconceptions during therapy sessions.

1. *Self-examination.* Therapists actively encourage and support clients as they look more closely at themselves and assess how their lives are affected by their personal beliefs and styles of relating with others.
2. *Explanation.* Therapists use questions, reflections, interpretations, and confrontations (see Chapter 3) to focus clients on examining their beliefs and expectations.
3. *Self-demonstration.* Therapists use the process of therapy to help clients observe their own behavior. This is done by examining transactions between the therapist and client as they occur in therapy.
4. *Experience.* Clients may be encouraged to experience the effects of various beliefs on their feelings and on the reactions they receive from others. This can be done with imagery and with homework assignments.

Accepting Life's Realities

Clients learn a number of "lessons" in therapy about the importance of accepting and learning to cope with life's realities. These lessons, which are outlined by Strupp (1973), are similar to the kinds of beliefs described by Ellis (1987).

1. The world has good and bad aspects. Although, unfortunately, we need to accept many bad things in life, we can also learn to appreciate and live for the many things that are good.
2. We will benefit by learning to be less demanding of other people. Some of our demands for praise and admiration from others can never be satisfied, and we will be happier if we give them up.
3. We need to learn how to give ourselves pleasure for our accomplishments, rather than demanding recognition or approbation from others.
4. An important lesson in life is to learn how to delay gratification and endure the inevitable frustrations, tensions, and privations that life bestows on us.
5. Separation is painful, but even when significant others are physically removed, they are still symbolically present.

6. Setting realistic goals and accepting the responsibility to expend the necessary effort to reach them is worthwhile.

7. We have more strength than we give ourselves credit for in surviving life's inevitable tensions, anxieties, suffering, pain, and deprivations. We are better off in the long run working through these challenges than attempting to avoid them.

8. Certain interpersonal maneuvers (such as ingratiation, negativism, aggression) are often self-defeating. We are not helped by blaming ourselves for using these tactics, but we can gain by perfecting our interpersonal skills.

9. We should appreciate the benefits of a cooperative attitude toward others, while recognizing that some people will take advantage of us if we allow them to do so.

10. Honesty about our feelings and motives is a good policy.

11. Every person has rights, and we need to learn to stand up for these in a way that communicates respect for others.

12. It is difficult to avoid the fact that some people will have authority over us. We need to develop skills for coping with this dilemma.

13. We are responsible for our actions.

14. An important task in life is to develop our own sense of identity, individuality, self-esteem, self-acceptance, and self-sufficiency.

Achieving Insight

According to Dinkmeyer, Dinkmeyer, and Sperry (1987), "The insight phase of counseling is concerned with helping clients become aware of why they choose to function as they do" (p. 115). Clients need to examine their styles of relating to other people and of coping with the demands and challenges in their lives, and they need to ask themselves whether these styles are in their best interest and are really getting them what they want. As Sullivan put it, "A person achieves mental health to the extent that he becomes aware of his interpersonal relationships" (Chapman, 1978, p. 40). This attitude toward insight follows the compensatory model of responsibility described earlier in this chapter. Clients are not held responsible for the causes of their unsatisfactory coping styles, but they are responsible for learning to improve them. "When we increase clients' awareness of patterns in their lives, they can no longer get away with acting in self-defeating ways without realizing what they are doing and why" (Kottler, 1991, p. 151).

Insight as Part of the Therapeutic Relationship

Because clients enact their relationship and coping styles with the therapist, much insight that takes place during therapy occurs in the process of the therapeutic relationship—in the here-and-now. As Luborsky (1984) explains,

The reexperiencing with the therapist in the "here and now" of the conflictual relationship problems gives the patients the most impetus toward meaningful insight and permits greater freedom to change. Past relationships gain in meaning when they are related to the current ones. Keeping the relevance of the present in sight is one way for the therapist to insure that the insight is emotionally meaningful and not just intellectual. (p. 22)

In a similar vein, Michels (1983) asserts

The primary data of psychoanalysis are neither what happens in childhood nor what happens in adult life, and not even the cause–effect relationship between them; the primary data are what the patient says in the analyst's presence, how the analyst responds, and how the patient can make constructive use of the experiential and dialectical process. (p. 61)

Sullivan points out that, by acting as a "participant observer," the therapist can help clients achieve *consensual validation* of the pros and cons of their styles of relating with others (Chapman, 1978). The therapeutic relationship is a healing experience to the extent that it enables therapists to instruct clients about their maladaptive interpersonal behavior (Yalom, 1980, p. 404).

The preceding discussion was meant to impress the point that clients gain insight when the therapist joins them on a "journey of understanding." During this journey, the therapist's task is to "be with" and understand the client's feelings, actions, and thoughts as clearly as possible. What the therapist learns about the client is shared with the client. This is not done by making *interpretations* but, rather, with well-timed *reflections*. Interpretations are not recommended because they are likely to be experienced as criticism or disapproval and cause the client to become defensive (Strupp, 1989). Strupp paraphrases Frieda Fromm-Reichmann's (1950) famous dictum about interpretations in the following manner:

What is effective in therapy is patients' experiences of therapy as a helpful and constructive human relationship that undergirds their efforts to come to terms with a troubled past, not an explanation of how and why they became the kind of people they are. (Strupp, 1989, p. 723)

Insight into the Past

Insight into the roots of one's problems is neither necessary nor sufficient for therapeutic change. Clients can often make constructive changes in their life without understanding why they grew up the way they did. In addition, intellectual insight into one's past does not guarantee that any real change will take place (Marmor, 1990). Paul Watzlawick (1990a) points out that he could not recall a single case in which insight was sufficient to cause a person to change. The fact that recall of memories from the past is not necessary for change was recognized long ago by psychoanalysts Franz Alexander and Thomas French (1946).

It is not necessary—nor is it possible—during the course of therapy to recall *every* feeling that has been repressed. Therapeutic results can be achieved without the patient's recalling all important details of his past history; indeed, good therapeutic results have come in which not a single forgotten memory has been brought to the surface. Ferenczi and Rank were among the first to recognize this principle and apply it to therapy. However, the early belief that the patient "suffers from memories" has so deeply penetrated the minds of the analysts that even today it is difficult for many to recognize that the patient is suffering not so much from his memories as from his incapacity to deal with his actual *problems of the moment.* (p. 22, emphasis added)

Nicholas Hobbs (1962) outlined the limitations of insight in his Presidential Address to the Division of Clinical Psychology at the 1961 meeting of the American Psychological Association.

I suggest that insight is not a cause of change but a possible result of change. It is not a source of therapeutic gain but one among a number of possible consequences of gain. It may or may not occur in therapy; whether it does or does not is inconsequential, since it reflects only the preferred modes of expression of the therapist or the client. It is not a change agent, it is a byproduct of change. (p. 742)

Functions of Insight

Although insight is neither necessary nor sufficient for therapeutic change, it can still be beneficial. Insight into the roots of behaviors can be useful in therapy, especially for clients who believe such a process is important. "The value of insight may lie less in its inherent truth than in the process of discovering it" (Appelbaum, 1988, p. 205). There are two reasons insight into the past can be valuable for clients (Yalom, 1980, pp. 338–346). First, the process of looking into the past helps to solidify the therapeutic relationship. Second, insight into the past can empower clients to change.

Solidifying the therapeutic relationship   Heinz Kohut (1977) explains that the purpose of interpretation is less to produce insight than it is to provide the client a sense of being understood. When the therapist and client explore the client's past, the therapist communicates a sincere interest in the client. The client and therapist are united as partners working together to understand the client as fully as possible. "The intellectual venture, which Freud likens to an archaeological dig, provides a shared, apparently meaningful activity in which patient and therapist engage, while the real agent of change, the therapeutic relationship, unfolds" (Yalom, 1980, p. 350).

Empowering change   Insight into the past empowers clients to change because it reinforces the compensatory model. Insight into the past helps clients understand the reasons for their maladaptive coping styles. They come to realize that they are not to blame for their present dilemmas. This understanding also affords a sense of mastery by inspiring clients to say to themselves, "Now that I understand how I developed into the person I am, I can *choose* to change." As Yalom (1980, p. 343) points out, what particular theory is used to help clients understand their past is not so important as long as this theory makes sense to clients, satisfies their desire to know themselves better, and inspires them to take charge of their lives. Clients view the experience of coming to understand themselves and their problems more clearly as an important part of a therapy session (Martin & Stelmaczonek, 1988).

Being Sensitive to the Client's Individuality

When helping clients achieve insight, therapists must especially be sensitive to clients' individual needs and ways of thinking. First, some people are more interested than others are in self-exploration and in understanding the meaning and causes of their behaviors (Cacioppo & Petty, 1982; Fletcher et al., 1986). The amount and type of interpretation offered by the therapist must be matched to the cognitive style of the client. Second, the insights offered to the client must be both meaningful and acceptable (Garfield, 1990).

SUMMARY

The orientation taken in this book is that psychotherapy is not a "treatment" clients receive from therapists. It is, rather, a working relationship between therapists and clients to find solutions to clients' problems that are more advantageous than the solutions clients are using at the present time. The implications of this orientation are that (1) pathology is not necessary as an explanatory concept, (2) the goal is change rather than cure, and (3) clients are responsible for making changes in their lives.

There are four models of responsibility, based on whether or not clients are held responsible for the cause and solution of their problems. These are the moral model, the enlightenment model, the medical model, and the compensatory model. Clients are tempted to avoid responsibility by resorting to self-handicapping strategies, and it is the therapist's challenge to teach clients that they can solve their problems and that they are able to respond.

Six general therapeutic goals are (1) helping clients overcome demoralization and gain hope, (2) enhancing the clients' sense of mastery and self-efficacy, (3) encouraging clients to face rather than avoid their anxieties, (4) helping clients become aware of their misconceptions, (5) teaching clients to accept life's realities, and (6) helping clients achieve insight. Overcoming demoralization and gaining hope is accomplished by helping clients gain a sense of agency, energy, and determination and learn to find pathways for reaching goals. A client's self-efficacy is enhanced through the process of guided mastery. Clients learn to take pleasure in small accomplishments, to take credit for their accomplishments, to view self-efficacy as part of their personal identity, and to have realistic expectations. Clients are encouraged to face their anxieties with exposure, relabeling, and benevolence. Clients are also provided with support and guidance as they reevaluate their perceptions and interpretations about what they want and what they are getting from life. Insight is experienced as part of the therapeutic relationship in which the therapist provides the client with meaningful feedback. Seeking insight into the past serves to solidify the therapeutic relationship and empower change. Therapists are sensitive to the client's individuality, and they offer insights that are meaningful and acceptable.

SUGGESTIONS FOR FURTHER READING

Bandura, A. (1986). *Social foundations of thought and action: A social cognitive theory*. Englewood Cliffs, NJ: Prentice-Hall.

Beck, A. T., Freeman, A., & Associates. (1990). *Cognitive therapy of personality disorders*. New York: Guilford.

Ellis, A., & Dryden, W. (1987). *The practice of rational-emotive therapy*. New York: Springer.

Kleinke, C. L. (1991). *Coping with life challenges*. Pacific Grove, CA: Brooks/Cole.

Yalom I. D. (1980). *Existential psychotherapy*. New York: Basic Books.

CHAPTER 3

Psychotherapy Skills

Psychotherapy occurs within an interpersonal relationship. It therefore stands to reason that successful therapeutic outcomes will depend on therapists' interpersonal skills as well as on their technical expertise. After analyzing the research on psychotherapy outcome, Lambert (1989) concludes that the skills and personal characteristics of the therapist have eight times as much effect on psychotherapy outcome as does the therapist's theoretical orientation or treatment techniques. Hans Strupp (1984) argues that therapists' personalities and technical abilities are "inextricably intertwined" and that "they reflect the totality of the therapist's personality and professional experience" (p. 57). Strupp (1984) also points out that although the therapist's technical expertise is not unimportant, it can only be of benefit when therapists and clients have developed a favorable working alliance.

> Assuredly, technical operations may enhance changes achievable within a good therapeutic relationship. The preponderance of the available evidence, however, indicates that the human qualities of the patient and of the therapist and the nature of their relationship overshadow specific effects potentially attributable to technical maneuvers. (p. 59)

The focus of this chapter is on the skills therapists can develop to enhance the practice of their craft. We begin with an overview of therapist characteristics that various researchers have identified as desirable. Attention is given to more specific skills that are valuable for therapists to master and to mistakes that therapists should try to avoid. The chapter concludes with a discussion of measures that have been developed for assessing the quality of the working alliance between therapists and clients.

DESIRABLE THERAPIST CHARACTERISTICS: AN OVERVIEW

Lester Luborsky and his colleagues reached the following conclusion from their research on therapist factors in treatment outcome (Luborsky et al., 1985): "The major agent of effective psychotherapy is the personality of the therapist, particularly the ability to form a warm, supportive relationship" (p. 609). Two therapist qualities identified by Luborsky and his associates (1985, 1986) are (1) the therapist's interest in helping clients and (2) the therapist's psychological health and skill. Psychological health and skill is exemplified by therapists who appear to be well adjusted, who come across as capable and helpful, and who are not authoritarian and rigid. The study concluded that interest in helping and psychological health permit successful therapists to form a strong working alliance with their clients. Luborsky (1984, pp. 82–84) offers the following suggestions about how a strong working alliance between therapists and clients can be achieved.

1. Convey, through words and manner, support for the client's wish to achieve his or her goals.
2. Convey a sense of understanding and acceptance of the client.
3. Develop a liking for the client.
4. Help the client maintain vital defenses and activities that bolster his or her level of functioning.
5. Communicate a realistically hopeful attitude that the treatment goals are likely to be achieved.
6. Help clients recognize when they have made progress toward their goals.

A number of other writers have addressed this subject as well. Hellmuth Kaiser (1965) proposed the following useful therapist characteristics (Yalom, 1980, p. 495).

1. An interest in people.
2. Theoretical views on psychotherapy that do not interfere with the therapist's interest in helping the client to communicate freely.
3. The absence of neurotic patterns that would interfere with the establishment of communication with the client.
4. The mental disposition of "receptiveness"—being sensitive to duplicity or to the noncommunicative elements in the client's behavior.

Jeffrey Kottler (1991, p. 49) integrated the conclusions from Orlinsky and Howard's (1986) research review to suggest that the therapeutic relationship is most helpful when it has the following qualities.

1. An intense investment of energy both by the client and the therapist.
2. A reliance on roles in which the client demonstrates evidence of self-expressive attachment to the therapist, and the therapist demonstrates an active collaboration in the process.
3. Good personal contact, including a degree of mutual comfort, mutual trust, absence of defensiveness, spontaneity, and reciprocal understanding.
4. Sufficient support and goodwill to permit challenges and confrontation without jeopardizing the stability of the relationship.

Albert Ellis (1985, pp. 162–163) described effective therapists as having the following characteristics.

1. They are vitally interested in helping their clients and energetically work to fulfill this interest.
2. They unconditionally accept their clients as people, while opposing and trying to ameliorate some of the client's self-defeating ideas, feelings, and behaviors.
3. They are confident of their own therapeutic ability and, without being rigid or grandiose, strongly believe that their main techniques will work.
4. They have a wide knowledge of therapeutic theories and practices; are flexible, undogmatic, and scientific; and, are consequently open to acquiring new skills and to experimenting with these skills.
5. They are effective in communicating and teaching their clients new ways of thinking, emoting, and behaving.
6. They are able to cope with and ameliorate their own disturbances and consequently are not inordinately anxious, depressed, hostile, self-downing, self-pitying, or undisciplined.
7. They are patient, persistent, and hard working in their therapeutic endeavors.
8. They are ethical and responsible and use therapy almost entirely for the benefit of the clients and not for personal indulgence.
9. They act professionally and appropriately in the therapeutic setting but are still able to maintain some degree of humanness, spontaneity, and personal enjoyment in what they are doing.
10. They are encouraging and optimistic and show clients that, whatever difficulties clients may experience, they can change appreciably.
11. They try not only to help clients feel better and surrender their presenting symptoms but also to help them make a profound attitudinal change that will enable them to maintain their improvement, continue to improve, and ward off future disturbances.

12. They are eager to help virtually all their clients, they freely refer to other therapists those clients whom they think they can't help or are not interested in helping, and they try to be neither underinvolved nor overinvolved with clients they retain. They sincerely try to overcome their strong biases for or against their clients that may interfere with their therapeutic effectiveness.

13. They possess sufficient observational ability, sensitivity to others, good intelligence, and some judgment to discourage their clients from making rash and foolish decisions and from seriously harming others.*

Finally, Hans Strupp (1989) provides the following description of desirable therapist characteristics.

> Patients reasonably expect a therapist to be human—keenly attentive, interested, caring, respectful, and empathic. His or her manner should be natural and unstudied; there should be a willingness to respond to patients' questions and concerns; a therapist should never criticize, never diminish the patient's self-esteem and self-worth, and should leave no doubt about his or her commitment and willingness to help. There may be occasions when reassurance and even advice are appropriate. The patient should never feel that he or she is "just another patient." The therapeutic relationship should be experienced as a "real" relationship rather than an artificial or contrived one. This should be possible even though its "professional" aspects are observed. A good therapist should obviously refrain from fueling power struggles or reciprocating angry provocations. The therapist's language should be simple, straightforward, and understandable. The patient should feel that the therapist understands his or her feelings, at least a good part of the time. (p. 723)

RESPONSIVENESS

Responsive therapists are able to communicate to clients that they understand and are in touch with what the client is saying. When working with a responsive therapist, clients are reassured that the therapist is "with them." A responsive therapist communicates to the client, through verbal and nonverbal behaviors, "I am concerned about you, interested in what you have to say, and willing to listen" (Berg & Archer, 1980). The concept of responsiveness was originally applied by researchers to social interactions (Davis & Perkowitz, 1979). However, responsiveness is very pertinent to therapeutic interactions and will be discussed here in this context. A responsive therapist is able to exercise the following skills.

*From *Overcoming Resistance: Rational-Emotive Therapy with Difficult Clients*, by A. Ellis, pp. 162–163. Copyright © 1985 Springer Publishing Company, Inc., New York 10012. Used by permission.

1. Responding *actively* to what the client is saying, both verbally and nonverbally.
2. Responding in a way that is *congruent* with the message and feelings that the client is communicating. Being responsive requires the ability both to respond accurately to what the client is saying and to convey a sincere interest in the client's experiences (L. Miller & Berg, 1984).

The Value of Therapist Responsiveness

Therapists develop their skills at being responsive to have a positive impact on clients (Omer, 1987). Therapist responsiveness serves a number of important functions in facilitating therapy (Berg, 1987; Davis, 1982; Davis & Holtgraves, 1984).

1. Therapist responsiveness functions to maintain a smooth therapeutic interaction and to keep the focus of the interaction on issues that are important to the client.
2. Therapist responsiveness provides clients with a sense of validation—a feeling that their problems are real and understandable.
3. Therapist responsiveness solidifies the therapeutic relationship by reinforcing a sense that the client and therapist are "connecting" and becoming closer emotionally.
4. Therapist responsiveness enhances the client's attention to what the therapist has to say. A responsive therapist wins credibility in the eyes of the client.
5. Therapist responsiveness encourages openness and self-disclosure on the part of the client.

Responsiveness Skills

Being responsive requires the following skills.

1. *Ability to attend to what the client is attempting to communicate.* This requires following what the client is saying as well as having sensitivity to the client's tone of expression and other nonverbal behaviors.
2. *Motivation to develop an intimate relationship with the client.* The therapist must be willing to engage the client in the kind of close working relationship that responsiveness is likely to promote.
3. *Energy to respond at the rate "demanded" by the client.* The therapist must have the energy to work at the client's pace. This requires keeping up with energized or agitated clients who are speaking at a fast pace as well as persevering with depressed or dysphoric clients who are speaking at a very slow pace.

4. *Ability to identify with the client's frame of reference.* The therapist must be able to understand what the client is communicating from the client's point of view. This requires skill in understanding and appreciating people who come from different backgrounds.

5. *Being trained in basic interviewing skills.* The therapist must be proficient in basic interviewing skills.

Eliciting Self-Disclosure

The Opener Scale was developed to learn more about how good listeners are able to elicit self-disclosure from others (L. Miller, Berg, & Archer, 1983). This scale is made up of the following 10 items, which are answered on a 5-point scale (4 = strongly agree to 0 = strongly disagree).

1. People frequently tell me about themselves.
2. I've been told that I'm a good listener.
3. I'm very accepting of others.
4. People trust me with their secrets.
5. I easily get people to "open up."
6. People feel relaxed around me.
7. I enjoy listening to people.
8. I'm sympathetic to people's problems.
9. I encourage people to tell me how they are feeling.
10. I can keep people talking about themselves.

People with high scores on the Opener Scale appreciate the viewpoints of others and are able to take their perspective. People with high scores on the Opener Scale are also more successful in eliciting self-disclosure than are people with low scores. People with high scores on the Opener Scale are particularly successful in eliciting self-disclosure from others whose self-disclosure is normally very low. What makes these "high openers" so successful? Analysis of nonverbal behaviors of people with high and low scores on the Opener Scale indicates that high openers display more enjoyment, comfort, and attentiveness than do low openers (Purvis, Dabbs, & Hopper, 1984). In short, they are more verbally and nonverbally responsive.

Nonverbal Responsiveness

Beginning therapists often find it instructive to observe themselves on videotape to become aware of the nuances of their nonverbal behaviors. Sensitivity to one's own nonverbal behaviors, as well as to those of the client, is an important clinical skill. Communication occurs not only with words but also through body language. Some nonverbal behaviors that deserve attention from therapists are *gaze, facial expressions,* and *body posture.* Generally speaking, eye contact, smiling, forward leaning, and an open body posture communicate feelings of interest and caring for another person (Burgoon, Buller, Hale, & deTurck, 1984; Harper, Wiens, & Matarazzo, 1978; Kleinke, 1986; Kleinke & Taylor, 1991). Research has also indicated that therapists are better liked and are viewed as having more expertness, empathy, and trustworthiness when they engage in high rather than low levels of eye contact, smiling, open body posture, and forward leaning toward clients (Barak, Patkin, & Dell, 1982; Lee, Uhlemann, & Haase, 1985; Wiener, Budney, Wood, & Russell, 1989). However, this should not be taken to mean that therapists who make eye contact, smile, and lean forward with an open body posture will always be more successful. It is obvious that the therapist's nonverbal behaviors have to match the mood of the therapy and the context of what is occurring between the therapist and client. Research studies have indicated that what is important is not the *amount* of responsive nonverbal behaviors used by therapists but rather the *congruence* of these nonverbal behaviors with the emotions present in the therapy session (Hill et al., 1981; Lee & Hallberg, 1982).

On the basis of research studies of nonverbal behavior, the following advice can be given. Therapists should make a point to be aware of their own and the client's nonverbal behaviors during the therapy session. By attending to nonverbal behaviors, therapists can learn to use them as effective channels of communication. Nonverbal responses from the therapist are often helpful when the client is feeling stuck or having difficulty opening up. At other times, the therapist may decide that the client needs some "space" and will honor this need with reduced nonverbal intimacy.

The client's nonverbal behaviors can give important information about how the client is feeling. Therapists are especially encouraged to notice incongruities in the client's verbal and nonverbal communication. For example, if the client is smiling while talking about a sad event, this may be worth mentioning to the client. A client who reports feeling fine in an unenthusiastic tone of voice is communicating a different message than a client who shares the same information in a lively tone of voice and with a smile. A client who reports an infuriating experience with no signs of anger would deserve a different kind of response from the therapist than would a client who communicates the experience as well as the anger.

Nonverbal behaviors are a rich source of information and a valuable channel of communication in psychotherapy. However, they must be tailored to fit the style of the therapist and the individuality of the client.

Client Responsiveness

As suggested earlier, an important benefit of therapist responsiveness is that it encourages responsiveness from clients. This is important for several reasons. First, an important factor in the successful therapeutic outcome is the client's willingness and ability to become actively involved in the therapy process (Gomes-Schwartz, 1978; Windholz & Silberschatz, 1988). Client responsiveness is also important because, as Sullivan (1953; 1978) points out, clients often come to therapy with problems stemming from unsatisfactory interpersonal relationships. Sullivan's observation has been supported by a growing body of research studies demonstrating that people who are lonely or otherwise dissatisfied with their relationships are particularly lacking in social skills (Kleinke, 1991). The therapist's ability to model and teach responsiveness and other beneficial social skills to clients can be a valuable service.

VERBAL IMMEDIACY

Another way to communicate responsiveness to clients is to be verbally immediate with them. When being immediate, the therapist attempts to focus on the therapeutic relationship in the present. There is a sense of directness, intimacy, and willingness to experience with the client what is happening at the moment. Therapists attempt to be immediate by personalizing what is happening between them and the client. Here are some examples of therapist statements that communicate immediacy.

- "You say you get angry with people who aren't there when you need them. I wonder if you are angry with *me* when I'm not available for you."
- "Your separation from your wife is a very painful experience, and I can feel that pain right now as I see the tears in your eyes."

Wiener and Mehrabian (1968) defined immediacy by developing the following categories for scoring the amount of nonimmediacy present in a verbal communication.

Spatial-Temporal Categories

Statements tend to be nonimmediate when there is a spatial distance implied in a statement. For example, the demonstratives *that* and *those* are more distant than *this* or *these*. Nonimmediacy is also characterized by a statement that refers to the past or future rather than to the present. Here are some statements that are rendered nonimmediate because of spatial/temporal characteristics.

- "Those feelings of depression we have been discussing are expected, given what you have been experiencing."
- "Does the relationship between your parents have any connection to that problem between you and your wife?"
- "I've sensed those angry feelings you have are also directed toward me."

Here are more immediate forms of the preceding statements.

- "Your feelings of depression, which I can sense right now, are expected given what you have been experiencing."
- "Does the relationship between your parents you just shared with me have any connection to the lack of sexual satisfaction between you and your wife?"
- "At this moment, I can feel some of your anger being directed at me."

Denotative Specificity

A statement is nonimmediate if it focuses on only part of the issue, if it depersonalizes the issue from an individual to a general class, or if it refers to the speaker or recipient of the communication implicitly rather than explicitly. Here are some statements that are rendered nonimmediate because of diminished denotative specificity.

- "My primary feeling toward you is one of respect."
- "Anxiety is a common experience among college freshmen."
- "It's a fair conclusion that you can be a warm and interesting person when you want to be."

Here are more immediate forms of the above statements.

- "I respect you."
- "This is your first year in college. Many things are new to you. It is not surprising that you feel anxious."
- "I know from our relationship together that you can be a warm and interesting person when you want to be."

Action/Agent/Object Categories

A statement is not immediate if it contains a separation between the speaker and recipient of the communication or between a person and that person's problems. An occurrence or feeling that is described as unilateral is less immediate than one that is described as mutual. Statements implying passivity are less immediate than statements implying action or personal responsibility. Qualifiers such as "sort of," "kind of," "you know," or "I guess" decrease the immediacy of a statement. Here are some statements that are rendered nonimmediate by these categories.

- "I've come to understand you better during the course of therapy."
- "What will you do next time when depression overcomes you?"
- "There is sort of a wall between us."
- "It is, you know, important for you to do the homework I suggest."

Here are more immediate forms of the preceding statements.

- "We understand each other better from working together in therapy."
- "What will you do next time when you are depressed?"
- "I feel a wall between us."
- "It is important for you to do the homework we agree on together."

VERBAL SKILLS

A number of verbal skills have been identified as useful for students of psychotherapy to master (Cormier & Cormier, 1991; Ivey, 1988). These skills appear to be most successfully learned when students are encouraged to study them, practice them in their own mind, and then practice them overtly in simulated interviews (Baker et al., 1984; 1986). After sufficient practice, these skills become so automatic that experienced therapists don't give them much thought. However, they are active ingredients in successful therapy sessions.

Probe

A probe is a question therapists use to gain information. Probes are used judiciously because therapists want to avoid making therapy into a question-and-answer session. Some skills for using probes include allowing sufficient time for clients to answer, separating questions with other kinds of verbal responses, and making probes in a nonaccusatory tone. Often therapists can avoid using questions by expressing an interest in further information with statements such as "I'm wondering how that actually felt to you" or "I'm trying to more clearly understand what you were actually thinking when that happened."

Clarification

A clarification is a question used to obtain greater clarity about what the client is saying. Clarifications are used to (1) encourage the client to elaborate, (2) confirm with the client that you accurately understood her or his message, and (3) better understand vague or confusing statements. Therapists use clarifications to assure themselves that they fully understand what the client has told them and that there are no ambiguities that need to be clarified or details that require further exploration.

Paraphrase

A paraphrase is a rephrasing of the client's statement in a way that communicates to the client the therapist's understanding of what the client has said. The paraphrase is used to focus the communication on issues that appear to be most relevant and appropriate. When paraphrasing, therapists don't simply parrot or repeat the client's exact words. By making an active attempt to rephrase the client's statement in their own words, therapists are able to maintain the flow and focus of the conversation.

Reflection

A reflection is a rephrasing of the emotion or affect present in a client's statement. Therapists use reflections to communicate to clients an understanding of how they are feeling. Reflections encourage clients to experience and express their feelings, and, by doing this, they have the opportunity to put their feelings into clearer perspective. Reflections are a major way for therapists to communicate empathy for clients and acceptance of clients' feelings.

Information Giving

Information giving is not a regular response for therapists because the thrust of therapy is to help clients take responsibility and find solutions to their own problems. However, sometimes it is obvious that misinformation or lack of information is compromising the client's ability to make an informed decision. Under these circumstances, the therapist is obliged to step out of the therapist role and either provide the information or tell clients where they can obtain the information they need to know.

Confrontation

Confrontations are used to identify clients' mixed messages and to explore alternative ways of perceiving or interpreting problem situations. Mixed messages usually occur when the tone of a client's expression doesn't match the experience being described or when there is an inconsistency between a client's statements and his or her actions. When making confrontations, therapists must be aware of their own feelings and motives. Confrontations should not be made out of anger or frustration with the client but in a supportive and caring manner. Confrontations are indicated when clients are stuck and are having a hard time owning their feelings or meeting their goals. The confrontation is aimed not at the person of the client but at the difficulty the client is having. It has been said many times that therapists must "earn" the right to confront their clients by establishing a strong working alliance. When making confrontations, therapists obligate themselves to giving the time and energy necessary for seeing clients through their difficulty. If confrontations are made prematurely, too forcefully, or without a sense of support, clients are likely to react defensively in the following ways (Cormier & Cormier, 1991, p. 119).

1. Discrediting the therapist
2. Persuading the therapist that his or her views are wrong
3. Devaluing the importance of the issue
4. Seeking support elsewhere
5. Agreeing with the therapist on the surface, but not taking the confrontation seriously

Interpretation

An interpretation is used to help clients find meaning and understanding about their feelings, thoughts, or behaviors. Interpretations are beneficial to the extent that they help clients view their problems from a different perspective and motivate them to use this new perspective for making changes in their lives. The use of interpretations in therapy has a long history, ranging from Freud's belief that interpretations are essential to Carl Rogers' disavowal of their value. One great danger of interpretations, which Rogers (1957) articulated, is that they often have a blaming or pejorative quality (Strupp, 1989). Interpretations also pose the risk of placing the therapist in the role of "expert." Another problem with interpretations is that they may promote an intellectualized way of avoiding the here-and-now (Safran & Segal, 1990). Because interpretations pose these kinds of risks, Strupp (1989) cautions against their use. The fact that interpretations can lead to defensiveness on the part of clients explains why research studies do not show consistent evidence that interpretations are related to successful therapeutic outcome (Orlinsky & Howard, 1986).

Four criteria for effective interpretations are optimal timing, minimum dosage, concrete detail, and individual focus (Karasu, 1992). Therapists are also advised to restrict interpretations to whats or hows rather than to whys (Claiborn, 1982; Singer, 1970). Anderson and Goolishian suggest that therapists adopt a "not-knowing" position, whereby they communicate a genuine interest in being informed by the client (1992). Therapists do not provide clients with the meaning or an answer to their problems. Instead, they collaborate with clients using data from the clients' own experiences (including those in the therapy session) to understand their dilemmas and identify their options. Other suggestions for helping clients appreciate the ramifications of their thinking styles and behaviors include emphasizing the positive connotations of clients' openness to looking at themselves (J. T. Beck & Strong, 1982) and making interpretations tentatively rather than absolutely (Jones & Gelso, 1988).

Summarization

Summary statements are used to provide focus and structure to a therapy session. Therapists use summarizations to identify common themes, to review progress, and to provide focus when a client's statements appear to be disjointed. Summarizations can be used at the beginning of therapy sessions to get them off on a clear track. They can be used during the middle of sessions if the client is rambling or going off on a tangent. Summarizations can also be used at the end of therapy sessions to tie things together and suggest a starting point for the therapy session to follow.

Questions

Questions can be used to accomplish four general purposes in a therapy session (Tomm, 1988). The most obvious use of questions is to obtain facts. Fact-finding questions that focus on when, where, what, and why are called *lineal* questions.

• "What problems are troubling you?"
• "How long have you had these problems?"
• "When do they occur?"

Lineal questions are necessary for completing a basic assessment of a client's problems. They are generally safe and nonthreatening. Lineal questions can become a problem if they lead to a question/answer kind of interaction between the therapist and client. There is also the danger of focusing too much on "pathology"—analyzing and dissecting the client's problems rather than attempting to place her or his life into perspective. Skilled therapists know how to avoid the overuse of lineal questions.

A second type of question explores how a client's problems are related to his or her life. Exploratory questions that attempt to identify patterns and connections between a client's problems and his or her coping styles, ways of thinking, and interpersonal relationships are called *circular* questions.

• "How do other people react when you get so down on yourself?"
• "What are you thinking when your anger gets out of control?"
• "What kinds of situations make you particularly anxious?"

Circular questions take the focus off pathology and allow clients to gain a broader perspective on what is troubling them.

A third type of question attempts to influence or correct the client in some way. Corrective questions are called *strategic* questions.

- "Why haven't you told your wife about how unhappy you are?"
- "What stops you from setting limits with people who make unreasonable demands?"
- "Can you see why it would be good to take more responsibility for your life?"

Strategic questions may successfully challenge clients to change their behaviors or ways of thinking. However, because they are so direct, strategic questions are risky. Unless they are used tactfully, strategic questions are likely to cause the client to become defensive.

A fourth type of question attempts to help the client see his or her problem in a different light. Questions that are intended to facilitate a new perspective on the client's problems are called *reflexive* questions.

- "Imagine that you told your wife about how unhappy you are. What do you think would happen?"
- "Let's say you decided to set some limits with people who make unreasonable demands. How would they react?"
- "What might be some benefits of taking more responsibility for your life? What would be the drawbacks?"

Reflexive questions enable the client to generate and consider new possibilities. They are not as threatening as strategic questions because, instead of demanding that the client change, they only invite the client to consider "what if." Reflexive questions encourage the therapist and the client to approach the client's problems with a sense of open-mindedness and creativity.

SPEAKING SKILLS

Speaking skills refer not only to what one says but also to how one says it. A review of research on impressions conveyed by speaking styles revealed the following suggestions for speaking in a manner that reinforces a sense of competence and credibility (Kleinke, 1986).

Be Active

For therapy to be productive, therapists and clients must talk to each other. This does not mean that there cannot be periods of silence or time spent just being together. However, verbal activity by clients is important and is related to a successful therapeutic outcome (Orlinsky & Howard, 1986). Two studies have suggested that the preferred scenario is for the therapist to speak about one-third of the time in a therapy session (Friedlander, Thibodeau, & Ward, 1985; Kleinke &

Tully, 1979). Although this is by no means a definite rule, it does indicate that clients are likely to be uncomfortable with therapists who provide only minimal verbal responses.

Use an Expressive Tone

Therapists should try to match their speaking tone to the context of the discussion and mood of the therapy session. Within this guideline, therapists are most effective when they are spirited and communicate emotion and feeling in their tone of expression.

Speak Fluently

Therapists are encouraged to practice speaking fluently and avoiding speech disruptions. Even if therapists must pause to gather their thoughts, they should try to speak without stammers and repeated words. Therapists are also advised to speak without "ahs," "uhms," and "you knows." The trick is to express oneself clearly and concisely. A body of research suggests that people are viewed as more competent, persuasive, and enthusiastic when they don't talk too slowly. Although speaking at a fast pace is not generally characteristic of therapists, this research does reinforce the value of learning how to be verbally responsive and articulate. Finally, therapists should avoid using big words. What is best is to speak the client's language and to use only jargon with which the client is familiar.

THE POWER OF HUMOR

An admonishment often given by Arthur Brayfield was to practice Rule 11: *Never take yourself too seriously.* Freud recognized the value of humor and described it as the "highest of the defense mechanisms" (Lefcourt & Davidson-Katz, 1991). Freud viewed humor as "a rare and precious gift" that allows us in the face of stress to say, "Look here! This is all that this seemingly dangerous world amounts to. Child's play—the very thing to jest about!" (1928; quoted in Lefcourt & Davidson-Katz, 1991, pp. 43, 220). Gordon Allport (1958, p. 92) wrote "The neurotic who learns to laugh at himself may be on the way to self-management, perhaps to cure." Harry Stack Sullivan (1970, p. 182) described humor as a gift that provides the "capacity for maintaining a sense of proportion as to one's place in the tapestry of life." Humor is a useful coping skill (Kleinke, 1991) and therapists can often help their clients by teaching them how to use it. Miriam Polster (1990) described the power of humor in communicating to clients that "The problem is serious, but you are a little sturdier than you may have thought you were." To put it another way, where there is humor there is hope.

A survey of research literature on humor and health suggests the following conclusions about the value of humor as a coping skill (Lefcourt & Davidson-Katz, 1991).

1. People with a good sense of humor are less likely to react with negative moods and dysphoria when faced with stressful experiences than are people whose sense of humor is lacking. Humor is particularly helpful when it allows people to cope with feelings of depression and dysphoria by coming to terms with a negative event and putting it into perspective. However, humor does not necessarily decrease a person's anxiety in the face of a threatening experience.

2. Humor is an effective method for coping with negative emotions, such as anger, sadness, and depression. People with a good sense of humor are more likely to take an active stance toward their negative emotions and try to rise above them. A sense of humor allows us to carry on in the face of adversity. People who are lacking a sense of humor are more likely to be passive and to allow their negative emotions to control them.

3. People with a good sense of humor have a better chance of experiencing good physical health. Studies have linked humor to positive immune functioning and lowered physiological indices of stress.

The kind of humor that appears to be most healthy is a gentle self-directed form of jesting. This is, as suggested earlier, a sense of not taking oneself too seriously. This healthy kind of humor can be contrasted with a less healthy form of humor involving sarcasm and hostility. The value of humor in psychotherapy has been recognized by so many therapists that it is impossible to quote everyone who has extolled its virtues. However, three points about humor should be made.

First, as Viktor Frankl (1963) explained, humor is paradoxical. You can't feel truly sorry for yourself and laugh at yourself at the same time. The paradoxical nature of humor makes it a useful adjunct in systematic desensitization (Ventis, 1987). The anxiety- or anger-eliciting properties of stimuli are diminished when they are associated with thoughts or images that evoke humor. Second, humor is a uniquely human quality that provides a sense of choice and control by allowing people to detach themselves from their pain and suffering (Frankl, 1969, p. 17). Third, self-directed jesting is a form of self-affirmation. Laughing at yourself is a way of saying *I like myself and I accept myself as a fallible person.*

Therapist-initiated humor that is shared by the client can enhance feelings of comfort and closeness between therapists and clients (Megdell, 1984). Laughter in therapy sessions serves a number of useful purposes (Mahrer & Gervaize, 1984). Hearty laughter can indicate a desirable shift in the client's self-concept or self-perspective. Laughter can also communicate energy, optimism, zest, acceptance, mastery, and inner harmony. Another function of laughter is as an expression of warmth and intimacy between the client and therapist. Finally, laughter is an indication of enhanced willingness by clients to express and experience their feelings. Laughter that is desirable in therapy sessions is spontaneous, enthusiastic, and energetic. It often occurs when clients have taken a risk and are openly acknowledging their sense of pleasure in this accomplishment.

How do therapists facilitate humor during a therapy session? Falk and Hill (1992) identify two therapist interventions that are correlated with client mirth: *release of tension* and *therapist humor.* Release of tension is characterized by the therapist's willingness to discuss such tension-filled subjects as sex, anxiety, conflict, and the therapeutic relationship. An openness by the therapist to talk about issues that need to be talked about but that have previously been avoided gives clients a great sense of relief. Therapists are also able to facilitate client laughter by modeling humor with word play, anecdotes, facial expressions, and unexpected statements and reactions.

Albert Ellis, who has been a proponent of humor throughout his career, wrote a number of songs to help clients put their problems into perspective. Here are some examples (Ellis, 1985, pp. 55–58).

WHINE, WHINE, WHINE
(To the tune of the Yale Whiffenpoof Song, by Guy Scull)

I cannot have all of my wishes filled—
Whine, whine, whine!
I cannot have every frustration stilled—
Whine, whine, whine!
Life really owes me the things that I miss,
Fate has to grant me eternal bliss!
And since I must settle for less than this—
Whine, whine, whine!

*(Lyrics by Albert Ellis, copyright 1977 by the
Institute for Rational-Emotive Therapy. Reprinted by permission.)*

WHEN I AM SO BLUE
(To the tune of Johann Strauss' "The Beautiful Blue Danube")

When I am so blue, so blue, so blue
I sit and I stew, I stew, I stew!
I deem it so awfully horrible
That my life is rough and scarrable!
Whenever my blues are verified,
I make myself doubly terrified,
For I never choose to refuse
To be blue about my blues!

*(Lyrics by Albert Ellis, copyright 1980 by the
Institute for Rational-Emotive Therapy. Reprinted by permission.)*

As a final note on humor, we may all wish to heed Thomas Szasz' advice: "Beware of the psychoanalyst who analyzes jokes rather than laughs at them" (1973, p. 85).

COMMUNICATION

Everything that has been discussed so far in this chapter has to do with communication. This section acknowledges the importance of communication between the therapist and client. Hellmuth Kaiser's one rule of advice to therapists is *communicate* (Yalom, 1980, p. 406). Jerome Frank (1986) also emphasizes the importance of communication in psychotherapy.

> The therapeutic tool of all therapists is symbolic communication conveyed primarily by words but in some therapies also involving meaningful activities or exercises. So in the last analysis the effectiveness of all therapies rests on the therapist's communication skills. Basic to the success of all therapies is the therapist's ability to convey his or her understanding of the patient's problems or feelings as well as total commitment to the patient's welfare. These are the essential components of the therapeutic alliance, on which the success of all therapeutic encounters ultimately depends. (p. x)

Harry Stack Sullivan advises therapists never to assume they know what clients are talking about without first checking it out with the client. In the same vein, therapists should not assume that clients know what they are talking about until the accuracy of their communication is confirmed in what Sullivan called an *alert dialogue* (Chapman, 1978).

One aspect of therapeutic communication that is worth considering here is the therapist's *linguistic competence* (Edelson, 1975; Jenkins, 1991). The therapist must possess the linguistic skills necessary to "disambiguate" clients' statements so clients can get better control over what is being experienced. To do this, the therapist must be able to hear all possible meanings of the client's language, including those underlying meanings not suggested by the immediate context (Edelson, 1975; Jenkins, 1991). Two linguistic skills used by therapists to communicate with clients are the language of metaphor and the language of paradox.

The Language of Metaphor

Metaphors allow therapists to follow a piece of advice given by Milton Erickson many times during his career: *Learn and use the client's language.* Metaphors can be viewed as "cognitive instruments" that create analogies or connections that were not previously recognized (Muran & DiGiuseppe, 1990). Metaphors enable clients to see their problems from a fresh perspective. Metaphors provide clients with a new paradigm (Kuhn, 1970), and they encourage clients to develop "different emotional attitudes and different ways of interpreting the world around them" (Barker, 1985, p. 21). By offering a different paradigm or assumptive world, metaphors suggest possibilities that clients previously could not have considered. In this sense, metaphors create something new (Berlin et al., 1991) and provide therapists with a "language of change" (Watzlawick, 1978).

Milton Erickson (Erickson & Rossi, 1976/1980) is famous for communicating metaphors to clients in the form of hypnotic suggestions. Other therapists use metaphors with clients on a conscious level. In both cases, metaphors avoid direct confrontation and allow clients to consider ideas and feelings that would otherwise be avoided or denied. Evans (1988) describes the function of metaphors in psychotherapy in the following way.

> The client develops a kind of freedom, often an initially quite terrifying freedom to abandon his or her familiar perspective, assume different vantage points, and otherwise reexperience the world through the various phases of conscious metaphor. . . . psychological freedom is gained not by achieving a metaphor of liberation but rather by the liberation of metaphorizing. (p. 550)

Metaphors can be communicated in therapy by relabeling a feeling, experience, or problem or by using anecdotes, parables, and short stories. Barker (1985) describes how stories can be used metaphorically in psychotherapy, explaining that stories are beneficial for the following purposes.

1. Stories are usually more interesting than is a straight exposition of a point the therapist may wish to make.
2. Clients are less threatened when a new idea or perspective is communicated in a story than when it is directly presented by the therapist.
3. Clients have the freedom to interpret messages communicated in stories according to their own goals, purposes, and values.
4. Clients are less likely to resist an insight communicated in a story because it affects them at an unconscious level.
5. Stories are flexible and can be used to communicate several messages at one time.
6. A therapist can use characters in a story to say things to the client (who is represented by someone in the story) in a more direct way than the therapist could say during the therapy session.
7. Stories provide a good means of establishing rapport.
8. Stories model a useful fruitful style of communication.

According to Muran and DiGiuseppe (1990), metaphors are used in therapy to convey:

1. The relationship between cognitions, emotions, and behaviors.
2. The illogical and anti-empirical bases of maladaptive thoughts.
3. The lack of heuristic value in maintaining such thoughts.

Research suggests that metaphors can sometimes be more effective than direct feedback is in helping clients appreciate their feelings, emotions, and affective reactions to challenges in their lives (Martin, Cummings, & Hallberg, 1992). Metaphors can also motivate clients by creating a feeling of closeness with the therapist and by clarifying clients' problems as well as their goals.

Here are some steps for working with metaphors (Muran & DiGiuseppe, 1990).

1. Clearly define the concept you wish to communicate or teach.
2. Attend to the client's language and search for an arena that he or she understands and has comfortably mastered.
3. Search for an analogue construct in the client's arena of knowledge that includes the core elements of the concept that you wish to teach.
4. If none exists or comes to mind, start over with a new arena about which the client has knowledge.

Another suggestion for using metaphors is to adopt a discovery-oriented collaborative process with the client (Angus & Rennie, 1988). Therapists who take this approach convey a genuine curiosity about the client's ideas and associations, even if they are not going in the direction anticipated by the therapist. By helping clients elaborate their own metaphors, therapists communicate their interest and attentiveness, and they reinforce a lively and spontaneous sense of sharing and joint exploration. Therapists who take a noncollaborative approach and attempt to convince clients to understand metaphors in their chosen way are less likely to be successful. With the therapist as "expert," clients have no sense of shared discovery and are likely to react with confusion and puzzlement about the therapist's interpretations.

The Language of Paradox

Although many therapists do not intentionally use paradoxical strategies when working with clients, they often communicate in paradoxical language. Therapists use paradoxical language for the following reason. On the one hand, therapists are persuaders who are attempting to convince clients to take risks and make changes in their ways of thinking and behaving (Frank, 1961). On the other hand, since people are naturally reactive, they will resist attempts by others to persuade them (Brehm, 1966; Brehm & Brehm, 1981). Therapists therefore use paradoxical language to persuade clients while fostering the illusion that any risks clients end up taking are actually those of the client's choosing (Haley, 1963). Here are some methods for doing so.

Accepting the client's symptomatology   Therapists do not immediately challenge clients' symptoms. Their language implies acceptance of clients' solutions to their problems. Even if these solutions have disadvantages, they are the best alternatives the clients could find (Kercher & Smith, 1985).

Deemphasizing power and control   Therapists use noncoercive language to deemphasize their control and to place responsibility for change on the client. Therapists often eschew the role of expert and present themselves as "one-down" and unable to effect any change without the collaboration of the client. Any improvements that do occur are attributed to the client.

The double bind   The double bind provides clients with an illusion of choice while assuring that any choice the client makes will be therapeutic (Erickson & Rossi, 1975). For example, Milton Erickson's example of asking the client, "Do you want to deal with this symptom first or that symptom first?" implies that the client *will* deal with a symptom. Also, by wondering outloud whether the client will notice improvement on Wednesday, or possibly Thursday, or maybe even Friday provides the client with the choice of when to improve while demanding that improvement will occur.

Reframing   Therapists use reframing to provide clients with a new way of looking at or interpreting a situation or problem (Greenberg & Safran, 1981; Watzlawick, Weakland, & Fisch, 1974). When a different meaning is ascribed to the problem, solutions that were not previously apparent become a possibility (Duncan, 1989). For example, a client who is bewildered by feelings of depression may be encouraged to realize that this depression is quite understandable given the life events recently experienced. A client whose professional work is compromised by anxiety can learn to perceive the "symptom" as a natural response in a competitive career and one that indicates confronting a challenge rather than personal weakness. One valuable function of reframing is to help clients attribute their difficulties to life circumstances rather than to personal traits (Cormier & Cormier, 1991). A situational rather than dispositional analysis of one's problems offers a greater possibility of exercising self-efficacy and utilizing one's problem-solving skills (Kleinke, 1978; 1991).

SENSITIVITY TO PROCESS

Chapter 1 explained how the therapist attempts to provide the client with a corrective experience by not becoming an accomplice in the client's maladaptive style of relating to people. As Safran and Segal (1990) point out, the therapist's ability to become fully aware of the feelings and responses elicited by the client is an essential psychotherapy skill. Psychotherapists use this skill by first noticing when they are being engaged or "hooked" by the client to respond in a certain way (Kiesler, 1988). The therapist uses this process as a cue to assess the interpersonal style of the client as well as his or her personal reactions to the client's behavior. Rather than acting on the responses the client is pulling from the therapist, the therapist analyzes this process with the client in an attempt to determine which interpersonal styles are (and are not) in the client's best interest.

HELPFUL AND NONHELPFUL THERAPIST BEHAVIORS

Boxes 3.1 and 3.2 summarize a number of helpful and nonhelpful therapist behaviors that were identified in a research study conducted by Robert Elliott (1985). Other studies suggest the following conclusions about helpful and nonhelpful therapist behaviors (Beutler, Crago, & Arizmendi, 1986; Cooley & LaJoy, 1980; Elliott & James, 1989; Friedlander, Thibodeau, & Ward, 1985; Henry, Schacht, & Strupp, 1986; Orlinsky & Howard, 1986; Patterson & Forgatch, 1985; Strupp, 1989).

1. Helpful therapists attempt to be understanding and accepting. They are aware of the benefits of focusing on affect and taking a supportive and facilitative approach toward clients that emphasizes encouragement, support, willingness to help, a sense of hope, understanding, and a feeling of collaboration.
2. Helpful therapists assist their clients with achieving goals and solving problems. They work with clients to gain a better sense of self-understanding, and they serve as a catalyst for change by providing useful feedback.
3. Helpful therapists avoid taking the role of experts who are either nonresponsive or who interrogate their clients and give advice. Therapists are counterproductive when they respond to clients in a manner that is intellectual, judgmental, belittling, and blaming.

Helpful and nonhelpful therapist behaviors can also be identified from studies of the therapeutic process (Greenberg & Pinsof, 1986). There are two measures of therapeutic process that are particularly relevant for this chapter. The Vanderbilt Psychotherapy Process Scale (Suh, Strupp, & O'Malley, 1986) contains the following scales related to skills of the therapist.

Box 3.1 Helpful Therapist Behaviors

Offering a new perspective: Therapist encourages clients to achieve a new perspective: for example, by asking clients to consider the effects of their behaviors on others. Clients experience having an insight they hadn't thought of before.

Problem solving: Therapist suggests a problem-solving strategy. Clients learn a new way of acting or thinking.

Problem clarification: Therapist helps clients clarify the nature of the problem. Clients experience a clearer way of defining what is bothering them.

Focusing awareness: Therapist focuses clients' attention on critical issues related to the problem. For example, a client discussing difficulties with school work is asked about the possibility of failing and the effects of failure on his self-concept. Clients experience a sharper degree of awareness about how their problem might affect them.

Understanding: Therapist gives a clear reflection of the clients' problems and their feelings about these problems. Clients experience a feeling of being understood and appreciated.

Client involvement: Therapist provides a summary of the clients' problems and enlists the clients' involvement and commitment to work on them. Clients experience a desire to respond to the therapist's analysis.

Support: Therapist supports an action or accomplishment by clients. Clients experience being backed up by therapist's encouragement.

Personal contact: Therapist expresses personal interest and attention. Clients experience therapist as a person truly interested in them.

Source: Adapted from "Helpful and Nonhelpful Events in Brief Counseling Interviews: An Empirical Taxonomy" by R. Elliott, 1985, *Journal of Counseling Psychology, 32,* pp. 307–322. Copyright 1985 by the American Psychological Association. Adapted with permission of the author.

Therapist exploration is a measure of the therapist's attempts to examine the client's feelings and behaviors and the reasons behind them. Examples of specific therapist behaviors on this scale are:

- Tried to help the patient recognize his or her feelings.
- Tried to help the patient understand the reasons behind his or her actions.
- Placed the patient's report in a new perspective or reorganized the patient's experience.
- Conveyed expertise.

Box 3.2   Nonhelpful Therapist Behaviors

Misperception: Therapist makes response that indicates a misperception of clients' problem. Clients experience the therapist being off the track.

Negative reaction: Therapist is abrupt, critical, or impersonal. Clients feel the therapist is not interested in them or is unsympathetic to their problems.

Nonresponsiveness: Therapist appears uncertain about what to say. Therapist is nonresponsive or gives a response that does not meet clients' need. Clients experience a feeling of awkwardness and lack of direction.

Repetition: Therapist repeats what clients have shared without adding anything new. Clients experience lack of helpfulness from therapist.

Misdirection: Therapist gives reassurance or advice but misses clients' main concern. Clients experience lack of understanding from therapist about what is really bothering them.

Unwanted thoughts: Therapist suggests a thought or idea that discourages and confuses clients. For example, therapist reminds clients of possible negative event that is beyond clients' control. Clients feel pushed to consider issues they don't feel will help them.

Source: Adapted from "Helpful and Nonhelpful Events in Brief Counseling Interviews: An Empirical Taxonomy" by R. Elliott, 1985, *Journal of Counseling Psychology, 32*, pp. 307–322. Copyright 1985 by the American Psychological Association. Adapted with permission of the author.

Therapist warmth and friendliness is a measure of the therapist's acceptance of the client. Examples of therapist behaviors on this scale are:

• Helped the patient feel accepted in the relationship.
• Showed warmth and friendliness toward the patient.
• Supported the patient's self-esteem and confidence.
• Was involved.

Therapist negative attitude is a measure of therapist behaviors to be avoided. These include:

• Being judgmental.
• Being authoritarian.
• Lecturing the patient.
• Being defensive.
• Being intimidating.
• Confronting the patient in a negative manner.

The Penn Helping Alliance Scales (Alexander & Luborsky, 1986) measure a number of therapist behaviors, from the client's, therapist's, and observer's point of view. The therapist's *facilitating behaviors* are rated by observers on a 10-point scale (1 = very little; 10 = very much).

1. The therapist is warm and supportive.
2. The therapist conveys a sense of wanting the patient to achieve treatment goals.
3. The therapist conveys a sense of hopefulness that treatment goals can be achieved.
4. The therapist conveys a sense that he or she feels a rapport with the patient, that he or she understands the patient.
5. The therapist conveys feelings of acceptance and respect for the patient as opposed to behavior in which the patient is put down.
6. The therapist says things that show that he or she feels a "we" bond with the patient, that he or she feels a sense of alliance with the patient in the joint struggle against what is impeding the patient.
7. The therapist conveys recognition of the patient's growing sense of being able to do what the therapist indicates needs to be done.
8. The therapist shows acceptance of the patient's increased ability to understand his or her own experiences.
9. The therapist acknowledges and confirms the patient's accurate perceptions of him or her.
10. The therapist can accept the fact that the patient also can reflect on what the patient and he or she have been through together.

COMMON THERAPIST MISTAKES

A good way to perfect one's psychotherapy skills is to become aware of common mistakes, such as the ones described here (Buckley, Karasu, & Charles, 1979; Pipes & Davenport, 1990).

1. *Wanting to be liked by the client.* Beginning therapists often have trouble getting used to the fact that therapy sessions can be uncomfortable and can provoke feelings of anger, sadness, anxiety, and hostility from clients. It is important to deal with clients' feelings therapeutically and not to personalize them.
2. *Getting caught in intellectualizations.* This is especially difficult to avoid with clients who have an intellectualizing style. The therapist should attempt to shift the focus to the client's feelings and experiences, particularly to the here-and-now.
3. *Difficulty tolerating silence.* Silence is a therapeutic process that can be used advantageously. Therapists need to be aware of si-

lences and make an informed decision about whether the silence should be broken by them or by the client.

4. *Engaging in inappropriate behaviors.* Chatting, nervous laughter, and personal disclosures are generally not appropriate in a therapy session.

5. *Attempting to "cure" the client prematurely.* Beginning therapists often feel pressured by the need to do something for the client. Therapists must avoid the temptation to push the client toward "cure" before understanding the client's entire problem and assessing the client's ability and motivation to change.

6. *Focusing on people other than the client.* Clients often relate that their problems are due to other people in their lives. When this happens, therapists must bring the focus back onto the client.

7. *Asking too many questions.* Beginning therapists often fall into the trap of asking too many questions because they have not learned how to use the verbal skills discussed earlier in this chapter.

8. *Staying on the surface of issues.* Therapists need to find the balance between pushing clients to deeper levels of experiencing and feeling, on the one hand, and honoring clients' vulnerabilities, on the other. Therapists must be willing to take risks. It is precisely the client's sensitive issues that are to be addressed in therapy.

9. *Difficulty dealing with countertransference issues.* A fundamental skill is to recognize one's personal feelings toward clients while not acting them out in the therapy session. What is particularly important for therapists to deal with is the inevitable anger, frustration, or dislike they will experience toward certain clients (Strupp, 1980b). Although these kinds of negative reactions are real and should be accepted, the therapist must make every effort not to act on them. When therapists respond to disagreeable clients in a cold, aloof, or distancing manner, a self-fulfilling prophecy is created that results in an inevitable dissolution of the therapeutic relationship.

10. *Avoiding or not allowing sufficient time for termination.* Termination is an essential part of therapy and it needs to be planned by therapists and clients (see Chapter 10).

Another mistake therapists need to avoid is confusing the client's expression of positive or negative feelings toward the therapist as transference reactions when they are actually straightforward responses to something the therapist has said or done. Positive and negative expressions by clients that are motivated by transference (that is, they are more a function of the client's style or personality than of the therapist's behavior) are characterized by the following (Karasu, 1992).

1. The expressions appear inappropriate or irrational because they don't fit the context. Nothing has happened in the therapeutic relationship to explain why the client might be expressing these feelings.
2. The expressions are more intense than one would expect, given what has transpired during the therapy session.
3. The client holds on to these feelings in a way that is persistent and tenacious. The client's expression of positive or negative feelings toward the therapist occurs regardless of what is being discussed.
4. There is an obvious origin to the client's displaced feelings. The client may have given sufficient information to explain where these positive or negative feelings are coming from and to make clear that they are not generated by the behavior of the therapist.

A detrimental mistake is for the therapist to respond with a transference interpretation when the client's expression of positive or negative feelings is genuine. To avoid this error, the therapist should use interpretations with caution and should also be sensitive about the effects of his or her behaviors on the client.

TEACHING PSYCHOTHERAPY SKILLS

A review of research on the teaching of therapeutic skills indicates that this process can be quite helpful (Matarazzo & Patterson, 1986). What is of interest to note is that there was a time when "the psychotherapeutic hour was considered so mysterious and sacrosanct that a supervisor could not observe it nor could it be recorded for later discussion" (Matarazzo & Patterson, 1986, p. 822). Things have changed. Now teaching psychotherapy skills from recordings of therapy sessions is considered essential because therapist's reports of what occurred during a session are notoriously unreliable. Psychotherapy skills training programs are based on the theory that the progress of clients in therapy is affected not only by the dynamics of the client but also by the interaction between the client and the therapist. The therapist's behaviors during the therapy session are therefore very important. Anything that can be done through research and training to enhance the effectiveness of the therapist's behaviors is considered well worth the effort. Psychotherapy skills training programs are also useful because they provide therapists with a heightened sense of self-efficacy (Larson et al., 1992).

The following steps are included in a typical psychotherapy skills training program (Ivey, 1988; Ivey & Authier, 1978).

1. Study the skills to be learned.
2. Observe the skills as they are modeled.
3. Practice the skills in "counseling sessions."

4. Obtain feedback from observing one's tapes and from supportive colleagues and supervisors.
5. Practice further to implement what was learned in feedback sessions.

SUMMARY

The therapist's interpersonal skills are a critical component of success in psychotherapy. Clinicians are therefore interested in identifying these skills and devising methods for teaching them to students of psychotherapy. The skills proposed by clinicians who have written on this topic include an enthusiasm and interest in other people and an ability to work with them in a confident, encouraging, patient, accepting, and nonjudgmental manner. Skillful therapists are technically well trained and are able to implement therapeutic interventions flexibly with a sense of collaboration with the client. They are able to manage their own problems.

The responsive therapist communicates to the client a vital interest in what the client has to say. Responsive therapists are able to engage in an active dialogue with a client, and they know how to reply with statements that are congruent with the message the client is communicating. Responsiveness by therapists encourages a smooth dialogue in which clients experience validation, trust, and encouragement to participate actively in the therapy session. Nonverbal responsiveness is communicated through eye contact, attentive facial expressions, and open body postures. The amount of nonverbal responsiveness by therapists is less important than the congruence of nonverbal behaviors with the context of the therapy session. Therapists find it useful to pay attention to the congruency between the verbal and nonverbal behaviors of their clients.

Therapists are also advised to develop skills for communicating immediacy in their verbal statements. Nine verbal skills are the probe, clarification, paraphrase, reflection, information giving, confrontation, interpretation, summarization, and questions. Speaking skills include being verbally active, using an expressive tone, and speaking fluently.

Humor is useful in psychotherapy when it is employed to convey hope and to assist clients in looking at their problems from a new and different perspective. Humor is a valuable coping skill when people can use it to take an active stance with their problems, to carry on in the face of adversity, and to avoid taking themselves too seriously.

Two aspects of linguistic competence that enhance a therapist's ability to communicate are the language of metaphor and the language of paradox. Metaphors enable clients to gain a fresh perspective on their problems and to see solutions they had not recognized before.

Paradoxical language is used to persuade clients to take risks while reinforcing their sense of choice and self-control.

Ten common mistakes made by therapists are wanting to be liked by the client, getting caught in intellectualizations, having difficulty tolerating silence, engaging in inappropriate behaviors such as chatting and nervous laughter, attempting to "cure" the client prematurely, focusing on people other than the client, asking too many questions, staying on the surface of issues, having difficulty dealing with countertransference issues, and avoiding or not allowing sufficient time for termination. Studies of the psychotherapeutic process have been useful in identifying helpful and nonhelpful therapist behaviors.

Five steps generally included in programs for teaching psychotherapy skills are studying the skills to be learned, observing the skills as they are modeled, practicing the skills in "counseling sessions," obtaining feedback by observing one's tapes and from supportive colleagues and supervisors, and further practicing to implement what was learned in feedback sessions.

SUGGESTIONS FOR FURTHER READING

Cormier, W. H., & Cormier, L. S. (1991). *Interviewing strategies for helpers.* Pacific Grove, CA: Brooks/Cole.

Hutchins, D. E., & Cole, C. G. (1992). *Helping relationships and strategies.* Pacific Grove, CA: Brooks/Cole.

Ivey, A. E. (1988). *Intentional interviewing and counseling: Facilitating client development.* Pacific Grove, CA: Brooks/Cole.

Karasu, T. B. (1992). *Wisdom in the practice of psychotherapy.* New York: Basic Books.

Safran, J. D., & Segal, Z. V. (1990). *Interpersonal processes in cognitive therapy.* New York: Basic Books.

CHAPTER 4

The Therapeutic Relationship

Probably the most recognized commonality in psychotherapy is the significance of the therapeutic relationship. Yalom (1980, p. 401) reiterated a maxim that is learned by most therapists at some point in their training: *it is the relationship that heals.* As explained by Strupp (1982, p. 46), the goal of the therapeutic relationship is not to impose change on the client but to create a condition that allows change within the client to occur. In other words, the therapeutic relationship permits therapists to function as *instruments of change* (Korb, Gorrell, & Van De Riet, 1989). Carl Rogers (1961) described his insight into the value of the therapeutic relationship.

> One brief way of describing the change which has taken place in me is to say that in my early years I was asking the question, How can I treat, or cure, or change this person? Now I would phrase the question in this way: How can I provide a relationship which this person may use for his own personal growth? (p. 32)

The importance of developing a good therapeutic relationship for successful therapy has been documented in a wide range of research studies (Luborsky, Barber, & Crits-Christoph, 1990; Orlinsky & Howard, 1986; Saltzman et al., 1976; Waterhouse & Strupp, 1984).

DEFINING THE THERAPEUTIC RELATIONSHIP

The therapeutic relationship is defined by Gelso and Carter (1985) as *the feelings and attitudes that counseling participants have toward one another, and the manner in which these are expressed.* Gelso and Carter (1985) identified the following three components of the therapeutic relationship, each of which offers a particular challenge to

81

the therapist's skills. The therapist's task is to find the correct balance among these different levels of relating with a client.

The Working Alliance

Research indicates that the quality of the working alliance is related to therapeutic outcome (Horvath & Symonds, 1991). Greenson (1965) points out that the quality of the therapeutic alliance determines the client's capacity to work purposefully in the therapy session. A good working alliance requires a bond between therapist and client that reinforces collaboration toward agreed-upon tasks and goals (Bordin, 1979). The working alliance does not in itself cause change, but it is a necessary precondition for therapeutic progress to occur (Gaston, 1990; Tichenor & Hill, 1989). In developing a good working alliance, the therapist is challenged to win the client's trust and to communicate to the client a feeling of competence, acceptance, and respect. The working alliance is composed of the following three components (Bordin, 1979): tasks, goals, and bonds.

Tasks are the responsibilities taken on by the therapist and client. In a good working alliance, the therapist and client agree on their roles and believe them to be relevant and worthwhile. The client's satisfaction with the tasks of a working alliance are measured on the Working Alliance Inventory by the following kinds of statements (Horvath & Greenberg, 1986, 1989).

- My therapist and I agree about the things I will need to do in therapy to help improve my situation.
- I believe the way we are working with my problem is correct.

Goals are agreed-upon targets and outcomes of therapy. The client's satisfaction with the goals of a working alliance are measured by the following kinds of statements.

- My therapist accurately perceives what my goals are.
- The goals of these sessions are important to me.

Bonds represent the closeness of the relationship between the therapist and client and include issues such as mutual trust, acceptance, and confidence. Bonds are measured on the Working Alliance Inventory by the following kinds of statements.

- I believe my therapist is genuinely concerned for my welfare.
- My relationship with my therapist is very important to me.

Transference

Transference is the second component of the therapeutic relationship. The concept of transference was discussed in Chapter 1; it is the repetition of past conflicts with significant others. The therapist's challenge is to help the client resolve the conflict he or she is enacting with the therapist by responding to the client in a new and different manner.

Interpersonal Sharing

This is the personal part of the relationship in which clients and therapists share their feelings. There is a sense that the client and therapist are "in this together." Interpersonal sharing occurs when clients and therapists communicate their here-and-now experiences as they work toward common goals. The therapist's challenge is to be genuinely interested in the client.

THE POWER OF THE THERAPEUTIC RELATIONSHIP

One of the notable contributions made by Carl Rogers was defining the power of the therapeutic relationship in helping clients make changes in their lives. According to Rogers (1957), three ingredients of effective helping relationships are genuineness, empathy, and unconditional positive regard.

Genuineness

Genuine therapists are authentic. They can respond to the client in a congruent manner because they are not biased by their own moods, feelings, values, and needs. Therapists can share their personal reactions to clients but own these reactions by saying "*my* feeling is . . .," or "at this point I feel . . .". Genuineness is made up of the following four components (Cormier & Cormier, 1991).

1. *Role behavior.* Genuine therapists are comfortable in their role as therapists. They do not use their "expertness" to be dominant over or emotionally distant from clients.
2. *Congruence.* The therapist's words and nonverbal behaviors are consistent with the feelings being shared with the client. There is a sense of *resonance* between therapist and client (Larson, 1987). The client can tell from the therapist's responses that the therapist is fully in tune with what he or she is saying.
3. *Spontaneity.* Spontaneous therapists can express themselves naturally. They don't hesitate or deliberate before responding to something the client says. They know how to be tactful without appearing artificial.
4. *Openness.* The therapist is immediate with the client and is open to sharing herself or himself in the here-and-now.

Empathy

Therapists attempt to communicate to clients "You are not alone" and "You are understandable" (Combs, 1989). Empathic therapists try to see things from the client's point of view. As Carl Rogers (1951) explains, therapists "adopt the client's frame of reference" by communicating the following message.

> To be of assistance to you I will put aside myself—the self of ordinary perception—and enter into your world of perception as completely as I am able. I will become, in a sense, another self for you—an alter ego of your own attitudes and feelings—a safe opportunity for you to discern yourself more clearly, to experience yourself more truly and deeply, to choose more significantly. (p. 35)

Empathy means attempting to share with clients their subjective worlds. Therapists communicate empathy to their clients by encouraging them, in a nonjudgmental manner, to look at themselves and to explore the effects that their feelings, actions, and thinking patterns have on their life. Therapists who rely too much on advice giving or on making interpretations are not viewed as particularly empathetic (Barkham & Shapiro, 1986). According to Truax and Carkhuff (1967), empathic therapists:

- communicate in their manner and tone that they take their relationship with the client seriously.
- are aware of how the client is feeling at the moment.
- are able to communicate their understanding of the client's feelings in a manner that is congruent with these feelings.
- are sensitive to the client's feelings toward them and to their feelings toward the client.
- are flexible and able to correct themselves when they have misread the client's meaning.
- effectively communicate their support and belief that the client can find his or her own answers.

Carkhuff and Pierce (1975) defined five levels of empathy. These levels can be understood by considering various responses a therapist could give to the following clients.

> *Client A:* I've tried so hard to get along better with my wife, but it just doesn't work out. I feel stuck.
>
> *Client B:* I've been so worried about my grades at school, and now I have a big math test coming up next week.

Level 1 empathy is essentially lack of empathy, whereby the therapist's response either does not recognize or detracts from the client's feelings. A therapist at Level 1 empathy typically asks a question or gives reassurance or advice. A Level 1 response to Client A could be "Do you think you have really been able to see her point of view?" A Level 1 response to Client B could be "I'm sure you'll do OK. You just need to relax."

Level 2 empathy is a response to only the content of what the client says; the client's feelings are ignored. A Level 2 response to Client A could be "You tried unsuccessfully to get along better with your wife." A Level 2 response to Client B could be "Your grades are not what you want them to be and now you have an important test coming up in your math class."

Level 3 empathy is a repetition of the client's feelings without adding anything new to what the client said. The feeling words expressed by the client and therapist are essentially interchangeable. A Level 3 response to Client A could be "You feel stuck because everything you have tried with your wife has not worked out." A Level 3 response to Client B could be "You're worried about your grades and you have a big test coming up."

Level 4 empathy adds something to the feelings expressed by the client. It acknowledges the client's desire to find a solution to the problem and inability to do so. A Level 4 response to Client A could be "It is discouraging to try so hard and still not find a way to get along better with your wife." A Level 4 response to Client B could be "You have some real worries about your grades and are particularly concerned about your math exam next week."

Level 5 empathy contains the same sensitivity to the client's feelings as Level 4 empathy and adds an action step that the client can take to reach the goal. A Level 5 response to Client A could be: "It is discouraging to try so hard and still not find a way to get along better with your wife. Coming to therapy is a big step and maybe your wife would be interested in coming in sometime as well." A Level 5 response to Client B could be: "You have some real worries about your grades and are particularly concerned about your math exam next week. We can take some time to look at your progress in school and also decide whether there are some study skills or test-taking skills that would be good for you to know."

Batchelor (1988) identifies four different ways in which therapists can express empathy to clients. *Facilitative empathy* involves a reformulation or interpretation by the therapist that helps the client gain a new perspective on the problem. *Affective empathy* gives clients a feeling of comfort and satisfaction because it communicates that the therapist understands the client's feelings. *Sharing empathy* reassures clients that they are not alone and that they and the therapist have something in common; it encourages clients to believe there are potential solutions for their problems with which the therapist has had personal experience. *Nurturant empathy* provides clients with emotional support and a feeling of security.

Another way to understand empathy is to distinguish between cognitive empathy and affective empathy (Gladstein, 1983).

Cognitive empathy refers to the therapist's ability to take the client's role and to understand the client's way of thinking and responding to events in his or her life. Cognitive empathy means perceiving the world from the client's point of view . Cognitive empathy is helpful in establishing a good working relationship between the therapist and client and serves a useful purpose throughout all stages of therapy.

Affective empathy refers to the therapist's predisposition to feel the client's emotions. When affective empathy is present, the therapist is experiencing the same emotional state the client is experiencing. Affective empathy can be useful in promoting a good working relationship, and it can facilitate self-exploration on the part of the client. Affective empathy has limits; it is obviously not therapeutic for a therapist to become so involved with the client's emotions that she or he loses objectivity. Although it may be helpful for a therapist to feel at least some of what the client is feeling, affective empathy must be controlled. If the therapist experiences too much "emotional contagion," therapy will get stuck on the feelings of the therapist.

Unconditional Positive Regard

Unconditional positive regard means "I am on your side and I prize you as a person." The therapist communicates to the client: "My purpose is not to judge you, but to be with you as you search for new ways of acting, thinking, and feeling. Your ups and downs won't influence my commitment toward you as a person, and deep down, I know you can do it." Receiving unconditional positive regard is such a unique event that it is quite often a corrective experience. Strupp (1973) describes this corrective element in the following way.

> [The therapist's] attitude is respectful, accepting, nonvaluative, noncondemning, noncriticizing, and thus invariably in contrast to the patient's experiences with significant adults in his early life. The therapist, unlike significant people in the patient's past and present life, minimizes *his* emotions, feelings, and needs, and maximizes the patient's. Usually for the first time in his life, the patient has the unique experience of hearing himself, of experiencing himself. The importance of the therapist's attitude, as communicated nonverbally or by minimal verbal cue, can hardly be overestimated. The message to the patient is that of simple acceptance and worthwhileness as a human being, regardless of the symptoms and personality characteristics about which the patient and others (including the therapist) may have misgivings or regrets. In this way the therapist helps the patient toward greater self-acceptance and self-esteem ("If the therapist is tolerant and noncondemning, perhaps I can accept myself better too"). (pp. 37–38)

Arnold Lazarus (1985) reminds us that although therapists may vigorously attack maladaptive behaviors, therapists always support the dignity of the client. Albert Ellis and Windy Dryden (1987, p. 29) explain that "therapists strive to *unconditionally accept* their clients as fallible human beings who often act self-defeatingly but are never essentially bad (or good)." Esther Menaker (1990) paraphrased Heinz Kohut by saying the therapist's task is to affirm the *person* of the patient. In addition to honoring the client's dignity, therapists communicate positive regard by being *nondefensive* (Kahn, 1991). Therapists must accept clients when their behaviors or responses in therapy are undesirable, and they must avoid the temptation to "fight back" by making interpretations about the client's pathology or resistance.

Albert Ellis has argued on many occasions against overemphasizing the importance of the relationship in therapy, because it is not therapeutic to reinforce clients' desires for the therapist to like them (Ellis & Dryden, 1987, p. 29). This, however, does not contradict the basic therapeutic philosophy of acceptance, which is conveyed in an experience shared by Jeffrey Kottler (1991).

> I recall attending one of Albert Ellis's "road shows" during the 1970s and listening to his very strident presentation on the values of rational-emotive techniques while ridiculing Carl Rogers's emphasis on the therapeutic relationship, which he considered mostly a waste of time. He told us that therapy should be businesslike, direct, rational, and logical, concentrating on incisive confrontations of irrational beliefs. When I volunteered to be a "client" for demonstration purposes, I discovered that although I felt better after my therapeutic experience, it was *not*, as Ellis promised, because of his rational-emotive interventions. What helped me more than anything in dealing with the impending death of my mother was Ellis's caring and warmth. Ellis—a caring and warm clinician? He had always seemed so cold and analytic to me from afar. But even before an audience of hundreds on a stage, I could feel that, for those few moments, I was the most important person in the world to him. (p. 49)

Being In, Being For, and Being With

Another way to understand the power of the therapeutic relationship is by looking at the therapist as being in, being for, and being with the client (Moustakas, 1986). *Being In* is being empathic, being in the client's body and mind to whatever degree is possible. It is being open to whatever is shared by the client with complete absence of judgment, evaluation, or analysis. *Being For* is being the client's advocate and ally. It means offering one's support and guidance during the client's therapeutic journey. *Being With* means working together. It is an attitude of collaboration and a pooling of the client's and therapist's resources for the client's benefit.

The preceding discussion would not be complete without acknowledging that, although genuineness, empathy, and unconditional positive regard can enhance the progress of psychotherapy (Beutler, Crago, & Arizmendi, 1986, p. 279), they are not always predictive of successful therapeutic outcome (see Garfield, 1980, pp. 75–82). There are certainly cases in which the therapeutic relationship is not sufficient for helping clients make changes in their lives. Similarly, there are cases in which successful therapeutic change occurs without a therapeutic relationship characterized by genuineness, empathy, and positive regard. Nevertheless, these still are qualities that therapists should strive to achieve for the sake of the many clients who do respond positively to the power of the therapeutic relationship (Patterson, 1984).

HOW THE THERAPEUTIC RELATIONSHIP DIFFERS FROM FRIENDSHIP

Kanfer and Goldstein (1991, p. 2) outline three characteristics that differentiate therapeutic relationships from friendships.

1. Therapeutic relationships are *unilateral* because the focus is on the client. The relationship is one-sided because the problems and issues facing the client are important, whereas the therapist's problems and issues are not discussed. The interaction between therapist and client is directed toward helping the client resolve certain problems and achieve certain goals.
2. Therapeutic relationships are *formal* because the interaction is confined to specific times and places. The therapeutic relationship is restricted to helping clients achieve their goals. The therapist has no other roles, duties, or obligations than those defined in the therapeutic contract.
3. Therapeutic relationships are *time limited.* The relationship ends when the agreed-upon objectives and goals have been reached.

Another distinction between the therapeutic relationship and friendship is that the therapeutic relationship offers more than support; it also offers the opportunity for clients to take risks and to generalize what they have learned in therapy to the outside world. Therapeutic relationships are process oriented and are focused on the here-and-now. It would "overload" most friendships if friends spent as much energy as therapists and clients do looking at what is going on between them. In his book *Psychotherapy: The Purchase of Friendship*, Schofield (1964) cautions therapists against falling into the role of "surrogate friends." Schofield argues that therapists need to teach clients how to achieve friendships in their outside life so they don't develop the faulty belief that "only a therapist could love me."

THE THERAPIST AS MENTOR AND TEACHER

Throughout his career, Freud viewed psychoanalytic therapy as a form of "reeducation" or "after-education," in which the therapist role was analogous to that of a mentor or teacher (Strupp, 1982). The belief that the therapeutic relationship should be a collaboration between therapist and client is so common that it is impossible to cite all of the therapists who have used this term. As one example, Harry Stack Sullivan (1953) uses the term *collaboration* to describe a mutually rewarding relationship between therapist and client that promotes a reciprocal validation of personal worth. By taking the role of a collaborator, the therapist joins the client in a "shared experience" (Fisher, 1990).

The therapist is not an authority who provides clients with answers. Rather, the therapist collaborates with the client by sharing his or her knowledge, helping the client gain a more flexible perception of life and its possibilities, and serving as a good role model. Strupp (1986) describes the skill of the therapist in serving as a mentor and teacher.

> Wherein is this skill demonstrated? It encompasses the ability to (a) maintain and strengthen the patient's alliance with the therapist as a "good model" of reality and adult behavior while (b) fostering exploration and better understanding ("insight") of those cognitions, attitudes, feelings, fantasies, symptoms, and so on that prove self-defeating, self-contradictory, and maladaptive to the patient. In this endeavor, the therapist succeeds in bypassing or outflanking the patient's persistent tendency to ward off the therapist's efforts. Patients cling to the status quo, thereby defeating themselves and the therapist. In common parlance, patients should come to experience the "errors of their ways," and circumstances are arranged so that they will find it easier to remedy these errors. This process often involves the reliving of painful childhood experiences, the necessity to separate from the significant figures of one's childhood, to complete grieving for losses of various kinds, to give up unfulfilled wishes, and to accept oneself as an adult, together with the opportunities and responsibilities that adult status connotes. (p. 126)

CONTENT AND PROCESS

Hellmuth Kaiser (1965) describes working with a client who began to discuss some rather personal sexual experiences. Having been trained as an analyst, Kaiser's immediate reaction was one of great interest in the details of the client's story. However, it also occurred to Kaiser to wonder "Why is this person disclosing this information to me?" In asking himself this question, Kaiser was analyzing the process between himself and the client. The *content* of the interaction included the details of the story being told by the client. The *process* was the meaning of the client's willingness to share such personal information at this time. What was going on between the client and therapist to prompt the client to discuss a sexual experience? This inquiry led Kaiser to conclude that talking about the client's choice to disclose this sexual experience was more relevant to the therapy session than hearing about the sexual experience itself.

The content of a communication can be defined as the literal message of the words being spoken. It is analogous to a written transcript of what a person is saying. The process in a communication refers to the meaning of the words being spoken in this particular relationship. For example, assume that halfway through a session a client asks "What time is it?" A content response to this question would be "It's 5:30." A process response to this question, depending on the circumstance, could be "Are you anxious for this session to end?" or "Do you have something you've been waiting to bring up?" or "I wonder why you ask." In other words, the content response focuses on the literal meaning of the client's words. The process response focuses not on the client's words but on the message that the client is communicating. Some other examples can help explain the concepts of process and content.

- A client who is discussing marital difficulties asks the therapist whether he is married.

A content response would be "Yes" or "No."
A process response would be "Are you wondering whether I can appreciate your difficulties?"

- A client asks a therapist how many other clients she sees a week.
- A content response would be "I see an average of 20 clients a week."

A process response would be "Are you wondering whether I will have enough energy to give to you?" or "I do see other clients, but when you and I are meeting, my full attention is on you."

- At the end of the session, the client says "I'll probably see you next week."

A content response would be "Call me if you can't make it."
A process response would be "Are you having some doubts about continuing therapy?"

- The client says "I was annoyed that you were late for our last appointment."

A content response would be "Yes, I'm sorry. My car broke down and I did everything I could to be here on time."
A process response would be "I'm struck by the fact that you can tell me when you are angry with me."

Therapeutic relationships are characterized by the fact that the focus is primarily on process. This is another distinction between therapeutic relationships and friendships that was not mentioned earlier. It would strain the friendship if friends spent as much time looking at what is going on between them as therapists and clients do.

FOCUS ON THE HERE-AND-NOW

Because the therapeutic relationship pays a good deal of attention to process, the focus is necessarily on the here-and-now. Harry Stack Sullivan argued that therapy is an interpersonal process between therapist and client in which the therapist functions as a participant observer (Chapman, 1978). It is important, according to Sullivan, that therapists attend to events that are observable in their interpersonal relationship with the client. By attending to the here-and-now, the therapist can provide the client with *consensual validation* of the effects that his or her behaviors have on others. Lester Luborsky (1984) explains the value of attending to therapeutic process as it unfolds in the here-and-now.

> The reexperiencing with the therapist in the "here and now" of the conflictual relationship problems gives the patient the most impetus toward meaningful insight and permits greater freedom to change. Past relationships gain in meaning when they are related to the current ones. Keeping the relevance of the present in sight is one way for the therapist to insure that the insight is emotionally meaningful and not just intellectual. (p. 22)

The therapeutic relationship is used to help clients recognize patterns or themes in the way they have related to others in the past, how they relate to others in the present, and how they are relating to the therapist in the here-and-now. Luborsky explains that clients are provided with an experience of control and mastery as they learn and practice new interpersonal styles while receiving support and encouragement from the therapist. For an example of attending to process in the here-and-now, consider a client who has difficulty trusting others. An important goal of therapy would be to focus on the client's experiences as she learns to take risks in trusting the therapist. As another example, take a client who has a harsh and aggressive manner and tends to "turn other people off" and keep them at arm's length. As the client acts out this interpersonal style with the therapist, the therapist does not allow herself to be pushed away. Instead, the therapist focuses on the client's behaviors at the moment and explores with the client the effects that his behaviors have on their relationship. Finally, consider a client who has a passive and dependent style and who waits for the therapist to tell him what to do. Instead of getting angry or impatient with the client's passivity, the therapist engages the client to experience the effects of his passivity on their work together as they search for solutions to the client's problems.

CLIENT FRUSTRATION

The client in psychotherapy is very likely to become frustrated from time to time. Clients come to therapy hoping the therapist will provide answers to their problems. It is naturally disappointing when therapists explain to clients that therapists don't have answers and that finding a more satisfactory solution to their problems will involve a significant amount of work, risk, anxiety, and pain. Clients also enter therapy with a wish to have their dependent longings gratified (Gelso, 1979). They have desires to be taken care of and to be loved that are not generally satisfied by the therapist. Therapists don't respond with the reassurances (or reprimands) that clients attempt (often unconsciously) to "pull" from them. Rather, therapists experience these needs *with* the client and help the client determine where the needs are coming from and how to solve them (Waterhouse & Strupp, 1984). The goal is to help clients understand what roles their needs play in their life or in their "psychic economies" (Goldberg, 1978, p. 448).

How can therapists find an appropriate balance between developing a trusting and empathic working relationship with a client on the one hand, and reinforcing the client to take responsibility and be self-sufficient on the other? A number of suggestions can be helpful.

Recognizing Needs for Nurturing

Therapists must recognize their own feelings about nurturing clients. Therapists whose personal style makes it difficult to be nurturant should consider learning how to honor a client's dependency in a way that is comfortable for them. Therapists who achieve gratification from nurturing others should take care to separate their own needs from those of the client.

Deciding When to Nurture Clients

Gelso's (1979) first rule for gratifying clients' dependency needs is to provide gratification as little as possible and only when it is really needed. This doesn't mean that the therapist can't communicate empathy about how painful and difficult it is to feel unloved, worthless, lost, and anxious. The question is whether it is in the client's best interest to be "rescued" by the therapist or whether the client will gain more in the long run by finding his or her own solutions to these dilemmas.

Gelso's (1979) second rule for gratifying clients' dependency needs is to recognize that nurturance may be particularly valuable during the early phases of therapy, especially for clients who require at least some gratification to keep them in therapy. Many psychoanalysts recognize that the classical "blank screen" posture taken by analysts is not the most effective strategy for developing a working alliance between therapist and client (Basescu, 1990; Lane & Hull, 1990; Marmor, 1990; Menaker, 1990). Therapists must be sufficiently responsive to clients that clients will be motivated to work with them. After "proving" to a client their sensitivity to the client's needs for nurturance, therapists can gradually shift greater amounts of responsibility and independence to the client. Yalom (1980) explains this process.

> One priceless thing the patient learns in therapy is the limits of a relationship. One learns what one can get from others but, perhaps even more important, one learns what one *cannot* get from others. As patient and therapist encounter another on a human level, the former's illusions inevitably suffer. The ultimate rescuer is seen in the full light of day as only another person after all. It is an isolating moment but also . . . an illuminating one. (pp. 406–407)

By working through the inevitable frustration of not having their dependency needs consistently gratified by the therapist, clients determine to get these needs met by using their own resources. They are often ready to leave therapy when they realize they want—and can get—more from other people in their life than the therapist is able to offer.

SELF-DISCLOSURE BY THE CLIENT

Chapter 2 explains that psychotherapy is not a treatment and that clients don't come to therapy to be cured. Rather, the goal of therapy is to help clients make changes in their lives. For change to occur, clients must assume certain responsibilities. In addition to taking the risk to come to therapy in the first place, clients must be willing to cooperate with the therapist by sharing themselves, exploring emotionally painful issues, and experimenting with new ways of thinking and acting. An important requirement for a good therapeutic relationship is client self-disclosure. Self-disclosure by the client is necessary in psychotherapy for a number of reasons. Some of these are obvious, and others are not so obvious.

Self-Disclosure as a Necessary Condition for Therapy

It stands to reason that the therapist can be of help only to clients who are willing to disclose themselves. The therapist and client can't explore what is working and not working in the client's life unless the client is willing to talk about these things. Although this is not surprising, it does remind us of the tremendous challenge faced by therapists in facilitating clients' trust, motivation, and willingness to work with them.

Self-Disclosure for Experiencing Intimacy

A second reason for clients to engage in self-disclosure is to promote an experience of intimacy with the therapist. Martin Fisher (1990) argues that when clients come to therapy, "they are looking for a solution to loneliness, or more specifically, a 'cure' for a lack of intimacy." (p. 3).

> I believe that patients present themselves for psychotherapy because of the inability (with or without awareness) to have and/or be in intimate relationships. Somewhere, somehow, because of intrapsychic and/or interpersonal deficits, the individual comes to feel his/her aloneness, fear, and vulnerability. The patient, through the transference as well as the real relationship with the therapist, tries to capture (or recapture) this state of grace referred to as intimacy. (p. 3)

> It is my thesis that intimacy is the desired goal in life and that *self-disclosure* is the route to intimacy. (p. 8)

The therapeutic relationship offers clients the opportunity to develop their skills for achieving greater intimacy in their life by experiencing intimacy with the therapist. For this to happen, the clients (and therapists) must be willing to share themselves through self-disclosure.

Self-Disclosure as a Coping Skill

As explained above, self-disclosure is a coping skill because it allows people to pursue intimacy with others. Self-disclosure also serves as a coping skill by offering the opportunity to understand, assimilate, and find a resolution to painful experiences. George Stricker (1990) explains that clients reveal themselves to the therapist for the purpose of discovering themselves, and by doing so they are freed to live more authentic and fulfilled lives.

The value of self-disclosure as a coping skill was demonstrated in a study comparing three groups of people (Pennebaker & Susman, 1988). One group of people had never experienced a serious trauma (death of a family member or close friend, divorce or separation, sexual trauma, violence). A second group of people had experienced a serious trauma but had never talked to anyone about it. A third group of people had experienced a serious trauma and had confided their feelings to others. What is interesting is that people who had never experienced a serious trauma had a history of fewer illnesses than those who had experienced a trauma. Even more interesting is the fact that those who experienced a trauma and shared this experience with others had fewer illnesses than did those who had experienced a trauma and had kept it to themselves. In another study, surviving spouses of people who had died traumatic deaths (car accidents, suicide) were asked whether they had talked about this experience with other people after it had happened (Pennebaker & O'Heeron, 1984). Results of this study were similar; people who had talked about their spouse's death had fewer health problems than those who had not.

Looking at self-disclosure from the opposite direction, Larson and Chastain (1990) developed the concept of *self-concealment*. Self-concealment is defined as "a predisposition to actively conceal from others personal information that one perceives as distressing or negative" (p. 440). Self-concealment is not simply the inverse of self-disclosure, because people can engage in relatively low self-disclosure without making an active attempt to hold back sensitive feelings, thoughts, and experiences.The Self-Concealment scale includes the following kinds of items.

1. I have an important secret that I haven't shared with anyone.
2. My secrets are too embarrassing to share with others.
3. I have negative thoughts about myself that I never share with anyone.
4. There are lots of things about me that I keep to myself.

Significant correlations were obtained between people's scores on the Self-Concealment scale and measures of anxiety, depression, and physical symptoms. In addition, the Self-Concealment scale contributed significant variance over experiences of trauma, social support, and self-disclosure in predicting anxiety, depression, and bodily symptoms.

The studies just summarized indicate that people who don't talk to others about traumas tend to ruminate about their experiences and never have an opportunity to resolve these experiences and reach closure. These studies also suggest that making an active effort to disclose traumatic experiences can be a useful coping skill. This theory was tested in a series of studies conducted by James Pennebaker and his colleagues (Pennebaker, 1989). Participants in these studies volunteered to write or talk about "the most upsetting or traumatic experience of their entire life." This assignment was very emotional for participants, and it was crucial that the experimenters offered informed consent.

> I should warn you that many people find this study quite upsetting. Many people cry during the study and feel somewhat sad or depressed during and after it. (Pennebaker, 1989, p. 215)

In addition, the experimenters made a particular effort to establish rapport with each participant. Confidentiality was guaranteed, and the experimenters carefully monitored each participant throughout the study. After completing their self-disclosure assignment, participants were debriefed by experimenters who had clinical training. Counseling was readily available for participants who felt the need for it. The kinds of experiences disclosed in these studies included deaths, divorce and separation, family conflicts, illnesses, and (for participants who were college students) stresses associated with college. It is worth noting that most participants stated that they found the experience "valuable and meaningful" and that 98% of them said they would be willing to do it again (Pennebaker, 1989, p. 218). The value of the self-disclosure experience was expressed by the following kinds of statements.

- "It made me think things out and really realize what my problem is."
- "It helped me look at myself from the outside."
- "It was a chance to sort out my thoughts."

Results of these studies were dramatic. It was not unusual for participants to feel more depressed and anxious after disclosing their traumatic experiences. However, the long-term effects of this disclosure were beneficial. Compared with a matched group of participants who did not engage in the self-disclosure process, the self-disclosing participants had fewer health complaints, fewer stressful physiological responses, and a more healthy immune function (Pennebaker, Colder, & Sharp, 1990; Pennebaker, Kiecolt-Glaser, & Glaser, 1988; Pennebaker, Hughes, & O'Heeron, 1987).

The parallels between these self-disclosure studies and psychotherapy should be apparent. Confronting one's "traumas" is a painful but important experience in therapy. First, self-disclosure helps clients become aware of unfinished business that they have put out of awareness but that continues to take an emotional and physical toll. Through the process of self-disclosure, clients are able to assimilate, come to terms with, and reconcile the "demons" in their life. They can stop wasting precious energy avoiding thoughts, memories, and wishes that were previously intolerable.

SELF-DISCLOSURE BY THE THERAPIST

The Therapist as a Responsive Person

Few therapists would have trouble accepting the importance of self-disclosure by the client in therapy. Freud pointed out that clients need a safe environment that encourages self-disclosure with reassurances that their disclosures will be confidential and will be accepted by the therapist in a nonjudgmental manner (Lane & Hull, 1990). Freud also argued that therapists must be particularly cautious about revealing themselves to clients. According to Freud's writings, the analyst should "remain opaque to his patients, like a mirror, and show them nothing but what is shown to him" (Lane & Hull, 1990, p. 33). The image of the therapist as a "blank screen" has led to such jokes as "I knew my therapist was alive because I could hear him breathing" (Basescu, 1990, p. 47). It is unfortunate that some therapists have taken Freud's advice about the virtues of objectivity too far and have perpetuated the notion that the therapist should be an unresponsive person (Greben, 1981). Milton Erickson also describes the nonresponsive analyst (Haley, 1985):

> I can think of one psychoanalyst. He sits at his desk and the analysand enters. He turns, he stands, he walks over and he shakes hands. He's silent. The analysand lies down on the couch over here, and the analyst turns this way which is slightly back of the head of the couch. Now, when the hour's over, the analyst stands, silently shakes hands. Then the analysand walks out *that* door. It doesn't make a bit of difference who the analysand is. There's no deviation in that pattern. Three months, six months, a year, three years, five years. . . . That same rigid pattern day after day. (p. 153)

It is interesting to note that even though Freud wrote about the significance of the therapist as a blank screen, he did not always practice what he preached. Gay (1988, p. 33) described this as Freud's "sovereign readiness to disregard his own rules." Marmor (1990) explains that Freud's use of the blank screen was a research method, because it permitted analysis of the client's associations without bias or imposition from the therapist. However, as Marmor (1990) points out, a good research method is not necessarily a good clinical method: "Being relatively impassive and impersonal is not a neutral attitude at all, but an artificial one that always impacts on patients one way or another and can be misconstrued by some of them as coldness, disinterest, or rejection." Many therapists with an analytical orientation have come to accept Freud's practice rather than his preaching by accepting the value of self-disclosure by the therapist.

> Needless to say, no one questions the importance of a therapist being a good listener. But the assumption that the therapist should be a kind of neutral mirror who does not interact with patients but merely reflects their feelings and thoughts back to them is no longer considered to be the more desirable way or the most desirable way of conducting psychotherapy. (Marmor, 1990)

Basescu (1990) explains the value of therapist self-disclosure by distinguishing between the one-person model and two-person model of transference. According to the one-person model, transference comes purely from the client. The therapist has nothing to do with it and therefore must remain as "invisible" as possible. The two-person model acknowledges the impossibility of therapist neutrality and recognizes that the therapist is and must be an active participant in the therapeutic process. Therapy is a "shared experience" (Fisher, 1990) in which the client and therapist "create a history together" (Basescu, 1990). This thinking has led to an evolving concept of the therapist's role "from mirror, to participant observer, to human being" (Basescu, 1990).

Conclusions from Research

Although a large number of studies have been conducted to investigate the effects of therapist self-disclosure, researchers find it difficult to generalize this research to actual therapy sessions. Most of the research on therapist self-disclosure involves analogue studies, whereby research participants evaluate tapes or transcripts of therapy sessions in which the therapist engages in various levels of self-disclosure. It is unlikely that studies of this sort can capture the richness of a particular therapy session between a particular client and a particular therapist. In general, studies of therapist self-disclosure indicate that therapists who self-disclose are evaluated more favorably than are therapists who do not self-disclose (Doster & Nesbitt, 1979). In addition, therapist self-disclosure has generally been found to enhance self-disclosure by the client. Finally, a number of studies have found correlations between client self-disclosure and good therapeutic outcome. One study of actual therapy sessions concludes that therapist self-disclosure is viewed by clients as very helpful, and it encourages them to engage in deeper self-exploration (Hill et al., 1988). Probably the most useful way to communicate the contributions from research on self-disclosure in therapy is by discussing the following topics.

Importance of Process

Therapists must be acutely aware of what their self-disclosure communicates in the context of the therapeutic relationship. The most obvious question to ask about disclosing oneself to the client is "Whose needs are being met?" Therapists do not self-disclose to satisfy *their* needs or because it is something that will make *them* comfortable. Before making any communication with clients, therapists ask themselves "What is the point of this message and what purpose does it serve for therapy?"

Self-Disclosure Flexibility

Gordon Chelune (1977) defines self-disclosure flexibility as the ability to adapt one's disclosure to a particular person (or persons) in a given context. Highly flexible disclosers know how to monitor subtle social cues to determine how much disclosure is appropriate. Research studies have supported the expectation that therapists who accommodate their self-disclosure to a situation are more favorably evaluated than are therapists who do not (Neimeyer, Banikiotes, & Winum, 1979; Neimeyer & Fong, 1983).

Client Expectations

Self-disclosure by therapists must match the amount of disclosure expected by the client (Derlega, Lovell, & Chaikin, 1976; Doster & Nesbitt, 1979). Clients who come to therapy expecting the therapist to play the traditional "blank screen" role may be surprised when the therapist responds to them in a personal manner. Therapists benefit from reaching an agreement with clients about their mutual expectations for disclosure during the first few sessions of therapy (Simonson & Bahr, 1974; Wilson & Rappaport, 1974).

Disclosing Content versus Process

Therapists have the option of disclosing information about themselves (content) or of disclosing their feelings or perceptions about what is currently taking place in the therapy session (process). Disclosure about content is necessary to the degree that it is important for the therapist to be cordial and socially responsive. This entails sharing at least some personal information. However, it is worth noting that although college students expect counselors to share somewhat more information about themselves than they expect from either their physicians, their professors, or their haircutters, they don't expect counselors to share as much as their friends do (Hendrick, 1988).

Disclosure about process, which has also been called *self-involving disclosure* (McCarthy, 1982) or *interpersonal disclosure* (Nilsson, Strassberg, & Bannon, 1979), is the kind of disclosure that would generally be expected from therapists. This kind of disclosure fits the theory that therapy emphasizes process between therapist and client in the here-and-now. Research studies comparing people's reactions to therapists who were engaging in process disclosure versus content disclosure have found that disclosing therapists are preferred to non-disclosing therapists, but these studies have not identified a consistent preference for therapists who disclose about process versus content (Dowd & Boroto, 1982; McCarthy, 1979; Nilsson, Strassberg, & Bannon, 1979). This failure is most likely because participants in these studies were not in an actual therapy session and had not been socialized to understand or appreciate the role of process communication in psychotherapy. Clients do appear to react more favorably to *reassuring* disclosures, which support, reinforce, or legitimize the client's perspective, than to *challenging* disclosures, which confront or challenge the client's perspective (Hill, Mahalik, & Thompson (1989).

Four Approaches for Communicating about Process

Safran and Segal (1990) outline four approaches for communicating with a client about process as it unfolds in the here-and-now.

1. The therapist conveys his or her feelings to help clients become aware of the impact they have on others and thus become aware of their role in the interaction. Depending on the process, the therapist may say things such as "I feel like protecting you right now" or "I'm feeling put down right now," or "On the one hand I feel like apologizing to you, but on the other hand I feel angry."

2. By conveying his or her feelings to clients, the therapist is probing for the clients' internal experience. The therapist may say: "I'm feeling cautious with you right now. Does that fit with your experience?"; or "At this moment, I feel out of touch with you. What are you experiencing?"

3. The therapist identifies and points out the clients' interpersonal markers to help clients become aware of their role in the interaction. The therapist may say: "I experience you as being cautious and withdrawn right now"; or "I have a sense from the look on your face that you don't agree with what I'm saying"; or "I feel some anger coming from you about what I just said."

4. The therapist uses the identified interpersonal marker as a juncture for cognitive/affective exploration. The therapist may say: "I'm aware of you clenching your fists as you talk. Are you aware of that?"; or "I notice you are speaking very softly in a low voice. What are you feeling?"; or "I experience you as being impatient and somewhat irritable. What are you experiencing?"

Sharing Negative Feelings

It is not surprising that research participants are more favorable toward therapists who share positive versus negative feelings about what is going on in the therapy session (Andersen & Anderson, 1985). However, for therapists to honor process in the therapeutic relationship, negative feelings must sometimes be disclosed. This can be done tactfully and in a way that will strengthen rather than weaken the therapeutic relationship. Some suggestions for communicating negative feelings are provided by Carl Rogers (1962; see also Kahn, 1991).

1. Be selective about what you share. You don't have to communicate every passing irritation.
2. The most important negative feelings to share are those that are persistent, that say something about the client's style, and that interfere with the therapist's ability to be fully present with the client.
3. Before communicating a negative feeling, ask yourself whether you are doing this to enhance the authenticity of the therapeutic relationship or because of a personal need arising from anger or frustration.

4. Be tactful and try to avoid having the client take your disclosure as a criticism. Instead of saying "You're boring me" or "Much of what you are saying is irrelevant," say something like: "At the moment, I am feeling bored. Are you?"; or "Right now, I don't feel connected with you. What do you think is happening between us?"

SUMMARY

Three components of the therapeutic relationship are the working alliance, transference, and interpersonal sharing. According to Carl Rogers, three conditions for therapeutic change are empathy, genuineness, and unconditional positive regard.

Therapeutic relationships differ from friendships because they are unilateral, formal, and time limited. The therapeutic relationship offers clients the opportunity to take risks and to practice what they have learned in the outside world. Therapeutic relationships also differ from friendships in that much of the communication in therapy is focused on process rather than on content. The therapist is a mentor or teacher who engages in a collaborative relationship with the client. The focus is on the here-and-now, and the therapist provides the client with consensual validation about the effects of his or her behaviors on others.

Clients are often frustrated because their needs for nurturance are not always met by the therapist. This provides clients with an opportunity to learn what they can get and also what they cannot get from others. Self-disclosure by the client is a necessary condition for therapy, and it allows the client to experience intimacy with the therapist. Self-disclosure is also a useful coping skill that is related to physical health.

Self-disclosure by the therapist is generally accepted as a valuable part of therapy. Self-disclosure flexibility is recommended as a way of ensuring that therapists match their degree self-disclosure to a particular client in a particular context. Therapists are also advised to communicate with clients about their mutual expectations about self-disclosure in their relationship. Therapist self-disclosure focuses more often on process than on content, although some disclosure on content is necessary for the sake of cordiality. Sometimes therapists must share negative feelings about process, but this can be done tactfully in a way that will strengthen rather than weaken the therapeutic relationship.

SUGGESTIONS FOR FURTHER READING

Derlega, V. J., Hendrick, S. S., Winstead, B. A., & Berg, J. H. (1991). *Psychotherapy as a personal relationship.* New York: Guilford.

Kahn, M. (1991). *Between therapist and client: The new relationship.* New York: W. H. Freeman.

Patterson, C. H. (1985). *The therapeutic relationship: Foundations for an eclectic psychotherapy.* Pacific Grove, CA: Brooks/Cole.

Pennebaker, J. W. (1990). *Opening up: The healing power of confiding in others.* New York: Morrow.

Rogers, C. R. (1961). *Client-centered therapy.* Boston: Houghton Mifflin.

Safran, J. D., & Segal, Z. (1990). *Interpersonal processes in cognitive therapy.* New York: Basic Books.

◆ CHAPTER 5 ◆

Helping Clients Change

As suggested in Chapter 1, the road in therapy is not always smooth. There are ups and downs and impasses that need to be detoured. This chapter discusses the setbacks experienced by clients in psychotherapy and offers strategies for helping clients get around them.

THE CHALLENGE OF HELPING CLIENTS CHANGE

Many people naively believe that psychotherapy involves listening to clients talk about their problems and then telling them what to do. If this were the case, anybody could be a therapist and therapy would be boring. One of the things that makes therapy so fascinating is the challenge of first guiding clients as they set goals and priorities in their life and then helping them achieve these goals. The notion that the clinician's function is to *help clients change* is expressed in the titles of two influential books on this subject: *Helping People Change* (Kanfer & Goldstein, 1991) and *Helping Families to Change* (Satir, Stachowiak, & Taschman, 1976). The process of helping clients change involves four basic principles: (1) clients must work at their own pace, (2) the client is the agent of change, (3) change requires action, (4) change requires risks.

Clients must work at their own pace   Clients must work at their own pace in therapy. They are not ready to change until they feel the need and decide for themselves this is something they want to do. It is important that therapists appreciate the fact that encouraging people to take their time and not take risks until they are ready will often motivate change more effectively than prodding and coercing.

The client is the agent of change Clients must be their own change agents for two reasons. First, it is not appropriate for therapists to take responsibility for clients' lives. Second, the successes clients experience in therapy should be attributed to them and not to the therapist. This is the only way clients will feel empowered to continue taking control of their life.

Change requires action Clients are active participants in therapy and not simply passive recipients of treatment. Clients don't just *talk*—they *do*.

> The therapist must court action. He or she may pretend to pursue other goals—insight, self-actualization, comfort—but in the final analysis, change (that is, action) is every therapist's secret quarry. (Yalom, 1980, p. 287)

Change requires risks To effect change, clients must take risks, and this requires courage. As expressed by Julius Heuscher (1980),

> Freedom, the genuine ability to step away temporarily from one's constituted world and to begin viewing new horizons, can be frightening. It is only the very beginning of this genuine viewing that is commonly experienced as delightful or beautiful. Then it easily turns into terror. (p. 468)

Thomas Szasz (1973) makes a similar point: "Success in psychotherapy—that is, the ability to change oneself in a direction one wants to change—requires courage rather than insight" (p. 199).

Clients must give up ways of thinking and behaving that are familiar and safe and must venture into unexplored territory. Change is painful and scary and can be accomplished only by clients who are convinced of its benefits, who have decided to take control of their life, and who are encouraged to feel pride in their accomplishments.

RESISTANCE

On the surface, it might seem paradoxical that clients would come to psychotherapists for help and then resist making changes that would be beneficial. However, after a little thought, it is not surprising that even clients who are motivated to do something about their problems will find it hard to change.

Why Change Is Difficult

It is difficult for people to change for a number of reasons, some of which are given here.

Change is scary   The lifestyles people develop may not always work in their best interest, but they are lifestyles that are familiar and that provide at least some protection from the threats and anxieties of life. There is great risk in giving up familiar ways of acting and thinking for lifestyles that are new and untested. Michael Mahoney (1991) explains that resistance is a form of self-protection. To change, people have to give up part of themselves. Clients who are willing to risk adopting new behaviors and thinking patterns deserve credit for their courage. Those who are reluctant to change deserve empathy for their fears.

People are reactive   People have a natural tendency to react against or resist pressures or influence from others (Brehm, 1966; Brehm & Brehm, 1981). The stronger the threat to one's personal freedom, the stronger the reactance. Although reactance might be viewed as stubborness or obstinacy, a more helpful interpretation in a therapeutic context is as individuality and self-protection. In any case, it is a fact that clients, to one degree or another, will naturally resist when they are pushed too hard and their sense of personal freedom is threatened. For this reason, therapists must be sensitive to their clients' reactivity and match their therapeutic approach accordingly.

Interference from other people   Psychotherapy does not occur in a vacuum, and many factors in a client's life can interfere with the client's attempts to change. Probably the greatest interference with therapy comes from other people. Friends and family members may experience as much fear about clients making changes in their behaviors and ways of thinking as clients themselves do. If therapy is to be successful, these other people must be taken into consideration. Some therapists accomplish this by including a client's entire family in the therapy (Minuchin, 1974). In other cases, it might suffice if therapists help clients learn skills for negotiating with others who might resist the clients' efforts to make changes in their life.

Secondary gains   In some cases, clients receive some kind of payoff or secondary gain from the symptoms they bring to therapy. It stands to reason that clients will find it difficult to give up these symptoms unless they learn to satisfy the needs fulfilled by the symptoms in another, more adaptive, manner.

Lack of skills   Therapists must take care to assure that clients have the necessary skills to carry out changes agreed upon in therapy. Sometimes clients do not succeed in their goals because they have not been sufficiently trained to achieve them.

Hopelessness and pessimism   Clients must believe in their ability to make changes in their life. Clients who are hopeless and convinced they will fail are not likely to carry out their therapeutic goals.

Defining Resistance

Turkat and Meyer (1982, p. 158) define *resistance* as a client behavior that the therapist labels antitherapeutic. This definition is interesting because of its subjectivity. It is reminiscent of a comment a number of clinicians have made: resistance is when clients don't do what therapists want them to do. Thomas Szasz's (1973) definition is "Resistance: the term the psychoanalyst uses to register his disapproval of the patient who talks about what he himself wants to talk about rather than about what the analyst wants him to talk about" (p. 82). Perhaps a better definition of resistance is "any client *or* therapist behavior that interferes with or reduces the likelihood of successful therapeutic process and outcome (Cormier & Cormier, 1991, p. 551).

More important than how resistance is defined is the therapist's attitude toward it. Resistance is a natural and expected occurrence in therapy, and therapists should not feel compelled to "do something about it" (Whitaker & Keith, 1981, p. 214). A better attitude is that working through resistance *is* therapy (Anderson & Stewart, 1983, p. 5). As Bugental (1965, p. 43) points out, "the therapist who thinks of the resistance as a warding off of his own efforts misses the point and confuses the patient." The point is that clients are expected to have difficulty making changes in their life, and it is the therapist's job (and challenge) to help clients achieve the appropriate attitudes, skills, and life conditions to make change possible. Another thing to understand about resistance is that it resides in the therapist as much as it resides in the client (Lewis & Evans, 1986).

To Freud, resistances were similar to defense mechanisms, and they served to protect clients from the anxiety associated with achieving awareness of unresolved psychic conflicts. Much of Freudian therapy involved working through the transference neurosis, a process to which clients were understandably resistant. Resistances presented a useful avenue to the client's unconscious, and analysis of resistance became an essential feature of psychoanalysis. Because the term *resistance* is often associated with psychoanalysis, nonanalytic therapists often use other terms to describe clients' difficulties with change. Two of the most common of these terms are *noncompliance* and failure of *treatment adherence.* Noncompliance should not be misunderstood to mean that clients refuse to comply with the therapist's directives or "orders." The meaning of noncompliance is that clients do not always comply with or adhere to the goals and contracts that they have agreed to follow. In this sense, noncompliance and treatment adherence have the same meaning.

Types of Resistance

Otani (1989) defined the following four types of resistance.

Response-quantity resistance consists of responses characterized by a limited *amount* of information communicated to the therapist. The client may speak very little or engage in quick verbal responses, such as "hmm-mmm," "yes," "nope," and so on. Another kind of response-quantity resistance consists of verbosity with little or no meaningful content.

Response-content resistance consists of responses that are restricted in the *type* of information communicated to the therapist. One example of this kind of resistance is intellectual talk. A second example is emotional display, characterized by emotional outbursts that impede the exploration of the client's deeper feelings. A third example is symptom preoccupation, characterized by ruminations over issues not pertinent to the client's major issues. A fourth example is small talk, and a fifth example is the use of rhetorical questions, characterized by a variety of seemingly appropriate but irrelevant questions: "What is the purpose of . . ."; "What is your opinion about . . .".

Response-style resistance consists of idiosyncratic response patterns through which the client manipulates the *manner* of communicating information to the therapist. There are ten examples of response style resistance. Clients may engage in (1) discounting ("Yes, but . . ." kinds of statements), (2) setting limits on topics they are willing to discuss, (3) censoring or editing their thoughts, (4) externalizing, (5) second-guessing the therapist's intentions, (6) stroking or pleasing the therapist, (7) being seductive, (8) forgetting critical information, (9) making last minute disclosures, and (10) making false promises.

Logistic-management resistance consists of violating the *rules* of therapy by missing appointments, missing payments, and asking personal favors.

Reasons for Resistance

Beck, Freeman et al. (1990) offer the following reasons for clients' getting stuck in therapy and failing to make progress.

1. *The client may lack the skill to collaborate.* Therapists must often role play with clients to assure clients that they have the skills to carry out agreed-upon tasks.
2. *The therapist may lack the skill to develop collaboration.* This could happen when therapists lack experience with a particular client population, such as adolescents or the elderly.
3. *Environmental factors may interfere.* These factors usually involve significant others but may also include particular demands or stresses in the client's life that make change difficult.

4. *Clients may feel too hopeless to change.* Clients may convince themselves that there is no hope and that it is not worth even trying.

5. *Clients may fear the effects that their changing will have on others.* Clients may convince themselves that changing will result in negative consequences in their relationships with others.

6. *Clients may doubt their ability to survive with their "new self."* It may be too scary to give up one's style of survival for something new and untested.

7. *The therapist may lack the objectivity to perceive the client's problem.* If the therapist looks at the world the same way as the client does, the therapist will not be able to help the client change his or her way of thinking.

8. *The therapeutic alliance may not be developed sufficiently.* The therapeutic alliance must be developed to the point at which the client understands the therapist's ways of thinking and can relate to the therapist as a role model.

9. *The client may be receiving secondary gains.* It is difficult to give up symptoms that are used to gain special favor and consideration.

10. *There may be poor timing of treatment interventions.* Treatment interventions must be timed to coincide with a client's readiness to cooperate.

11. *Clients may lack motivation.* Clients who have been sent to therapy against their will are particularly lacking in motivation.

12. *A client's personality may be rigid to change.* Clients with rigid personality styles (such as obsessive compulsives and paranoids) may have particular difficulty changing.

13. *The client may have poor impulse control.* Clients with poor impulse control will have trouble adhering to treatment goals.

14. *Therapeutic goals may be unrealistic.* Therapeutic goals may be unrealistic and doomed to failure.

15. *Therapeutic goals may be unclear or unstated.* Therapeutic goals should be part of an explicit contract that both the client and therapist agree to follow.

16. *The client or therapist may become frustrated because of lack of progress.* Clients and therapists must have realistic expectations about the course and progress of therapy.

17. *Clients may resent being in the "patient" role.* Therapists must be sensitive to the client's feelings of being stigmatized for having problems.

18. *The client and therapist are mismatched.* Sometimes clients and therapists are simply mismatched, and it is appropriate for the therapist to refer the client to another clinician.

Some Warning Signs

Sooner or later, it becomes obvious when a client is stuck and not making progress. However, there are some warning signs that are worth the therapist's attention (Pipes & Davenport, 1990, pp. 174–175).

1. *Disarming behaviors.* Disarming behaviors include telling humorous stories, flirting mildly, praising the therapist, asking the therapist personal questions, and making psychologically sophisticated but "safe" self-disclosure.
2. *Innocuous behaviors.* Innocuous behaviors include changing the subject away from affect-laden issues, becoming helpless and passive, becoming confused, retreating into silence, and unemotionally recounting a powerful memory or experience.
3. *Provocative behaviors.* Provocative behaviors include accusing the therapist of being unhelpful and uncaring, demanding more attention or a closer relationship, adopting patterns of missed sessions and tardiness, and making sexual overtures to the therapist.

Warning signs that a client is having trouble focusing and making progress in therapy should not be ignored. Pipes and Davenport (1990) suggest following Bugental's (1978) three-part process of "joining" and supporting clients when they are stuck. By communicating with the client in an open and nondefensive manner, the therapist can model the process of openly discussing what is going on in the therapy session. First, the therapist makes the client's behaviors the focus of attention in a nonthreatening and accepting manner. The therapist may say, in a noncritical tone of voice: "We're spending a lot of time with small talk today. I wonder why?"; or "I've noticed that you've been late for the last few meetings. Have you noticed this as well?"; or "During the last few minutes I've felt like there is a wall between us. Did you feel this?"

The second part of the process is somewhat deeper, with focus on immediate feelings. Here, the therapist may point out: "Just before you changed the subject away from your mother's death, I noticed tears in your eyes"; or "It's interesting that when we approach the issue of your going back to work you seem to get angry with me"; or "I feel like I want to reach out to you, but when I do so I experience you as pulling back."

In the third part of the process, the therapist encourages the client to explore his or her feelings at the moment—in the here-and-now. Again, this is done with a noncritical attitude and feeling of caring. The therapist might say: "You're not looking at me, but I sense something important is going on inside you. Do you want to share this?"; or "You've been finding it difficult to complete your homework and I have a feeling it is because you are angry with me. Do you want to talk about it?" As another example, the therapist might say: "When your divorce came up a few minutes ago, you changed the subject. Take a minute to bring yourself back to our conversation. What was going on inside of you when this happened?"

Managing Resistance

Before taking the necessary risks to change, clients need to have satisfactory answers to the following questions (Kanfer & Schefft, 1988, pp. 128–131).

1. *What will it be like if I change?* The outcome of therapy must be acceptable to the client and fit the expectations and image of what he or she would like to be.
2. *How will I be better off if I change?* The payoffs of therapy must outweigh the hard work and risks that are required for change.
3. *Can I change?* Clients need encouragement from the therapist that change toward realistic goals is possible.
4. *What will it cost to change?* Clients must make an informed decision about the costs and benefits of therapy.
5. *Can I trust this therapist and setting to help me get there?* The client and therapist must establish a working relationship with common goals, expectations, and agreed-upon methods for change.

Once clients have found satisfactory answers to these questions, it is possible to use the following suggestions to help them manage the resistance they are likely to feel as they go about making changes in their life. Before considering suggestions for managing resistance, therapists should appreciate two general principles related to change. First, clients must come to terms with the fact that change requires pain and effort. This is a reality that clients must accept if they are to achieve success in therapy. Second, given the necessity of pain and effort, therapists are challenged to set the pace of therapy in a way that will make the risks and sacrifices required from clients as rewarding as possible.

The following suggestions for managing resistance are provided by Cormier and Cormier (1991, Ch. 20).

When clients lack necessary skills or knowledge Provide specific instructions. Outline with clients exactly what steps to take to accomplish their goals. Don't take for granted that clients understand what you are trying to explain. Practice with the client during the therapy session. Role play with the client to be sure that she or he can demonstrate mastery of the agreed-upon assignment.

When clients have pessimistic expectations   Acknowledge the client's pessimism. Be empathetic: "Yes, it does sometimes seem difficult and even hopeless." Explore the client's negative fantasies and thoughts. Be supportive and allow the client to talk about why he or she is feeling doubtful. Examine with the client the advantages and disadvantages of changing. Analyze what forces will help and what forces will stand in the way. Set goals that the client is likely to achieve and that will be rewarding. Use role playing to help clients (1) anticipate negative outcomes and discouraging responses from others and (2) practice strategies for dealing with them.

When environmental factors are incompatible with change   Teach clients to manage their environment to make it easier for them to accomplish their goals. Help clients arrange an environment that is compatible with the task they are trying to achieve. Help clients look for new and more fruitful patterns and routines.

When a problem is maintained by the environment   Find new ways for clients to meet their needs without engaging in symptomatic behaviors. Help clients master appropriate social skills, and teach them to reward themselves so they won't have to rely so much on attention from others. Involve significant others as "allies" and as support people for therapeutic goals.

Other suggestions for managing resistance include:

- Not taking resistance personally.
- Encouraging the client to be an active participant in therapy.
- Using good timing and pacing.
- Making sure that therapeutic strategies and goals are meaningful and relevant to the client.
- Understanding the client's special needs (such as being independent, being different, being accepted, or being needy).
- Asking clients to try a contract for one week, with the promise of reevaluating it during the following session.
- Taking a one-down position by admitting your limitations. This approach requires clients (or gives them permission) to take responsibility.
- Identifying potential impediments to change; then working together to find strategies for overcoming these impediments.

PARADOXICAL INTERVENTIONS

There has been a good deal of interest recently in the use of paradoxical interventions for managing resistance (Riebel, 1984; Seltzer, 1986; Weeks & L'Abate, 1981). The strategy of *paradoxical intention* was developed by Viktor Frankl (1967b, 1969) and is based on the premise that clients are more likely to change if the therapist accepts them as they are and does not threaten to force them to make changes they are not ready to make. The term *paradox* is used because this form of intervention is a *directive* from the therapist for the client to do something *voluntarily* (Raskin & Klein, 1976). Paradoxical interventions give clients the illusion that they are in control of the therapy session, even though the therapist is still exerting influence (Haley, 1963). Paradoxical interventions allow clients to experience the fact that they indeed *can* control their symptoms. Paradoxical interventions are also designed to place clients in a position in which their symptoms no longer serve a useful purpose. The philosophy of paradoxical interventions is that encouraging clients to accept, experience, and flow with their symptoms is more likely to be effective than cajoling and admonishing them to give up their symptoms.

Paradoxical interventions can be divided into two categories: *compliance based* and *defiance based* (Rohrbaugh, Tennen, Press, & White, 1981; Tennen, Rohrbaugh, Press, & White, 1981). In compliance-based interventions, the therapist *prescribes the symptom.* Symptom prescription allows clients to gain a sense of control by flowing with and experiencing their symptoms. Compliance-based interventions are appropriate for clients who are not highly reactive (Brehm, 1966; Brehm & Brehm, 1981) and whose symptoms don't appear to be motivated by secondary gain. In defiance-based interventions, the therapist *restrains* the client from changing. By "forbidding" change, the therapist communicates to the client "If you change, it is because of your power, initiative, and choice. I had nothing to do with it." Defiance-based interventions are appropriate for clients who are highly reactive and who may have some investment in their symptom.

Symptom Prescription

Symptom prescription follows the principles of paradoxical intention. By taking control of their symptoms, clients confront the "very thing they fear" (Frankl, 1967a, p. 146). They replace their habitual avoidant style with one of self-efficacy and self-control. By engaging in symptoms by choice, clients are faced with the fact that their symptoms are amenable to change. Here are some examples of symptom prescription.

• A client who suffers from anxiety might be encouraged to intentionally make himself or herself anxious, with the goal of experiencing and learning more about the kinds of thoughts and bodily feelings that occur when he or she is anxious. By cultivating rather than avoiding anxiety, the client learns that anxiety is something he or she can tolerate and even control.

- A client who wishes to quit smoking may be encouraged to smoke more. Intentionally increasing smoking (or any other habit) "proves" that the habit is controllable. Clients who intentionally smoke at a higher than usual level also pay the price of smoking beyond their physical comfort, and sooner or later they will ask "Why do I (choose to) do this?"
- A client who complains "I can't stop these feelings of depression" might be told: "You shouldn't try to stop your depression. In fact, feeling depressed is good because it keeps you from taking the positive things in life for granted."

Restraining

Therapists use restraining as a dramatic way of communicating to clients that they do not intend to coerce them to make changes they are not ready to make. In addition to saying "I won't force you," restraining communicates to clients that they are acceptable "just the way they are." Here are some examples of restraining (Weeks & L'Abate, 1982).

1. The therapist might suggest *delaying* change by saying "go slowly," "take your time," "we don't want to rush things." This communicates to clients that they are in control and responsible for their life.
2. The therapist might *forbid* change by suggesting that it would be best if the client did not attempt to change at this time. Instead, the client should continue with his or her symptom until its meaning and purpose is fully understood. Forbidding change elicits a natural reaction on the part of the client to change "in spite of the therapist."
3. The therapist might declare *hopelessness*. This is a potentially effective technique with the "yes, but" client. The therapist tells clients that there is very little chance for change and that they will probably have to learn to live with their problems. This challenges clients to "prove the therapist wrong."
4. The therapist might *predict a relapse*. If a client is improving, it is generally safe to suggest that the client will have a relapse. If a relapse occurs, it doesn't appear catastrophic because it was anticipated as a normal course of therapy. If a relapse does not occur, so much the better.
5. The therapist might *prescribe a relapse*. If it seems certain that the client will experience a relapse, the therapist might suggest that the client should intentionally have one. This approach functions to make the relapse predictable and places it under the client's control.

Another method for restraining is to withhold therapy until the client feels ready and motivated for this process (O'Connell, 1984;

Omer, 1985). The client is told that therapy cannot begin until the client "cooperates" with the therapist to lay the necessary groundwork to ensure that therapy will be successful. The client is asked to do one or more of the following tasks.

1. *Test conventional cures.* Clients are asked to confirm their need for psychotherapy by testing out all other possible approaches toward solving their problem. If the client succeeds in solving the problem, so much the better. If not, he or she will be more motivated to work in psychotherapy.

2. *Rehearse symptoms.* Clients are instructed to consciously and deliberately rehearse and exaggerate their symptoms. Again, it is fine if the symptoms decrease as a result of this task. If not, the client's willingness to engage in this assignment is seen as a sign of motivation to prepare properly for the process of psychotherapy.

3. *Reframe.* Clients are asked to reflect on what life problems their symptoms may actually alleviate. To put it another way, clients spend time considering what other problems they might face if their present symptom disappeared.

4. *Slowly develop insight.* Clients are promised therapy only after they have developed their capacity for "heightened awareness." Clients are requested to pay attention and become more sensitive to their behaviors and feelings. This assignment teaches clients to be responsible for their actions and emotions and allows them to "prove" they are ready to participate in self-exploration during therapy.

5. *Pretend to be cured.* This exercise helps clients identify some potential sources of resistance. It also provides the freedom, without any obligation for the future, to experience a different way of thinking or acting. In this way, it can become a self-fulfilling prophecy.

6. *Pretend to be sick.* This exercise helps clients identify some potential secondary gains from their problems. Since they are only "pretending," they can't be blamed for their actions. At the same time, they experience the fact that they actually have control over their life.

7. *Spontaneously change.* This task reinforces the idea that any change clients ultimately experience must come from themselves. It sets the stage for the kind of self-responsibility that will be required during therapy. The request to spontaneously change offers clients an opportunity to save time and money they would otherwise have to devote to therapy. It also emphasizes areas in which clients most strongly need the therapist's help.

8. *Gather information.* This task motivates clients to "do something different." A good assignment here is to teach clients how to self-

monitor the antecedents, behaviors, and consequences relevant to their problems. The information gathered by clients can be helpful later in therapy. In the meantime, the process of doing something for oneself is therapeutic.

Relabeling and Reframing

Underlying most paradoxical interventions is the *relabeling* of a client's problems to give them a different meaning and a *reframing* of the context in which the problem is understood. Relabeling and reframing are used to help clients perceive their problems in a way that makes them more amenable to change. Although there are subtle differences between the definitions of relabeling and reframing (Grunebaum & Chasin, 1978), most therapists use these terms interchangeably (Seltzer, 1986, p. 106). Relabeling and reframing serve to alter the context of therapy *from* (1) a relationship in which clients are "problem people" because they engage in undesirable behaviors that the therapist is expected to cure *to* (2) a relationship in which clients are coping as well as they can, but have agreed to work with a therapist to seek alternative solutions. Here are some examples of how relabeling and reframing can render a client's problems more manageable and responsive to change (Weeks, 1977; Weeks & L'Abate, 1982).

- Instead of calling a procrastinating client "lazy," a therapist can empathize with the client's use of procrastination as a way of protecting himself from threat and anxiety. The therapist can then offer to help the client explore alternative coping strategies.
- Clients who withdraw are taking care of themselves.
- Clients who are seductive or attention seeking are feeling a great need to be accepted and liked.
- Impulsive clients have the ability to be spontaneous.
- Oppositional clients are independent.
- Self-deprecating clients are modest.
- Clients use self-mutilation as a means of expressing their individuality and independence.
- Clients with eating disorders are seeking some way to exert control over their lives.

Some Cautions about Using Paradoxical Interventions

Therapists need to consider several factors before attempting paradoxical interventions (Weeks & L'Abate, 1982). First, paradoxical interventions require the establishment of a supportive therapeutic relationship in which the client is willing to take an active role. Second, the therapist must have a clear definition of the client's problem, and the therapist and client must agree on their goals. How the client's problem is perpetuated and what functions it serves for the client should be evident. The therapist should then track the client's progress and reevaluate the approach if it is not working.

Therapists must also evaluate ethical issues associated with using a paradoxical intervention. Such interventions require appropriate training and supervision. Therapists should be trained to recognize (1) when to use paradoxes, (2) how to use paradoxes, and (3) how to recognize when a paradox is unnecessarily manipulative or dangerous. Paradoxical interventions are not recommended for clients who are in crisis, who have been victimized, or who are suicidal or potentially violent (Weeks & L'Abate, 1982, pp. 242–243).

USING METAPHORS

One method for communicating messages to clients that might otherwise cause anxiety and defensiveness is through the use of metaphors (see Chapter 3; Angus & Rennie, 1988; Barker, 1985; Evans, 1988; Gordon, 1978). Milton Erickson is recognized as a master in the use of metaphors in psychotherapy, and the interested reader is encouraged to explore his work (Haley, 1967, 1973). Some examples of metaphors in therapy are:

- With a rigid client, the analogy of a steel beam and the advantages of using the kind of steel that can bend under pressure.
- With an impulsive client, the image of a sport (downhill skiing, windsurfing, skydiving) that requires speed and daring as well as precaution and control.
- For a parent with childrearing problems, the metaphor of tending one's garden.
- For the procrastinator, the image of a slow but methodological turtle.
- For the angry client, picturing tight steel bands around one's body and the relief of pressure that would come if these bands were slowly released through reconciliation.
- For the shy or anxious client, the image of taking the risk to open a door, to first peek at and then maybe join an exciting and challenging new world.

Jeffrey Zeig (1985) uses the metaphor of the wind to communicate to clients the value of taking control of their life.

- If people battle against the wind to get where they want to go, they end up frustrated and angry.
- If people are like leaves and let the wind blow them wherever it blows, they wind up where they don't want to be and feeling depressed.

- If people are like ostriches and hide their head in the sand to avoid the wind, they wind up confused and muddled.
- People gain control by negotiating the wind currents and tacking.

Using Imagery

Imagery is recognized as a useful skill for facilitating change by therapists from a wide range of backgrounds (Anderson, 1980; Singer, 1974; Singer & Pope, 1978). There are a number of ways in which imagery can be used to help clients change.

1. A client's imagery (fantasies, dreams, daydreams) can help identify important issues and areas of concern in the client's life. Imagery provides a clearer picture of the client's perceptions, needs, values, and assumptive world.
2. Imagery can help clients get "in touch" with their emotional responses to particular issues and problems. When therapy is stuck at an intellectual level, imagery moves the focus toward feelings and emotions.
3. Imagery offers an opportunity for clients to rehearse skills they are trying to learn before risking these new ways of acting and thinking in the outside world. With imagery, clients can anticipate the consequences of their actions and plan suitable responses when they meet with frustration or failure.
4. Imagery is a coping skill because it allows clients to monitor their thoughts, plans, and feelings. Self-monitoring increases clients' power over their life because it enables them to plan their actions rather than react symptomatically or impulsively. Imagery can also be used to enhance one's enjoyment of life's pleasures and distract oneself from life's pains.

One promising imagery procedure suggested by Michael Mahoney (1991) is *streaming.* Streaming is a modified free association technique in which clients report on their stream of consciousness about a particular event or issue in their life. Streaming differs from classical free association in two respects. First, clients put together their train of thought and report only what is comfortable for them to disclose to the therapist. Second, the therapist does not make interpretations. Instead, the client and therapist collaborate to find meaning in the client's thoughts that are relevant to the client's personal life.

When employing imagery in therapy, therapists must assess clients' comfort with imagery and their ability to use it. Clients who are not accustomed to imagery often need some instruction. Some simple techniques involve closing one's eyes, placing oneself in a situation, and describing what one sees, feels, and senses. Therapists can teach the practice of imagery with metaphors and by modeling for clients how they picture things in their minds.

GOOD MOMENTS IN THERAPY SESSIONS

Another way to help clients change is to maximize the number of "good moments" in therapy sessions (Mahrer & Nadler, 1986). Box 5.1 illustrates that good moments in psychotherapy occur when clients are able to communicate openly with the therapist, when they are focused on their therapeutic work, and when they are experiencing some success in achieving their goals. Good moments in therapy are also characterized by the free expression of feelings (Hoyt et al., 1983; Mahrer et al., 1990). Good moments in therapy have a sense of charge, force, energy, and spontaneity. Clients are actively engaged in therapy, and they readily express their positive and negative feelings with a sense of ownership and self-responsibility (Orlinsky & Howard, 1986).

Good moments in therapy sessions can be defined in terms of the stages identified by the Patient Experiencing Scale (Klein, Mathieu-Coughlan, & Kiesler, 1986). The Patient Experiencing Scale is used to score the client's involvement in the therapeutic process.

- *Low involvement* is characterized by an impersonal and detached client attitude. At this stage, clients distance themselves from events in their lives. Feelings are externalized, and there is little sense of ownership of one's problems and emotions.
- *Medium involvement* is characterized by more immediacy and personalizing of problems and emotions. Issues are not presented abstractly but are brought into the here-and-now.
- *High involvement* occurs when clients are open to discussing their problems and emotions as they occur at the moment. There is an acknowledgment of responsibility and interest in exploring one's role in maintaining or perpetuating certain difficulties. There is an active collaboration with the therapist to recognize the ramifications of one's thoughts, feelings, and behaviors and an active exploration of constructive ways these can be modified.

A somewhat different perspective on good moments in therapy is offered by Stiles (1980), who identifies two important factors in the therapy session. The first factor has to do with the client's perception of the *smoothness* and *ease* of the session. A smooth and easy session is rated by clients as smooth, pleasant, easy, and safe. The second factor is based on the therapist's rating of the *depth* and *value* of the session. A deep and valuable session is rated by therapists as special, full, valuable, good, and deep. The most productive therapy sessions seem to be those that are smooth (from the perception of the client) and deep (from the perception of the therapist). This conclusion is diagrammed in Table 5.1. Type 1 sessions, which are "good therapy hours," can be described as deep and smooth or as *smooth sailing* (Orlinsky & Howard, 1977). Type 2 sessions are shallow and smooth or *coasting.* Type 3 sessions are deep and rough or *heavy going.* Type 4 sessions are shallow and rough or *foundering.*

Box 5.1   Good Moments in Psychotherapy

Provision of significant material about self and/or interpersonal relationships. The client is open about sharing personal feelings and experiences as well as hopes, dreams, wishes, thoughts, images, and fantasies.

Description/exploration of the personal nature and meaning of feelings. The client is willing to explore the nature and meaning of feelings that are immediate and ongoing rather than distant, intellectual, or removed.

Emergence of previously warded-off material. The client is willing to explore issues that were warded off earlier in therapy.

Expression of insight/understanding. The client expresses insight into feelings, thoughts, and behaviors and the effects of these on his or her life.

Expressive communication. The client communicates in an expressive manner, indicating an active involvement in the therapeutic process.

Expression of a good working relationship with the therapist. The client communicates a feeling of trust and confidence in the therapist and a willingness to accept responsibility and to collaborate in reaching agreed-upon goals.

Expression of strong feelings toward the therapist. The client is willing to express positive as well as negative feelings toward the therapist.

Expression of strong feelings in personal life situations. The client is experiencing and expressing feelings about his or her personal life.

Expression of a qualitatively different personality state. The client manifests new ways of thinking, acting, and feeling.

Expression of new ways of being and behaving. The client expresses an improved state of well-being, characterized by achieving therapeutic goals and expression of an increased sense of self-acceptance, self-efficacy, and self-esteem.

Source: From "Good Moments in Psychotherapy: A Preliminary Review, a List, and Some Promising Research Avenues," by A. R. Mahrer and W. P. Nadler, 1986, *Journal of Consulting and Clinical Psychology, 54,* 10–15. Copyright 1986 by the American Psychological Association. Adapted with permission of the authors.

FACILITATING TREATMENT ADHERENCE

In their book *Facilitating Treatment Adherence,* Meichenbaum and Turk (1987) outline many useful suggestions for enhancing the working relationship between therapists and clients. These suggestions are discussed in the following section.

Table 5.1   Therapy Sessions Defined by Smoothness and Depth

Client's rating of smoothness	Therapist's rating of depth	
	Deep, full, valuable	Shallow, empty, worthless
Smooth, easy, pleasant	Type 1 Deep/smooth (smooth sailing)	Type 2 Shallow/smooth (coasting)
Rough, difficult, unpleasant	Type 3 Deep/rough (heavy going)	Type 4 Shallow/rough (foundering)

Source: From "Measurement of the Impact of Psychotherapy Sessions" by W. B. Stiles, 1980, *Journal of Consulting and Clinical Psychology, 48,* 176–185. Copyright 1980 by the American Psychological Association. Adapted with permission of the author.

Goal Setting

Clients are more likely to cooperate and to work toward making changes if they have clear, obtainable goals that are meaningful to them. Some suggestions are provided by Meichenbaum and Turk (1987).

1. *Goals must be owned by the client.* It is important that clients participate in goal setting. Clients need to feel a sense of choice and personal control as they work toward defining goals with the therapist.
2. *Goals should be specific.* Goals should be specific enough that clients can record on a daily basis exactly how they did or did not meet their goals.
3. *Goals must be realistic.* If clients are to gain any sense of accomplishment, goals must be realistic and achievable. Goals that will take some time and effort to achieve should be broken down into smaller steps or subgoals. Therapists need to determine that clients possess the necessary skills to reach their goals. Otherwise, these skills must first be mastered.
4. *Goals should be meaningful and rewarding.* Therapists and clients both will benefit from taking some time to explore the pros and cons of the goals clients are considering. This exploration will help clients select goals that are meaningful. It will also enable them to anticipate and prepare for obstacles or setbacks they may encounter as well as for possible disadvantages their goals may bring.

5. *Success in reaching goals should be attributed to the client.* Therapists are urged to encourage clients to take pride in their improvements and accomplishments.

6. *Encouragement from others is helpful.* Although the most important source of reinforcement for success should come from the client, encouragement from others also helps (as long as it does not imply coercion). In addition to receiving encouragement from the therapist, clients can enlist friends and family members to provide positive feedback when they are successful.

Contracts

Meichenbaum and Turk (1987) offer the following suggestions about enhancing the success of therapist/client contracts (see also Kanfer & Gaelick-Buys, 1991). Many of these suggestions are similar to those for setting goals. Contracts should be specific enough that the therapist and client can determine clearly whether the contract is being followed. Contracts should be owned by the client. Clients are more likely to honor contracts that they helped to devise, that they feel are meaningful and appropriate, and to which they have given personal and public commitment. Careful records should be kept by the client about his or her adherence to the contract. Specific rewards and penalties should be defined for following or failing to follow the contract. It is important that these rewards and penalties be as immediate as possible.

Self-Monitoring

A good way to involve clients in therapy is by having them monitor their progress. Self-monitoring includes the following steps (Cormier & Cormier, 1991; Kanfer & Gaelick-Buys, 1991).

1. *Providing a rationale.* Clients must understand why it is in their best interest to monitor their progress. A Socratic approach, in which the therapist helps the client "discover" the benefits of self-monitoring, is sometimes useful.

2. *Defining the best behaviors to monitor.* The therapist and client agree on exactly what the client will monitor. Behaviors recorded by the client are very specific and easy for the client to determine. In most cases, clients will probably choose to monitor positive behaviors, although there are times when the monitoring of negative behaviors is also appropriate. It is best to limit the number of behaviors monitored to one or possibly two.

3. *Making a recording sheet.* The therapist helps the client construct a recording sheet that will show specifically how and when the behavior to be monitored should be recorded. A wise course is for clients to practice filling out the recording sheet with the therapist to

ensure that the client understands fully how the recording sheet works.

4. *Agreeing on contingencies.* The therapist and client agree on (1) how often and for how long the client will monitor her or his progress and (2) how they will use the data on the recording sheet. They also agree on rewards for completing the self-monitoring project and on penalties for failing to complete the self-monitoring project.

Self-Reward

Although it is certainly appropriate for the therapist to encourage clients and show enthusiasm about their progress, clients benefit more from taking credit for meeting their goals. This is often accomplished through the client's sense of pride and mastery. However, sometimes a client's progress can be enhanced with the deliberate use of self-reward. As with other procedures for facilitating treatment adherence, self-reward procedures are most effective if they are set up in collaboration with the client. Self-reward involves the following steps (Cormier & Cormier, 1991; Kanfer & Gaelick-Buys, 1991).

1. *Selecting appropriate rewards.* Clients can reward themselves with tangible goods, although it is generally better to teach clients how to reward themselves with activities, with self-praise and positive self-statements, or with positive imagery.

2. *Defining contingencies.* Clients need not be stingy about taking pride in their accomplishments. However, it often helps to break goals into small steps, with the completion of each step followed by a self-reward.

3. *Timing.* Self-rewards follow completion of a goal as soon as possible. Self-rewards are not given for promising to complete a goal or before the goal is accomplished.

MAINTAINING THERAPEUTIC GAINS

Helping clients make constructive changes is difficult enough; assuring that these changes last for more than a few months is even harder (Glass & Kliegl, 1983). How can therapists help clients maintain the gains they have accomplished in therapy? A number of useful suggestions have been summarized by Marlatt and Gordon (1985) in their book *Relapse Prevention.*

The first thing therapists must help clients realize is that therapy (as well as life) is a journey with ups and downs, successes and failures. If clients take this attitude, they are less likely to look at relapses as failures and are more likely to view them as challenges for coping. Therapy is not a "treatment" that wears off over time. Therapy is an opportunity for clients to master skills and learn new ways of acting and thinking. Clients must therefore continue their learning, practicing, and growing process even after therapy is over. Before terminating therapy, therapists should arm clients with the skills and strategies for coping with the ups and downs they will experience. The process of relapse prevention can be seen as a "meta-skill," because clients learn to combine a "package" of strategies to maintain the gains they have made in therapy (Higginbotham, West, & Forsyth, 1988, pp. 177–178).

Identifying High-Risk Situations

Clients need to learn to identify situations that will make it particularly difficult to maintain the gains they have achieved in therapy. For example, a client who has worked on his anxiety may predict having particular difficulty in the future if he is faced with the need to negotiate a deal or make a bargain. A client who has completed therapy for depression might anticipate a hard time ahead when her parents die. A client who has worked on his anger might realize that a high-risk situation will occur when he is evaluated for promotion within the next year.

A good way to anticipate high-risk situations is to be in touch with our emotions. Often our feelings tell us when trouble is brewing. Changes in eating, sleeping, or exercise habits are often useful warning signs. The more effectively clients can anticipate high-risk situations, the more prepared they will be to cope with them when they occur.

Preparing to Cope

Keeping high-risk situations in mind, clients can prepare to cope by practicing adaptive responses.

What are you going to tell yourself?   Clients anticipate possible setbacks and ask themselves "What am I going to say to myself when this happens?" Some possible self-statements are:

- Keep calm. Don't panic. I can handle this.
- OK, this may be tough, but it isn't the end of the world.
- Even if my response is not perfect, it doesn't mean everything I learned in therapy is wasted.
- I can cope better now than I could before.

What are you going to do?   Clients are prepared to use their problem-solving skills to outline possible courses of action. These responses can then be analyzed to determine which ones are likely to be most effective.

Therapists and clients are advised to practice these coping responses before terminating therapy. By role playing, the therapist can determine whether the client possesses the skills necessary to cope with setbacks when they happen. Clients can also intentionally experience a setback during therapy as a "fire drill" or "life boat drill" for them and the therapist to practice together (Marlatt & Gordon, 1985, Ch. 4).

Avoiding Self-Blame

Clients generally are not helped by putting themselves down when they experience setbacks to their achievements in therapy. Rather than faulting themselves for "failing," clients should practice taking responsibility for coping and finding solutions. An attitude of coping and problem solving will also help clients avoid excessive anxiety about when and how they might fail. Setbacks are not to be feared or dreaded; they need to be accepted as part of life.

Using Support Systems

Clients are well-advised to identify people on whom they can rely for assistance and emotional support. There may be support groups or other services in the community to help the client maintain her or his achievements in therapy. It is also possible for the client and therapist to agree to meet, as needed, for follow-up sessions.

SUMMARY

Four principles of helping clients change are: (1) clients must work at their own pace, (2) the client is the agent of change, (3) change requires action, and (4) change requires risks. Resistance, which is defined as client or therapist behaviors that interfere with successful therapeutic process and outcome, has also been called noncompliance and failure of treatment adherence. Therapeutic change is difficult because change is scary, people are reactive, others often interfere, problems produce secondary gains, clients don't always possess necessary skills, and clients are sometimes hopeless and pessimistic.

Strategies for managing resistance include teaching clients necessary skills, empathizing with their pessimism, helping clients master their environments and not take resistance personally, encouraging active participation by clients, using good timing and pacing, using strategies and goals that are meaningful to clients, understanding clients' special needs, and preparing clients to overcome obstacles.

Paradoxical interventions include symptom prescription and restraining. Reframing and relabeling serve to reinforce a collaborative working relationship between therapists and clients. Metaphors can be used to communicate ideas that might otherwise cause anxiety or defensiveness. Imagery and streaming provide a useful method for clients to look at difficult issues in their lives. Clients can be helped in their efforts to change by maximizing the number of "good moments" in therapy sessions. Good moments are characterized by high client involvement and therapy sessions that are smooth and deep.

Suggestions for facilitating treatment adherence include goal setting, contracts, self-monitoring, and self-reward. To assist clients in maintaining therapeutic gains, therapists are advised to identify high-risk situations, prepare clients to cope, teach clients to avoid self-blame, and encourage the use of support systems.

SUGGESTIONS FOR FURTHER READING

Anderson, C. M., & Stewart, S. (1983). *Mastering resistance: A practical guide to family therapy.* New York: Guilford.

Ellis, A. (1985). *Overcoming resistance: Rational-emotive therapy with difficult clients.* New York: Springer.

Kanfer, F. H., & Schefft, B. K. (1988). *Guiding the process of therapeutic change.* New York: Pergamon.

Marlatt, G. A., & Gordon, J. R. (1985). *Relapse prevention: Maintenance strategies in the treatment of addictive behaviors.* New York: Guilford.

Meichenbaum, D., & Turk, D. C. (1987). *Facilitating treatment adherence: A practitioner's guidebook.* New York: Plenum.

Seltzer, L. F. (1986). *Paradoxical strategies in psychotherapy: A comprehensive overview and guidebook.* New York: Wiley.

Weeks, G. R., & L'Abate, L. (1982). *Paradoxical psychotherapy: Theory and practice with individuals, couples, and families.* New York: Brunner/Mazel.

CHAPTER 6

Professional Challenges

This chapter discusses a number of professional challenges faced by psychotherapists. These include burnout and stress, difficult clients, and the need to develop multicultural competence and gender awareness. Although professional challenges can be a burden, they also can offer gratifying experiences. It is in this spirit that they are reviewed here.

PSYCHOTHERAPY AS A SATISFYING CAREER

Before discussing the professional challenges confronting clinicians, we might want to consider why people would choose a career as a psychotherapist in the first place. In spite of its demands, stresses, and possible isolation, psychotherapy is a satisfying career for many reasons (Guy, 1987, Ch. 1). Results of two surveys show that 87% of clinical psychologists would make the same career choice again after a year of professional experience; and 89% of these same clinical psychologists would make the same career choice after eight years of professional experience (Walfish, Moritz, & Stenmark, 1991; Walfish, Polifka, & Stenmark, 1985).

Independence

In a survey of clinicians, independence was the most often reported element leading to career satisfaction (Tryon, 1983). Therapists can practice their profession according to their personal strengths and preferences. They are usually free to personalize their work and to take satisfaction in their accomplishments. Other benefits of the profession are the control over appointments and schedules and the freedom to bring variety and diversity into one's work.

Financial Rewards

Clinicians are able, within some limits, to determine how hard they want to work and how much money they wish to make. Therapists often can set their own fees, and they have the option of supplementing their incomes by giving seminars, consultations, and taking on extra clients.

Variety

Psychotherapy offers clinicians a wide range of experiences and challenges and an opportunity to work with many different kinds of interesting people with a large range of problems.

> In a very real way, the psychotherapist has a "front row seat" in the lives of musicians, scientists, movie stars, blue collar laborers, politicians, doctors, salespeople, lawyers, and vagrants. . . . As a result, therapists are exposed to people and events which would not likely be encountered in their own private life and social arena. In this way, no two clients are alike and each new encounter provides the clinician with a unique individual with whom to work. (Guy, 1987, p. 5)

Recognition and Prestige

Psychotherapists are generally respected and regarded for their special training, experience, and professionalism. People are naturally curious about psychotherapy and typically perceive clinicians as being educated and sensitive people.

Intellectual Stimulation

Psychotherapy is a craft that requires problem solving, searching for clues, testing hunches, and conducting and reading scientific research. The profession offers the opportunity to share and debate ideas and theories with colleagues, to read professional journals dedicated to one's particular interests, and to socialize with one's colleagues at professional conferences. As noted by Bugental (1964), "there is no other career which allows the individual to immerse himself or herself in the workings of psychological processes in their natural condition to the same degree (Guy, 1987, p. 7)." Clients provide myriad worldviews and are a continual source of interest, challenge, and stimulation.

Emotional Growth and Satisfaction

Therapists report that clinical practice provides significant opportunities for personal and emotional growth in areas such as assertiveness, self-assurance, self-reliance, introspection, and personal sensitivity (Farber, 1983b). A significant amount of satisfaction can be gained from developing intimate relationships with clients and helping them learn about themselves and find solutions for their problems.

> It is also inspiring to encounter the depth of courage, integrity, and sincerity of some individuals as they struggle to live out their destiny. The psychotherapist is in a privileged position to witness this battle, to share the pain of defeat and the joy of victory. (Guy, 1987, p. 8)

Kottler (1991) also describes the rewards of being a therapist.

> In an initial encounter with a client, there is nervous anticipation and excitement. A new challenge. A new test of our resources and powers to be inventive and creative. We are offered a new life to study, a new person we will come to know. We are presented with a puzzle to put together, one that has stumped many others before us. We are invited to witness the client's life story, to be privy to his or her deepest, darkest secrets. And with each journey we take to the furthest reaches of human experience, we return, as from any trip, wiser and renewed. (p. 184)

BURNOUT

Burnout is a state of emotional exhaustion, depersonalization, and reduced personal satisfaction that is experienced by professionals whose work involves helping others with their problems (Freudenberger, 1975; Maslach & Jackson, 1986). Burnout is characterized by the following difficulties (Ackerley, Burnell, Holder, & Kurdek, 1988).

- Physical and emotional exhaustion
- Responding negatively toward others
- Decreased satisfaction with oneself and one's accomplishments

Some of the symptoms of burnout include: (1) a bit too much celebration when a client calls to cancel, (2) daydreams and escapist fantasies, (3) a cynical and pessimistic attitude toward one's profession, (4) loss of spontaneity and vigor in therapy sessions, (5) a falling behind in case notes and other paperwork, (6) drug abuse, (7) feelings of lethargy and lack of enthusiasm for work, (8) diminished activities and social life, and (9) reluctance to explore causes and solutions for one's burned-out condition (Kottler, 1986).

Given the challenges presented by clients with various kinds of social, emotional, physical, and personality problems, we should not be surprised to find that burnout is an occupational hazard for people working in mental health professions.

Prevalence of Burnout among Psychotherapists

Three categories of burnout identified by Maslach and Jackson (1986) are *emotional exhaustion, depersonalization,* and *low sense of personal accomplishment.* A national survey of clinical psychologists indicated the following levels of burnout experienced by respondents (Ackerley et al., 1988).

• For *emotional exhaustion,* 32.7% were in the moderate burnout range and 39.9% were in the high burnout range.
• For *depersonalization,* 24.7% were in the moderate burnout range and 34.3% were in the high burnout range.
• For *low sense of personal accomplishment,* 3.8% were in the moderate burnout range and 0.9% were in the high burnout range.

Although 73.5% of the respondents said they would choose the same profession again, 4.5% said they would choose a different area of psychology, and 21% said they would choose a career not related to psychology. It is not clear why these rates of career satisfaction are lower than those reported in the surveys mentioned at the beginning of this chapter. Possibly, more of the therapists in this latter survey had jobs in stressful settings. In any case, even for therapists who are happy with their job choice, burnout is an occupational hazard for which they should be prepared.

Factors Related to Burnout

A survey of psychologists, psychiatrists, and social workers found that "lack of therapeutic success" was the single most stressful aspect of therapeutic work (Farber & Heifetz, 1982). This finding suggests the value of developing professional support systems, negotiating one's professional caseload, and maintaining realistic expectations. A study of factors related to burnout among clinical psychologists resulted in the following conclusions (Ackerley et al., 1988).

• Clinicians troubled by *emotional exhaustion* tend to be younger and overinvolved with their clients, who often have medical as well as psychological problems. These clinicians experience limited feelings of control over the demands of their work.
• Clinicians troubled by *depersonalization* tend to be younger and overinvolved with their clients, who are often negative and uncooperative in therapy. The clinicians studied also had a large number of clients with personality disorders and legal issues. They experienced limited feelings of control over the demands of their work.
• Clinicians troubled by *low sense of personal accomplishment* earn lower incomes, experience limited feelings of control over their work, and do not have sufficient professional support.

Coping with Burnout

The first step in coping with burnout is to recognize when it is a problem. When it is, you must take personal responsibility for dealing with it. Psychotherapists are obligated to be as competent in their work as possible, and they owe it to themselves to make their profession as enjoyable as they can. Three areas for therapists to explore when suffering from burnout are personal issues, client factors, and demands of the workplace.

Personal issues Two personal issues identified in the research on factors related to burnout are youth and overinvolvement with clients. Younger clinicians are probably more prone to burnout because they have had less time to develop their coping skills. In addition, it is possible that younger clinicians are more idealistic and have expectations that are not always possible to achieve. Other personality characteristics that can cause increased stress for therapists are a need for intimacy and closeness, a need for control, and a "type A" style of competitiveness and striving for success (Guy, 1987). It might be useful for therapists whose work is not meeting their expectations to consider some of the irrational beliefs of therapists outlined by Albert Ellis (1985).

- I have to be successful with all my clients practically all of the time.
- I must be an outstanding therapist, clearly better than other therapists I know or hear about.
- I have to be greatly respected and loved by all my clients.
- Since I am doing my best and working so hard as a therapist, my clients should be equally hard working and responsible, should listen to me carefully, and should always push themselves to change.
- Because I am a person in my own right, I must be able to enjoy myself during therapy sessions and to use these sessions to solve my personal problems as well as to help my clients.

The problem of overinvolvement with clients is probably best remedied by taking advantage of consultations with other therapists and professional supervision.

Client factors Obviously, clients with serious problems and difficult personality styles will cause more stress for therapists than will clients who are personable and motivated. Clients who cause the most stress for therapists include those who are suicidal, hostile, and aggressive; who suffer from personality disorders; and who are unreliable about keeping appointments and remaining in therapy (Guy, 1987). Although it is not easy to restrict one's professional work to "good" clients, therapists need to take advantage of professional support systems when a difficult caseload is getting the best of them.

Workplace   Three sources of stress related to a therapist's professional roles are role ambiguity, role conflict, and role overload (Farber, 1983a). *Role ambiguity* is associated with lack of clarity about one's job responsibilities and one's accountability. *Role conflict* occurs when therapy is complicated by interference from the client's family members or by legal issues, such as divorce and child custody disputes. *Role overload* generally involves having more responsibilities than time and energy permit. A fourth source of stress is a feeling of *inconsequentiality* that occurs when therapists feel they are facing insurmountable obstacles to therapeutic success. Therapists must take the responsibility to use assertiveness and negotiation skills to achieve a reasonable work environment.

Here are some other strategies for coping with burnout (Corey, 1991; Guy, 1987; Kottler, 1986):

• Maintain a good sense of humor.
• Learn new therapeutic approaches. Attend workshops and lectures to get new ideas and perspectives.
• Teach others; this is a great way to invigorate yourself.
• Learn your limits, and learn to set limits with others.
• Become more active in professional organizations.
• Take care of your health by getting adequate sleep, diet, and exercise.
• Find meaning in life outside of your profession by developing hobbies, playing, and traveling.
• Form a support group with colleagues for sharing solutions to professional frustrations. Finding a supportive clinical supervisor can be particularly helpful (Ross, Altmaier, & Russell, 1989).
• Evaluate your goals, priorities, and expectations to see whether they are realistic and are getting you what you want.
• Avoid assuming responsibilities that belong to others.

HELPING IMPAIRED THERAPISTS

As with any profession, therapists should expect to have ups and downs in their careers. When life stresses become too great, a therapist's ability to practice can be compromised. Therapists are considered to be *impaired* when their professional functioning suffers from chemical dependency, personality disturbances, or personal conflicts (Laliotis & Grayson, 1985). To provide effective assistance for impaired therapists, one must assess the need, determine who will operate a program, and decide on a process of referral.

What Is the Scope of the Problem?

Although the challenges of working as a therapist are often recognized, people sometimes forget that therapists have lives outside of therapy. Psychotherapists are vulnerable to the same kinds of life stresses that affect everyone else (Norcross & Prochaska, 1986a; 1986b). A survey of licensed psychologists indicates that 27% of respondents believe that drug or alcohol abuse by psychotherapists is a "serious" or "very serious" problem (Wood, Klein, Cross, Lammers, & Elliott, 1985). Over 40% of the respondents believe that depression or burnout is a serious or very serious problem. Almost 40% said they were aware of colleagues who had drug or alcohol problems, and 63% said they were aware of colleagues who were suffering from depression or burnout. In another survey, 36.7% of psychotherapists responding said they had experienced personal distress during the past three years that had interfered with their quality of patient care (Guy, Poelstra, & Stark, 1989). It seems safe to conclude that impairment among psychotherapists is a professional issue that deserves attention. Impairment among psychotherapists is exacerbated by the fact that clinicians often don't get help when they need it. This is partly because clinicians, as helpers, are reluctant to admit that they might also need help. In addition, there is little professional monitoring of clinical work, especially by private practitioners. Finally, clinicians are often reluctant to question the performance of their colleagues.

What Sorts of Programs Are Possible?

Probably the best type of program for assisting impaired clinicians would be one run by professional organizations, at either the state or the local level. The American Medical Association has been ahead of psychological organizations in developing programs for assisting impaired physicians (Laliotis & Grayson, 1985). This advancement is because there are more physicians than there are clinical psychologists in the United States and because the range of problems for the American Medical Association is wider. However, efforts have been made by some psychological organizations to develop programs for assisting impaired psychologists (Schwebel, Skorina, & Schoener, 1987), and the scope of these programs should increase in the future.

What Is a Good Procedure for Referrals?

Clinicians have an ethical obligation to maintain quality control over their profession. Naturally, referring a colleague for professional assistance requires tact and diplomacy. However, if clinicians don't take responsibility for their profession, they are likely to face increased monitoring from state licensing agencies. Not surprisingly, the majority of psychotherapists prefer a voluntary program for obtaining assistance over a state-mandated system of required supervision and mental health checkups (Wood et al., 1985).

Self-Referral and Prevention

The best way for clinicians to cope with the stresses of their work is to monitor their performance and avail themselves of professional support and assistance when they need it. The profession of psychotherapy poses a danger for clinicians because it can be physically as well as psychically isolating (Guy, 1987, Ch. 3). Suggestions for maintaining a high level of professional performance include participating in continuing education, being active in professional organizations, and taking advantage of consultations and supervision. Norcross and Prochaska (1986a, 1986b) concluded in their study of female psychotherapists that helping relationships can be particularly useful to psychotherapists because they know how to take advantage of them.

DEALING WITH DIFFICULT CLIENTS

It is no surprise that some clients are more difficult to deal with than others are. Difficult clients are likely to cause the most stress and potential for therapist burnout, but they also offer a challenge to therapists who are willing to work with them. Eighty-four percent of psychiatrists interviewed about difficult clients indicate that there are some clients who are so difficult that they dread working with them (Bongar, Markey, & Peterson, 1991). The most troublesome client behaviors for these psychiatrists are manipulativeness, suicidal gestures, addiction problems, and noncompliance. A survey of psychotherapists identified two categories of client behaviors that are particularly stressful: psychopathological symptoms and resistance (Farber, 1983c). *Psychopathological symptoms* include incoherent speech, agitated anxiety, compulsive behaviors, intense dependency, aggression, seductive sexual behavior, paranoid delusions, impulsive behavior, and hypersensitivity. These problems are experienced most often by clinicians who worked in institutional settings. *Resistance* behaviors are attempts to avoid genuine therapeutic engagement, such as missed appointments, lateness, reluctance to end a therapy session, erratic payment of fees, and premature termination of therapy. The following three behaviors are rated as most stressful by the clinicians.

• suicidal attempts
• aggression and hostility
• premature termination of therapy

The fact that premature termination of therapy is disturbing to clinicians led the author of the study to this conclusion.

> This finding suggests that therapists are not simply detached observers of the psychotherapeutic process and are not likely to consider their patients as replaceable parts. Therapists appear to be personally as well as professionally invested in the emotional growth and welfare of individual patients. (p. 792)

Another noteworthy finding is that stressful client behaviors are as troublesome to experienced clinicians as they are to clinicians in the early stages of their careers. It appears that one's attitudes and expectations toward clients are more important for coping with client behaviors than is length of professional experience.

A second study identified two slightly different categories of client behaviors that are particularly annoying to therapists: impositions and threats (Fremont & Anderson, 1988). The most annoying *imposition* is when clients make noncrisis calls to the therapist's home at odd hours. *Threats* by clients to harm the therapist or to harm themselves are also rated as highly annoying.

In a third survey, therapists ranked the following seven client behaviors or conditions as causing them the greatest stress (Deutsch, 1984).

1. Clients' suicidal statements.
2. Inability to help an acutely distressed client to feel better.
3. Seeing more than the usual number of clients in a week.
4. Client expression of anger toward you.
5. Lack of observable progress with client.
6. Severely depressed client.
7. Client apathy or lack of motivation.

Therapists who work in agencies generally report greater stress than therapists who work in private practice. Five irrational beliefs that cause the greatest stress for the therapists include:

1. I should always work at my peak level of enthusiasm and competence.
2. I should be able to handle any client emergency that arises.
3. I should be able to help every client.
4. When a client does not progress, it is my fault.
5. I should not take time off from work when I know that a particular client needs me.

The fact that clients with troublesome behaviors pose a challenge to clinicians is documented in a study in which clinicians evaluated clients who had comparable types of problems but who had either positive or negative personal characteristics (Lehman & Salovey, 1990). Although therapists agreed that clients with negative personalities are in greater need of therapy than are clients with positive personalities, the therapists are more inclined to work with clients who have positive personalities. Therapists said they would be less comfortable and less confident about their therapeutic skills when working with negative clients. They also believe the prognosis for negative clients is poorer and that negative clients would be less cooperative, more troublesome, and would require a more directive approach, including a greater need for medication.

The Aggressive Client

Professionals who work with the public are inevitably subjected to harassment, and therapists are no exception. In a national survey of psychotherapists, 81% of the respondents reported that they had experienced at least one incident of verbal or physical harassment from a client (Tryon, 1986). Verbal harassment includes annoying phone calls, threats to sue, and threats to harm or kill. Physical assault is less commonly experienced by therapists in general, but it is an occupational hazard for clinicians who work in institutional settings or with clients who have histories of violence. Depending on the clinicians who are sampled, reports of having been assaulted by clients range from 14% to 24% (Bernstein, 1981; Whitman, Armao, & Dent, 1976). Therapists working in institutional settings report being battered by a variety of items including shoes, bed slats, lamps, fire extinguishers, chairs, and canes (Tryon, 1986).

Over 50% of the therapists responding in Tryon's (1986) survey said they did not accept certain types of clients in order to avoid placing themselves in potentially dangerous situations. Therapists most often avoid clients with histories of violent behavior, paranoid schizophrenics, and drug addicts. Female therapists are more likely than male therapists are to be selective about accepting clients. In addition to screening their clients, therapists take precautions against violent or abusive incidents by having unlisted phone numbers, maintaining private practices in offices with security guards, and seeing certain clients only when others are around.

Psychotherapists responding to a national survey indicated that the following responses are most useful for potentially dangerous clients (Botkin & Nietzel, 1987):

- hospitalization
- rapport building
- environmental management (making the environment less lethal)

Therapists who are older and more experienced are more likely to recommend building rapport and setting contingencies with clients for acceptable and unacceptable behaviors.

Kanfer and Schefft (1988) suggest that it is particularly important to develop a therapeutic contract with aggressive clients. This contract should contain the following two elements.

1. The contract clearly defines therapy limits indicating that violence, verbal threats, and other offensive behaviors are not acceptable. Clients and therapists agree on specific consequences that will follow if the client violates the contract.
2. Clients agree to inform the therapist when they sense they are becoming angry or upset. It is important for clients and therapists to talk about anything the therapist might have done to contribute to the client's upset and how the therapist might help to reduce this tension.

Kanfer and Schefft (1988, p. 351) offer other suggestions as well.

- Giving clients an opportunity to communicate that they are becoming upset and allowing them time to calm down.
- Allowing clients to describe their feelings verbally.
- Keeping a calm, low, and reassuring tone of voice.
- Modeling relaxation and adaptive self-talk.
- Maintaining relaxed and nonthreatening nonverbal behaviors.
- Accepting clients' feelings, but reminding them of the therapeutic contract and their commitment to follow it.
- Encouraging clients to generate options and potential coping strategies.

The Suicidal Client

A more complete discussion of suicidal clients is given in Chapter 7. However, because suicidal clients pose such a professional challenge, they are also considered here.

With suicidal clients, it is important that clients and therapists agree on a contract with strict contingencies, including a commitment for clients to inform the therapist when they are in danger of harming themselves. Suicidal clients are particularly challenging because the directive caretaking response they demand from the therapist is contradictory to a collaborative therapist/client relationship in which clients assume primary responsibility for their well-being. For this reason, some therapists contract with clients from the beginning that they will be referred for crisis intervention or hospitalization if they become suicidal.

Aaron Beck (1985) suggests engaging potentially suicidal clients so much in the therapeutic process that they will want to come back to see the next chapter. To build a bridge from one therapy session to another, therapists encourage clients to take an interest in their "hot cognitions." Clients agree to write down their thoughts whenever they feel suicidal so they can bring them in for discussion. The therapist attempts to intrigue the client to analyze the relation between his or her past experiences, thinking patterns, and emotions.

The Boring Client

Although boring clients may not be particularly stressful, they challenge therapists who wish to seek an interesting, creative, and meaningful interaction. Yalom (1980) describes this challenge.

> I listen to a woman patient. She rambles on and on. She seems unattractive in every sense of the word—physically, intellectually, emotionally. She is irritating. She has many off-putting gestures. She is not talking to me; she is talking in front of me. Yet how can she talk to me if I am not here? My thoughts wander. My head groans. What time is it? How much longer to go? I suddenly rebuke myself. I give my mind a shake. Whenever I think of how much time remains in the hour, I know I am failing my patient. I try then to touch her with my thoughts. I try to understand why I avoid her. What is her world like at this moment? How is she experiencing the hour? How is she experiencing me? I ask her these very questions. I tell her that I have felt distant from her for the last several minutes. Has she felt the same way? We talk about that together and try to figure out why we lost contact with one another. Suddenly we are very close. She is no longer unattractive. I have much compassion for her person, for what she is, for what she might yet be. The clock races; the hour ends too soon. (p. 415)

Coping Strategies

Therapists responding to a national survey were asked to think of a particularly difficult client and to specify how much they used various coping strategies for dealing with this client (Medeiros & Prochaska, 1988). Clients who cause the most stress are borderlines, clients who are depressed and suicidal, and clients who are psychotic. Substance abusing, sociopathic, acting out, and physically violent clients were also listed as causing significant stress, as were clients with an organic disorder. The least effective coping responses are wishful thinking (hoping things would improve on their own) and being too self-critical about one's therapeutic responses to the client. Therapists who cope best are those who do not engage in self-blame or passivity but rather maintain an optimistic sense of perseverance.

Helping Difficult Clients Accept Themselves

A helpful technique for dealing with difficult clients is to search for their strengths—for some aspect of the client you can approve of and like (Luborsky, 1984, p. 83). However, as Carl Rogers pointed out in his writing and teaching, it is not as important to like your clients as it is to have empathy for them. Difficult clients are likely to have experienced rejection and negative reactions from many people in their lives. Helping these clients *accept themselves* will go a long way toward building a satisfying therapeutic relationship (Ellis, 1985, Ch. 8).

MULTICULTURAL THERAPY

Outlined in Chapter 7 are five areas of competence that therapists are ethically obligated to maintain: knowledge, clinical skills, technical skills, good judgment, and personal effectiveness. All of these areas are relevant for competent therapeutic work with clients from different cultures. Multicultural therapy can be defined as any therapeutic relationship in which two or more of the participants differ with respect to cultural background, values, and lifestyle (D. W. Sue et al., 1982).

Developing Multicultural Competence

Therapists have an ethical responsibility to receive training and supervision appropriate for working with all clients they encounter in their practice. There has been a great deal of interest in multicultural therapy in recent years, and graduate schools are beginning to incorporate cross-cultural issues into their clinical and counseling training programs (Hills & Strozier, 1992; Lopez et al., 1989; Mio & Morris, 1990). Pedersen (1978) designed a model for training therapists in cultural sensitivity that includes four skills: (1) articulating the client's problems within a cultural framework, (2) anticipating and dealing with client resistance, (3) recognizing and dealing with one's defenses, and (4) recovering from one's mistakes in the counseling session. White as well as black counselors who participated in a 4-hour training program based on this model received significantly more favorable evaluations from black clients than did white and black counselors who did not receive this training (Wade & Bernstein, 1991).

Steps have also been taken to amend the ethical codes of various professional organizations to specify competence in multicultural therapy as a requirement for therapists (Corey, Corey, & Callanan, 1993). To become competent with clients from different cultures, therapists need to develop an understanding of the following issues.

Understanding Oppression

It is important for therapists to understand that many clients come from cultures with histories of being oppressed. This understanding will help explain a client's reluctance to engage in a trusting relationship, especially if the therapist is from a culture responsible for oppression. Therapists need to realize that a client's behavior in therapy may have as much to do with the client's background as it does with the client's personality.

When developing sensitivity about oppression, therapists must avoid the pitfall of allowing feelings of guilt to interfere with their therapy (Jones & Seagull, 1977). Therapists who feel guilty about oppression may err by letting their feelings of sympathy prevent them from engaging in necessary confrontation. It does not help the client when therapists ingratiate themselves with clients and become over-zealous in their desire to compensate for the oppression. Sensitivity to oppression can also cause therapists to feel anxious when working with clients from cultures that have been oppressed. This anxiety is likely to instill discomfort and defensiveness in clients. Another potential problem caused by sensitivity to oppression is the therapist's discomfort with clients' expressions of rage and anger. Clients from oppressed cultures may feel reluctant to share their feelings with a therapist who is ingratiating, anxious, and trying too hard to be helpful.

Building Trust

Building a trusting relationship with clients from other cultures is likely to require extra time and patience, and it may necessitate a willingness to talk about clients' interests and incidental events in their lives. A therapist can often build trust by helping clients find solutions to immediate tangible problems (S. Sue & Zane, 1987). For example, the therapist may teach clients skills for coping with anxiety or depression. The therapist can also help clients clarify their problems and find options for solving them. Another way to build trust is to provide clients with hope and reassurance. Clients are often reassured when their suffering is normalized. Normalization takes the focus off self-blame and reinforces clients' feelings that the therapist is making a personal effort to understand them.

Taking a Pragmatic Focus

Therapy devoted to self-exploration may not be appropriate for clients who are facing immediate life challenges, such as unemployment and lack of food and housing. Also, a 50-minute meeting once a week may not be as helpful as briefer meetings several times a week. Therapists need to be flexible about how they can best help their clients.

Being Sensitive to Language Differences

Clients from different cultures may have been raised with a different language, or they may use terms and expressions not familiar to the therapist. This communication barrier should be openly acknowledged so the therapist and client can work together to obtain effective communication.

Being Directive When Necessary

Some clients expect therapists to be directive, and it may be necessary for the therapist to accept this role. Clients' passivity needs to be understood within the context of their background and culture and not necessarily viewed as resistance. However, being directive does not mean telling the client what to do. A therapist can take a directive stance by helping clients identify alternatives and choices and by encouraging clients to decide on a course of action (Thomason, 1991).

Developing Nonverbal Sensitivity

People from different cultures vary in their use of nonverbal behaviors. Therapists must be sensitive to these cultural differences if they wish to have comfortable interactions with their clients (D. W. Sue, 1990). *Proxemics* refers to the use of personal space; people differ in their comfort levels for physical closeness and seating arrangements. *Kinesics* include bodily movements, gestures, and eye contact. Therapists must realize that smiling can sometimes communicate discomfort, anxiety, and even anger. In addition, lack of facial expressions does not necessarily imply lack of feelings. In some cultures, eye contact communicates interest and attentiveness. In other cultures, eye contact is viewed as aggressive or challenging, and avoidance of eye contact communicates respect. Other gestures, such as head shaking, have different meanings in different cultures. *Paralanguage* refers to vocal cues such as loudness of voice, pauses, hesitations, and silences. Some people are comfortable with conversations that are fast and loud; others prefer low speech volumes and periods of silence. Misunderstandings can result when people who are vocally expressive perceive those who are quiet as shy, sullen, or embarrassed. Those who prefer low speech volumes and periods of silence are likely to view expressive people as overemotional and aggressive. When in doubt, therapists will benefit from talking with clients about their respective styles of nonverbal communication.

Being Appropriately Intimate

Therapists are advised not to take self-disclosure for granted. Clients from some cultures may be reluctant to share personal feelings and issues. Clients may also react uncomfortably to direct questions and interrogation. Intimacy between therapists and clients is best negotiated in a sensitive and thoughtful manner.

Being Sensitive to Family Structure

For clients from cultures with extended family structures, therapy will necessarily involve the family. Therapists with multicultural training understand that decisions about a client's life cannot always be made individually by the client; other people must sometimes be included.

Understanding Differences in Values

Not all cultures value individuality and achievement. Therapists attempt to match the skills they plan to teach with clients' cultural backgrounds. Some concepts of adjustment taken for granted by many therapists, such as self-efficacy, mastery, internal control, expression of feelings, and assertiveness may be foreign to clients from other cultures. Clients from other cultures may also have different perceptions of the meaning of time and punctuality. Being late for appointments and failure to provide 24-hour cancellation are not necessarily signs of resistance or lack of motivation. They may stem from client habits that are quite benign.

Being Cognitively and Emotionally Empathetic

Being emotionally empathetic means sharing clients' feelings and letting them know you are with them. Cognitive empathy involves understanding where clients' feelings are coming from. Cognitive empathy, which can be defined as *cultural role taking* (Scott & Borodovsky, 1990) requires that the therapist make an active attempt to understand the relation between clients' feelings, emotions, and dilemmas and their backgrounds and cultures. To be truly emotionally empathetic with clients, therapists must appreciate how clients' emotions stem from their cultures.

Characteristics of Culturally Skilled Therapists

A task force of the American Psychological Association suggested that the following competencies would be useful for culturally skilled therapists (D. W. Sue et al., 1982).

BELIEFS AND ATTITUDES
1. Being aware of one's own beliefs, attitudes, and biases, and being sensitive to how these may influence one's work with clients from other cultures.
2. Developing an appreciation for diverse cultures and an attitude of comfort, challenge, and satisfaction when working with clients from different backgrounds.
3. Being sensitive to one's limits of competence when working with clients from different cultures. Seeking supervision when necessary and making appropriate referrals.

KNOWLEDGE
1. Understanding the history, traditions, and values of their clients' cultures.
2. Being aware of different cultures' views of mental health, adjustment, and helping.
3. Matching therapeutic approaches to the needs and backgrounds of their clients.

4. Developing sensitivity to institutional barriers and prejudices that impinge on clients from different cultures.

SKILLS
1. Being flexible in utilizing approaches that are compatible with the cultures of clients with whom they are working.
2. Communicating effectively with clients by using appropriate language and nonverbal behaviors.
3. Being familiar with referral sources, agencies, and programs that are appropriate for clients from different backgrounds and cultures.

In addition to the APA's suggestions, several other factors are associated with effective multicultural therapists.

The Multicultural Therapist as Advocate

To be effective, multicultural therapists must be client advocates (Robinson, 1984) and take a proactive role. One important task for multicultural therapists is *prevention*. Multicultural therapists don't focus exclusively on remedies; they work actively for social change. Four roles for multicultural therapists as advocates are as facilitators of self-help, outreach, consultation, and social change (Atkinson, Morten, & Sue, 1989).

Self-help Multicultural therapists are interested in teaching clients to help themselves. This includes encouraging changes in client personal behaviors, cognitions, and coping styles as well as taking an active role to influence society. Clients are taught how to utilize existing support systems and how to lobby for services and programs beneficial to people with similar problems.

Outreach To be effective in multicultural settings, therapists expand their activities into the community. This may include home visits and participation in neighborhood programs.

Consulting Consulting may include lending one's expertise in needs assessments and assisting with the development of programs for mental health services. The multicultural therapist provides workshops, training, and supervision for other mental health professionals.

Social change Multicultural therapists are committed to social change. This is accomplished by consciousness raising among colleagues and within one's professional organizations. It may also include lobbying legislators and funding agencies. Multicultural therapists promote social change by supporting the efforts of people in need to create changes for themselves.

Gender Sensitivity

Another type of multicultural competence is awareness of the relation between gender socialization and problems brought to therapy by clients (Good, Gilbert, & Scher, 1990). Therapists are urged to practice a *gender-role analysis* by understanding that a client's problems from the point of view of the client's gender (Brown, 1986; 1990). Some aspects of gender-role socialization that are particularly relevant to women include:

• expressing anger
• being assertive
• developing a sense of independence and internal locus of control
• developing a sense of competence in making life decisions and career choices
• finding a comfortable balance between competitiveness and compliance
• being satisfied with one's physical appearance
• engaging in sexual behavior

Some aspects of gender-role socialization that are particularly relevant to men include:

• expressing nurturance
• experiencing feelings of dependency
• finding a comfortable balance between independence and loyalty and commitment
• expressing fear and sadness
• being satisfied with one's physical appearance
• engaging in sexual behavior

Therapists are advised to explore clients' developmental experiences with gender-role socialization (Brown, 1986; 1990) by exploring in therapy questions such as these.

• "What was it like growing up as a male or female in your family?"
• "How were you taught to deal with feelings of anger, sadness, and dependency?"
• "What lessons did you learn about expressing your sexuality?"
• "What kind of encouragement (or discouragement) did you receive about developing your independence and making career choices?"
• "What experiences have affected the development of your self-esteem?"
• "How were you taught to set goals and to react to success and failure?"

Therapists should always ask clients about their experiences with physical and sexual abuse and should take particular care to develop competence in working with clients who have been victimized (Sesan, 1988).

Gender also impinges on the therapeutic relationship (Gilbert, 1987). For example, because women are often socialized to be dependent on men, they may find it difficult to achieve a sense of independence and assertiveness with a male therapist. Although men may not easily form a trusting relationship with a male therapist, they might have even more difficulty with a female therapist who arouses "sexual scripts" that men are socialized to have toward women.

REFLECTIONS ON THERAPEUTIC PRACTICE

A good way to end this chapter on professional challenges is by considering the following reflections on therapeutic practice offered by Michael Mahoney (1991, p. 371).

1. Prepare for each session in private reflection. No matter how briefly, always take time to center your attention on the individual(s) you are about to serve.
2. Cultivate your commitment to helping; respect and honor the privilege of your profession.
3. Appreciate the complexity and uniqueness of each life you counsel.
4. Accept the fact that your understanding is limited; give yourself permission not to know.
5. When you get lost in a session and don't know what to say or do, take a moment to recenter in your intentions to help.
6. Trust in your clients' capacities to endure and harvest their individual struggles.
7. As much as possible, be emotionally present to their suffering; feel *with* them.
8. Recognize that you cannot take away anyone's pain (although you may often wish that you could).
9. If you are frightened by intense feelings (theirs or yours), remember to breathe and, if appropriate, express what you are feeling.
10. Offer comfort and encouragement as you can.
11. Foster faith in the possibilities and process of personal development.
12. In the dynamic dance of a client in process, learn both to lead and to follow.
13. Whenever possible, let the client do most of the work.
14. Honor a client's pacing and encourage his or her empowerment, especially in the process of your parting.
15. Cultivate your faith in yourself as a person and in the value of your services as a professional.
16. Be gentle with yourself; be patient with your own process.
17. Pace yourself; honor your limits and back off when you need to.
18. Establish personally meaningful routines of self-care.

19. Protect your private life.
20. Cherish your friendships and intimate relations.
21. Rest, play (repeat often).
22. Be willing to ask for and accept comfort, help, and counsel.
23. Keep the Faith (however you experience it) and share it when you can.*

SUMMARY

Psychotherapy is a satisfying career because it offers independence, financial rewards, variety, professional recognition, intellectual stimulation, and opportunity for emotional growth and personal satisfaction. However, being a therapist also presents the occupational hazard of burnout. Suggestions for coping with burnout include being aware of one's personal needs, not overburdening oneself with difficult clients, and maintaining a satisfying work environment. Keeping one's sense of humor, maintaining one's physical health, and using support systems are also recommended.

There is a growing interest and commitment among therapists to set up programs for assisting colleagues who are under particular stress and whose work is impaired. Clients who pose particular difficulties for therapists include those who are suicidal, aggressive, or who have inordinate pathology. A number of suggestions for dealing with these clients are provided.

Therapists have an ethical obligation, when working with clients from different cultures, to develop multicultural competence. This requires that the therapist understand oppression, build trust, know when to take a pragmatic focus and to be directive, be sensitive to language differences and nonverbal behaviors, be appropriately intimate, be sensitive to family structure, understand differences in values, be cognitively as well as emotionally empathetic, and understand one's role as an advocate.

Therapists are also ethically obligated to practice gender-sensitive therapy. This involves understanding a client's problems from the point of view of his or her gender-role socialization.

SUGGESTIONS FOR FURTHER READING

Brenner, D. (1982). *The effective therapist.* New York: Pergamon.
Guy, J. P. (1987). *The personal life of the psychotherapist.* New York: Wiley.
Kottler, J. A. (1986). *On being a therapist.* San Francisco: Jossey-Bass.
Kottler, J. A. (1991). *The compleat therapist.* San Francisco: Jossey-Bass.

Pedersen, P. (Ed.). (1985). *Handbook of cross-cultural counseling and therapy.* Westport, CT: Greenwood Press.

Sue, D. W., & Sue, D. (1990). *Counseling the culturally different.* New York: Wiley.

Woody, R. H., & Robertson, M. (1988). *Becoming a clinical psychologist.* Madison, CT: International Universities Press.

CHAPTER 7

Ethics

As professionals providing an important service to other people, psychotherapists are obliged to maintain high ethical standards. Ethical handling of client relationships is a distinctive skill to be valued, mastered, and practiced by clinicians. This chapter provides an overview of ethical issues that are relevant for therapists. Most of the ethical principles discussed here are adopted voluntarily by psychotherapists because they ensure the most effective therapy. A number of legal issues with which therapists should be familiar are outlined in this chapter as well.

COMPETENCE

The *Ethical Principles* of the American Psychological Association (APA, 1992) and the *Ethical Standards* of the American Counseling Association (ACA, 1988) require that psychologists and counselors maintain high standards of competence. Psychotherapists are expected to recognize the boundaries of their competence and the limitations of their techniques. They should provide only the services and use only the techniques for which they are qualified by training and experience. Overholser and Fine (1990) have outlined five areas of competence that therapists should maintain: knowledge, clinical skills, technical skills, good judgment, and personal effectiveness.

Knowledge

It has been estimated that one-half of a psychologist's knowledge base will become obsolete in 10 to 12 years (Dubin, 1972). Clearly, therapists need to keep abreast of developments in areas such as psychological processes, assessment, ethics, and other areas relevant to their professional work. This can be done by attending conferences, reading professional journals, and engaging in consultations and discussions with colleagues. A crucial area of knowledge for clinicians is awareness of clinical techniques that are most (or least) effective for various kinds of problems (Beutler, 1979). Psychotherapists should be able to identify the most appropriate treatments for each of their clients (Seligman, 1990).

In addition to maintaining a current knowledge base, therapists need to be aware of their own professional limitations. When faced with problems or issues for which they are not trained, therapists are ethically obligated to seek training and supervision and to provide adequate referrals.

Clinical Skills

Chapter 3 described the basic clinical skills of establishing a productive therapeutic relationship with clients and communicating a sense of genuineness, warmth, and competence. Therapists must have the necessary skills to communicate caring and sensitivity as well as the ability to maintain their composure in crisis situations and to be firm when challenges and confrontations are necessary. Therapists are expected to develop an objective picture of their clinical skills. Participating in case presentations and receiving supervision are the best ways to assess these skills. Along with being aware of their clinical skills, clinicians must know the effects that their personalities and styles have on others. We need to know how our personal nuances and idiosyncrasies influence other people. With this insight, we can understand why clients react to us in certain ways, and we can learn to use our personal styles to their best advantage.

Another important clinical skill for therapists is the ability to work with people from other ethnic groups and cultures. The ethical responsibility for clinicians to receive multicultural training has received a good deal of attention in recent years (see Chapter 6).

Technical Skills

The field of psychotherapy has developed to the point at which there is a vast technology of skills therapists can use in particular cases. Some of these technical skills include desensitization and flooding, aversion therapy, relaxation training, self-modeling, hypnosis, role playing, Gestalt experiments, paradoxical interventions, problem solving, cognitive interventions, metaphors, and imagery. Therapists must also possess technical skills in various areas of assessment, ranging from intelligence and personality tests to neuropsychological instruments. These skills include administration, scoring, and interpretation of test results as well as knowledge of applications and limitations of test data.

It is clear that no therapist can be an expert in all of these areas. Again, therapists have an ethical responsibility to be aware of their technical skills in various areas and to seek consultation or provide referrals for services they are not qualified to perform.

Judgment

Therapists are called upon to use sound judgment in crisis situations and when dealing with problems that are unique, puzzling, or confusing. In cases of clinical uncertainty, it is important that therapists obtain consultation. Therapists need to avoid the pitfall of following a course of action with a client because of their own unclear (or possibly biased) assessment of the issue.

Another area of clinical judgment involves making proper decisions about when to accept clients for treatment, when to refer them to other therapists, and when to recommend avenues for the client other than psychotherapy. Therapists must also make sensible judgments about termination. It is unethical to keep a client in therapy if the client is not benefiting from working with you.

Personal Effectiveness

Therapists are encouraged to maximize their personal effectiveness with clients, part of which requires recognizing their own needs and personal values. Therapists need to be sensitive to their countertransferences. How do we react to clients who intellectualize or who are obsessive, impulsive, seductive, or aggressive? When do we rely on clients to satisfy our needs to nurture, to be admired, and to wield power? To maintain good personal effectiveness, therapists should participate in case presentations, consultations, and supervision.

Another area of personal effectiveness to which therapists must attend is their own emotional and physical health. In a survey conducted by Pope, Tabachnick, and Keith-Spiegel (1987), 60% of psychotherapists admitted to having worked with a client when they were too distressed to be effective. APA *Ethical Principles* and ACA *Ethical Standards* require that psychologists and counselors recognize personal problems and conflicts that may interfere with their professional effectiveness. Under these conditions, therapists should seek professional assistance and refrain from working with clients.

INFORMED CONSENT

Thomas Szasz (1985b) explained his approach to informed consent by saying "What I promise to do, I do, and what I promise not to do, I don't do." Psychotherapy clients are buying a service, and they have a right to know what they are paying for. Failure to provide adequate information about the therapeutic contract can place the therapist in jeopardy for malpractice judgments (Bray, Shepard, & Hays, 1985; Lakin, 1991). To be properly informed, clients should be given the following information (Everstine et al., 1980; Lakin, 1991).

- An explanation of therapeutic procedures and their purpose.
- The role of the therapist and his or her professional qualifications.
- Potential discomforts or risks to be expected. This should include a reminder that therapy often involves talking about painful memories and emotions, and it can engender feelings of anxiety, sadness, and anger. Assurance can be given that the therapist will support the client through these experiences.
- Benefits that can reasonably be expected.
- Possible alternatives to therapy, such as community agencies, support groups, and training programs.
- A guarantee that questions about the therapy will be answered at any time.
- Affirmation that the client can withdraw from therapy at any time.
- A statement about the limits of confidentiality.

Written Consent Forms

Psychotherapists are obligated to use a written informed-consent form, along with any verbal contract they wish to establish with their clients. Several legal scholars have argued that written consent forms should be mandatory (Cohen & Mariano, 1982; Furrow, 1983), and some states have laws requiring psychologists to present certain information to their clients in writing (Handelsman, 1990).

Given the importance of informed consent, it is interesting to know that only 29% of licensed clinical psychologists responding in a 1986 survey said they currently used written consent forms (Handelsman, Kemper, Kesson-Craig, McLain, & Johnsrud, 1986). Some psychologists not using written consent forms said they preferred to communicate informed consent orally. Others worried that the use of written consent forms would undermine the therapeutic relationship. This is a legitimate concern. Written consent forms that resemble legal documents might compromise feelings of trust between the therapist and client. In addition, written contracts are potentially detrimental to therapists (or clients) if they become subject to legal scrutiny.

A Suggested Written Format

A good way to achieve a balance between honoring one's legal and ethical responsibilities while avoiding the potential contentiousness of a legal document is by giving clients an "information sheet," such as the one shown in Box 7.1. An information sheet provides clients with

Box 7.1   Information Sheet for Clients

Information You Have a Right to Know
When you come for therapy, you are buying a service. Therefore, you need information to make a good decision. Below are some questions you might want to ask. We've talked about some of them. You are entitled to ask me any of these questions, if you want to know. If you don't understand my answers, ask me again.

I. Therapy
   A. How does your kind of therapy work?
   B. What are the possible risks involved? (like divorce, depression)
   C. What percentage of clients improve? In what ways?
   D. What percentage of clients get worse?
   E. What percentage of clients improve or get worse without this therapy?
   F. About how long will it take?
   G. What should I do if I feel therapy isn't working?
   H. Will I have to take any tests? What kind?

II. Alternatives
   A. What other types of therapy or help are there? (like support groups)
   B. How often do they work?
   C. What are the risks of these other approaches?

III. Appointments
   A. How are appointments scheduled?
   B. How long are sessions? Do I have to pay more for longer ones?
   C. How can I reach you in an emergency?
   D. If you are not available, who is there I can talk to?
   E. What happens if the weather is bad, or I'm sick?

IV. Confidentiality
   A. What kind of records do you keep? Who has access to them? (insurance companies, supervisors)
   B. Under what conditions are you allowed to tell others about the things we discuss? (Suicidal or homicidal threats, child abuse, court cases, insurance companies, supervisors)
   C. Do other members of my family, or of the group, have access to information?

V. Money
   A. What is your fee?
   B. How do I need to pay? At the session, monthly, etc.?
   C. Do I need to pay for missed sessions?
   D. Do I need to pay for telephone calls or letters?
   E. What are your policies about raising fees? (for example, How many times have you raised them in the past two years?)

(continued)

Box 7.1 *(continued)*

    F. If I lose my source of income, can my fee be lowered?

    G. If I do not pay my fee, will you take me to small claims court? Do you use a collection agency or lawyer? Under what circumstances?

V. General

    A. What is your training and experience? Are you licensed? Supervised? Board certified?

    B. Who do I talk to if I have a complaint about therapy which we can't work out? (e.g., supervisor, State Board of Psychologist Examiners, APA ethics committee)

The contract [or brochure, or our conversation] dealt with most of these questions. I will be happy to explain them, and to answer other questions you have. This will help make your decision a good one. You can keep this information. Please read it carefully at home. We will also look this over from time to time.

Source: Adapted from "Facilitating Informed Consent for Outpatient Psychotherapy: A Suggested Written Format," by M. M. Handelsman and M. D. Galvin, 1988, *Professional Psychology: Research and Practice, 19,* 223–225. Copyright 1988 by the American Psychological Association. Adapted with permission of the authors.

information required by ethical guidelines without the awkwardness of a legal document. Psychotherapists who are uncomfortable with the formality of written documents might be interested to know that written consent forms enhance positive perceptions of professionals who use them (Handelsman, 1990). In addition, the use of a consent form reinforces a collaborative relationship between therapist and client and places the client in the role of a responsible and competent person.

DUAL RELATIONSHIPS

A dual relationship occurs when a therapist has a relationship with a client that is outside the realm of their formal therapy sessions. APA *Ethical Principles* and ACA *Ethical Standards* state that psychologists and counselors are expected to respect the integrity and protect the welfare of people with whom they work. There are a number of potential dual relationships that therapists must deal with in a sensitive and conscientious manner. These include social relationships, financial involvements, friends or family members as clients, nonerotic physical contact, and sexual intimacy.

Social Relationships

It is difficult to see how one could combine the essential features of a therapeutic relationship (emotional intensity, confrontation and challenging, corrective experience, transference and countertransference) with a social relationship. However, this depends partly on how one defines social relationships. Arnold Lazarus (1985), for example, believes that taking a walk or playing tennis can help a therapist and client get to know each other on a broader level. For this reason, it might not be reasonable for therapists to take a firm stance against social relationships with clients under all circumstances (Corey, Corey, & Callanan, 1993). But therapists are advised to ask the following questions before engaging in social relationships with clients.

• Whose needs are being met?
• Will a social relationship interfere with our therapeutic interactions?
• Am I placing the client or our therapy in jeopardy?

A national survey of psychologists, psychiatrists, and social workers obtained the following opinions about the ethics of various social interactions with clients (Borys & Pope, 1989; Pope, Tabachnick, & Keith-Spiegel, 1987).

• 66% of respondents felt it was ethical under some or most circumstances to accept a client's invitation to a special occasion. 26.3% felt this was ethical under rare conditions, and 6.3% felt it was never ethical.
• 44.3% of respondents felt it was ethical under some or most circumstances to become friends with a client after termination. 38.4% felt this was ethical under rare conditions, and 14.8% felt it was never ethical.
• 17% of respondents felt it was ethical under some or most conditions to go out to eat with a client after a session. 37.9% felt this was ethical under rare conditions, and 43.2% felt this was never ethical.
• 50% of respondents felt it was clearly unethical and 34% of respondents felt it was unethical except under rare circumstances to invite clients to a party or social event.

Financial Involvements

Therapists should not enter into business relationships with clients. They should not sell goods to clients, and they should not lend clients money. When it comes to accepting gifts from clients, the key question is what this gift means within the context of the therapeutic relationship. National surveys generally indicate that accepting gifts worth less than $10 does not pose an ethical problem, whereas accepting gifts worth more than $50 is questionable (Borys & Pope, 1989; Pope, Tabachnick, & Keith-Spiegel, 1987, 1988). Therapists are generally advised not to give gifts (especially expensive gifts) to clients.

Most psychologists believe that it is preferable to charge some kind of fee for therapy but that it is certainly acceptable to offer a reduced fee for clients with limited resources. It is not a good practice to allow clients to run up large unpaid bills, and it is not ethical for therapists to accept services from clients in lieu of fees.

Friends or Family Members as Clients

It is not ethical (or practical) to accept friends, employees, or family members as clients.

Nonerotic Physical Contact

In a national survey, Holroyd and Brodsky (1977) reported that 27% of the responding therapists said they had occasionally engaged in nonerotic hugging, kissing, or affectionate touching with clients. Nonerotic physical contact was viewed as most appropriate in the following circumstances.

- For socially or emotionally immature clients, such as those with histories of parental deprivation.
- For clients experiencing acute distress, such as grief, depression, or trauma.
- For providing emotional support during stressful therapy sessions.
- For greeting and termination.

Clinicians differ widely in their attitudes toward physical contact with clients (Goodman & Teicher, 1988). When it comes to engaging in nonerotic touch, therapists should ask themselves the following questions (see Holub & Lee, 1990).

- Am I sensitive to the fact that I, as therapist, have greater power in this relationship?
- Whose needs are being met by my physical contact with the client?
- What is the meaning of physical contact in my relationship with this client? How will it be interpreted by the client?

Before engaging in physical contact with a client, therapists should also consider the client's gender and cultural background. Some necessary preconditions for appropriate physical contact with clients include the following (Gelb, 1982; cited in Goodman & Teicher, 1988, p. 496):

- The therapist and client should be able to talk openly with each other about their feelings regarding physical contact.
- The client should feel in control.
- Physical contact should not be experienced as fulfilling the needs of the therapist.
- Physical contact should be congruent with treatment goals and the therapeutic contract.
- Physical contact should be congruent with the client's emotions.

Touching of clients by therapists does not necessarily lead to sexual intimacy (Holroyd & Brodsky, 1980) and does not appear to be inherently harmful. Some clinicians believe that touching is a positive form of communication in therapy, especially in work with children (Willison & Masson, 1986).

Sexual Intimacy

It is understandable that therapists will sometimes experience sexual attraction toward clients (Pope, Keith-Spiegel, & Tabachnick, 1986; Pope, Tabachnick, & Keith-Spiegel, 1987). The important question to be answered is "What does the therapist do about it?" Therapists in training need to be made aware that attraction to clients is not uncommon. It will help these therapists if they are encouraged to discuss this issue openly and, when necessary, to seek supervision and advice from professional colleagues (Stake & Oliver, 1991). Most professionals view it as unethical and unprofessional for therapists to tell clients when they are sexually attracted to them (Pope et al., 1986; 1987). Sexual relationships with clients are unethical and, in some states, illegal. Arnold Lazarus (1985) put it very clearly: "I certainly don't think that sex and therapy can ever mix. There are some clinicians who seem to think that they can. I think they're crazy, you see. I think they are flirting with plutonium, do you follow?"

Pope and Vetter (1991) report that out of 647 clinical psychologists who responded to a national survey, 50% had seen at least one client who had experienced sexual relations with a previous therapist. In another national survey, 5.6% of male therapists and 0.6% of female therapists stated they had been sexually intimate with clients (Holroyd & Brodsky, 1977). Although this percentage is not large, it does involve a critical number of therapy clients who are harmed. Bouhoutsos and her associates (1983) reported that 90% of 559 clients who became sexually involved with their therapists were negatively affected. Adverse effects of sexual intimacy with therapists include ambivalence, guilt, emptiness and isolation, sexual confusion, impaired ability to trust, boundary disturbance and diffusion of identity, emotional lability, suppressed rage, depression and increased suicidal risk and cognitive dysfunction, particularly in the area of attention and concentration, frequently involving intrusive thoughts, unbidden images, flashbacks, and nightmares (Pope, 1988; Pope & Bouhoutsos, 1986).

Masters and Johnson (1975) argue that therapists who have sexual relations with clients should be prosecuted for rape. Clients put their trust in therapists to provide a constructive, growth-producing experience. It is difficult to see how sexual intimacy can be therapeutic in a relationship in which the power and control shared by participants is not equal.

Given the fairly obvious reasons that sex and therapy don't mix, it is surprising to know that efforts to establish ethical guidelines and to raise therapists' consciousness about refraining from sex with clients have met with many obstacles (Pope, 1990).

Admitting that therapist/client sex was a problem   Psychologists did not recognize therapist/client sex as an issue until the 1960s, when survey data collected in California indicated higher rates of therapist/client sex than one would have anticipated. Data from these early surveys were repressed by psychological organizations, who maintained that it was not in psychology's best interest to make them public. It was not until the early 1970s that data on the prevalence of therapist/client sex were accepted for publication in professional conferences and journals. Another factor contributing to the denial of therapist/client sex as a problem was the chauvinistic insistence that complaints by women of sexual improprieties by male therapists were not credible. Finally, there was denial that therapist/client sex was harmful. In fact, a number of professionals argued that therapist/client sex could indeed be helpful.

Professional accountability   Even when therapist/client sex was accepted as harmful, it took a long time for professional organizations to accept responsibility for this problem. Male-dominated professional organizations were very slow to make rules and policies that could place their members at risk for malpractice judgments.

Another issue standing in the way of professional accountability is the fact that sexual abuses are not limited to the least-qualified or worst-trained professionals. Prominent and highly respected therapists are equally likely to engage in these practices. In addition, sexual misconduct is a serious offense that, by all rights, should result in revocation of one's professional license. It is difficult to see how a guilty therapist could undergo "rehabilitation" or make some kind of restitution, only to return to professional practice in the future.

Blaming the victim   It has always been easy to justify therapist/client sex by claiming that the client gave consent or even initiated the sexual relationship. There are surely clients who will testify they suffered no harm and possibly experienced some benefit from having sex with their therapist. However, this does not negate the fact that the therapist/client relationship is not egalitarian. Clients are not in a position to give informed consent for sex with a therapist, and legal precedent places responsibility for therapist/client sex squarely on the therapist.

Given the preceding obstacles, it is perhaps not surprising that it took until 1990 for someone to propose that professional organizations should establish committees whose purpose is to assist clients who have experienced harmful effects from sexual intimacy with a therapist (Gottlieb, 1990). The Committee on Women in Psychology (1989) recently published a paper informing the public about the harmful effects of therapist/client sexual intimacy. Here are some things clients (and therapists) should know.

1. *Therapists should not have sex with clients.* This includes any kind of sexual or erotic behavior. Sex is not therapy and can only interfere with any kind of productive work a therapist and client can accomplish together.

2. *Sex after termination of therapy is also unethical.* Many therapists have argued that it is not ethical for therapists to have sex with former clients (Brown, 1985; Gottlieb, Sell, & Schoenfeld, 1988; Sell, Gottlieb, & Schoenfeld, 1986). Therapists are not excused from ethical charges if they terminate therapy for the purpose of engaging in a sexual relationship. The APA *Ethical Guidelines* state that sexual relations with former clients may be permissible two years after termination if a number of conditions protecting the client have been satisfied.

3. *Clients can fall in love with therapists.* It is normal for people undergoing therapy to have feelings of love, affection, and even sexual attraction toward their therapist. When this occurs, therapists are expected to address these feelings professionally so they result in a positive therapeutic experience. It is unethical for therapists to exploit clients' vulnerability for their own gratification.

4. *Clients have rights.* Clients have the right to be treated in a respectful and professional manner by therapists. Clients can legitimately discuss concerns with their therapist, and, if the therapist's response is not satisfactory, clients should seek a different therapist.

5. *There are legitimate channels for complaints.* It is difficult for clients who are under stress and feeling vulnerable to summon up the energy to bring a formal complaint against a therapist. However, legitimate complaints can be made to state licensing boards and to professional associations. If the therapist is employed by an agency, complaints can be lodged with the agency director.

CONFIDENTIALITY

Psychotherapists responding in a national survey ranked confidentiality as one of their most serious dilemmas and issues of concern (Haas, Malouf, & Mayerson, 1986). The APA *Ethical Principles* and the ACA *Ethical Standards* require that psychologists and counselors maintain confidentiality of their clients' identities and of the information their clients disclose. To begin our discussion of confidentiality, we define two terms: *confidentiality* and *privileged communication*.

Confidentiality   Confidentiality is an ethical principle that protects clients from disclosure of information without their expressed permission. Confidentiality is intended to honor the client's privacy and freedom to choose when and if personal information should be shared with others. Policies regarding confidentiality are made and sanctioned by professional organizations.

Privileged communication   Privileged communication is a right that exists by legal statute and protects the client from having personal information revealed publicly during a legal procedure. Laws regarding privileged communication vary from state to state, but it is generally true that psychotherapist/client privilege is more limited than attorney/client privilege or clergy/client privilege. In California law, for example, a psychotherapist is legally mandated not to divulge information in a legal proceeding without the client's permission, except under the following circumstances when the right of privilege *must* be breached (Everstine et al., 1980, p. 837).

- When criminal action is involved.
- When the information is made an issue in a court action.
- When the information is obtained for the purpose of rendering an expert's report to a lawyer.
- When the psychotherapist is acting in a court-appointed capacity.
- When the psychotherapist believes that the client is a danger to himself, herself, or others and feels that it is necessary to prevent an actual threat of danger from being carried out.
- When a client is under the age of 16 and the therapist believes that the client has been the victim of a crime (e.g., incest, rape) and judges such disclosures to be in the client's best interest.

It is interesting to compare the exceptions to psychotherapist/client privilege to the exceptions for attorney/client privilege and clergy/client privilege. Attorneys (in California) are required to breach privilege only if criminal action is involved or if information is made an issue in a court action. Clergy/client privilege cannot be breached for any legal reason; it is absolute.

What Should Be Kept Confidential

Therapists should make every effort to honor the following kinds of confidentiality. First, therapists should never reveal the identity of their clients without the client's written permission. Case records should be secured and therapists should never discuss their clients with friends, family members, or acquaintances. If you happen to meet a client in public, the best principle is not to acknowledge the client unless he or she acknowledges you first. (This is something you can discuss with clients ahead of time.) Second, therapists should never share information about clients (such as case records, or even their identity) with other professionals or agencies without the client's written permission.

It is acceptable for therapists to discuss their clients when therapists are receiving professional supervision. Therapists should attempt to withhold the client's identity (this is not always possible in agencies or inpatient settings). The best practice is for therapists to advise clients at the beginning of therapy about the procedures for obtaining consultation and supervision.

The Limits of Confidentiality

As explained earlier, courts can order therapists to breach privileged communications with clients under circumstances defined by state law. States also have laws requiring therapists to break confidentiality to protect clients from harming themselves or others. It is imperative that therapists be familiar with the laws regarding "duties to report" for their state. Most states now require that therapists report any information about physical or sexual abuse of children that may be revealed in therapy sessions. Other states have similar laws requiring that therapists report abuse of the handicapped or elderly.

The most famous legal precedent for laws requiring that therapists break confidentiality is the case of *Tarasoff* v. *Regents of the University of California* (1976). This case involved a male student who disclosed to a therapist at the university counseling center that he was planning to kill a woman (who was readily identifiable as Tatiana Tarasoff). The campus police were informed of this threat and did take the client into custody for questioning. The client was released when he gave evidence of appearing "rational." However, no attempt was made to warn the intended victim, and the supervisor of the counseling center ordered the contents of the clinical record to be destroyed. Shortly after these events, the client killed Tatiana Tarasoff. A suit brought by the Tarasoff family was upheld by the California Supreme Court and was settled out of court in July, 1977. The main implication of the court's decision is that therapists are required to use *reasonable care* to protect the safety of potential victims. The court reached its decision on the basis of the California Evidence Code which states "There is no privilege . . . if the psychotherapist has reasonable cause to believe that the patient is in such mental or emotional condition as to be dangerous to himself or to the person or property of another and that disclosure of the communication is necessary to prevent the threatened danger" (Everstine et al., 1980, p. 836). The court reached a conclusion that has important implications for confidentiality: "The protective privilege ends where the public peril begins" (*Tarasoff*, 1976, p. 337).

Legal requirements for therapists to break confidentiality place therapists in an awkward position of being called upon to serve as "gatekeepers of the criminal justice system" (Everstine et al., 1980). Not surprisingly, some psychologists have reacted bitterly to the court's "blow against individual freedom of conscience" (Siegel, 1976). Other therapists argue that reporting requirements will do more harm than good because people with legal problems who need psychological help will be discouraged from seeking it (Lakin, 1991, p. 193). No matter how you feel about it, however, the reality is that therapists' duty to protect the public will be the subject of litigation and legislation for many years to come (Everstine et al., 1980; Fulero, 1988). The following facts are fairly certain:

- At this point there is a great deal of confusion about the legal responsibilities of therapists. Statutes of different jurisdictions often disagree or even work at cross-purposes. Unfortunately, this confusion is likely to remain for some time.
- It seems clear that psychotherapists will never again be able to practice "behind closed doors, in strict confidence, out of the public's view, and away from legal scrutiny" (Finkel, 1988, p. 119).
- Psychotherapy organizations should work with lawmakers, judges, and attorneys in developing reasonable guidelines for safeguarding the public.
- Psychotherapists need to stay informed about legal requirements, precedents, and rulings (Cohen, 1983).

Knapp, Vandecreek, and Shapiro (1990) suggest that the following guidelines proposed by J. Beck (1987) can serve as a useful model for what a legal statute should include.

1. Therapists should not be held liable for behaviors of their clients if (1) they have made reasonable efforts to assess the likelihood of such dangerous behavior, and (2) those efforts have failed to yield evidence of imminent danger of harm against a clearly identified or reasonably identifiable victim or victims.
2. When therapists determine that their patients pose danger to identifiable victims, they may discharge the legal duty to protect by any professionally reasonable course of action. Such actions may include but are not limited to communicating the danger to the victim or victims, notifying the appropriate law enforcement agency, arranging for the patient's hospitalization voluntarily or petitioning for involuntary hospitalization, and developing a therapeutically indicated treatment plan with a reasonable likelihood of reducing the violent behavior and protecting the identifiable victim or victims.
3. Therapists should not be held liable for confidences disclosed to third parties in an effort to discharge these duties.

As therapists, we all face the challenge of maintaining a comfortable balance between our personal values, the ethical principles of our profession, and the law.

Handling Confidentiality

Although the issue of confidentiality is complex, it is possible to give some suggestions for keeping it in perspective and in harmony with your work as a therapist.

Give informed consent   Research studies indicate that clients value and expect confidentiality from their therapists (McGuire, Toal, & Blau, 1985; Miller & Thelen, 1986). For this reason, it is imperative that therapists disclose limitations on the confidentiality of their therapy sessions at the outset of therapy. Although this may sound awkward, guidelines on confidentiality can be presented in a fairly unobtrusive manner if they are given in written form during the time of informed consent. Muehleman, Pickens, & Robinson (1985) report that providing clients with information about limits of confidentiality does not inhibit their willingness to engage in self-disclosure.

Be prepared for incidental encounters   Eighty-two percent of the therapists responding to a national survey reported they had experienced public encounters with clients who were currently in therapy (Sharkin & Birky, 1992). The feelings experienced by the therapists during these encounters include surprise, uncertainty, and discomfort. The therapists also reported concerns about potential violation of confidentiality and therapeutic boundaries.

If there is any likelihood that you might encounter a client outside of therapy, it is a good idea to discuss with the client ahead of time how you both want to handle the situation. It is common practice to tell clients that you will not acknowledge them during an incidental encounter unless they acknowledge you first. If clients choose to acknowledge their therapist, it is usually most appropriate to restrict the interaction to a brief social greeting.

Seek consultation   When in doubt, seek supervision or consultation. In the survey by Haas, Malouf, and Mayerson (1986), therapists ranked discussion with colleagues as the most useful mode of ethics education. Furthermore, consultation gives evidence of willingness to seek "professional consensus" about a course of action (Fulero, 1988). Decisions reached in collaboration with other professionals are much easier to justify than are decisions made alone.

Document   Make it a habit to keep documentation. Get informed consent from your clients in writing. Keep records of all consultations with other professionals.

Confidentiality with Clients Who Have AIDS

An issue that is bound to become more important in coming years is the question of when, and under what circumstances, to break confidentiality with clients who have AIDS. What would you do if you were working with a client who had AIDS but refused to engage in safe sex practices? How do you satisfy the legal requirement of "duty to protect" under such circumstances? Not surprisingly, there is currently a great deal of disagreement among psychotherapists about this question. Saenger (1987) conducted a survey asking sex therapists whether they would inform partners of clients with AIDS about the clients' condition if clients did not wish their partners to know. In response to this question, 31.9% said therapists should inform the partner, whereas 33.3% said therapists should not. The remaining 34.8% did not answer the question.

Psychotherapists writing in professional journals show equal amounts of disagreement. Gray and Harding (1988) argue that therapists are obligated to take an active role in protecting the public from potential harm by clients who have AIDS. On learning that a client has AIDS, Gray and Harding recommend that therapists use their therapeutic relationship to assist the client in assuming responsibility for informing his or her partner(s). However, if after a reasonable attempt the client refuses to take this responsibility, Gray and Harding suggest that the following steps should be taken.

1. Therapists should inform the client of their duty and intention to break confidentiality.
2. The client's partner(s) should be directly informed.
3. If the client's partner(s) are not known, the therapist should inform the state public health officer.

Posey (1988) offers additional suggestions for therapists who have clients with AIDS. First, refer the client to a support group. Support groups can reinforce the clients to take responsibility for their condition. Second, offer to work with or provide referrals for the client's family and sexual partner(s).

Other professionals who endorse breaking confidentiality when a client with AIDS is not willing to do so include Annas (1987) and Kaplan, Sager, and Schiavi (1985). The American Medical Association asserts that doctors must warn the sexual partners of patients infected with the AIDS virus if the patient is not willing to do so (AMA, 1988).

On the other hand, another group of professionals argues that the therapist/client relationship comes first and that breaching confidentiality is inconsistent with the therapist's obligation to be an advocate for the client (Francis & Chin, 1987; Greene, 1985; Kain, 1988). Francis and Chin (1987) assert:

> Maintenance of confidentiality is central to and of paramount importance for the control of AIDS. Information regarding infection with a deadly virus, sexual activity, sexual contacts and the illegal use of IV drugs and diagnostic information regarding AIDS-related disease are sensitive issues that, if released by the patient or someone involved in health care, could adversely affect a patient's personal and professional life. (p. 1364)

Needless to say, the question of breaking confidentiality with a client who has AIDS is not easy to resolve. This issue is likely to be the subject of legislation, litigation, and ethical statements by professional organizations for some time to come. In the meantime, Lamb and his colleagues (1989) offer the following suggestions.

- Therapists must inform themselves about the medical dimensions of AIDS, including how one does (and does not) become infected.
- Therapists should become familiar with the short- and long-term issues facing HIV-positive individuals, AIDS patients, and significant others potentially affected by such diagnoses.
- Therapists should be aware of their own attitudes, biases, and prejudices as they may relate to individuals who have or are at high risk of contracting some form of AIDS.
- Therapists must not hesitate to inform and encourage all clients in high-risk groups to consider the use of safer sex (or drug use) procedures.
- Therapists should refer clients with AIDS to legal counseling.
- Therapists should be familiar with existing laws in their states that relate to AIDS legislation.

As a therapist, you need to determine your policy for confidentiality with clients who have AIDS and communicate this policy at the outset of therapy as a measure of informed consent.

Confidentiality with Clients Who Are Suicidal

Therapists must expect to be confronted with suicidal threats and gestures. Chemtob and his associates (1988) report that 22% of a sample of psychologists had been faced with a client's suicide. This is a traumatic experience for which therapists themselves might wish to seek support or counseling.

The first point to make in discussing suicide is that therapists should be prepared. It is not a bad idea for therapists to receive training in suicide treatment and assessment. Some of the most common warning signs include the following (Fujimura, Weis, & Cochran, 1985; Pope, 1985; Wubbolding, 1988).

- Direct verbal warnings; these are one of the best predictors of suicide.
- Previous suicide attempts or gestures.
- Expressions of depression, helplessness, or loss of hope about one-self or the world.
- Recent losses and traumas.
- Lack of support systems.
- Inability to express reasons to continue living or to articulate steps one would take to protect himself or herself.
- Having a suicide plan and the resources to carry it out.
- Having a history of drug or alcohol abuse.
- Giving away prized possessions, finalizing business plans, or revising wills.

The second point is that therapists must take suicide risks seriously. When confronted with a potentially suicidal client, therapists need to document that they took a proactive approach in helping this person maintain his or her life. Corey (1991) and Corey, Corey, & Callanan (1993) offer the following suggestions.

- Provide the client with phone numbers for crisis or emergency treatment centers. If possible, have the client sign a contract agreeing to call for help if self-harm or suicide is imminent.
- Have a list of hospitals to which you can make referrals.
- Communicate your caring, but be firm with your contracts and don't allow yourself to be manipulated.
- Develop a contract with the client, which can include increasing the frequency of therapy sessions if the client is willing to use these sessions productively.
- Assess the availability of weapons, drugs, or other methods of harming oneself and make a contract with the client to put these objects out of reach.
- Do not allow yourself to be the only person responsible for the client's actions. Make the client as responsible as possible with contracts and get the client to involve other people as a support network.
- Let the client know you will be seeking consultation.

By certifying you took the preceding steps and that you received consultation from other professionals, you can document your role in taking *reasonable care* with a potentially suicidal client. Again, it is important for you as a therapist to develop a policy for working with clients who are suicidal. This policy is most easily incorporated into your practice by making it part of your informed consent procedure.

When it comes to breaking confidentiality or going as far as committing the client to hospitalization, the issues become more complex. Szasz (1986) argues that, by taking over the lives of suicidal clients, we are invalidating their rights and responsibilities. Should mental health workers assume the role of caretaker by labeling people as "mentally ill" and committing them to "treatment?" Widiger and Rinaldi (1983) argued that suicide should not be viewed as psychopathological. Auld and Hyman (1991) make the distinction between a therapist being responsible *for* a client and a therapist being responsible *to* a client.

> The therapist who feels responsible *for* a patient will likely react to the threat itself, acting to assuage whatever anxiety is aroused by the threat. These actions may include hospitalizing the patient, warning relatives, or some other extratherapeutic intervention. The therapist who feels responsible *to* a patient by contrast will recognize that the patient is free to do what she or he wishes with her or his life, that the therapist has no way, realistically, to prevent a suicide if the patient intends to kill herself or himself, and that the therapist's responsibility is to analyze the communication of the patient in the same way that other, less dramatic communications are analyzed. (p. 103)

When psychotherapists participate in suicide prevention to the extent of forced "treatment" or commitment, they are acting as agents of societal norms. They are, however, abandoning the basic principles of psychotherapy that emphasize respect for the client's autonomy and self-responsibility. This is a moral and philosophical issue that all therapists must consider.

PROFESSIONAL RELATIONSHIPS

APA *Ethical Principles* and ACA *Ethical Standards* require that psychologists and counselors act with due regard for the needs, competencies, and obligations of their colleagues. Clinicians are expected to acknowledge the competencies of other professionals and to refer clients for their services if this is in the best interest of the client. Therapists should always make a point to ask new clients whether they are currently receiving therapy from another therapist or agency. It is unethical to take on for therapy a client who is currently working with another therapist without first contacting that therapist (with a signed release from the client).

Psychologists and counselors are also obligated to take responsibility when they are aware of ethical violations of other therapists. The first course of action is to communicate your concerns to the therapist. Although this can be awkward, the therapist in question has a right to respond to your concerns. If necessary, get support and consultation from your colleagues. If the therapist's response to your concerns is not satisfactory or if the ethical violation in question is serious, you have little alternative except to go to higher sources. Again, the therapist in question should be informed of your intentions. If the therapist works for an agency, you can contact his or her director. You should also report the violation to the relevant professional organizations, which are listed at the end of this chapter. In addition, your state licensing board should be contacted.

Thirty-five percent of psychologists responding to a national survey reported having had occasion to file an ethics complaint against a colleague (Pope, Tabachnick, & Keith-Spiegel, 1987). In the same survey, 81% of the respondents believed that filing an ethics complaint against a colleague is itself ethical.

Ironically, a therapist who is acting in a manner that is unethical but not illegal might be subject to very limited sanctions. Professional organizations can only censor or revoke the membership of therapists who are members. Licensing boards and certifying agencies can only revoke licenses and certifications of therapists who are licensed or certified. None of these actions will necessarily prohibit the offending therapist from continuing to see clients.

RECORD KEEPING

The value of documentation was suggested earlier in the discussion of confidentiality. More needs to be said about documentation because it is becoming increasingly important that therapists keep thorough records of their work with clients. The significance of good record keeping is well known to professionals who work in hospitals or community agencies that require accreditation. Site visitors are very fastidious when they review client records, and hospitals and agencies go to great lengths to see that their records are up to standards in anticipation of their accreditation reviews. Nothing can make therapists look good (or poor) the way their written records can.

Record keeping is an ethical and legal obligation, and that is a good enough reason to do it. Another good reason is that good records are the best way to document an acceptable level of care: one that meets the standards of the average practitioner. Finally, an inadequate record by itself may be taken as indicative of negligence or poor care. Here are some things to bear in mind with regard to record keeping (Soisson, VandeCreek, & Knapp, 1987).

1. Make good records of your assessment and diagnosis. It is important to document that you took care to understand the client to determine appropriate treatment.
2. If the client has had previous therapy, make a careful determination whether you should obtain these records. This would be most appropriate if the client were at risk of self-harm or of harming others.
3. Record all of your instructions or contracts with clients to document the client's level of cooperation with therapy. Also record the

level of cooperation given by the client's family or other significant people related to the therapy.

4. Document all consultations and supervision sessions.

5. Be conservative about your expectations and honest about limitations of your treatment. If you have doubts or concerns, state them in the record. This will indicate that you were appropriately thoughtful about potential problems and were not negligent.

6. Retain your records for as long as required by the laws of your state.

For all practical purposes, clinical records are not private. Although clinical records are the property of the provider, many states allow clients access to their records. In addition, therapy records can be subpoenaed by a court at any time. For this reason, it is wise not to write anything potentially embarrassing either to you or your client in your case records. Some therapists keep separate notes for their personal use that are not made part of the client's official case record. Many jurisdictions honor this practice and allow clinicians' personal notes immunity from subpoena. You should become aware of the laws pertaining to personal notes in your state and act accordingly.

PUBLIC REPRESENTATION

Two ethical issues involving the public that are important to consider are advertising and giving personal advice.

Advertising

APA *Ethical Principles* and ACA *Ethical Standards* require that psychologists and counselors represent their services in a manner that allows the public to make informed choices and judgments. It is not ethical to publicize selective successful cases without disclosing cases in which success did not occur or was limited. The most acceptable kind of ad gives the therapist's name, highest relevant degree earned from an accredited institution, types of certifications, and types of services offered. The ad could also include information about fees and third-party payment policies. If the advertisement specifies the therapist's professional memberships, it must do so in a way not to imply that the therapist's services are *endorsed* by the professional organization. It is not ethical for clinicians to use their professional identification (certified counselor, psychologist, psychiatrist, social worker,) to promote services or products.

Advice Giving

Psychologists responding to Pope, Tabachnick, and Keith-Spiegel's (1987) survey were divided in their opinions about providing personal advice on radio, TV, and other media. This practice was judged as never ethical by 18.4% of respondents, rarely ethical by 28.3%, sometimes ethical by 22.1%, fairly often ethical by 23.7%, and very often ethical by 6.4%. The ethical issue in question regards the representation of psychological data in a balanced and accurate manner. No research findings should be publicized as "facts" without disclosure of the study's limitations. Psychologists must be conscientious and tactful to ensure that their public statements are represented accurately.

SUMMARY

APA *Ethical Principles* and ACA *Ethical Standards* include competence, informed consent, dual relationships, confidentiality, professional relationships, record keeping, and public representation. Psychotherapists are expected to be competent in their knowledge, clinical skills, technical skills, judgment, and personal effectiveness. To maintain informed consent, clients should be provided with a written consent form. Dual relationships between therapists and clients are unethical. Therapists particularly should avoid entering into financial relationships with clients. It is unethical to have sex with present as well as former clients. Therapists are obligated to maintain confidentiality about the identity of their clients unless required to break confidentiality by the jurisdiction in their state. Most states have laws requiring that therapists reveal the identity of clients who are a threat to themselves or to others or who are victims or perpetrators of child abuse. To avoid problems involving confidentiality, therapists are advised to give informed consent to clients about the limits of confidentiality, to seek consultation when uncertain about a procedure, and to keep good documentation. Suicidal clients and clients with AIDS present particular challenges to therapists in the area of confidentiality.

Therapists also have ethical obligations regarding professional relationships. These include not only acknowledging the competencies of their colleagues but also taking appropriate actions when they are aware of another therapist's ethical violations. Therapists are ethically obligated to keep adequate records, and they should remember that clinical records are subject to subpoena. In their public representations, therapists should maintain professional standards with regard to advertising and giving advice publicly.

ADDRESSES OF PROFESSIONAL ORGANIZATIONS

For further information on ethical standards, you may wish to contact the following professional organizations.

American Counseling Association, 5999 Stevenson Avenue, Alexandria, VA 22304   (703) 823-9800

American Psychiatric Association, 1400 K Street NW, Washington, D.C. 20005   (202) 682-6000

American Psychological Association, 1200 Seventeenth Street NW, Washington, D.C. 20036   (202) 955-7729

National Association of Social Workers, 7981 Eastern Avenue, Silver Spring, MD 20919   (301) 565-0333

SUGGESTIONS FOR FURTHER READING

Corey, G., Corey, M.S., & Callanan, P. (1993). *Issues and ethics in the helping professions.* Pacific Grove, CA: Brooks/Cole.

Keith-Spiegel, P., & Koocher, G. (1985). *Ethics in psychology: Professional standards and cases.* New York: Random House.

Lakin, M. (1991). *Coping with ethical dilemmas in psychotherapy.* New York: Pergamon.

Pope, K. S., & Bouhoutsos, J. C. (1991). *Sexual intimacies between therapists and patients.* New York: Praeger.

Pope, K. S., & Vasquez, M. J. T. (1991). *Ethics in psychotherapy and counseling: A practical guide for psychologists.* San Francisco: Jossey-Bass.

Van Hoose, W. H., & Kottler, J. A. (1985). *Ethical and legal issues in counseling and psychotherapy* (2nd ed.). San Francisco: Jossey-Bass.

CHAPTER 8

Getting Therapy Off to a Good Start

This chapter describes how therapeutic outcome can be enhanced by getting psychotherapy sessions off to a good start. A review of outcome studies suggests that therapists can increase the likelihood of success in psychotherapy by adopting the following guidelines (Beutler, Clarkin, Crago, & Bergen, 1991; Meichenbaum, 1990).

1. Assess the client's likelihood of success.
2. Prepare clients for therapy.
3. Match therapy to the client.

Before discussing characteristics of clients that appear to be related to successful therapeutic outcome, we will consider the process by which people come to psychotherapy in the first place. You may be surprised to discover that the clients who come to psychotherapy represent a select and very small proportion of the population. Another problem impairing the success of therapy is the large number of clients who prematurely drop out.

WHO SEEKS PSYCHOTHERAPY?

It has been estimated that some 20% of American adults have a diagnosable "mental disorder" (Norcross & Prochaska, 1986a; Wills, 1987b). However, only about one-quarter of these people who could potentially benefit from psychotherapy decide to work with a professional therapist. The majority of people with adjustment problems turn to friends or rely on themselves to find solutions to their problems. Those who do choose professional help are as likely to take their problems to a member of the clergy or to a physician as they are to seek psychotherapy (Wills & DePaulo, 1991). Overall, only 2 to 3% of the population receives mental health services in any given year (Norcross & Prochaska, 1986a; Wills & DePaulo, 1991). These data are interesting because they indicate that clients of psychotherapists constitute a select sample from a small minority of the population.

Why do only a select group of people take advantage of psychotherapy? Financial constraints may be important, but there are other issues that must be considered. Although there is limited research on this question, it seems safe to assume that people's perceptions of the meaning of psychotherapy are an important factor influencing their choice of professional help for life problems (Parish & Kappes, 1979). Psychotherapy suffers from the stigma (largely perpetuated by psychotherapists) that therapy clients necessarily suffer from some kind of disorder, which is listed numerically in a diagnostic manual. This stereotype of psychotherapy is likely to dissuade those who are uncomfortable with the idea of placing themselves in a dependent position in a relationship with a therapist whose role is to offer treatment and to cure them of some disorder that the therapist is obliged to uncover. Research studies have shown that people are less willing to consider psychotherapy when they view life problems as resulting from an illness rather than from ineffective social learning skills (Fisher & Farina, 1979).

Psychotherapy clients are often perceived and treated negatively. This negativism was demonstrated in a study in which pairs of previously unacquainted college students carried on 10-minute conversations (Sibicky & Dovidio, 1986). In half the experimental sessions, one of the two participants (the perceiver) was truthfully told that the other person (the target person) was a student in a psychology course. In the remaining experimental sessions, one of the two participants (perceiver) was falsely told that the other person (target) was currently seeking psychotherapy (the target person was not aware of this false information). The description of the target person had dramatic effects. Perceivers gave significantly fewer favorable personality ratings to target persons who were supposedly seeking psychotherapy. They also behaved in a less friendly manner toward the supposed psychotherapy clients during their conversation. The unfavorable behaviors of perceivers toward target persons who were introduced as clients also rubbed off on the target persons. Target persons were less friendly and less responsive when they had been falsely described as psychotherapy clients.

The perception of psychotherapy as a treatment of illness is incompatible with the following factors that influence people's willingness to ask for help (Wills & DePaulo, 1991).

- People prefer to ask for help when they don't feel they will have to give up control to another person.
- People prefer help that encourages them to develop skills they can use to help themselves.
- People prefer to seek help when they are assured they will have control over the duration of the help and the type of help that is offered.

The common principles of psychotherapy described in this book are very much in line with the preceding factors that influence help seeking. However, many people appear to be unaware of the possibility that psychotherapy can involve a collaborative relationship between a therapist and client in which goals and processes are openly negotiated. This lack of awareness is unfortunate, because it means that only those who are willing to risk taking advantage of psychotherapy in the first place can have the opportunity to discover what it has to offer.

People are most likely to enter psychotherapy when they are suffering from difficult events in their life and are feeling the need to reduce the stress they are experiencing (Wills & DePaulo, 1991). A person under stress who has support people available will turn to them first. Often it is these support people who help this person sort out his or her options, of which psychotherapy may appear most suitable. With some luck, the support people will be able to convince the person suffering from life difficulties that a psychotherapist might be able to assist with discovering solutions to their problems. Those who are suffering from life problems and who do not have support people may seek psychotherapy as a last resort. All in all, it appears that the process through which people get themselves into psychotherapy is often a matter of chance. It is no wonder that such a small proportion of people who could benefit from psychotherapy ever end up in a therapist's office.

Psychotherapy suffers from a problem that has been pointed out by Thomas Szasz (1961; 1988) throughout his professional career, which was also articulated by Hans Strupp (1982). To be eligible for reimbursement under health insurance, psychotherapists are compelled to medicalize psychotherapy and advertise it as a treatment for health-related disorders. Although promoting psychotherapy as a treatment for a disorder has financial benefits, it causes misunderstanding among the public about exactly what psychotherapy has to offer. The point of view expressed in this book is that seeking help from a psychotherapist is a coping skill (Wills, 1987b). Clients do not submit themselves to a psychotherapist to be analyzed; they engage a psychotherapist to provide encouragement and empathy and to help them learn skills that will be useful for making necessary changes in their ways of thinking and acting (Goldfried, 1980a). Whether this type of service is appropriate for health insurance reimbursement is an issue for debate (Kisch & Kroll, 1980; Maher, 1982; Strupp, 1982; Szasz, 1990a). However, it is a more accurate portrayal of what actually happens in psychotherapy.

Given the current reimbursement system in America, psychotherapy is destined to be represented to the public as a medically relevant treatment. People who wish to take advantage of psychotherapy may have to reconcile themselves with the stereotype of a patient who is suffering from some kind of mental disorder. Only when clients enter the psychotherapy session will they have an opportunity to be disabused about the contradiction between what many psychotherapists publicly claim to be doing and what they actually do in practice. This clarification, which is called *structuring*, was described in Chapter 1 and is discussed in this chapter in greater detail.

The Dropout Problem

The difficulties of communicating the benefits of psychotherapy to those who could gain from it are compounded by the fact that a sizeable number of clients who do begin psychotherapy drop out prematurely. Research reviews indicate that the *median* number of psychotherapy sessions for clients in the United States is six. Furthermore, roughly 40% of clients fail to return after the first interview. Another way to appreciate the problem of dropouts is to recognize that the majority of mental health providers have terminated or lost half of their therapy clients before the eighth session (Garfield, 1986). Donald Meichenbaum (1990) put the problem more dramatically by reporting that the *modal* number of therapy sessions in North America is −1; that is, the majority of prospective clients make an initial appointment and then never show up at all.

As explained earlier in this chapter, people's willingness to take advantage of psychotherapy could be enhanced by changing public attitudes of the psychotherapy process. Two other approaches toward involving those who could benefit from psychotherapy are to assess a client's likelihood of success and ensure that clients and therapists get their relationship off to a good start.

ASSESSING THE CLIENT'S LIKELIHOOD OF SUCCESS

What conclusions can be reached from research studies that attempt to identify characteristics of clients who are most likely to benefit from psychotherapy? Generally speaking, very few client-related factors are consistently related to therapy outcome (Garfield, 1986). This is not surprising when one considers the multitude of variables involved when specific clients with specific problems meet with specific therapists who suggest specific interventions. Client characteristics such as age, sex, social class, intelligence, and personality styles are difficult to correlate with the likelihood of success because their importance depends so much on the problem, the therapist, and the intervention. The following generalizations have been advanced about clients who are most likely to succeed in psychotherapy (Strupp & Binder, 1984; Weiner, 1975):

1. Clients are more likely to succeed in therapy when they are feeling sufficient distress to be motivated but do not have severe enough personality disturbances to keep them from changing.
2. Clients are more likely to succeed in therapy when they have a positive attitude toward therapy, are seeking it out of free choice, are willing to actively participate in therapy, and expect that therapy can help them.
3. Clients are more likely to succeed in therapy if they possess minimal social skills, are able to express themselves, and have the capacity for trusting others and for relating on a personal level.
4. Clients are more likely to succeed in therapy if they are willing to examine and communicate their feelings.
5. Clients are more likely to succeed in therapy if they are willing to take responsibility for their behaviors and to consider the effects of their actions on others.
6. Clients are more likely to succeed in therapy if they accept the fact that therapy will require that they take risks and make certain sacrifices.

The client characteristics just listed are not surprising and have prompted clinicians to remark that psychotherapists who desire to bolster their record of "successes" should accept only clients who meet these criteria. Few therapists have this luxury! Therapists can, however, size up their clients to determine how much special effort will be necessary to solidify a good working relationship and negotiate the goals, responsibilities, and interventions that will be part of the therapeutic contract. One way of predicting a client's likelihood of success is by assessing his or her motivation to be actively engaged in the therapy sessions (Gomes-Schwartz, 1978; Windholz & Silberschatz, 1988). *Active engagement* consists of the following kinds of client behaviors (Rosenbaum & Horowitz, 1983).

- The client presents goals for therapy that are carefully thought out, elaborated, and clear.
- The client willingly engages as an active participant in the therapy sessions.
- The client's goals for therapy are realistic.

- The client finds the initial interview with the therapist to be a good fit to what he or she wanted and relevant and appropriate to his or her concerns and goals.
- The client indicates a willingness to change, explore, and experiment.

PREPARING CLIENTS FOR THERAPY

Research indicates that the outcome of psychotherapy is enhanced when the therapist and client share similar values, philosophies, and ways of viewing the world (Beutler et al., 1991). Therapists and clients must agree on their expectations about the goals and processes of therapy. Four dimensions of the psychotherapeutic interaction about which clients may have particular preferences have been identified (Tracey & Dundon, 1988).

- *Approval.* The degree to which the client wants the therapist to provide support and emotional guidance.
- *Advice.* How much the client feels the therapist should provide guidance, advice, and evaluation.
- *Audience.* The client's wish for the therapist to act as a sounding board and listen to what he or she has to say.
- *Relationship.* The client's desire to self-disclose to the therapist within a comfortable, egalitarian relationship.

Preferences for approval and advice are associated with more dependency on the part of a client than are preferences for audience and relationship, which reflect a more mature manner of relating with the therapist. The sample of clients studied by Tracey and Dundon (1988) at a university counseling center indicate that clients want to receive advice but not necessarily approval from their therapist. Clients also express preference for a close therapeutic relationship. Since therapists generally don't provide approval and do offer a close relationship, it appears that the issue of advice is in particular need of negotiation during the first therapy sessions.

It is not feasible to match clients and therapists on all of the above dimensions ahead of time, so it makes sense that therapists should take some time during their first sessions to prepare their clients for therapy and assure that the groundwork has been laid for a productive working relationship. The usefulness of taking the time to prepare clients for therapy has been demonstrated in a large number of research studies (Frank, 1978; Garfield, 1986; Orlinsky & Howard, 1986). There are three ways in which preparation of clients for psychotherapy is generally accomplished: instruction, films and tapes, and contracts (Beutler et al., 1991).

Instruction

Instructing clients about the therapy process is referred to by many clinicians as *structuring*. Structuring is defined as an interactional process between therapists and clients in which they arrive at similar perceptions of the role of the therapist, an understanding of what occurs in the therapy process, and an agreement on which outcome goals will be achieved (Cormier & Cormier, 1991, p. 51). The structuring process is accomplished with what is often called a *role induction interview* (Frank, 1978), which is based on the concept of the *anticipatory socialization interview* outlined by Orne and Wender (1968).

It is important that the therapist engage in structuring with the client's collaboration and cooperation to reinforce the client's motivation and active participation in the therapy process. The philosophy of structuring is that the client is a consumer, and it is ethically indicated that clients should be involved in negotiating the service they are purchasing (Morrison, 1979). The following suggestions can be made about the structuring procedure (Cormier & Cormier, 1991; Day & Sparacio, 1980).

1. Structuring is negotiated with the client, not coerced.
2. The therapist clearly explains his or her purposes for certain procedures and answers all of the client's questions.
3. Structuring is flexible. It is tailored to the individuality of the client.
4. Structuring is done in a timely manner. It occurs only when it seems appropriate, and it is not given out of context.
5. Structuring is accomplished in a manner that stimulates the interest and involvement of the therapist and client. It is not lengthy, boring, and drawn out.
6. Structuring is a collaborative effort and does not involve a recitation of rules, demands, restrictions, and sanctions.

The specific processes that are worked out with the client during structuring depend on the individual therapist and client and on the client's presenting problem. The following issues are generally covered during the structuring process (Frank, 1978).

1. Agreement on scheduling of therapy sessions and the approximate number of sessions until termination.
2. Agreement on fee amount and on fees for missed and uncanceled appointments.
3. Specification of the client's and therapist's respective roles and responsibilities.
4. An understanding that therapy requires time, patience, and practice. Acknowledgment that the therapy process is not linear but is characterized by setbacks, discouragements, and relapses.

5. Acknowledgment that the client will experience a variety of potentially uncomfortable emotions during psychotherapy.
6. Acceptance of the fact that the client will at times be reluctant to carry out activities suggested by the therapist.

Films and Tapes

Another way to prepare clients for psychotherapy is with films or audiotapes that describe typical therapy sessions (Truax & Carkhuff, 1967; Truax & Wargo, 1969; Strupp & Bloxom, 1973). These audiovisual devices can provide prospective clients with a good model about what kinds of interactions and interchanges occur during so-called good and productive therapy sessions. Clients can also be given an opportunity to develop their relevant therapeutic behaviors ahead of time in practice sessions (Warren & Rice, 1972). A 30-minute videotape was developed by Wilson (1985) to prepare clients for psychotherapy. Dropout rates after the first session of therapy were 12% for clients who were shown the video and 33% for a comparable group of clients who did not see the video. The videotape, *A Time for Change: It's Okay to See a Therapist,* presented four clients involved in the following behaviors that research has suggested are effective in getting psychotherapy off to a good start.

1. Talking candidly to the therapist about problems.
2. Exploring and expressing feelings.
3. Actively collaborating with the therapist.
4. Working on concerns over the course of several weeks.
5. Beginning to change ineffective ways of behaving.
6. Coping with the stresses resulting from therapy.
7. Realizing that talking to a psychotherapist can be helpful in resolving problems.
8. Demonstrating a moderate level of positive expectancy.
9. Experiencing the therapist's responses as warm, accepting, understanding, patient, and uncritical.

The videotape also included an informational component, which instructed the viewer that psychotherapy is most helpful when clients do the following things.

1. Express personal feelings to the therapist.
2. Realize and accept that talking about troublesome feelings can be useful.
3. Understand that change requires hard work that clients must do for themselves.
4. Realize that some physical problems are caused by psychological stress.
5. Accept that some of their difficulties are self-inflicted.

6. Realize that there are adaptive and maladaptive ways of expressing emotions.
7. Expect no miracles and understand that personality change requires time.
8. Learn that difficulties in living are common and that talking about them is an effective way of finding solutions.
9. Accept that there are no "cures" for life's difficulties, only more or less adequate ways of dealing with them.
10. Expect psychotherapy to be stressful at times, but nonetheless helpful.

Contracts

A third way to prepare clients for psychotherapy is through the process of contracting (Kirschenbaum & Flaner, 1984). Contracting can be used for structuring as well as for facilitating the therapeutic process of defining and pursuing therapeutic goals (Emmelkamp, 1986). When structuring, the use of contracts is very much related to the processes of negotiation, which are discussed next.

NEGOTIATING THE CLIENT/THERAPIST RELATIONSHIP

There are two kinds of negotiation that take place between therapists and clients (Higginbotham, West, & Forsyth, 1988). The first negotiation centers around defining the type of interaction therapists and clients will have and their respective roles and responsibilities. The second negotiation is for therapists and clients to find a common ground for understanding the client's problems and identifying viable goals and solutions.

Therapist/Client Interaction

Before discussing negotiations, we should remind ourselves that the process of negotiation implies that the negotiating parties are attempting to arrive at compatible goals by means of cooperative communication. Through the process of negotiation, therapists and clients attempt to gain "a better appreciation of what is probable, possible and impossible, and what the opportunity costs might be" (Higginbotham et al., 1988, p. 78). Therapists and clients both want their relationship to be conducive for helping clients make constructive changes in their life. Clients want to be assured that they will be taken seriously, will be respected, and will not be pushed to do things they are not ready to do. Therapists desire a relationship that will make it possible for them to have a positive influence on the client. While negotiating the guidelines of their interaction, therapists and clients usually feel the need to address the following issues. Some of these issues are negotiated in open conversation between the therapist and client. Other issues are not actually discussed but are worked out during the course of the therapy session.

1. Clients should be given information about ethical guidelines the therapist promises to honor.

2. Clients may want to talk about different kinds of topics and issues than therapists do. Therapists must sometimes be willing to allow time for conversation that to them is off the track before shifting the conversation back to areas of importance for the therapist.

3. Therapists need to be sensitive about how willing clients are to talk about personal issues. Although clients are ultimately responsible for sharing personal information, the therapist has to avoid pushing the client faster than he or she is comfortable being pushed. Sometimes clients are willing to share personal issues more quickly than appears appropriate, and the therapist must take actions to slow the client down.

4. Therapists and clients need to find a level of intimacy that is comfortable for both of them during the therapy session.

5. Therapists and clients need to learn each other's style of communicating. This is particularly important when therapists and clients are from different backgrounds or cultures. To repeat Milton Erickson's advice mentioned in Chapter 3, therapists should learn and use the client's language. Harmony in communication between therapists and clients needs to be maintained at verbal as well as at nonverbal levels. For this reason, the verbal and nonverbal skills discussed in Chapter 3 are very important.

Understanding the Client's Problems

Before embarking on a course of psychotherapy, therapists and clients must reach a shared definition of the client's problem and agree on viable goals and solutions. Therapists and clients attempt to find a common language for answering the following questions (Higginbotham et al., 1988). These questions, which are generally included in an assessment interview, are important here because they must be negotiated to both the client's and the therapist's satisfaction.

What are the causes of the problem?   This question may be of greater interest to clients than to therapists (who are often less interested in "causes" and more interested in antecedents and consequences). However, it is important that clients get some reassurance from therapists that their concern about *whys* ("why me?") has been addressed. When the diagnosis of cause does appear relevant to the therapist, the therapist's conclusions should be communicated to the client in a manner the client can understand and accept.

Why is the problem present at this time?   This question can be the subject of a collaborative investigation by the client and therapist about what is happening in the client's life at this time. Often the therapist can be a source of comfort by normalizing the client's condition: "Given what is happening to you and what you've been through, it is no wonder that you are feeling depressed." "You have a lot of stresses in your life and anxiety is a natural reaction."

How is the problem experienced in the client's everyday life? As the therapist and client explore this question together, they can gain some insight about how the client's problem is maintained or exacerbated by other people. They can also learn about the advantages or disadvantages that may result from the client's problem in his or her interactions with significant others.

How severe is the problem? How much does it interfere with the client's life?   Therapists need to get some idea about whether the client is blowing the problem out of proportion or denying its significance. This takes tact because clients who are suffering are not interested in having someone tell them that their problems are unimportant. "Catastrophizing" clients require empathy and acceptance from the therapist before they can be persuaded to alter their perceptions. "Denying" clients also must be taken seriously until they trust the therapist sufficiently to share their pain.

What is the most suitable way of solving this problem? Therapists always find it useful to ask clients what solutions they have already attempted. Therapists also want to ask clients how they think the therapist can assist them. These questions will help to ensure a good working alliance between therapist and client. Generally speaking, the therapist should not *prescribe* solutions but should "figure them out" with the cooperation of the client.

Hans Strupp (1989) is one of the many therapists who advise against using technical terms and jargon during this period of negotiation with clients.

> I see little room for the large array of traditional analytic interpretations. A frequent consequence of these abstract, highly inferential pronouncments may be to antagonize the patient, diminish his or her self-esteem, and merely teach a vocabulary of jargon that may become a weapon to be turned against the therapist. (p. 723)

Rather than using technical language that is likely to keep the client at a distance, therapists should engage the client using the linguistic skills of paradox and metaphor that were described in Chapter 3. For example, instead of providing obsessive clients with a diagnostic label, it may be more fruitful to experience with them the troubling consequences of their obsessions ("it must be difficult carrying around so much baggage"). Although clients may not appreciate being diagnosed and labeled, they are likely to find comfort from a therapist who can appreciate their suffering. In this light, paranoid clients can be shown empathy about how exhausting it is always to have to be on guard to protect themselves from others. Narcissistic clients can be touched by acknowledging their deep desire to be loved and appreciated. Histrionic clients can be engaged on the theme of what it's like to feel "obliged" to charm and entertain others. Although a therapist and client may have different ways of understanding and labeling the presenting problem, they both can reach a common bond by acknowledging the essence of the client's pain (Watzlawick, 1990a).

MATCHING THERAPY TO THE CLIENT

A Multimodal Approach

There has been a growing concern among psychotherapists about the importance of tailoring therapy to fit the client rather than attempting to "tailor" the client to fit the therapy (Lazarus, 1986). The value of adapting therapy for the individual client was recognized many years ago by Alexander and French (1946), who proposed a principle of therapeutic *flexibility*.

> As long as the psychoanalytic method of treatment was considered a single procedure, the analyst—whether he was aware of it or not—selected his patient to fit his technique; only a few tried to adapt the procedure to the diversity of cases they encountered. In all medicine there are very few instances in which the therapeutic tool is rigidly fixed and the patients made to conform. The logical solution to the problems of therapy is rather the converse. Not only do their ailments differ greatly, but the patients themselves present many physical and psychological differences. In psychotherapy, as in all therapy, the physician must adapt his technique to the needs of the patient. (p. 25)

Although we may appreciate the value of therapeutic flexibility, we must acknowledge that therapeutic flexibility has not been the procedure followed by many clinicians throughout the history of psychotherapy. The battle for dominance and superiority of various schools of psychotherapy has reinforced a rigid adherence to the ideology, theoretical framework, and practices defined as "sacred" by a school's founder. Paul Watzlawick (1985) made this point by quoting the philosopher Hegel, who said "If the facts don't fit the theory, so much the worse for the facts." This can be translated to "If the client doesn't fit the therapy, so much the worse for the client."

Recognition of the drawbacks of becoming a disciple of a particular psychotherapeutic school has led an increasing number of psychotherapists to identify themselves as *eclectics* (Jensen, Bergin, & Greaves, 1990; Smith, 1982). Taken at face value, this trend means that the majority of therapists don't believe that one particular theory or school of therapy provides the complete answer to the question of how to help their clients. There is a need to develop as a therapist by incorporating methods and procedures that have been demonstrated as useful by other therapists, *regardless of their theoretical persuasion.* In this spirit, Corsini (1989, p. 9) suggests that "all good therapists are eclectic." Unfortunately, the term *eclectic* has been taken too literally by some clinicians who have accused therapists who call themselves eclectics as being "muddleheaded" (see Norcross, 1986b) and creating a "methodological porridge" (Slavney & McHugh, 1987, p. 4) and a "mish-mash of theories, a hugger-mugger of procedures, a gallimaufry of therapies, and a charivaria of activities" (Eysenck, 1970).

A number of terms can be suggested to describe the attempt to open oneself up to therapeutic procedures that have been demonstrated as successful in controlled research studies. These include *eclecticism, integration, synthesis,* and *pluralism* (Okum, 1990, pp. 405–406). To avoid unnecessary semantic discourse, it is probably best to adopt Arnold Lazarus' (1986) use of the term *technical eclecticism* to describe the process of employing proven psychotherapeutic techniques and procedures, without necessarily subscribing to any of their underlying theories. Lazarus (1986) contends that the day may come when there is a theory that can successfully explain the operation of all of the procedures identified through controlled research as being effective for different kinds of clients with different kinds of problems. However, that day is far away, and in the meantime therapists must do their work as effectively as they can. This requires keeping abreast of current research findings and maintaining the flexibility to match therapeutic procedures to individual clients. As Matarazzo (1984) pointed out, this is where psychotherapy becomes an art as well as a science.

The aim of a technically eclectic (or multimodal) approach is to formulate a consistent framework that allows the therapist to accomplish the following tasks (Lazarus, 1986).

- Specify problems and goals.
- Specify treatment techniques.
- Measure systematically the relative success of these techniques.

Specific guidelines and procedures for a multimodal psychotherapeutic approach have been outlined by Lazarus (1976; 1981). Recognition of the necessity of matching therapy to clients has important implications for the therapy process (Duncan, Parks, & Rusk, 1990). Therapists must acknowledge that clients' problems have to be understood in terms of the meaning the problem has for the client. Since clients' meanings for their problems may not correspond with those of the therapist, the therapist is challenged to be accepting and nonjudgmental. The therapist's task is to base the goals and procedures of therapy on the client's reality. Change occurs in therapy when clients are persuaded to alter their realities in a way that will enable them to decrease their pain and achieve more of what they desire from life. This is done by encouraging clients to take risks with new ways of thinking and acting as well as by helping clients to ascribe different meanings to their conflicts.

Important Client Dimensions

Beutler and Clarkin (1990) proposed that therapy will get off to a better start if therapists attempt to match their approach to the client's problem severity and reactance level.

Problem severity   Therapists widely believe that clients have to be under a minimal amount of discomfort to be motivated to work in therapy (Arkowitz & Hannah, 1989). It is also understood that therapy requires that clients take risks and expose themselves to thoughts, feelings, and activities they have previously avoided. However, the amount of arousal or risk encouraged by the therapist must be matched to the client. Clients with very severe problems may require support and even reassurance before they are ready to engage in the hard work of psychotherapy. Clients whose problems are less severe may be more ready to jump into risk-taking activities. Therapists practice the art of finding the optimal level of arousal or discomfort for each individual client (Rapee, 1987).

Reactance level   Therapists need to match their directiveness to the reactance level of the client. Blau (1988) defines the therapist's level of directiveness along the continuum from *unintrusive*, to *moderately intrusive*, to *probative*. When being unintrusive, the therapist offers acceptance, empathy, and encouragement. Metaphors and analogies are used to help the client look at the world in a different way. The moderately intrusive therapist attempts to clarify and challenge the client's ideas and sets limits when they seem appropriate. The probative therapist offers interpretations and uses directed activities such as role playing, imagery, and behavioral expression. Clients who are open to change are generally comfortable with a therapist who is probative. However, reluctant or reactive clients need to be approached in a less intrusive manner.

Seligman (1990) recommends taking a *directive* approach with the following kinds of clients.

- Clients who are willing to take direction.
- Clients who are motivated primarily to achieve specific goals.
- Clients who are severely disturbed and fragile.
- Clients in crisis.
- Clients who have difficulty setting limits.

An *experiential* approach is recommended (Seligman, 1990) for the following kinds of clients.

- Clients who can establish their own direction.
- Clients who are guided by broad and long-term goals.
- Clients who are functioning acceptably but not up to their potential.
- Clients who are not in crisis.
- Clients who are able to establish appropriate interpersonal boundaries.

A *supportive* approach is indicated for clients with low motivation who are fragile and dysfunctional and who are externally oriented (Horowitz et al., 1984; Seligman, 1990). A *probing* approach is most appropriate for clients who are motivated, reasonably well functioning, insightful, psychologically minded, and internally oriented.

SOME USEFUL PSYCHOTHERAPEUTIC STRATEGIES

The following psychotherapeutic strategies were developed to be sufficiently flexible to fit the methods, goals, and procedures of most psychotherapists (Omer & Alon, 1989).

Define a hierarchy of therapeutic goals   Therapists need to agree on more than one goal with a client, so that if movement toward a particular goal is blocked, the therapy can shift to the next goal in the hierarchy. It is wise to stick with goals that are realistic and that fit the resources of both the client (time and money) and the therapist (expertise). Goals should be defined clearly enough that therapists and clients can judge their progress. When working toward goals, the therapist needs to devise strategies for overcoming the following kinds of impediments.

- Behavioral and cognitive avoidance.
- Ineffective repetitive solutions.
- Rigid patterns, rules, beliefs, and myths.
- Unreflective dysfunctional behavior.

Therapists should always help clients enhance their sense of independence, assumption of responsibility, self-efficacy, and whatever social skills may augment their motivation and commitment to working in therapy.

Perform small interventions   Small interventions allow the therapist and client to test what they are doing together. Clients who are reluctant to attempt large goals can often be convinced to try something for one week as an experiment. When small interventions are called trials or experiments, lack of success is viewed not as a failure but as an opportunity for modifying the approach.

Avoid attacking points of maximum resistance   This is a commonsense piece of advice related to the theme of honoring the client's resistance and not fighting battles that one can't win. The only exception would be if the probability of overcoming the resistance with a strong attack is very high. For example, techniques of in vivo exposure for phobias and obsessions, therapeutic ordeals (Haley, 1984), and strong doses of reality (Glasser, 1965) are used when the therapist is confident about their chance of success.

Exploit propitious timings   Clients are often particularly open to change during a crisis, life transition, or meaningful anniversary. With tact and creativity, therapists can use these occasions to therapeutic advantage. Propitious moments can also be created by therapists when they say or do something unexpected. Spontaneous actions that catch the client by surprise are the basis of the corrective emotional experiences that were described in Chapter 1.

Concentrate the therapeutic influence at strategic points   Instead of taking a generalized broad-based approach, therapists often prefer to identify and confront specific points of resistance. For example, the impediments outlined earlier in defining a hierarchy of goals are possible points for therapeutic focus. When appropriate, the therapist can challenge particular blocks to therapeutic progress with high-impact techniques such as focusing, role playing, or other exercises involving emotional expression.

Take advantage of other resources   Arnold Lazarus (1990b) has been a strong proponent of integrating all of a client's available resources into therapy. These resources may include friends and family members as well as support groups and other services provided in the community. Since clients must learn to live in the outside world, therapy should not be conducted in a vacuum. Resources that can be integrated into the therapy process will still be available to clients after they have terminated their sessions with the therapist.

Stabilize partial achievements   Clients' achievements can be stabilized by generalizing them as much as possible. For example, new skills learned by a client are practiced in a variety of contexts until they become a natural part of the client's repertoire. Clients can be taught to appreciate the benefits of their achievements in their everyday life so that these achievements will become self-reinforcing.

Seek a middle course when the client is stuck between competing goals   When the client becomes stuck between competing goals, the most fruitful response is to find a course of action that can be therapeutic for either goal. For example, a client who can't decide whether to continue or end a relationship will benefit from assertiveness training in either case. A client suffering from obsessive thinking about a traumatic event can be offered a compromise solution in which he or she is allowed to obsess but agrees to do this with self-control, in the spirit of a planned life review.

Plan for possible failures   Since failures are unavoidable, they must be anticipated. The straightforward approach is to own the failure as a team and say to the client "What we tried did not work, so let's try something different." Another way to anticipate failure is to predict relapses and interpret failure as a natural and expected event in therapy. Paradoxical interventions described in Chapter 5 are often useful for clients who are prone toward interpreting failures as an indictment of the therapist or of the therapeutic process.

When you get stuck, change the therapeutic framework   When a therapist is stuck with a client, the therapist is ethically obligated to obtain supervision and consider making a referral. The therapist should also be flexible and consider taking an approach that is sufficiently new and different that it alters "the rules of the game." First, the original goals of therapy may be postponed in favor of a series of new and more feasible goals. Second, the therapist can alter the therapeutic context by changing the length, frequency, or location of sessions, involving other people, and adding new therapeutic techniques and procedures (which the client may be enlisted to develop or which may be instituted without warning because the client is now "ready").

ENHANCING THE EFFICIENCY OF PSYCHOTHERAPY

Time-Limited Therapy

One important element of getting therapy off to a good start is coming to terms with clients regarding the expected number of therapy sessions. It is interesting to recognize that the perceptions held by clients and therapists about the optimal length of therapy are often quite divergent (Garfield, 1986). Compared with therapists, clients commonly expect therapy to be shorter (and more effective). For example, the majority of clients surveyed by Garfield and Wolpin (1963) expected improvement by the fifth therapy session and felt that therapy should not last more than ten sessions. Kupst and Schulman (1979) asked nontherapists and therapists to respond to the following statement: "If I saw a professional helper, I would expect it to take a long time before I solved my problems, maybe years." Whereas only 17% of nontherapists agreed with this statement, 96% of the therapists felt the statement was valid. Based on data reported earlier in this chapter about the average number of therapy sessions that clients attend before dropping out, it appears that clients' expectations about how many therapy sessions are realistic are frequently more accurate than those of therapists.

The argument that time-limited therapy may be indicated for many clients is also supported by research data. An examination of the dose-effectiveness relationship in psychotherapy resulted in the following conclusions (Howard, Kopta, Krause, & Orlinsky, 1986). By the eighth session of therapy, approximately 50% of clients show measurable improvement, and by the 26th session, almost 75% of clients have improved. When therapy is carried out to 52 sessions, approximately 83% of clients are improved. As far as psychotherapy is concerned, it appears that more is not always better (Johnson & Gelso, 1980). It is ethically questionable whether psychotherapy should be advertised as a treatment in which the more one gets the greater cure one can expect (Bugental, 1988). There is a point of diminishing returns at which the benefits of continued therapy are minimal and not cost-effective (Cummings & VandenBos, 1979). This point of diminishing returns differs from client to client. For over half of therapy clients, it seems to come by the tenth session. Research studies have also concluded that only a small minority of prospective clients require long-term psychotherapy (Bennett & Wisneski, 1979; Cummings & VandenBos, 1979) and that most clients prefer brief rather than lengthy therapy (Koss, 1979).

In addition to clients' preferences and data outlining cost-effectiveness, there are other pressures on therapists to limit the number of therapy sessions for most clients (Bauer & Kobos, 1984). First, there is a growing commitment by professionals to provide immediate relevant and practical services to all members of the community. Second, there is an increasing emphasis on preventive mental health services (Albee, 1990). Third, there has been increasing consumer demand for economically feasible services. These demands have been enforced by limits on payments for therapy offered by insurance companies. These pressures for time-limited therapy have been recognized by directors of mental health agencies, who have begun revamping their services to balance the needs of disadvantaged people with the parameters of third-party payments (Burlingame & Behrman, 1987).

The practical fact is that only therapists who have wealthy clients with plenty of time on their hands can afford to keep their clients in therapy for years on end. In this vein, it is interesting to recognize that Freud was originally a short-term therapist (Budman & Gurman, 1988, p. 1; Strupp & Binder, 1984, p. 8). It was only later in his life that Freud began seeing his patients for lengthy periods. This was due partly to Freud's ill health and the ease of keeping current patients in therapy rather than recruiting new ones. Freud was also not entirely satisfied with the outcome of his therapy and he began to experiment with longer-term therapy to see whether his results might improve.

Characteristics of Time-Limited Therapy

Budman and Gurman (1988) remind us that the chief difference between what is called *time-limited* therapy and other forms of therapy is that the time limit in time-limited therapy is by plan rather than by default. Typical time-limited therapy lasts from 6 to 15 sessions, with an upper limit at 25 sessions (Koss & Butcher, 1986). What are some characteristics of therapy that is introduced to clients as time-limited from the beginning of the first interview? A survey comparing the beliefs of therapists who prefer short-term therapy with those who prefer long-term therapy found two major differences (Bolter, Levenson, & Alvarez, 1990). First, short-term therapists are more likely than long-term therapists to believe that setting a time limit for therapy would increase and intensify the work accomplished: "Time is the lever that motivates and moves the patient" (Mann, 1973, p. 16). Second, short-term therapists are more inclined than long-term therapists to believe that clients can experience psychological change outside of therapy. An examination of the major features of time-limited therapy indicates that many of its practices are consistent with those recommended in this chapter for getting therapy off to a good start (Bauer & Kobos, 1984; Budman & Gurman, 1988; Koss & Butcher, 1986).

1. *Maintaining a clear and specific focus.* The therapist and client agree on clear and realistic goals that are made the focus of each therapy session. Attention is on the present and the here-and-now more than on the past.
2. *Communicating an attitude of confidence and hope.* The therapist makes a special attempt to communicate to the client an attitude of confidence and hope.
3. *Combining assessment and therapeutic work.* Assessment is not neglected but is continued throughout the course of therapy. New information is incorporated into the therapeutic work as the client and therapist collaborate toward achieving therapeutic goals.
4. *Maintaining a high level of therapist activity.* The therapist is highly responsive and participates in sessions with probes, clarifications, and other verbal skills outlined in Chapter 3. There is a high level of therapist/client exploration and collaboration.

5. *Rapidly establishing the therapeutic alliance.* Because therapists are accessible, clients get to know and trust them relatively quickly. Therapists don't press clients to the point of "resistance," but use the techniques for minimizing resistance outlined in Chapter 5.

6. *Encouraging ventilation.* A climate is established in which the client feels accepted and safe. Clients are encouraged to express and experience their feelings.

7. *Incorporating the client's outside life into therapy.* The client's outside life is incorporated into the therapy to facilitate generalization of changes accomplished in therapy. There is a liberal use of homework assignments (see Chapter 1). Significant others are recruited to assist the client with his or her goals. Support groups and other services offered in the community are utilized.

8. *Actively tracking progress.* Since goals are clearly formulated, they can be actively tracked during the course of therapy.

9. *Using time flexibly.* Therapy need not be restricted to weekly 50-minute sessions. Sessions can be shorter (or longer) and can be spaced out gradually to biweekly or monthly meetings.

10. *Planning follow-up meetings.* A planned follow-up session (six months to one year) emphasizes the "permanence" of the therapeutic work. It reinforces the therapist's continued interest in the client. It also implies a commitment on the part of the client to maintain the changes and to continue practicing the skills that were acquired in therapy.

Characteristics of Efficient Therapy

In addition to enhancing the efficiency of therapy with regard to its length, Albert Ellis (1980) proposed the following characteristics of efficient psychotherapy.

Pervasiveness in psychotherapy is defined as helping clients apply what they have learned in therapy to their entire lives rather than just to a specific complaint or problem. For example, a client who engages in a great deal of self-blame over a divorce may work not only on coping with the divorce but also on reevaluating the tendency to engage in so much self-blame.

Extensiveness in psychotherapy means that clients can be helped not only to decrease their negative feelings but also to develop their potential for enhancing their positive feelings. Therapy is not simply a matter of helping clients solve problems; it is also focused on teaching clients to maximize their capabilities.

Throughgoingness in psychotherapy refers to taking a multimodal approach (Lazarus, 1976; 1981). As Ellis (1980) argues, "The more comprehensive a therapist's armatmentarium of techniques is, the more likely he or she is to find suitable procedures for especially unique or difficult clients" (p. 416).

Maintenance of therapeutic progress is accomplished with strategies for relapse prevention that were discussed in Chapter 5. For the sake of efficiency, therapy should strive for changes that will be relatively long-lasting.

Preventive psychotherapy is geared toward helping clients develop coping skills and ways of thinking and acting that will enable them to bear up to challenges and problems that face them in the future.

SUMMARY

One of the first points to recognize in getting therapy off to a good start is that only a small proportion of people who could benefit from psychotherapy ever end up in a therapist's office. An important reason for people's reluctance to take advantage of psychotherapy is the stigma of being diagnosed as having some kind of "disorder." Psychotherapists must accept responsibility for the stereotype of therapy as a "treatment of disorders" because they have chosen to be part of the health insurance system. Given this reality, it is important that psychotherapists make it as comfortable as possible for clients to come to them and ask for help.

Once clients begin therapy, they will learn about the close kind of interpersonal relationship it has to offer. Although therapists don't often have the luxury of choosing clients who are most likely to be successful, therapists find it useful to assess a client's potential for success at the beginning of therapy. Therapists should also use a procedure of structuring to assure that they and the client are in agreement about the processes and goals of psychotherapy. Among the issues that therapists and clients must negotiate are their roles and responsibilities and a framework for defining the client's problem.

Therapists must have the skill and flexibility to match their therapeutic approach to specific clients. A multimodal approach was developed by Arnold Lazarus for this purpose. Some useful psychotherapeutic strategies that will fit the methods and goals of most therapists include (1) defining a hierarchy of therapeutic goals, (2) performing small interventions, (3) avoiding attacking points of maximum resistance, (4) exploiting propitious timings, (5) concentrating the therapeutic influence at strategic points, (6) taking advantage of other resources, (7) stabilizing partial achievements, (8) seeking a middle course when the client is stuck between competing goals, (9) planning for possible failures, and (10) when stuck, changing the therapeutic framework.

Time-limited therapy is becoming more common for many reasons, and research indicates that a large proportion of clients are suited for this approach. Some characteristics of time-limited therapy include (1) maintaining a clear and specific focus, (2) communicating an attitude of confidence and hope, (3) combining assessment and therapeutic work, (4) maintaining a high level of therapist activity, (5) rapidly establishing of the therapeutic alliance, (6) encouraging ventilation, (7) incorporating the client's outside life into therapy, (8) actively tracking progress, (9) using time flexibly, and (10) planning follow-up meetings. Characteristics of efficient therapy suggested by Albert Ellis are pervasiveness, extensiveness, throughgoingness, maintenance, and prevention.

SUGGESTIONS FOR FURTHER READING

Beutler, L. E., & Clarkin, J. (1990). *Systematic treatment selection: Toward targeted therapeutic interventions.* New York: Brunner/Mazel.

Budman, S. H., & Gurman, A. S. (1988). *Theory and practice of brief therapy.* New York: Guilford.

Garfield, S. L. (1989). *The practice of brief psychotherapy.* New York: Pergamon.

Okum, B. F. (1990). *Seeking connections in psychotherapy.* San Francisco: Jossey-Bass.

Seligman, L. (1990). *Selecting effective treatments.* San Francisco: Jossey-Bass.

Strupp, H. H., & Binder, J. L. (1984). *Psychotherapy in a new key: A guide to time-limited dynamic psychotherapy.* New York: Basic Books.

CHAPTER 9

Assessment

This chapter focuses on a number of issues related to the process of assessment. An attempt is made to find a useful balance toward assessment by considering both a *pathological approach* (focusing on what makes people unhealthy) and a *salutogenic approach* (focusing on what makes people healthy) for understanding clients and their problems (Antonovsky, 1979; 1990).

The orientation taken in this book is that clients who come for psychotherapy are suffering from what Harry Stack Sullivan (Chapman, 1978, p. 1) and Thomas Szasz (1961) call *problems in living.* Essentially, the coping skills or solutions clients are using for certain problems are not working to their satisfaction, are causing distress, and in many cases are disadvantaging them in their relationships with other people (see Kanfer & Schefft, 1988, pp. 98–99). As Richard Fisch (1990) explains; "The principal job of the expert in psychotherapy is to assess where the clients are stuck, what mainly they are doing to get unstuck, and how to influence them to stop doing what they regard as logical or necessary" (p. 271).

In other words, it is the psychotherapist's challenge to help clients change from implementing a "more of the same" solution that is not working and learn new strategies, coping skills, and ways of looking at and understanding their problem (Watzlawick, 1988). "Most problems are not viewed as internal pathologies but as the natural result of solving developmental demands in ways that do not fully work for the people involved" (Lankton, 1990, p. 364).

In his book *Personality Disorders,* Theodore Millon (1981) articulates the process of interpreting personality disorders not as the result of diseases, but as the product of ineffective coping skills.

The archaic notion that all mental disorders represent external intrusions or internal disease processes is an offshoot of prescientific ideas such as demons or spirits that ostensibly "possess" or cast spells on the person. The role of infectious agents and anatomical lesions in physical medicine has reawakened this archaic view. Of course we no longer see demons, but many still see some alien or malevolent force as invading or unsettling the patient's otherwise healthy status. This view is an appealing simplification to the layman, who can attribute his/her irrationalities to some intrusive or upsetting agent. It also has its appeal to the less sophisticated clinician, for it enables him or her to believe that the insidious intruder can be identified, hunted down, and destroyed. . . . Such naive notions carry little weight among modern-day medical and behavioral scientists. Given our increasing awareness of the complex nature of both health and disease, we now recognize, for example, that most physical disorders result from a dynamic and changing interplay between individuals' capacities to cope and the environment within which they live. (p. 5)

Millon believes that personality disorders should be conceived as reflecting the same interactive pattern. In other words, disorders of personality (problems in living) are a result of a dynamic interplay between people's environments and their coping skills and adaptive flexibilities. It is the psychotherapist's job to help clients adapt more flexibly to the demands and stresses in their lives. As Fox, Barclay, and Rodgers (1982, p. 307) suggest, the professional psychologist is concerned with "enhancing the effectiveness of human functioning."

A COPING SKILLS MODEL OF ASSESSMENT

DeNelsky and Boat (1986) outline a coping skills model of assessment that is focused on assessing people's strengths and deficiencies in coping in three areas of their lifes: interpersonal relationships, thinking and feeling, and approaches to self and life. Identifying particular strengths and deficiencies in these coping skills will help the therapist and client define some useful therapeutic goals.

Interpersonal Relationships

General social skills   General social skills that are useful for therapists to assess include common social courtesies, the ability to make conversation and be a good listener, and an acceptable balance between assertiveness and respect for the rights of others.

Intimate social skills   These include the ability to manage the unique rewards and frustrations of relationships with mates, lovers, children, and parents. Skills that are useful to assess include the client's success in selecting and maintaining viable love relationships, interpersonal commitments, and appreciation for and protection of another person's vulnerabilities. Other intimate social skills involve self-disclosure, risk taking, and the ability to express love in a variety of ways, as well as the ability to end relationships and manage personal loss through separation, divorce, or death.

Appropriate socialization This category of coping skills refers to age-appropriate internalization of rules, guidelines, and attitudes that govern functioning in society. Examples of relevant coping skills are the ability to manage impulses and to delay gratification, respect for societal norms, and the ability to negotiate and empathize with others.

Thinking and Feeling

Intellectual competencies Examples of these skills include the ability to concentrate on tasks and a certain amount of flexibility in finding solutions to problems.

Awareness of feelings This refers to the ability to recognize, label, experience, and, when appropriate, express feelings within a reasonable period from when the feelings begin. The skill is to avoid either denying one's feelings and suppressing them with drugs or wallowing in them and letting them take over one's life.

Appropriate emotional arousal People need to be able to generate appropriate arousal to motivate themselves toward accomplishing their goals. They must also be able to moderate their arousal in situations that are stressful, challenging, or characterized by close (negative or positive) interpersonal involvement.

Reasonable balance between intellect and feeling This skill includes the ability to draw from both intellect and feeling when making major decisions such as mate selection, vocational choices, and significant purchases. It is valuable to monitor both feelings and intellect during daily life activities.

Approaches to Self and Life

Realistic self-regard and self-expectations The primary coping skill here is a positive yet realistic view of oneself, recognition and tolerance of one's weaknesses, and a desire to grow and maximize one's strengths. People need to have sufficient self-esteem to experience a meaningful life without defending themselves with grandiosity.

Appropriate expectations of life   People's expectations of life must help them cope with disappointments, unfairness, loss, and suffering. However, expectations must be sufficiently positive and optimistic to motivate people to reach their goals and find satisfaction.

Ability to experience healthy pleasure and satisfaction   It is important to find an appropriate balance between enjoying the pleasures of life and knowing how to delay gratification sufficiently to accomplish one's goals. Problems occur when a person derives little or no pleasure out of life or is preoccupied with seeking pleasure through excessive use of drugs, alcohol, food, or sexual activity.

Ability to sustain goal-directed effort   This involves having sufficient self-motivation and frustration tolerance to stick with tasks until some reasonable level of completeness has been achieved. This skill is developed by teaching people to cope with both failure and boredom as they pursue meaningful goals.

The coping abilities just described have to do with skills that can be learned through modeling and guided practice. We could also define coping as a style of confronting life challenges. For example, there are *internalizing* and *externalizing* styles of coping, both of which can cause disadvantages if they become too extreme or rigid to change (Beutler & Clarkin, 1990). *Repression* and *sensitization* are also styles of coping that can become disadvantageous when they are exaggerated and inflexible (Weinberger, Schwartz, & Davidson, 1979).

ASSESSING MALADAPTIVE SCHEMAS

A good way to understand people is by gaining a sense of their schemas for themselves and for their interpersonal relationships (see Chapter 1). Jeffrey Young (1989) outlines another useful model for assessing clients on the basis of their maladaptive schemas. Maladaptive schemas can affect people in the following areas of their life: autonomy, connectedness, worthiness, and limits and standards.

Autonomy

Problems within the realm of autonomy include dependence, subjugation, vulnerability, and loss of control.

Dependence is the belief that one is unable to function independently and needs the constant support of others. The schema for dependence includes the following kinds of thoughts: "I can't function on my own." "I need someone else to help me." "I can't support myself." The consequences of dependence are being passive, alienating others, and underachieving.

Subjugation is the sacrifice of one's own needs to satisfy others. The schema for subjugation includes the following kinds of thoughts: "If if do what I want, something bad will happen." "I must sacrifice myself for others." "My needs are not as important as those of others." The consequences of subjugation are feeling stressed and worn out and having feelings of deprivation and anger.

Vulnerability is the fear that disaster is imminent. The schema for vulnerability includes the following kinds of thoughts: "Something terrible will happen to me." "I worry about things going wrong." "I feel anxious and defeated." The consequences of vulnerability are anxiety, panic, and hypertension.

Loss of control is the fear of losing control over one's own behavior, body, impulses, and emotions. The schema for loss of control includes the following kinds of thoughts: "I am losing control." "I can't control myself." "I have no power over myself." The consequences of loss of control are anxiety, tension, rigidity, and overcontrol.

Connectedness

Problems within the realm of connectedness include emotional deprivation, abandonment, mistrust, and social isolation.

Emotional deprivation is the expectation that one's needs for nurturance, empathy, and caring will never be adequately met by others. The schema for emotional deprivation includes the following kinds of thoughts: "No one is ever there to meet my needs." "I don't get enough love and attention." "No one really cares about me." The consequences of emotional deprivation are anger, resentment, and manipulativeness.

Abandonment is the fear that one will imminently lose significant others and then be isolated forever. The schema for abandonment includes the following kinds of thoughts: "I will be alone forever." "No one will ever be there for me." "I will be abandoned." The consequences of abandonment are loneliness, isolation, and fear of making commitments.

Mistrust is the expectation that others will willfully hurt, abuse, cheat, lie, manipulate, or take advantage of oneself. The schema for mistrust includes the following kinds of thoughts: "People will hurt me, attack me, or put me down." "I must protect myself." "I'll attack them before they get me." The consequences of mistrust are hostility, mistrust, and aggressiveness.

Social isolation is the feeling that one is isolated from the rest of the world, different from other people, and not a part of a group or community. The schema for social isolation includes the following kinds of thoughts: "I don't fit in." "I'm different." "No one understands me." The consequences of social isolation are isolation and loneliness.

Worthiness

Problems within the realm of worthiness include defectiveness, social undesirability, incompetence, guilt, and shame.

Defectiveness is the feeling that one is defective, flawed, and unlovable. The schema for defectiveness includes the following kinds of thoughts: "No person I desire will ever love me." "No one would want to stay close to me." "I am flawed and defective." The consequences of defectiveness are depression and low self-esteem.

Social undesirability is the belief that one is undesirable to others. The schema for social undesirability includes the following kinds of thoughts: "I'm a social outcast." "People don't like me." "I'm boring and ugly." The consequences of social undesirability are loneliness, depression, and low self-esteem.

Incompetence is the belief that one cannot perform competently in areas of achievement, daily responsibilities, and decision making. The schema for incompetence includes the following kinds of thoughts: "Nothing I do is ever good enough." "I'm incompetent." "I screw up everything I try." The consequences of incompetence are underachievement, rigidity, and low self-esteem.

Guilt is the belief that one is morally bad or irresponsible and deserves harsh criticism or punishment. The schema for guilt includes the following kinds of thoughts: "I am a bad person." "I deserve to be punished." "I don't deserve pleasure or happiness." The consequences of guilt are depression and low self-esteem.

Shame is the recurrence of feelings of shame, embarrassment, and self-consciousness. The schema for shame includes the following kinds of thoughts: "I am humiliated by my own failure and inadequacy." "I am too inferior to get close to someone." "If others found out about my defects, I couldn't face them." The consequences of shame are anxiety, self-consciousness, and avoidance.

Limits and Standards

Problems within the realm of limits and standards include unrelenting standards and entitlement.

Unrelenting standards is the relentless striving to meet extremely high expectations of oneself at the expense of one's happiness, pleasure, or satisfaction. The schema for unrelenting standards includes the following kinds of thoughts: "I must be the best." "I must be perfect." "I have to work harder." The consequences of unrelenting standards are hypertension, isolation, and lack of satisfaction.

Entitlement is the insistence that one should be able to do, say, or have whatever one wants. The schema for entitlement includes the following kinds of thoughts: "I should always get what I want." "I'm special and shouldn't have to accept restrictions placed on others." "I deserve immediate satisfaction." The consequences of entitlement are impulsiveness, anger, and alienation.

COMMON THEMES FOR ASSESSMENT

Budman and Gurman (1988) outline five themes that often become the focus of psychotherapy: losses, interpersonal conflicts, symptoms, personality disorders, and developmental dysynchronies. Although clients won't necessarily fall into one of these categories, these themes may serve as useful guidelines when working on a clinical assessment.

Losses

Loss is a common theme in therapy. After a loss, clients may come to therapy seeking the therapist's assistance in finding some kind of reconciliation. It is also not uncommon for clients to come to therapy with some other kind of problem and to discover during the course of therapy that they have not successfully resolved certain losses in their lives.

Interpersonal Conflicts

Interpersonal conflicts are a common complaint of clients seeking psychotherapy. One of the therapist's first decisions is whether these conflicts are best resolved by working with the client individually or whether it would be more fruitful to include other people involved in the conflict in the therapy sessions.

Symptoms

Common symptoms brought to therapy by clients include anxiety, depression, pain, compulsions, and habits related to smoking, eating, and use of alcohol. Substance abuse may be part of the picture in any client's problems and use of drugs by clients must always be carefully assessed.

Personality Disorders

Clients rarely come to therapy complaining of a personality disorder. However, the therapist will want to assess whether there are patterns in the client's ways of thinking and acting that seem to cause chronic problems for the client in his or her life.

Developmental Dysynchronies

Therapists often want to assess where clients are in terms of their development. There are a number of ways to look at human development, which can include focusing on physical growth, cognitive understanding, intrapsychic processes, and interpersonal relations (Achenbach, 1986; Levinson, 1986).

Cognitive Development

Therapy is likely to be most effective if the therapist can communicate at the client's level of cognitive development. Four levels of cognitive development are outlined by Ivey (1986, 1991).

1. Sensorimotor: Focusing on the elements of immediate experience   The client presents concerns in a random, disorganized fashion and frequently jumps around on topics. The client has a short attention span and has an intense concentration on here-and-now experiences. Defenses are characterized by denial, distortion, projection, and repression. The therapist may wish to provide this kind of client a fair amount of direction and environmental structuring.

2. Concrete-operational: searching for situational descriptions   The client gives concrete, linear descriptions of individuals, often with a fair amount of detail. Emotions may be described but not reflected upon. Defenses are characterized by intellectualization, rationalization, and failure to bring actions in concert with ideas and feelings. The therapist may wish to provide structure by coaching the client to participate in the therapy process.

3. Formal-operational: Discerning patterns of thought, emotion, and action   These clients can talk about themselves and their feelings. Their conversation tends to be abstract, and they can look at the world from the perspective of others. Defenses are characterized by humor, suppression, and sublimation. For this client the therapist may wish to act as a consultant who provides warmth, support, and feedback.

4. Dialectic/systematic: Integrating patterns of emotion and thought into a system   The client is aware of systems of knowledge and is learning how he or she is affected by the environment. This is an abstract form of thinking characterized by the ability to analyze and challenge one's beliefs, interpretations, and perceptions. Defenses are not immediately apparent. The therapeutic relationship is characterized by an egalitarian search for more effective solutions to the client's problems.

Social Development

Erik Erikson's (1963) model of psychosocial development can be useful for psychotherapists because it encompasses the entire life span (see Box 9.1). Erikson's model of psychosocial stages is not meant to define what is normal or abnormal; it should be used flexibly and should be adapted for people according to their individual experiences,

---

Box 9.1   Erikson's Psychosocial Stages of Development

Infancy (ages 0–1): *Trust versus Mistrust*
Developmental task is to gain a sense of trust in oneself and in other people. The growing person needs to be provided with caring and security.

Early Childhood (ages 1–3): *Autonomy versus Shame and Doubt*
Developmental task is to gain a sense of self-reliance. The growing person needs to explore and experiment, to make mistakes, and to test limits with encouragement and support.

Preschool (ages 3–6): *Initiative versus Guilt*
Developmental task is to achieve a sense of competence. The growing person needs to be taught to take risks, make decisions, take pleasure in successes, and cope with failures.

School Age (ages 6–12): *Industry versus Inferiority*
Developmental task is to learn basic social skills and to learn to set and accomplish personal goals. The growing person needs appropriate role models.

Adolescence (ages 12–18): *Identity versus Confusion*
Developmental task is to assert one's independence and to gain a sense of identity. The growing person needs support, guidance, and a feeling of respect and trust from significant others.

Young Adulthood (ages 18–35): *Intimacy versus Isolation*
Developmental task is to form intimate relationships. The growing person needs to have gained appropriate skills for social relationships during the previous stages of his or her life.

Middle Age (35–60): *Generativity versus Stagnation*
Developmental task is to gain satisfaction in one's achievements in life. The growing person needs to come to terms with the discrepancy between dreams and hopes and actual accomplishments.

Later Life (ages 60+): *Integrity versus Despair*
Developmental task is to become satisfied with one's life and reconciled with one's mortality. The growing person needs to know that her or his life was worthwhile.

Source: From *Childhood and Society*, Second Edition, by Erik H. Erikson, by permission of W. W. Norton and Company, Inc. Copyright 1950, © 1963 by W. W. Norton & Company, Inc. Copyright renewed 1978, 1991 by Erik H. Erikson.

background, and culture (Gilligan, 1982; Ivey, 1991). The point is for the therapist and client to explore how the client has managed to cope with life challenges, such as those outlined by Erikson, and to determine whether the client is satisfied and reconciled or whether the client has "unfinished business" to complete.

Sectors of Development

Basch (1992) explains how clients can be understood according to whether their problem resides in one of the following five sectors of development: attachment, autonomy, affect/cognition, creativity, and psychosexuality.

Life Tasks and Dreams

Another way to assess a client's development is in terms of the client's *life tasks* (Cantor & Kihlstrom, 1987; Cantor & Langston, 1989). What does the client wish to accomplish, what kinds of skills and strategies is the client using, and how is the client progressing in terms of success and satisfaction? Development can also be understood by exploring a client's *dream* (Levinson, 1978). It is often not as important whether a life dream has been achieved as it is for people to be reconciled and satisfied with how their dreams have turned out. This can be a fruitful path for therapists to explore with their clients.

A focus on developmental stages allows the therapist and client to explore the client's sense of purpose and meaning (Hobbs, 1962). The goal is to assist the client in developing a cohesive self (Kohut, 1977).

ARNOLD LAZARUS' BASIC-ID

One model for clinical assessment that is sufficiently broad to be useful to most clinicians is Arnold Lazarus' BASIC-ID (1976; 1986). This stands for behavior, affect, sensation, imagery, cognition, interpersonal relations, and drugs.

Behavior

Behaviors are acts, habits, gestures, responses, and reactions that are observable and measurable. Clients are asked what behaviors they would like to increase and what behaviors they would like to decrease. Behaviors can be measured by their frequency, intensity, and duration. They can be assessed by the client's report, by self-monitoring, and through the use of role playing. Once behaviors are defined, their antecedents and consequences should be identified. Examples of behaviors clients may wish to increase include physical activity, assertiveness, and social skills. Examples of behaviors clients may wish to decrease include inappropriate expressions of anger, symptoms of nervousness and anxiety, and avoidance.

Affect

Affect refers to emotions, moods, and strong feelings. Clients are asked which emotions they experience most often. They also specify the kinds of affect they would like to experience more often and the kinds of affect they would like to experience less often. Clients often wish to decrease feelings of guilt, anxiety, depression, and anger. They typically desire to experience more joy, amusement, satisfaction, love, and pride.

Sensation

Sensations include touching, tasting, smelling, seeing, and hearing. Common complaints that occur in the sensory modality are headaches, dizziness, stomach distress, fatigue, and various kinds of aches and pains.

Imagery

Imagery includes dreams, memories and mental pictures about the past, present, or future. Included in imagery is the client's self-image. Imagery can be assessed by asking clients to close their eyes and put themselves into the situation they are trying to describe. Clients vary in how "visual" they are about their life. They can often benefit by being taught how to picture themselves working on the goals they have decided to accomplish.

Cognition

Cognitions are attitudes, values, opinions, and ideas that either work or do not work in the client's best interest. Common maladaptive cognitions are "shoulds," "musts," and other unrealistic demands people place on the world. Clients are taught to change rigid expectations that result in distress to preferences. Clients are also taught to accept the fallibility, pain, and suffering that are unavoidable in life. Clients learn how their feelings and actions are influenced by their cognitions, and they learn skills for analyzing, questioning, and modifying their cognitions.

Interpersonal Relationships

Clients are asked to describe interpersonal relationships that are troublesome as well as those that are gratifying. An attempt is made to identify behaviors, affect, sensations, imagery, and cognitions that are relevant to various interpersonal relationships. Clients identify changes they would like to accomplish in their relationships with others.

Drugs

This area refers to drugs the client is using as well as to other health issues, such as physical fitness, diet, exercise, and general well-being. Clients are asked about their physical health and about hobbies, interests, recreational pursuits, and other activities. An assessment is made of what kinds of changes clients would like to make with regard to specific drug use and in their life activities.

CLINICAL DIAGNOSIS

One of the most common procedures followed when making a clinical assessment is to arrive at a diagnosis. We should consider the value of creating clinical diagnoses by asking what purpose the procedure serves. One very apparent purpose is that insurance companies require a clinical diagnosis for payment of services. Clinical diagnoses also help therapists communicate with each other. When a clinician seeks supervision about a client who has a particular diagnosis, the supervisor has a fair idea of the type of client the clinician is talking about. Whether clinical diagnoses assist psychotherapists in deriving a treatment strategy for the client depends on the orientation of the therapist. Diagnostic labels are based on a medical model of disease and treatment. For many medical problems, physicians must make an accurate diagnosis of the problem because, in a real sense, the diagnosis suggests the cure. This diagnostic necessity might occur in psychotherapy for certain problems for which there is a medication of choice. However, treatment that is restricted to medication is medical treatment and not psychotherapy. Interestingly, the diagnoses catalogued in the *Diagnostic and Statistical Manual of Mental Disorders* (DSM-III-R) are not intended to suggest a course of therapy; "It should be understood, however, that for most of the categories the diagnostic criteria are based on clinical judgment, and have not yet been fully validated by data about such important correlates as clinical course, outcome, family history, and treatment response" (American Psychiatric Association, 1987, p. xxiv).

Beutler and Clarkin (1990) point out that the DSM-III-R identifies symptom clusters that might be amenable to particular medications. It also allows clinicians to categorize clients with diagnoses that have been approved for reimbursement by insurance companies. Because the DSM-III-R takes little note of clients' interpersonal relations, environments, coping styles, and strengths and resources (Frances, Clarkin, & Perry, 1984), it is of limited value for suggesting a course of therapy for many clients. As far as therapy is concerned, it is more advantageous to understand the client as a person than it is to give the

client a clinical diagnosis (Persons, 1986). A survey of psychotherapists indicate that the majority of respondents believe that
the primary reasons for using DSM diagnoses is for insurance and
legal purposes (Kutchins & Kirk, 1988). When it comes to devising
plans for psychotherapy, therapists prefer social, interpersonal, and
behavioral assessments of their clients, and they don't see much value
in giving them diagnostic labels (Smith & Kraft, 1983).

Two additional issues need to be considered when evaluating the
practice of clinical diagnosis: (1) the name is not the thing and (2)
clinical diagnoses are subjective.

The Name Is Not the Thing

To point out a common fallacy, Paul Watzlawick (1990c) quoted Alfred
Korzybski, who said, in his book *Science and Sanity*, "The name is
not the thing." The mistake we often make is to assume that, because
there is a name for something, this "something" must necessarily
exist. Psychiatric diagnoses have become reified from descriptions of
behaviors to tangible disorders (Gergen, 1990). This fallacy has been a
major concern for Thomas Szasz (1961; 1987), who has argued that
labels for various types of "mental illness" are just that—labels. The
problem we face is when these labels are taken literally. Although the
existence of diagnoses for certain kinds of behavior patterns can help
therapists communicate more effectively with each other, we must
avoid the temptation to treat these diagnoses as entities.

Diagnoses Are Subjective

Clinical diagnoses are based as much as possible on objective behaviors of the person being diagnosed. However, they are necessarily
subjective because the people who derive diagnostic manuals must
agree on what kinds of diagnoses should be included and what kinds
of behaviors should be used as criteria for particular diagnoses. Clinical diagnoses are value judgments based on what is considered as
normal or abnormal in a particular society or group of professionals
(Weisskopf-Joelson, 1980). One example of the subjectivity of clinical
diagnoses is seen in the political and economic bases on which certain
diagnoses have been chosen. Benjamin Rush, a signer of the Declara-
tion of Independence, is considered to be the founder of American
psychiatry and is honored on the logo of the American Psychiatric
Association. One of Dr. Rush's contributions to psychiatry was the
psychiatric diagnosis of anarchia. Anarchia was a form of insanity
suffered by people who were dissatisfied with certain aspects of the
political structure following the American Revolution (slavery, restric-
tion of the vote to white male property owners) and who sought a more

democratic society (Brown, 1990; Szasz, 1970). In 1835, James Cowles Prichard, a British psychiatrist, coined the term *moral insanity*, which provided justification for hospitalizing young people (mainly women) who were not behaving according to their parents' wishes (Masson, 1988). In 1843, Dr. Samuel Cartwright identified the mental disease of drapetomania, which was suffered by black slaves who had a compulsion to run away (Thomas & Sillen, 1972). In the early 1900s, the psychiatric diagnosis of hypersexual behavior was given to sexually active women in the United States who were unmarried, widowed, or divorced (Lunbeck, 1987).

When I first began practicing as a clinical psychologist, I encountered a problem working with people who wished to quit cigarette smoking because many insurance carriers would not pay for helping clients break their smoking habit. This difficulty was addressed when the American Psychiatric Association made cigarette smoking a disorder and added the diagnosis of nicotine dependence to the DSM-III-R. The creators of DSM-III-R also wanted to include the diagnosis of paraphilic coercive disorder for sexual abusers of children. Given the growing concern about child sexual abuse in our country, there is a lucrative market for the psychiatric treatment of sex abusers. However, this diagnosis was left out of DSM-III-R because of complaints that it could be used to excuse adults who sexually abuse children from criminal responsibility. Feminists also pressured the creators of DSM-III-R to leave out the diagnosis of masochistic personality disorder for fear that this label would be used to blame women for "allowing" men to batter them (Kaplan, 1983). The creators of DSM-III-R agreed to compromise with the feminists by changing "masochistic personality disorder" to "self-defeating personality disorder." One psychologist who was invited to participate in the creation of DSM-III-R gave the following description of the process (Leo, 1985).

> The low level of intellectual effort was shocking. Diagnoses were developed by majority vote on the level we would use to choose a restaurant. You feel like Italian, I feel like Chinese, so let's go to a cafeteria. Then it's typed into a computer (p. 76).

Another example of the subjectivity of clinical diagnoses is found in research showing that diagnoses of pathology given by mental health professionals can be influenced by the opinions expressed by the person who is being diagnosed (Brajinsky & Brajinsky, 1974; Weisskopf-Joelson, 1980). People who express political views that are incompatible with the views held by the mental health professionals are more likely to be diagnosed as suffering from pathology. William Faulkner (1964, cited in Weisskopf-Joelson, 1980) expressed the subjectivity of diagnoses: "Craziness ain't so much what a fellow does, but it is the way the majority of folks is looking at him when he does it" (p. 223).

As Weisskopf-Joelson (1980) reminds us, people in some societies *suffer from hallucinations* whereas people in other societies *achieve visions.*

Millon (1981) articulates how his opinions about criteria for diagnosing various personality disorders differ from the criteria agreed upon by the clinicians who created the DSM-III. Kroll (1988) explains how his opinion of criteria for diagnosing borderline personality differs from the criteria devised by the creators of DSM-III-R. Given the difference of opinions about how various diagnoses should be conceptualized, it is not surprising that the reliability of DSM diagnoses is poor and that there is limited agreement among clinicians about which specific diagnoses should be given to particular clients (Beutler & Clarkin, 1990; Brown, 1990; Mirowsky, 1990). Another issue, which may or may not be a problem, is that the number of diagnosable "mental disorders" has grown from 66 in DSM-I, to 111 in DSM-II, to 206 in DSM-III, to 261 in DSM-III-R (Beutler & Clarkin, 1990, p. 34). There is little doubt that this number will increase with the publication of DSM-IV.

It should also be mentioned that the subjectivity of clinical diagnoses is not without benefits. For example, the creators of DSM-III decided to delete homosexuality as a mental disorder. As Paul Watzlawick (1990c) pointed out, this resulted in the most dramatic psychiatric success in human history. By the stroke of a pen, millions of people were "cured" of a mental disorder.

SOME BIASES IN CLINICAL ASSESSMENT

A good deal has been written about biases in clinical assessment (Brehm & Smith, 1986; Salovey & Turk, 1991). Since the focus of this chapter is on practical suggestions about how assessment can be used in the psychotherapy process, theoretical questions related to clinical decision making will not be summarized here. However, we will take a brief overview of some issues about assessment that are likely to affect most psychotherapists.

Labeling

In their book *Psychotherapy for Better or Worse*, Strupp, Hadley, and Gomes-Schwartz (1977) printed letters from 65 prominent psychotherapists giving their opinions about how and when negative effects can occur in therapy. Arnold Lazarus gave the following reply.

> One factor that seems prominently associated with a negative effect is the use of labeling. There are far too many people who have been labeled "schizophrenic" (or "homosexual," or "hysterical," etc.) and for whom this unfortunate label becomes either an excuse and/or a reason for repeated failures and bizarre conduct. (Strupp et al., 1977, p. 287)

The point is not that clients consciously choose labels they can use to excuse their behaviors (although this does happen). What needs to be understood is that, by giving labels to people, we construct a particular reality for the way we treat them and the way they respond. One important consequence of labeling is deindividuation (Hamilton, 1979; Wright, 1991). People who are placed into particular groups by virtue of a shared label lose their individuality. They are viewed and treated as prototypes of their group rather than as independent persons. Their behaviors are explained primarily on the basis of personality traits and dispositions, and the influence of environmental factors on their actions is often neglected. Deindividuation is particularly disadvantageous when the group into which a person is labeled has negative connotations. For psychiatric labels and clinical diagnoses, the connotation is virtually *always* negative. The client is sick, ill, disordered, and not living up to the standards of "normal" behavior in her or his society. Research studies have shown quite clearly that people who are labeled as mentally ill are viewed as having more serious problems with less hope of finding a solution than are people who are labeled as suffering from social problems (Brehm & Smith, 1986). Theodore Millon (1975) describes the hazards of labeling.

> Labeling *is* dangerous. It entails a reification, an impression that something has been identified as possessing intrinsic properties both salient and durable. Also, by virtue of deriving its official sanction from the approved classification system, the belief is strengthened that a label designates a significant and valid attribute. Further, what is reified suggests permanence, and thus a label endures long after the symptoms that gave rise to it have vanished. Because psychiatric labels convey pejorative implications, they remain as stigmas, result in social scapegoating and burdensome self-images, and thereby set the stage for self-fulfilling prophecies. (p. 460)

Millon (1975) suggests that some of the problems of labeling can be overcome by treating each client as an individual person rather than as a prototype of a diagnosis. This entails exploring the client's life history and attempting to understand the client's problem within the context of the client's personality style and current life circumstances. Beatrice Wright (1991) reminds clinicians to assess clients' environments and their personal strengths in addition to their so-called disorders. This can be done by attending to the following four issues.

1. The client's deficiencies and undermining characteristics.
2. The client's strengths and assets.
3. Deprivations and maladaptive forces in the client's environment.
4. Resources and opportunities in the client's environment.

The Vocabulary of Deficit

Kenneth Gergen (1990) points out that psychiatric diagnoses are focused on identifying deficits in people. The language of deficiency is degrading because it implies that people with psychiatric labels are functioning in a way that is unacceptable in our society (Goffman, 1961). People with deficits are expected to place themselves in the hands of experts who can treat their affliction. Gergen proposes that clinicians should cease assessing clients using a language of deficiency, which attributes their problems to an internal disorder. He argues that it would be more beneficial to assess clients with a language of *relatedness.* This would involve understanding clients' problems in terms of their family systems, social ecology, and communication processes.

Confirmatory Strategies

One bias that is particularly relevant to clinical assessment is people's tendency to find what they are looking for (Brehm & Smith, 1986; Salovey & Turk, 1991). Albert Einstein pointed out that theories are not realities in the world waiting to be discovered; rather, people's theories determine what they *can* discover (Watzlawick, 1990c). Research has demonstrated that when clinicians have a theory that psychotherapy clients must necessarily have personality disorders, they will find personality disorders in psychotherapy clients. For example, Langer and Abelson (1974) asked clinicians to observe a videotape of an actor being interviewed about his work experiences. When the clinicians were told the man being interviewed was a job applicant, they described him as realistic, enthusiastic, pleasant, and relatively bright. When told that the man was a patient, those clinicians with a psychodynamic orientation gave the following kinds of evaluations: "tight defensive person . . . conflicts over homosexuality; dependent, passive-aggressive; rigidity . . . considerable hostility, repressed or channeled" (Langer & Abelson, 1974, p. 8).

Temerlin (1968) conducted a similar study in which clinicians observed a videotape of man who acted as normally as possible. When the clinicians were informed that this man was psychotic, they were able to find evidence in the videotape for psychosis. Herbert, Nelson, and Herbert (1988) reported that clinicians found evidence for depression in a person who behaved normally when they expected this person to be depressed. The confirmatory bias is affected by clinicians' points of view as well as by their expectations. For example, research participants are more likely to interpret a client's behavior as personality based rather than as determined by situational factors when they place themselves in the role of a counselor (Snyder, Shenkel, & Schmidt,

1976). In the same vein, practicing therapists who identify themselves as dynamically oriented are inclined to interpret a "patient's" behaviors as determined by personality factors (Snyder, 1977). Behaviorally oriented therapists, on the other hand, tend to explain the same patient's behavior on the basis of situational factors.

A famous illustration of the confirmatory bias is found in Rosenhan's (1973; 1975) study in which "normal" people (the researchers) had themselves admitted to mental hospitals by claiming they were hearing voices. They were all given the diagnosis of schizophrenia. After gaining admission to the respective hospitals, the researchers acted normally. However, since members of the hospitals' staff had a theory that these researchers were mentally ill, they found evidence for this illness in their behaviors. As a simple example, when one of the researchers openly took notes to record what was going on in the hospital, a staff member wrote in this "patient's" chart "patient engages in writing behavior." When the researchers were finally discharged from the mental hospitals, they carried with them the label "schizophrenia in remission."

In another study, staff members of mental hospitals were told to be on the lookout for pseudopatients who might try to gain admission to their hospital (Rosenhan, 1973; 1975). In reality, no pseudopatients tried to gain admission to these hospitals, but because the staff members were expecting pseudopatients, 41 out of 193 patients who were admitted to the hospitals during the period of the study were alleged by at least one member of the hospital staff to be "normal."

An important issue raised by Rosenhan's study is the power of context in determining what we see in other people's behaviors (Rosenhan, 1975). Rosenhan claimed that the pseudopatients acted normally once they were admitted to their respective hospitals. However, critics of the study argue that acting cooperatively and replying that they were feeling fine are not "normal" behaviors because that is how mental patients typically behave (Millon, 1975; Spitzer, 1975; 1976). This is an ironic example of the power of context. If patients in a mental hospital act cooperatively, then acting cooperatively in a mental hospital is a sign of mental illness. These critics suggested that "normal" behavior would be to say "Look, I am a normal person who tried to see if I could get into the hospital by behaving in a crazy way and saying crazy things." However, it is very likely that if a patient in a mental hospital said something like this, it would simply be interpreted as another example of crazy behavior. As the patients in Rosenhan's study recommended, if you want to get released from the hospital: "Don't tell them you're well. They won't believe you. Tell them you're sick, but getting better. That's called insight, and they'll discharge you (Rosenhan, 1975, p. 472)!"

It is not surprising that Rosenhan's study was criticized for its use of deception (Spitzer, 1975; 1976). However, we cannot escape the fact that a clinician's theory about people's problems will have a significant impact on that clinician's assessment (and treatment) of those who have problems.

A Possible Compromise

A possible compromise to the problem of assigning diagnostic labels to clients is to view labels as falling into clusters that reflect a style of coping rather than a disorder. Budman and Gurman (1988) suggest three clusters of personality styles: the odd cluster, the dramatic cluster, and the anxious cluster.

The odd cluster   This includes people with schizoid, schizotypal, and paranoid styles. They are characterized by aloofness and detachment from others. There may be suspiciousness and some peculiarity in the person's manner, dress, or way of looking at the world. These people lack the ability to form interpersonal relationships.

The dramatic cluster   This includes people with borderline, antisocial, histrionic, and narcissistic styles. They behave in dramatic, exaggerated, and overly reactive ways. They often display anger, depression, and impulsivity, particularly in interpersonal relationships. They may also have a sense of grandiosity and entitlement and a lack of empathy for others. Interpersonal relations are characterized by instability and unpredictability of affect.

The anxious cluster   This includes people with avoidant, compulsive, dependent, and passive/aggressive styles. They are characteristically anxious, fearful, worried, and tense. These people use inadequate skills to cope with anxiety, such as avoidance, procrastination, and perfectionism. However, they are more flexible than those in the clusters described above. They can relate to others and often interact effectively if they feel sufficient reassurance to become relaxed.

SOME USEFUL ASSESSMENT QUESTIONS

The purpose of a clinical assessment is to learn enough about the client and his or her problems that meaningful therapeutic goals can be agreed upon and a direction for therapy can be established. It is taken for granted that more will be learned about the client as therapy progresses and that goals and procedures of therapy can be modified whenever the client and therapist feel it is appropriate. Some useful questions to consider when making an assessment are described in this section. More detailed outlines of clinical assessment procedures can be found in handbooks such as those edited by Ciminero, Calhoun, and Adams (1977) and Hersen and Bellack (1981).

1. *Explain the purpose of the assessment.* An advantageous method is to begin an assessment by explaining its purpose to the client (Cormier & Cormier, 1991). There are several reasons for structuring an assessment in this manner. First, clients are likely to be more cooperative when they feel that they are active participants in the assessment process. Second, clients need to know that while you are focusing on assessment you may ask many questions. However, when the therapy process begins, the client can expect that you will no longer ask questions and that the conversation will revolve around what the client has to say. A third reason for structuring the assessment is to present the process in a way that communicates a sense of hope and positive expectancy. Many clients are surprised to learn about the possibilities of therapy. The realization that they might find viable solutions to their problems and learn some effective coping skills is often encouraging.

2. *Define the problem.* The therapist asks the client to give a description—not an explanation (Watzlawick, 1990c)—of the problem, urging the client to be as objective as possible. If the client uses concepts that are difficult to objectify, the therapist asks for further description. For example, if the client complains about not being in touch with life, the therapist asks "What would it look like if you were in touch with life?" The therapist then asks the client to identify how he or she would be acting or thinking differently if the presenting problem were resolved. If the client's description of his or her problem is vague or ambiguous, the therapist plays dumb, which, as Donald Meichenbaum (1986; 1990) likes to say, "is not that difficult." Therapists must be careful not to fill in the gaps with their own ways of looking at the world. They should patiently obtain as much objective information from the client as possible.

3. *Obtain a history of the problem.* A common procedure when doing a clinical assessment is to obtain a history of the problem. When did it first begin? Has the problem been consistent or periodic? Is the problem related to identifiable events in the person's life? Does the problem have identifiable antecedents and consequences? How (and to what degree) does the problem interfere with or disrupt the client's life?

4. *Ask "why now?"* The therapist asks the client why she or he has chosen to seek therapy at this particular time. Are there any precipitating factors the therapist should know about?

5. *Ask "what for" rather than "why?"* Paul Watzlawick (1990b; 1990c) advises against asking *why* a person has a particular problem. It is more fruitful to ask *what for.* In other words, what purpose, function, or role does the client's problem play in his or her life? The purpose of asking "what for" is to understand the client's problem within the context of his or her life. Therapists need to appreciate the role of environmental factors affecting the client's life and to avoid the error of over-attributing the client's behaviors to dispositional factors (Wright, 1991).

6. *What if the client's problem were solved today?* This is another way to get at the "what for" question. Paul Watzlawick (1990b; 1990c) suggests asking clients what would happen if they left the therapy session today with their problems solved. It is the client's *second* answer that is important (the first answer, of course, is that everything would be fine). Therapists need to anticipate what price clients will have to pay to accomplish desired changes in their lives. Another way to make this assessment is to ask clients to list the short-term and long-term advantages and disadvantages of reaching their goals (Cormier & Cormier, 1991, p. 223).

7. *Find out how the client has attempted to solve the problem up to this point.* It helps to know how clients have attempted to solve their problems and what kinds of advice they have received from others. This knowledge allows the therapist to avoid prescribing the "more of the same" solution that has proven unsuccessful (Watzlawick, 1990b; 1990c).

8. *Assess the client's perception of how the therapist can help.* It is important to ask clients how they think therapy can help them. Knowing the client's expectations about therapy will enable the therapist to negotiate a therapeutic contract that is acceptable to both the therapist and the client.

9. *Ask the client how he or she will know when therapy has been successful.* This is another way of understanding the client's goals, hopes, and expectations.

10. *Assess previous experiences with psychotherapy.* Therapists always need to know whether the client has had psychotherapy in the past. The client should be asked what was helpful about his or her previous therapy and what was not helpful. The present therapist wants to be clear about the client's past therapeutic experiences to avoid past mistakes and to make the therapy as successful as possible.

11. *Find out who really wants the client to change.* Is the client in therapy for himself or herself? Or are there other people who have an investment in the client coming to therapy? Knowing whether the client has come to therapy out of free choice or at the behest of others is important.

12. *What feelings does the client pull from the therapist?* The kinds of feelings a client pulls from the therapist can be very diagnostic of the client's style of relating to others. Of course, any assessment of feelings elicited in the therapist by a client must be made with an appreciation of the therapist's unique way of interpreting and contributing to the interaction (Kiesler, 1988; Safran & Segal, 1990).

13. *What interpersonal or environmental processes may maintain or exacerbate the client's problems?* Assessment should focus not only on the client, but also on other forces in the client's life that may contribute to his or her problems.

14. *Ask about the clients use of drugs and alcohol, suicidal thoughts, and current life stresses.* All assessments should gather information about the client's use of drugs and alcohol and suicide potential. In addition, it is worthwhile to find out whether the client has recently undergone or is facing the prospect of losses, crises, or meaningful anniversaries.

15. *What are the client's strengths, support systems, and resources?* As suggested earlier in this chapter, it is always wise to assess a client's strengths, support systems, and resources.

SUMMARY

The orientation taken in this book is that clients who come for psychotherapy are suffering from problems in living. Assessment is therefore focused on discovering how clients are keeping themselves stuck and what they can do to get unstuck. A coping skills model of assessment helps to identify a client's strengths and deficiencies in coping with three areas of life: interpersonal relationships, thinking and feeling, and approaches to self and life.

Therapy can also be enhanced by assessing clients' maladaptive schemas for themselves and their interpersonal relationships. Five themes that often become the focus of psychotherapy are losses, interpersonal conflicts, symptoms, personality disorders, and developmental dysynchronies. Arnold Lazarus' BASIC-ID (behavior, affect, sensation, imagery, cognitions, interpersonal relationships, drugs-health) is a sufficiently broad assessment tool to be useful for most clinicians.

Clinical diagnoses are useful because they allow clinicians to communicate with each other about their clients. Diagnoses are also required by insurance companies for reimbursement. However, clinical diagnoses are subject to the following biases: (1) diagnoses are labels and not entities; (2) diagnoses are necessarily subjective; (3) as labels, diagnoses can be detrimental; and (4) diagnoses are subject to a confirmatory bias.

Some useful assessment methods are to: (1) explain the purpose of assessment; (2) ask the client to define the problem; (3) obtain a history of the problem; (4) ask "why now"; (5) ask "what for" rather than "why"; (6) ask what would happen if the client's problem were solved today; (7) find out how the client has attempted to solve the problem; (8) assess the client's perception of how the therapist can help; (9) ask the client how he or she will know when therapy has been successful; (10) assess previous experience with psychotherapy; (11) find out who really wants the client to change; (12) attend to feelings the client pulls from the therapist; (13) assess interpersonal or environmental processes that may exacerbate the problem; (14) assess use of drugs, alcohol, current life stresses, and suicide potential; and (15) assess the client's strengths, support systems, and resources.

SUGGESTIONS FOR FURTHER READING

Cohen, D. (Ed.). (1990). *Challenging the therapeutic state: Critical perspectives on psychiatry and the mental health system.* Special issue of *The Journal of Mind and Behavior, 11*, 1990.

Dixon, D. N., & Glover, J. A. (1984). *Counseling: A problem-solving approach.* New York: Wiley.

Hersen, M., & Bellack, A. S. (Eds.). (1981). *Behavioral assessment: A practical handbook* (2nd ed.). New York: Pergamon.

Lazarus, A. A. (1976). *Multimodal behavior therapy.* New York: Springer.

Lazarus, A. A. (1981). *The practice of multimodal therapy.* New York: McGraw-Hill.

Szasz, T. S. (1987). *Insanity: The idea and its consequences.* New York: Wiley.

Watzlawick, P. (1988). *Ultra-solutions.* New York: Norton.

Young, J. E. (1989). *Schema-focused cognitive therapy for personality disorders and difficult patients.* Sarasota, FL: Professional Resource Exchange.

CHAPTER 10

Goal Setting and Termination

This chapter focuses on two important processes in psychotherapy: goal setting and termination. These two topics are related because successful termination is a meaningful therapeutic goal.

GOAL SETTING

Goal setting in psychotherapy was strongly emphasized by Alfred Adler, who felt that the therapeutic relationship was a collaborative effort between therapists and clients in which clients took responsibility to work toward agreed-upon goals (Dinkmeyer, Dinkmeyer, & Sperry, 1987). Adler did not believe that clients come to therapy to be "cured." Rather, clients and therapists form a contract outlining each of their responsibilities in helping clients make constructive changes in their life. For this reason, specification of goals is important because it allows therapists and clients to evaluate their progress. The value of goal setting is demonstrated in a study that compared two kinds of clients: those who had dropped out of therapy after one session and those who stuck with therapy for a longer period of time (Epperson, Bushway, & Warman, 1983). One important predictor of which clients would stay in therapy was the clients' sense that the therapist clearly recognized their problems. An important function of goal setting is to assure clients that the therapist understands why the client has come to therapy and understands what the client hopes to achieve.

Purposes of Goals

Cormier and Cormier (1991) outlined the following purposes of goals in psychotherapy.

1. *Goals provide a direction for therapy.* Establishment of goals enables the client and therapist to ensure that they are on the same track and agree on what they want to accomplish in therapy. Clients are more likely to commit themselves to therapy if they believe the therapist understands them as individuals with particular needs and desires. If the therapist and client are to embark on a journey together, they need a destination.
2. *Goals allow therapists to evaluate their competence.* Goals allow therapists to determine whether they have the skills and training necessary for working with a particular client toward a particular outcome.
3. *Goals facilitate performance.* Goals facilitate performance because they are mentally rehearsed and they call attention to useful resources and coping strategies (Dixon & Glover, 1984, pp. 128–129).
4. *Goals suggest effective therapeutic strategies.* The changes a client desires provide therapists with a basis for choosing appropriate and relevant therapeutic strategies. Goals allow therapists to find a direction for their therapy and to proceed with a "rational basis" (Bandura, 1969, p. 70).
5. *Goals allow therapists and clients to track their progress.* By tracking their progress, clients and therapists can evaluate which strategies are working and which need to be modified.
6. *Goals are self-motivating.* The process of defining goals is self-motivating (Lloyd, 1983). Goals emphasize to clients and therapists that what they are doing is worthwhile and deserving of their best efforts.

Selecting Goals

Cormier and Cormier (1991) also outlined the following steps to be taken by therapists and clients in selecting goals for therapy.

1. *Explain the purpose of goals.* Cormier and Cormier (1991) recommend that therapists structure the goal-setting process by explaining the purpose of goals to clients. This reinforces the collaborative relationship between therapist and client and ensures that the client and therapist have compatible expectations.

2. *Identify goals.* Clients are typically vague about their goals in therapy, for several reasons. First, because many clients are not able to articulate their specific problems, it is not surprising that they cannot define their goals. Clients also have difficulty specifying goals because goal setting is a skill that many people have not acquired. A first step in identifying goals is to make the distinction between *choice* and *change* (Dixon & Glover, 1984). Some goals require that clients make

choices; other goals necessitate change. For goals that involve change, it is important to assess whether the client possesses the necessary skills and social and environmental support to make this change possible. If not, the skills must be learned or the environmental system must be altered.

Another important step in identifying goals is to be concrete and operational. When a client presents a goal that is difficult to define (such as, "improving my self-esteem," or "having better relationships"), it is worth asking the client to specify what he or she would be *doing* differently if this were to happen. Clients should be asked to be very specific about particular behaviors or thoughts that would change if their goals were accomplished. As a homework assignment, clients can make a list of things they can imagine themselves doing or thinking differently once have reached their goals. For clients who have difficulty thinking of specific behaviors or cognitions to define their goals, it may be helpful to provide them with a list of overt and covert behaviors and ask them to check the ones they would like to be doing more (and less) often (Cautela & Upper, 1975; 1976).

A final step in identifying goals is to state them in positive terms. Clients should not restrict their lists to things they want to do *less* often. It is important for clients to motivate themselves to master new behavioral and cognitive skills to replace the less adaptive ones they wish to abandon (Maultsby, 1984).

3. *Determine whether the goal is owned by the client.* Two points need to be made here: (1) Does the client really want to change? Or does the client believe his or her problems are caused by other people or circumstances? (2) Is the client in therapy for herself or himself or for someone else? This second question is relevant for all clients but is particularly important for clients with limited power, such as children, the elderly, and the handicapped.

4. *Determine whether the goal is realistic.* Therapeutic goals should be challenging. Challenging goals are more likely than mundane goals are to stimulate effort and enthusiasm from the client. However, goals must be realistic, and it is the therapist's responsibility to explore with clients whether their goals are feasible.

5. *Identify the goal's advantages and disadvantages.* It is a good idea to do a cost/benefit analysis of a client's goals. One way to accomplish this is to have the client make a list with four columns consisting of immediate advantages, long-term advantages, immediate disadvantages, and long-term disadvantages. The list of advantages will help motivate clients to take the risks and expend the effort necessary to reach their goals. The list of disadvantages is valuable because it keeps both clients and therapists aware of the fact that there will be times when it is difficult for clients to follow through with their "assignments." When this happens, the suggestions for enhancing compliance outlined in Chapter 5 are helpful guidelines.

6. *Make a commitment.* The client and therapist make a commitment to work together toward achieving the agreed-upon goals. This commitment may be formalized with a verbal or written contract. It implies that the therapist and client have agreed that the goals are realistic, that they are owned by the client, and that their advantages outweigh their disadvantages. A contract also implies that the therapist has the necessary training and expertise to assist the client. The contract should not be directed toward achieving *success*. Rather than looking at goals with a performance-oriented attitude, take a mastery-oriented approach (see Chapter 2). Achieving so-called success is not as important as developing personal skills and coping resources.

Defining Goals

Cormier and Cormier (1991) outlined the following steps for clients and therapists to follow in defining and operationalizing goals.

1. *Define overt and covert behaviors associated with goal.* As suggested before, goals must be defined operationally by asking clients how they would be acting or thinking if they were to achieve their goals. Again, therapists should focus on what clients want to *do* rather than on what they want to *stop doing.*
2. *Define the conditions or the context of the goal.* Clients are asked to specify *where, when,* and *with whom* they would like to implement their goals. It is more realistic to think of changing one's behaviors to suit particular contexts than it is to think of revamping one's entire personality.
3. *Define the level of desired change.* The therapist and client agree on a level of change the client can realistically achieve. Clients experience a greater sense of collaboration if they can decide *how much, how often,* and *how quickly* they would like to implement their goals.
4. *Identify subgoals.* It is generally easier to reach a final goal by identifying subgoals to accomplish along the way. By outlining a list of subgoals, the therapist and client can provide opportunities for the client to reward herself or himself as these subgoals are attempted or accomplished (Bandura, 1969).
5. *Identify obstacles.* The therapist and client identify obstacles to the client's goals. This gives them the opportunity to devise strategies for coping with these obstacles when they occur.
6. *Identify resources.* The notion that the therapist and client are involved in a collaborative effort to achieve the client's goals implies an openness to all available resources, which may include support people or programs in the community.
7. *Review progress.* Therapists and clients need a way of tracking their progress. This allows clients to take pleasure in their accom-

plishments. It also provides therapists and clients with the opportunity to identify obstacles and setbacks so that they can come up with suitable coping strategies.

SOME POSSIBLE THERAPEUTIC GOALS

Chapter 2 presented an overview of goals that are relevant to almost all therapeutic relationships. Here we will focus on some more specific therapeutic goals. Many clients come to therapy with definite problems they want to overcome, and these problems often suggest immediate goals. Solving a client's immediate problems or helping a client get over particular symptoms is, of course, important and not to be neglected. However, as Carl Rogers (1961; 1977) pointed out, therapists usually try to take a broader view of their clients and help them engage in a growth process through which they can become more fully functioning people. How can the therapist use what Martin Fisher (1990) calls the "shared experience" of psychotherapy to provide the client with what Donald Meichenbaum (1986) defines as an "irreversible experience?" One place to start is by identifying a client's schema, which includes the client's particular way of looking at the world and her or his hopes, demands, expectations, and desires (Beck, Freeman, et al., 1990). For example, a client who places her self-worth on what others think of her can be helped to explore this schema during the course of therapy. Similarly, a client who feels the need to be in control of all facets of his life can be encouraged to assess the advantages and disadvantages of this point of view. A client who feels the need to protect himself from interpersonal relationships because of the risk of being hurt might experience enough trust with the therapist to discover that the benefits of human relationships outweigh their liabilities.

Irvin Yalom (1980) discusses the four existential goals of coming to terms with the challenges of death, freedom, isolation, and meaninglessness. Albert Ellis and Windy Dryden (1987) offer the following criteria of psychological health as possible goals for therapists and clients to pursue in therapy.

1. *Self-interest.* It is good to sacrifice oneself for others, but not overwhelmingly or completely. Above all, people need to take care of themselves.
2. *Social interest.* People generally fare better when they can derive support and pleasure from interactions with others.
3. *Self-direction.* Healthy people assume responsibility for their own lives, but they know how to cooperate with others.
4. *High frustration tolerance.* High frustration tolerance enables people to cope with inevitable dissatisfactions and displeasures in life.
5. *Flexibility.* Flexibility enables people to adapt themselves to the demands of life's challenges.

6. *Acceptance of uncertainty.* Uncertainty can be scary, but it also brings excitement and fascination to life.

7. *Commitment to creative pursuits.* This is a source of gratification and meaning in life.

8. *Scientific thinking.* One should be objective about one's feelings and consider the long-term consequences of one's actions. Perceptions and interpretations about other people's actions can be verified through communication.

9. *Self-acceptance.* Self-acceptance means refusing to rate one's value as a person. Only actions, but not people, can be judged as good or bad.

10. *Risk taking.* Risks are necessary for achieving a full and meaningful life. People can't learn and grow unless they are able to take risks and cope with failure.

11. *Long-term hedonism.* We need to plan for our futures. This may require postponement of immediate pleasure for long-term gain.

12. *Nonutopianism.* Life is not a panacea, and there is no utopia. We need to accept the fact that there is pain and suffering as well as happiness and joy in life. It is wise to avoid the idea that there is what Paul Watzlawick (1988) has called an "ultimate solution."

13. *Self-responsibility.* We are responsible for ourselves. We need to ask ourselves what we can do to live self-fulfilling lives and how we can minimize what Albert Ellis (1987) has defined as our innate tendency to make ourselves miserable.

TERMINATION

Termination provides therapists and clients with an opportunity to say goodbye in a mutually satisfying manner. This is a new and important experience for many clients who have not learned how to separate from people who have become significant to them. As Maholick and Turner (1979) explain: "Termination of therapy can be thought of as a recapitulation of multiple preceding goodbyes of living. At the same time it is a preparation for being able to deal more adequately and openly with future goodbyes" (p. 584).

Teyber (1988) describes the learning experience offered by successful termination in the following manner.

> In most clients' pasts, they have painfully experienced endings with significant others as "just happening to them." In many cases, either they were not prepared in advance for the separation, they did not understand when or why this particular ending was occurring, or they were not able to participate in the leave-taking by discussing it with the departing person. These types of responses have left many clients feeling powerless and out of control in regard to some of the most important experiences in their lives. (p. 191)

An important goal of termination is to teach clients how to end relationships with a sense of mastery and fulfillment. For this reason, termination is an essential process in therapy that should not be avoided.

> Therapy, like life itself, ends. If as therapists we minimize the termination process or do not permit ourselves to be as emotionally available as we can be during the final sessions, what are we implying to the client about how to conduct one's waking activities during an experience that has a certain end? Might we not then be teaching the need to defend oneself against loss and death instead of the need to live life to its fullest? (Martin & Schurtman, 1985, p. 95)

The therapist's task is to remain emotionally available and to recognize, accept, and experience with the client whatever feelings of anxiety, denial, and pain may accompany the termination process.

Termination as a Process

In his paper "Analysis Terminable and Interminable," Freud (1937) pointed out that although the goal of cure in psychotherapy makes theoretical sense, it is not likely to occur in most cases. Freud cautioned that therapists who commit themselves to total cure are in jeopardy of keeping their clients in therapy forever. Freud's paper suggests a compromise to cure in which clients suffer less from their problems and gain sufficient self-knowledge and skills in living to cope more successfully in the future than they have in the past (Weiner, 1975, p. 265). Because psychotherapy often does not have an ideal ending point, it is more suitable to view termination as a *process* rather than as a discrete event (Ekstein, 1965; Weddington & Cavenar, 1979). As Freud and others have pointed out, the termination process begins during the first therapy session and continues until the client and therapist say goodbye.

Termination Goals

Before discussing goals of termination, we need to acknowledge that termination is itself an important goal in psychotherapy. Goldberg (1975) described how he handles termination as a therapy goal: "I must realize that unless I avoid colluding with my patient in guarantying him a future as a patient, therapy will never begin—for both of us will fuse in the magical notion of acting as if that which is not born can not die" (p. 342). Therapists and clients should look forward to the process of saying goodbye as an important experience in their work together. Three specific goals to be accomplished before termination is completed are outlined by Ward (1984): (1) assessing the client's readiness for termination, (2) reaching closure in the therapeutic relationship, and (3) preparing the client to transfer what was learned in therapy to his or her own life.

Assessing Readiness for Termination

Readiness for termination is assessed by having the therapist and client discuss their progress toward therapeutic goals. Ward (1984) suggests looking back to the first few therapy sessions to evaluate changes that have taken place for the client since that time. As Thomas Szasz (1965) reminds us, since psychotherapy is a contractual relationship in which the client is paying the therapist for a service, it is generally up to the client to decide whether satisfactory progress has been reached or whether there is more to be gained from staying in therapy.

Reaching Closure

The therapist and client must feel reconciled toward each other before ending their work together. This is accomplished when the therapist is willing to model acceptance and openness toward the many feelings that can occur when the therapist and client are ready to part company. The client and therapist should review their work together and share feelings they experienced during various points in the therapeutic relationship. Expression of mutual appreciation is a good way to arrive at closure. The therapist and client can end on a positive note by sharing particular things they value in one another.

Transferring Learning

The goal in the transfer of learning is to affirm that clients can apply what they have learned during therapy to their outside life. This is achieved by having the therapist and client discuss the client's plans for coping with future challenges. Therapists often choose to phase out therapy sessions gradually, with the understanding that clients can return for a follow-up or "booster" session if necessary. Termination should coincide with a sense that the client has sufficient confidence and self-reliance in her or his ability to maintain therapeutic gains after therapy has ended.

Deciding When to Terminate

If we accept the argument that therapy does not result in a cure, it becomes clear that the decision about when to terminate therapy is necessarily subjective. Freud (1937) suggested that therapy could be terminated when the following criteria are satisfied.

1. The client is no longer suffering from former symptoms.
2. The client has gained sufficient insight and developed enough coping skills that the symptoms are not likely to reappear.

3. The client is not likely to experience significant gains if therapy were to continue.

A longer list of criteria for assessing when to terminate therapy is proposed by Maholick and Turner (1979).

1. Examining the degree to which initial problems or symptoms have been reduced or eliminated.
2. Determining whether the stress that motivated the client to seek therapy has been dissipated.
3. Assessing increased coping ability.
4. Assessing increased understanding and valuing of self and others.
5. Determining increased levels of relating to others and of loving and being loved.
6. Examining increased abilities to plan and work productively.
7. Evaluating increases in the capacity to play and enjoy life.

Kramer (1990) proposes resolution of transference as an additional criterion for terminating therapy. Weigert (1952) believes this resolution occurs when the client is able to be candid and spontaneous. A therapist interviewed by Kramer (1990) for his research on termination gave this description of a favorable ending point in the client/therapist relationship: "Clients would fully acknowledge their relationship with me, expressing their feelings about me, especially what I mean to them. They would see me as a person who remains interested in them beyond my professional role" (p. 49).

Levenson (1976) suggests that the client should be able to view the therapist: "as a real person, not simply attacking him or forgiving him as a failed parent but bringing a loving and constructive effort in engaging him and changing him" (p. 340).

Kramer (1990) also echoes Freud's suggestion that there is a point of diminishing returns in therapy. He suggests that the therapist and client perform a cost/benefit analysis to determine whether further benefit from therapy would be sufficient to offset the further expenditure of emotional energy and financial cost.

Initiating Termination

Kramer (1990, p. 37) explains that the phrase *beginning the termination process* is a misnomer, because the process of ending therapy starts during the first therapy session. This is a concept that Kramer believes therapists should understand and keep in mind before entering into therapeutic relationships. However, even though the termination process begins at the onset of therapy, the time must come when the therapist and client agree to cease scheduling therapy sessions.

Client-Initiated Termination

Traditional therapists who view the psychotherapist as an expert who treats and cures the client believe that termination should be initiated by the therapist (Kupers, 1988). In their opinion, only the therapist could determine when termination was appropriate. Most contemporary psychotherapists do not endorse this approach. They view clients as autonomous people who should be encouraged to take responsibility for their life and for their work in therapy (Kramer, 1990; Kupers, 1988; Szasz, 1965). Raskin and Rogers (1989) also make this point: Clients can be trusted to select their own therapists, to choose the frequency and length of their therapy, to talk or to be silent, to decide what needs to be explored, to achieve their own insights, and to be the architects of their own lives. (p. 156)

Kramer (1990) argues that it is generally preferable for the client to decide when therapy should be ended. He also cautions therapists not to stand in the way of the client's decision.

> One of the best reasons for agreeing with the client is that disagreeing is not therapeutic or helpful. If the patient brings up thoughts and feelings about ending therapy and the therapist disagrees for any reason, the therapeutic relationship—assuming it was a good one—is frequently irrevocably damaged or flawed. This is true even if the practitioner disagrees in a seemingly nonintrusive and well-intended manner. (p. 41)

Therapist-Initiated Termination

An important ethical principal outlined in Chapter 7 obliges therapists to terminate or refer clients when therapists don't feel they can provide the client with a useful service. Weiner (1975, p. 273) states that "persuading a patient to remain in psychotherapy has no more place in an effective treatment contract than seducing him into beginning it." However, Kramer (1990) cautions therapists to ask themselves honestly whether their desire to terminate clients is motivated by boredom, dislike for the client, or other countertransference issues.

> It is also fair to acknowledge that it is all right for therapists to have negative feelings about their patients. Whether they should initiate termination because they have not come to grips with their own personal issues, however, is quite another matter. When having trouble handling an overly dependent client, for example, the therapist's task might be to arrange a consultation rather than to rationalize that termination is a proper means of dealing with the problem. If there are no cues or suggestions of termination coming from the patient, and no clearly observable criteria, then a therapist-initiated ending may well be based on countertransference. (p. 31)

When process issues in the therapeutic relationship are causing discomfort for the therapist, the therapist needs to seek supervision and turn this discomfort into a profitable learning experience. Allowing the discomfort to escalate until the only recourse is to terminate therapy is not in the best interest of the client or the therapist.

Premature Termination

Client-Initiated Premature Termination

It is unfortunate when therapy ends before a sense of closure has been reached. When termination must occur earlier than desirable, it is still possible for the therapist and client to make the best of it. Clients may have logistical reasons for wanting to stop therapy, ranging from moving to running out of money. Clients may also have an idea that differs from the therapist's of how much they are ready (or willing) to gain from therapy. When a client wishes to terminate therapy, the therapist is cautioned against arguing with the client or interpreting the client's desire as resistance. Generally, it is more beneficial to take some time to summarize the client's progress up to this point and help the client achieve an overview of where the client has been, how far the client has come, and where the client would like to go. Helping clients gain a perspective on their problems, along with an appreciation of possibilities that therapy offers, can greatly assist the client with his or her future plans. Just because a client wishes to stop therapy now does not mean that he or she may not be willing to resume therapy in the future. When a client wishes to terminate, however, therapy should not end during the session when termination is first brought up. Therapists are encouraged to ask their clients to come back for a special termination session.

Therapist-Initiated Premature Termination

Therapists should do everything possible to avoid surprising clients with unexpected termination. When therapists are unable to continue a therapeutic relationship, clients must be notified well in advance. Therapists need to plan sufficient time for a comfortable termination. Feelings about ending therapy sooner than desirable should be openly shared between the therapist and client to minimize the client's feelings of being abandoned (Dewald, 1965; Glenn, 1971). Even though it can be painful, premature termination can be a useful learning experience if it is handled in a sensitive manner.

One common situation in which premature termination cannot be avoided is in counseling centers where there are interns or residents who have a finite amount of time in their rotation. It goes without saying that therapists who know their time with a client is limited will discuss this issue with the client at the beginning of therapy so that the number of available sessions can be part of their therapeutic contract. It makes sense when faced with a limited number of therapy sessions to formulate goals that can be accomplished during that period. When the time for ending therapy is approaching, the therapist and client can sum up how far they have come and evaluate whether the client would like to continue his or her work with another therapist. If so, the therapist can assist the client by facilitating the transfer. This includes providing the client with a referral and helping the client work through her or his anxieties and hesitations about starting over with someone new. Therapists must be careful not to become too emotionally close to clients if they anticipate that the client will soon be transferred to another therapist.

When faced with premature termination initiated by the therapist, clients have a number of possible reactions (Penn, 1990). They may feel angry that the therapist is abandoning them. They may also experience anxiety about being deserted. Another common reaction by clients is self-blame. Clients may decide the therapist is leaving because they are unlikable, inadequate, and undesirable as clients. Therapists must anticipate these kinds of reactions and openly discuss with clients their feelings about having to end therapy sooner than they desire.

Therapists also anticipate premature termination with mixed emotions (Penn, 1990). They too may feel anxiety and a sense of loss about having to say goodbye to the client sooner than they would wish. The therapist is likely to experience some sense of guilt about "abandoning" the client. On top of their own feelings about premature termination, therapists must also deal with the feelings of the client. Anger, hurt, or depression directed by the client toward the therapist must not be taken personally but should be understood as a predictable and understandable response to be dealt with therapeutically. Therapists are challenged to handle their personal reactions to clients' expressions of dissatisfaction in a professional manner. As Schafer (1973) suggests, therapists want to perceive themselves as "having offered something good, having made a sincere effort, and having achieved some results (if that is that case) under very disadvantageous conditions" (p. 141).

How Termination Affects Clients

Therapists need to be sensitive to the fact that termination can be a traumatic experience for psychotherapy clients. Strupp and Binder (1984) describe how termination evokes memories of painful separations; Mikkelson and Gutheil (1979) make an analogy between termination and death. However, termination is not always an adversity, and for many clients the experience of ending therapy is positive. Marx and Gelso (1987) studied clients who had terminated therapy in a university counseling center and found little evidence of negative effects. Clients were far more likely to describe their experiences of ending therapy in positive rather than in negative terms. The majority of clients said they had the following kinds of feelings about ending therapy: calm, alive, healthy, thoughtful, and satisfied. Clients who did have negative feelings about termination said they experienced being afraid, alone, and nervous. Clients who had the most difficulty with terminating therapy were those who had experienced previous traumatic losses in their life. It was also more difficult for clients to end therapy when they had developed a close relationship with their therapist over a relatively long period of time.

When clients are overly dependent or have not learned to cope with loss, they may react to termination by devaluating the therapist, bargaining for more time, or by regressing and experiencing a relapse (Roth, 1987). When termination is planned, discussed ahead of time, and carried out with the suggestions given later in this chapter, it is usually a positive experience for clients.

How Termination Affects Therapists

Termination can be as emotionally involving for therapists as it is for clients. Greene (1980) developed the Therapist Termination Questionnaire to assess the following positive and negative reactions of therapists to termination.

Role shift is characterized by less concern about professional distance, becoming more of a "real" person, becoming more emotionally expressive, and the desire to share more personal information.

Denial is characterized by viewing the client as having no problems with termination, as having no troubles, and as feeling completely positive and reconciled toward the therapist.

Depression is characterized by experiencing therapy as less rewarding, difficulty concentrating on therapeutic tasks, and the desire to withdraw emotionally.

Anxiety is characterized by feeling upset and emotionally involved and worrying about the client's well-being.

Task satisfaction is characterized by increased satisfaction about therapeutic work, confidence that the client has improved, and feelings of self-confidence about one's competence as a therapist.

Goodyear (1981) and Martin and Schurtman (1985) outlined four problems that can be experienced by therapists when therapy is terminated.

Guilt

Therapists may experience feelings of guilt over abandoning the client. This guilt is exacerbated for therapists who have not resolved their own sense of independence and individuality.

Anxiety

Therapists may experience anxiety stemming from the loss of their professional role. During termination, therapists must give up their role as an expert who is valued by the client as a figure of authority. Another source of anxiety is concern for the client. Therapists may worry about the client's well-being and about the client's satisfaction with the therapy. Since termination is a potentially traumatic experience for clients, therapists may worry about their ability to end therapy in an appropriate manner.

Self-Doubt

Therapists may experience feelings of self-doubt, self-depreciation, and depression. They wonder whether they have really helped their client, and they question their competence. These feelings can result in the therapist clinging to the client for reassurance or attempting to provide the client with "something of worth" by giving advice.

Loss

Therapists may experience grief over the loss of a meaningful and significant relationship they have developed with the client. Therapists must also give up the vicarious experience of pleasure in watching the client develop, grow, and make improvements in his or her life.

Martin and Schurtman (1985) caution that therapists may attempt to defend themselves against the potentially negative experience of termination with the following kinds of maneuvers.

1. Therapists may make light of termination, deny its importance, and not devote sufficient time and energy to the termination process.
2. Therapists may project their negative feelings to the client and blame the client for not appreciating them and for not making the best use of therapy. This projection may be acted out by leaving the client before the client can leave the therapy or by provoking the client to drop out of therapy.
3. Therapists may deny their feelings by viewing termination as an academic exercise carried out solely as a learning experience for the client.
4. Therapists may become dependent on the client for reassurance about their clinical skills and personal value.

It is apparent that termination can be as meaningful an experience for the therapist as it is for the client. Therapists are encouraged to take advantage of whatever supervision they need to make this a useful experience.

A MODEL FOR TERMINATING THERAPY

In Marx and Gelso's (1987) survey of termination at a university counseling center, the majority of clients reported engaging in the following activities during the termination process.

- Thanking the therapist
- Summarizing their work together
- Assessing how much goals had been attained
- Discussing their plans for the future
- Therapist sharing his/her feelings about ending therapy
- Setting a date for the final session
- Sharing feelings with the therapist about ending therapy
- Therapist inviting client to return if client feels the need

Lamb (1985) outlined a procedure for terminating psychotherapy that begins seven weeks before therapy is scheduled for completion.

Seven Weeks before Termination

At this point, the therapist and client have agreed that therapy will end. It is clear to both of them that sufficient progress has been made to stop therapy or that other circumstances have occurred that require termination. The therapist and client outline their plan for terminating therapy and make explicit that they are headed toward their final therapy session.

Six to Five Weeks before Termination

During these sessions, the client and therapist review the course of therapy. They look at what they have experienced together and what changes the client has made in her or his life. The therapist and client analyze coping skills the client has learned as well as skills the client would like to learn in the future. They go over the emotions and feelings they have experienced together. The therapist reminds the client that in four weeks they will be saying goodbye. The client and therapist share their feelings about concluding therapy.

Four to Three Weeks before Termination

The therapist and client talk about their relationship. How have they felt about each other and how have these feelings changed during the course of therapy? What have they learned about themselves as they have interacted with each other? What kinds of feelings and emotions have they experienced during their therapy sessions? The client and therapist identify critical incidents in their therapy sessions that particularly influenced them during their work together. They also share their answers to the question "What has our relationship meant to me?"

This is also a time to discuss the transition from the therapist to other people as the client's support system. Who can the client use for support persons after therapy has ended? Are there still areas of unfinished business that the client wishes to address? What thoughts does the client have about resuming therapy again sometime in the future?

Finally, it is important during these sessions to acknowledge feelings of sadness and loss over the prospect of saying goodbye. How can the therapist and client use their therapeutic relationship to learn something about what it means when people must leave one another?

Two Weeks before Termination

It is time to focus on the client's plans for the future. What has the client learned in therapy that will make it easier to cope with challenges he or she will face after therapy has ended? The therapist and client can use imagery or role playing to prepare the client for responding to future problems. Both can review the client's previously less adaptive styles of responding to challenges and compare them with the client's current skills for handling the same difficulties.

The client is also reminded that, during the next session, the therapist and client will be saying goodbye. It is not uncommon for clients at this point either to bargain for one or two additional sessions or to suggest that having the last session is not important. This fear is understandable, and the therapist should be empathetic but firm. It is time to end therapy, but the final session must not be avoided.

Final Session

The task of the final session is to say goodbye. This session can be awkward because there is often no formal agenda. However, because the therapist and client have had several weeks to think about it and to prepare themselves for it, they can usually make it into a constructive experience. The therapist and client share appreciations and acknowledge that they are together as they go through the process of saying goodbye. Some therapists may schedule a follow-up session, but this must be done with caution because it might communicate an extension of the termination process. It may be preferable to leave the door open for clients to call if they should desire to schedule therapy sessions in the future.

GUIDELINES FOR SUCCESSFUL TERMINATION

Kottler (1991, p. 171) describes the importance of terminating therapy in a way that allows clients to feel good about their work and to continue being their own therapist in the future. Yalom (1985) emphasizes that "termination is more than the end of therapy; it is an integral part of the process of therapy and, if properly understood and managed, may be an important force in the instigation of change" (p. 368). Strupp and Binder (1984) view termination as an opportunity for clients to learn how to separate from significant others in a constructive and adaptive manner.

We conclude this chapter with a number of guidelines for successful termination of therapy that are based on the ideas discussed in the preceding pages (Kramer, 1990; Pipes & Davenport, 1990).

Discuss Termination Early

The therapist must begin talking about termination in the early stages of therapy and remind the client from time to time that, at some point, therapy will end and it will be time to say goodbye. Many therapists go as far as setting a termination date at the beginning of therapy. This is not done to make clients anxious (although Freud did set termination dates as a tactic for motivating recalcitrant clients); rather, the therapist's goal is to model a willingness to talk about uncomfortable issues in an open manner. It is better to be explicit about sensitive issues than to wait until they are acted out symptomatically.

Have Clear Goals

It is much easier for the client and therapist to work toward a satisfactory ending when they share mutual goals. The therapy goals should be as objective as possible so that the therapist and client can evaluate their progress during the course of therapy. When the client's gains are subtle, the therapist can help the client appreciate these accomplishments by reviewing the course of therapy. If the client is prepared to expect setbacks and relapses as a natural course of therapy, these can be taken in stride. The therapist must be sensitive about matching his or her "personal agenda" with the wishes, needs, capabilities, and limitations of the client.

Attend to Termination Cues

In addition to communicating with clients about their progress, therapists must also be sensitive to cues from clients that indicate they might be getting ready to end therapy. When termination cues are present, it is important that the therapist openly discuss with the client when ending therapy might be most appropriate. The most common termination cues are outlined next (Kottler, 1991; Kramer, 1986; 1990).

The client does not have as much to talk about   The issues the client does bring up are less substantive. Therapy sessions are less intense. The therapist needs to determine whether a plateau has been reached and there is more work to be done or whether therapy is beginning to wind down.

Clients begin relating to the therapist in a more egalitarian manner   The client no longer needs to idealize or depreciate the therapist. There is a feeling that the client and therapist have become peers. The client relates to the therapist in a less formal manner. The client is more open and immediate. Psychoanalysts refer to this phenomenon as resolution of the transference. Humanistic therapists perceive the client as having developed a stronger sense of self. In his essay "The Art of Psychoanalysis," Jay Haley (1963) gives the following description of the equalization of the therapist/client relationship.

> Ultimately a remarkable thing happens. The patient rather casually tries to get one-up, the analyst places him one-down, and the patient does not become disturbed by this. He has reached a point where he does not *really* care whether the analyst is in control of the relationship or whether he is in control. In other words, he is cured. (p. 201)

The client requires less input and feedback from the therapist   There is a sense that the client has internalized much of what has taken place in therapy. This is particularly evident when the client demonstrates the ability to cope with relapses or setbacks. The client can now do much of the therapy work for himself or herself.

There is a pattern of fewer therapy sessions   Clients either begin missing appointments or find reasons to schedule them less frequently. When this happens, the therapist should avoid taking it personally. Instead, the therapist should attempt to balance empathy for the client's apparent desire to phase out of therapy with an attempt to have the client honestly evaluate whatever issues and problems he or she may still need to address (either now or in the future).

Respect the Client's Autonomy

The point was made earlier that a major goal of psychotherapy is to enhance the client's sense of mastery, competence, and self-responsibility. Toward this end, therapists need to respect clients' views about when they wish to end therapy. This does not mean that therapists should not voice their own professional opinion and assist clients in considering all of the relevant issues. Therapists, however, would do well to avoid placing clients in the no-win situation of being labeled *resistant* when they want to end therapy and *dependent* when they desire to continue therapy (Kramer, 1986, p. 529).

Maintain a Professional Relationship

When therapy is approaching termination, it is not uncommon for therapists to act less formally, to focus less on process, and to share more about themselves. This is a natural reaction to the client's increased sense of comfort with the therapist as a "real person." However, it is wise to consider the value of maintaining the client/therapist relationship on a professional level. The therapist's major commitment, after all, is toward the client's personal growth. The therapeutic work the therapist and client have struggled through together could be compromised if the therapist were to disregard the sanctity of the therapeutic relationship and begin acting as the client's friend.

Keep the Door Open

Most contemporary therapists do not subscribe to the traditional view that, once therapy has ended, the therapist and client should never communicate with each other. As Arnold Lazarus (1981) argues: "Should those who return to physicians or dentists for more care be viewed as relapsers or treatment failures? We hope not. However, this terminology and the underlying mythology pervade mental health care" (p. 30).

Budman and Gurman (1988) recommend that therapists maintain a primary care perspective with their clients in which clients are offered the opportunity to schedule appointments in the future if they should feel the desire to take up more therapeutic work. As Budman and Gurman (1988) tell their trainees; "There is nothing easier than getting a patient *not* to come back" (p. 290).

> Indeed, many therapists seem to have exceptional innate skills in getting patients never to return to them. We believe that patients can and should return as needed. This perspective does not preclude doing therapy efficiently and effectively, and it encourages a more flexible perspective of "not needing to do it all at once." (Budman & Gurman, 1988, p. 290)

SUMMARY

Goal setting is important because it provides a direction for a collaborative effort between the therapist and client. The purposes of goals are to: (1) provide a direction for therapy, (2) allow therapists to evaluate their competence, (3) facilitate client effort and performance, (4) suggest useful therapeutic strategies, (5) allow clients and therapists to track their progress, and (6) provide self-motivation. Steps for selecting goals include: (1) explaining the purpose of goals, (2) identifying goals, (3) determining whether the goal is owned by the client, (4) determining whether the goal is realistic, (5) identifying the goal's advantages and disadvantages, and (6) making a commitment. Steps for defining goals include: (1) defining overt and covert behaviors associated with the goal, (2) defining the conditions or context of the goal, (3) defining the level of desired change, (4) identifying subgoals, (5) identifying obstacles, (6) identifying resources, and (7) reviewing progress.

Carl Rogers points out that therapists usually try to help their clients engage in a growth process and become more fully functioning people. Existential goals discussed by Irvin Yalom include coming to terms with the challenges of death, freedom, isolation, and meaninglessness. Albert Ellis and Windy Dryden offer the following criteria of psychological health as possible goals for therapists and clients: (1) self-interest, (2) social interest, (3) self-direction, (4) high frustration tolerance, (5) flexibility, (6) acceptance of uncertainty, (7) commitment to creative pursuits, (8) scientific thinking, (9) self-acceptance, (10) risk taking, (11) long-term hedonism, (12) nonutopianism, and (13) self-responsibility.

Termination provides therapists and clients with an opportunity to say goodbye in a mutually satisfying manner. This is a new and important experience for many clients, and it should not be avoided. Termination begins at the start of the first therapy session. It should be emphasized clearly at the outset of therapy that, at some point, the therapist and client will part company. Many therapists recommend setting a termination date that the client and therapist can work toward together. The best situation is one in which both therapist and client agree when it is an appropriate time for termination. However, if clients decide to end therapy, therapists should support them for taking responsibility for their life and help them gain an overview of what they have learned in therapy and what they could potentially gain from therapy in the future.

Ideally, termination occurs after clients have been able to find solutions to their symptoms or problems and have learned sufficient coping skills to maintain their gains and deal with similar problems in the future. Hopefully, the therapist and the client have reached a comfortable level of closure in their relationship. Often, however, termination of therapy does not come at an ideal time and it is the therapist's responsibility to call the client back for a termination session if at all possible. Termination can be a loss experience for both therapists and clients, and therapists should be open to discussing a wide range of feelings that can accompany the termination process. The following guidelines are suggested for successful termination of therapy: (1) discuss termination early, (2) have clear goals, (3) attend to termination cues, (4) respect the client's autonomy, (5) maintain a professional relationship, and (6) keep the door open.

SUGGESTIONS FOR FURTHER READING

Basch, M. F. (1992). *Practicing psychotherapy*. New York: Basic Books.

Cormier, W. H., & Cormier, L. S. (1991). *Interviewing strategies for helpers*. Pacific Grove, CA: Brooks/Cole.

Kramer, S. A. (1990). *Positive endings in psychotherapy*. San Francisco: Jossey-Bass.

Kupers, T. A. (1988). *Ending therapy*. New York: New York University Press.

Szasz, T. S. (1965). *The ethics of psychoanalysis*. New York: Basic Books.

CHAPTER 11

Some Philosophical Issues

The point of view expressed throughout this book is that psychotherapy is not a treatment intended to provide a cure; rather, it is a contractual arrangement between the therapist and client in which the therapist serves as the client's agent (Szasz, 1965). Freud (1949) viewed the therapist as a teacher and educator. It has also become clear that therapists, by the very nature of their work, are persuaders who exert a substantial amount of influence over their clients. Psychotherapy is an enterprise in which the norms, values, and beliefs of the therapist, client, and client's culture and environment must be brought into harmony.

> Psychotherapy is the name we give to a particular kind of personal influence: by means of communication, one person, identified as "the psychotherapist," exerts an ostensibly therapeutic influence on another, identified as "the patient." It is evident, however, that this process is but a special member of a much larger class—indeed, of a class so vast that virtually all human interactions fall within it. Not only in psychotherapy, but also in countless other situations, such as advertising, education, friendship, and marriage, people influence each other. *Who is to say whether such interactions are helpful or harmful, and to whom?* (Szasz, 1965, p. vii, emphasis added)

Perry London (1986) views psychotherapists as having both a scientific and a moralistic function. The *scientific function* of psychotherapists is to keep abreast of research developments in the field of therapy so therapists can offer their clients the most effective strategies for achieving change. A scientific approach to psychotherapy requires that therapists be accountable, and it is based on the following values (Singer, 1980).

1. As explicit a statement of assumptions as possible.
2. As precise definitions of constructs as possible.
3. The erection of theoretical propositions that are susceptible to empirical evaluations.
4. Some form of systematic collection of new data or reanalysis of accumulated data under carefully specified conditions.
5. Quantitative methods as a means of establishing the statistical reliability of findings that emerge from empirical investigations.
6. Careful and accurate communication of scientific procedures.
7. Dissemination of data so that new findings can be replicated by independent investigators.

London (1986) explains that the scientific function of therapists is analogous to that of a repairperson who assists clients with aspects of their life that are not working properly. London (1986) describes the *moralistic function* of psychotherapists as a secular priesthood in which the therapist serves as a moral agent. The moralistic function of therapists is to help clients find salvation, plan their futures, and live meaningful lives.

Because the goal of psychotherapy is to help clients find solutions to problems in living, we can appreciate Freud's characterization of the psychoanalyst as a secular pastoral worker (Breggin, 1991, p. 373) and Thomas Szasz's (1985b) description of therapy as *applied secular ethics*. Although many psychotherapists view themselves as scientists, they are in a very real sense philosophers with theories about the nature of people and their disturbances (Drane, 1982). Therapists need to appreciate the fact that the ideas, perceptions, and interpretations they offer their clients are necessarily subjective. The purpose of this chapter is to outline some of the philosophical issues that therapists might wish to consider as they work with their clients.

THERAPEUTIC VALUES

A Survey of Psychotherapists' Values

Jensen and Bergin (1988) conducted a national survey of values endorsed by professional therapists, which included psychiatrists, clinical psychologists, social workers, and marriage and family counselors. Respondents were asked to indicate how much they agreed or disagreed with a large number of values that had been identified in the psychotherapy literature and with input from prominent practitioners. The values on the survey were grouped by factor analysis into ten themes (see Table 11.1). The following conclusions can be reached from this survey. First, the majority of therapists agreed with the values contained in the following themes: 1, 2, 3, 4, 5, 6, and 7. The values proposed in themes 8, 9, and 10 did not receive endorsement by

Table 11.1 A Survey of Values' Importance in Psychotherapy

Value	Respondents Expressing High or Medium Agreement with Values' Importance (%)
1. Sensitivity to Feelings	
Increase sensitivity to other's feelings	92
Be open, genuine, and honest with others	87
2. Freedom/Autonomy/Responsibility	
Assume responsibility for one's actions	98
Increase one's alternatives at a choice point	96
3. Integration, Coping, and Work	
Develop effective strategies to cope with stress	97
Develop appropriate methods to satisfy needs	94
4. Self-Awareness/Growth	
Become aware of inner potential and ability to grow	90
Discipline oneself for the sake of growth	59
5. Human Relatedness/Interpersonal and Family Commitment	
Develop ability to give and receive affection	95
Increase respect for human value and worth	79
6. Self-Maintenance/Physical Fitness	
Practice habits of physical health	69
Apply self-discipline in use of alcohol, tobacco, and drugs	75
7. Mature Values	
Have a sense of purpose for living	85
Regulate behavior by applying principles and ideals	78
8. Forgiveness	
Forgive others who have inflicted disturbance in oneself	78
Make restitution for one's negative influence	51
9. Regulated Sexual Fulfillment	
Understand that sexual impulses are a natural part of oneself	85
Have sexual relations exclusively within marriage	49
10. Spirituality/Religiosity	
Seek spiritual understanding of one's place in the universe	41
Seek strength through communication with a higher power	31

Source: Adapted from "Mental Health Values of Professional Therapists: A National Interdisciplinary Survey," by J. P. Jensen and A. E. Bergin, 1988, *Professional Psychology: Research and Practice, 19,* 290–297. Copyright 1988 by the American Psychological Association. Adapted with permission of the authors.

as many therapists. This is most likely because themes 8, 9, and 10 are based on religious teachings with which not everyone agrees. Not surprisingly, some differences in agreement with various values were found for therapists of different ages, marital status, and theoretical orientation. For example, older therapists agreed with more of the values than did younger therapists. Married respondents gave stronger endorsement to marital fidelity than did unmarried and divorced respondents. Therapists with a behavioral orientation agreed less with values related to self-awareness and growth than did dynamically or humanistically oriented therapists. It is apparent from this survey that there are many values on which psychotherapists (and probably most people) agree. There are also some values on which psychotherapists do not agree. This survey is noteworthy because it provides an overview of how a national sample of psychotherapists responded to various values. In practice, however, it should be obvious that any discussion of values in therapy must be carried out with sensitivity and understanding of the client's culture and background.

Some Thoughts about Values

An important professional issue discussed in Chapter 6 is the therapist's obligation to develop multicultural competence. It stands to reason that discussions with clients about beliefs and values, as well as about changes they might wish to make in their life, must be carried out with sensitivity to their culture and environment. For example, when discussing assertiveness with clients, careful attention must be given to the consequences of assertive behavior in relationship to the clients' families, social groups, and workplace. As another example, helping a client evaluate his or her marriage or family situation must include attention to the client's cultural and religious norms. The values of therapists and their clients may differ around spiritual matters and with regard to such issues as premarital and extramarital sex, divorce, abortion, and a gay lifestyle (Bergin, 1980). It is incumbent upon therapists to learn and speak the language of their clients' values.

A client's participation in psychotherapy can have a significant impact on family members and on other people who share a close relationship with the client (Nietzel, Guthrie, & Susman, 1991). First, significant others may suffer feelings of inadequacy because the client chose to confide in someone else. Second, significant others may feel resentment and jealousy over the closeness and privacy of the therapeutic relationship. Third, there may be dissatisfaction about the time and money devoted by the client to therapy. Another issue deserving consideration is the fact that changes accomplished by a client in therapy are sometimes difficult for significant others to accept. Friends, family members, and other people close to the client may have trouble adjusting to clients who confront them with new ideas about how they wish to live their life.

It should be clear from this discussion that the therapist's role is not to tell clients what to do or what kinds of changes to make. The therapist's responsibility is to help clients become aware of *possibilities* and teach them to anticipate the *consequences* of these possibilities.

In his discussion of values in psychotherapy, Hans Strupp (1980a) reiterated Freud's belief that the purpose of therapy is to strengthen the client's adaptive capacities and provide whatever assistance may be necessary to enable the client to lead a more satisfying life as a responsible citizen in his or her culture. Strupp proposed seven therapeutic values.

1. People have the right to personal freedom and independence.
2. As adult members of a particular society, people have rights and privileges, but they also have responsibilities toward others.
3. To the greatest extent possible, people should be responsible for conducting their own life, without undue dependence on others.
4. People are responsible for their actions but not for their feelings, fantasies, and so on.
5. People's individuality should be fully respected, and they should not be controlled, dominated, manipulated, coerced, or indoctrinated.
6. People are entitled to make their own mistakes and learn from their life experiences.
7. People should be encouraged to use their abilities to search for and find their own solutions to basic life problems.

A number of other important values discussed in the psychological literature can also be suggested for consideration in psychotherapy. Each of these are discussed in turn in the following sections.

AUTONOMY

Autonomy is a value that most therapists would agree is useful to impart to their clients. Szasz (1965) defines autonomy in the following way: "Autonomy is a positive concept. It is freedom to develop one's skills, and achieve responsibility for one's conduct. And it is freedom to lead one's own life, to choose among alternative courses of action so long as no injury to others results" (p. 22). Autonomy offers clients increased freedom to determine what they want to do with their life. It is the therapist's role to help clients appreciate the possibilities that autonomy has to offer. Therapists can also teach clients to plan, foresee, and take responsibility for their autonomy. It is not the therapist's place, however, to encourage the client to use his or her autonomy in any particular way. As Szasz (1965) explains "It is more important that the patient be *free to choose* than that he choose to be healthy, wealthy, or wise" (p. 45, emphasis added).

LEARNED RESOURCEFULNESS

Learned resourcefulness is a concept suggested by Michael Rosenbaum (1990) to describe a style of relating to the world in which a person reacts to challenges with the following responses.

- Paying attention to one's thoughts and talking oneself through challenges.
- Using appropriate problem-solving strategies to come up with viable solutions.
- Having the ability to foresee the consequences of one's acts and to plan. Having the strength to delay immediate gratification for the sake of long-term goals.
- Believing in oneself and in one's ability to cope.

Learned resourcefulness is similar to the goal of self-efficacy outlined in Chapter 2. A client's learned resourcefulness can be developed in therapy by helping clients master useful coping skills and enhancing their confidence so that they can use these skills effectively (Kleinke, 1991).

SENSE OF COHERENCE

A person's sense of coherence is defined as a feeling of confidence that life challenges are understandable and that one has the necessary resources for coping with these challenges (Antonovsky, 1979; 1990). One's sense of coherence is made up of three components: comprehensibility, manageability, and meaningfulness.

Comprehensibility refers to people's ability to make sense of problems and challenges that confront them. Even though certain events in our life might not be desirable, we need to reconcile ourselves to the fact that they are a natural part of life, that they make sense, and that there is no need to react with panic and confusion.

Manageability is defined by the degree to which a person feels he or she has the necessary coping skills and resources to stand up to life's problems and challenges. People with high self-efficacy and resourcefulness are most likely to believe they can manage difficult situations.

Meaningfulness refers to the extent to which a person feels that life makes sense and has enough value to warrant the emotional energy and pain it sometimes requires. A person who views life as meaningful is willing to cope with problems and challenges with a sense of pride and dignity.

MINDFULNESS

The concept of mindfulness is used by Ellen Langer (1989) to describe the process that occurs when people think flexibly and take the time to consider many different options and possibilities before deciding on an appropriate response to a challenging life event. Mindlessness is the opposite of mindfulness; mindless behaviors are automatic. Some mindless behaviors are very useful. For example, when we have a lot on our mind, we are able to get up in the morning, take a shower, get dressed, make and eat breakfast, and even drive to work without having to think much about what we are doing. Because these morning chores are automatic, they don't require much of our attention. Other mindless behaviors include saying "excuse me" when we bump into somebody and replying "fine" when someone asks us how we are doing. Life would be more fatiguing than it already is if we couldn't rely on some mindless behaviors to get us through the day. We need to be able to accomplish some tasks mindlessly in order to reserve our energies for more important challenges. Problems can arise, however, when people don't take the time to be mindful about things that can have a genuine effect on their personal adjustment. Mindlessness is not a symptom of laziness as much as it is a habit or a pattern people develop without really thinking about it. Everyone is disadvantaged by mindlessness at one time or another, and it often helps to have another person (such as a therapist) suggest a new and different way of interpreting and solving a problem or dilemma.

When people are mindless, they make *premature cognitive commitments.* In other words, they make cognitive errors by reaching conclusions before considering all of the evidence. Some examples of cognitive errors that are particularly relevant for psychotherapy are making *faulty comparisons* and *underestimating the power of roles.* Psychotherapists can help their clients achieve greater autonomy by becoming more mindful of their faulty comparisons and of the roles they are playing.

Faulty Comparisons

Faulty comparisons occur when we suffer low self-esteem and put ourselves down because we don't measure up to our assessments of the accomplishments and strengths of others. It is a common experience to think badly of oneself because other people seem to handle their problems better or appear to be able to achieve things with much less difficulty. When we make faulty comparisons, we commonly lose sight of the fact that those other people experience the same self-doubts we do. Faulty comparisons are made on the basis of insufficient evidence.

We may assume that other people find things easier than we do, but, if we asked them about their difficulties, we would find them to be similar or even worse than our own. Faulty comparisons also occur when we choose to compare ourselves with people who are better at a particular skill than we are and we ignore the multitude of people who are worse.

Underestimating the Power of Roles

People underestimate the power of roles when they make a premature cognitive commitment about self-identity without appreciating the fact that their identity is a subjective perception that can be changed. Research studies have shown that when people are arbitrarily placed into roles, they begin to act according to these roles. In addition, they are perceived by others as having the qualities required for these roles (Kleinke, 1986).

A role very relevant to psychotherapy is that of being a patient. Thomas Szasz (1985a) provides some insight into the patient role using a model in which a person is either a patient or not a patient and either has a disease or does not have a disease. A person with no disease who is not a patient is healthy. A person with a disease who is a patient is sick and has decided to take advantage of medical help. A person with a disease who is not a patient is sick but has decided not to obtain medical help. A person with no disease who is a patient is an enigma. How could a person with no disease be in the role of a patient? This can happen when people become "patients" in order to obtain drugs and other kinds of attention. In Szasz's view, people assuming the role of patient when they have no disease is what characterizes the field of psychiatry. Whether or not psychotherapists accept Szasz's argument, their job is to help clients look at what roles they are playing in their life and to explore with clients the roles they have each adopted in the therapeutic relationship.

How can people learn to become more mindful? The following suggestions are offered by Langer (1989): (1) broaden one's perspective on a problem, (2) consider all possible alternatives, and (3) pay attention to the process of one's behaviors. All of these activities have been discussed in this book as within the realm of psychotherapy.

FLEXIBILITY

The concept of mindfulness reinforces the value of flexibility. Paul Watzlawick (1990b) explained that Darwin's theory of the survival of the fittest does not mean that the *strongest* survive but rather that those who can best *fit* survive. In other words, organisms must be sufficiently flexible to adapt to the changing demands of the world. *Functional flexibility* was defined in Chapter 1 as a useful skill for expanding one's worldview. Functional flexibility includes (1) having a wide range of coping responses in one's repertoire and (2) being able to match the appropriate response to the situation (Paulhus & Martin, 1988). Functional flexibility can be related to what Cantor and Kihlstrom (1987) call *social intelligence:* the efforts of individuals to solve problems of daily life and to work toward desired goals. Here are some examples of using one's social intelligence (Cantor & Harlow, 1992).

Avoiding "More of the Same" Solutions

Watzlawick (1990b) describes how people get stuck when faced with life challenges by using a "more of the same" coping response because they either don't have other coping responses in their repertoire or are unable to match the appropriate response to the present situation. Flexibility allows people to "break set" and to work out the best responses to different situations.

Setting Realistic Goals

It is not only important to set realistic goals (see Chapter 10) but also to modify one's goals as one's life situation changes. For example, people who value being independent and doing things for themselves will need to modify this goal in their old age by defining *independence* in a different way. Instead of viewing a wheelchair as a threat and stigma, one could "flexibly redefine" the wheelchair as a means of transportation and an opportunity for getting oneself around. As another example, a person who values the attention he or she receives from being physically attractive will have to develop other skills for achieving attention when the aging process causes physical attractiveness to wane.

Fitting One's Goals to the Situation

Flexible people are able to fit their goals to the situation. For example, someone who enjoys being in control and acting assertively may be able to fulfill this need very satisfactorily at work but not in his or her friendships or social relationships. People who enjoy being dependent and receiving nurturance may fruitfully achieve this goal with their spouse but wisely refrain from assuming this role with their boss.

The challenge of becoming flexible in deciding *what* goals to pursue, *when* and *where* to pursue them, and *how* to reach them (Cantor & Harlow, 1992) may sound mundane, but it is the basis of many people's problems. Epstein (Epstein & Meier, 1989) describes his reactions to a university class he taught on self-concept, in which students kept records of their most positive and negative emotional experiences each day: "One cannot help but be impressed, when observing students in such a situation, with the degree to which some otherwise bright people lead lives in a manifestly unintelligent and self-defeating manner" (p. 333).

Epstein and Meier (1989) use the concept of *constructive thinking* to define people's ability to react to life challenges in a thoughtful and flexible manner. Two major components of constructive thinking are emotional coping and behavioral coping.

Emotional coping includes the ability not to take things personally, not to be oversensitive to disapproval, and not to worry excessively about failure and negative responses from others. Emotional coping is characterized not so much by positive thinking as it is by the capacity to avoid getting bogged down in negative thinking. Good emotional copers don't catastrophize, and they make thoughtful primary and secondary appraisals (see Kleinke, 1991).

Behavioral coping refers to approaching challenges with a sense of optimism and with a strategy of seeking effective responses. Good behavioral copers don't hold grudges. They let bygones be bygones, and they focus their energies on planning and carrying out effective action. Behavioral copers know how to use problem-solving strategies (see Kleinke, 1991).

Other components of constructive thinking are the ability to avoid categorical thinking, superstitious thinking, and negative thinking. *Categorical thinking* is rigid and extreme. Categorical thinkers are judgmental and view the world (and its possibilities) in blacks and whites. *Superstitious thinking* is characterized by a belief that one has limited control over one's life because of the influence of unpredictable factors. *Negative thinking* is exemplified by a gloom and doom attitude toward life. It is a tendency to think "no matter what I do, things won't turn out right." Because negative thinkers are so pessimistic, they are not inclined to face life challenges with effective action.

TAKING A SALUTOGENIC APPROACH

In Chapter 2 we established that pathology is not a necessary construct when devising goals for psychotherapy. A pathological orientation in psychotherapy seeks to explain why people have a particular disorder (such as those listed in DSM-III -R). Clinicians who take a pathological orientation are biased by what Kenneth Gergen (1990) calls a *language of deficit*. Focusing exclusively on pathogenic factors leads therapists to take a narrow approach toward clients, in which the emphasis is on diagnosing a disorder and attempting to provide a treatment.

The term *salutogenic* was suggested by Aaron Antonovsky (1979; 1990) to define a focus on the origins of successful coping and adjustment. A salutogenic orientation in psychotherapy seeks to explain how people develop sense of psychological well-being. Psychotherapists who take a salutogenic orientation view their clients as people with strengths as well as weaknesses. Rather than defining the client's pathology, the goal is to provide strategies for helping clients develop their potentials and attain what Howard Friedman (1991) defines as a *self-healing personality.*

HAPPINESS

Freud (1930) recognized that, for most people, happiness is an overriding goal in life. People devote considerable energy toward seeking happiness and holding on to it whenever they find it. Given the significance of happiness as a human value, it makes sense to ask whether happiness is a viable goal in psychotherapy. There are at least two reasons for psychotherapists' reluctance to claim they can provide their clients with happiness. First, since happiness is so subjective, it is difficult to conceive of a strategy for finding happiness that would suit all clients. Second, happiness is elusive. Thomas Szasz (1990a) likens happiness to a wet bar of soap; the harder you grab for it, the more it slips out of your hands. Therefore, it is questionable whether psychotherapists could ethically offer happiness as a therapeutic goal. When asked about happiness as a goal for psychotherapy, Szasz (1990a) quoted Socrates, who said he'd rather be an unhappy philosopher than a happy cow.

Although it may not be ethical or practical to offer happiness as a therapeutic goal, the human desire for happiness is so pervasive that it cannot be ignored. For this reason, although psychotherapists can't guarantee their clients happiness, they can still help their clients appreciate some essential principles about happiness, such as those outlined next.

Defining Happiness

There are two general ways in which people define happiness (Baumeister, 1991). One way to define happiness is to equate it with intense pleasure. This is the kind of happiness that is unpredictable and elusive. Because states of happiness come to us on an intermittent schedule, they can be addictive (the harder one grabs, the more it slips away). These are what Thomas Szasz calls the "bonuses of life" (1990a). Although states of happiness may make life worth living, it is risky for people to devote their lives toward grabbing for them. It can be argued (as a value judgment) that many people have squandered their life by focusing their energies on achieving momentary highs rather than taking these highs as they come and devoting their talents toward long-term accomplishments. A second definition of happiness is a general satisfaction with life. Given this definition, happiness can be called *subjective well-being* (Diener, 1984), and it is characterized by items such as those on the Satisfaction with Life Scale (Diener, Emmons, Larsen, & Griffin, 1985).

1. In most ways, my life is close to my ideal.
2. The conditions of my life are excellent.
3. I am satisfied with my life.
4. So far I have gotten the important things I want in life.
5. If I could live my life over, I would change almost nothing.

Psychotherapists can help their clients appreciate the difference between states of happiness, which are exciting but elusive, and subjective well-being, which, while less exciting, is more predictable and stable. Subjective well-being can be attained by devoting one's energies to achievements that result in a satisfying life.

The Virtues of Frequent Rather Than Intense Pleasures
The notion of life satisfaction suggests that it is more fruitful to achieve happiness by seeking emotional stability and serenity than it is to live for the unpredictable peaks of excitement and suffer through the low points in between. Research studies have shown that overall happiness is correlated more with the *frequency* of small pleasures experienced rather than with the achievement of fewer but highly *intense* pleasures (Diener, Sandvik, & Pavot, 1989).

Happiness Comes from Inside
Most people lose sight of how much happiness is a result of their expectations and perceptions as well as of the demands they make of life. It is a mistake to assume that happiness is caused by external events. Many people truly believe they would be happy "if only" something (external) would happen. They say, "I would be happy *if only:*

• I could find the right romantic partner."
• I could win the lottery or make lots of money."
• the project I'm working on would be successful."
• some problem in my life would go away."

A good example of the fallacy of deriving one's happiness from external events is seen in a study of people who won their state lottery (Brickman, Coates, & Janoff-Bulman, 1978). These people, who received from $50,000 to $1 million, were naturally happy about their good fortune. However, this happiness was surprisingly short-lived. For one thing, the experience of winning so much money had the effect of making the other pleasures of life less valuable. It seemed that the lottery winners had forgotten how to find pleasure in activities that used to bring them satisfaction. Since they were blessed with the external gift of a lottery prize, the only thing worth looking forward to was winning an even larger lottery in the future. As suggested earlier, living one's life for elusive pleasures has costs. First, people waste a lot of time putting their life on hold waiting for their "lucky day" (which, of course, may never come). Second, although the pleasure of external events may be intense, it is short-lived and often undermines the gratification that can be achieved from smaller but more predictable enjoyments that come from inside (Diener, Colvin, Pavot, & Allman, 1991).

Positive and Negative Affect Are Independent

It would not occur to most people that positive and negative affect are independent (Watson & Tellegen, 1985). In other words, experiencing pleasure doesn't necessarily take away one's pain (although pleasure can serve as a temporary distraction). In the same vein, decreasing a negative feeling doesn't necessarily bring about an increase in positive feelings. In other words, it is a fallacy to think that "If only I could overcome this negative event in my life, I would be happy."

The relation between positive and negative affect and subjective well-being was outlined by Costa and McCrea (1980) using the diagram shown in Figure 11.1. Figure 11.1 suggests that people can improve

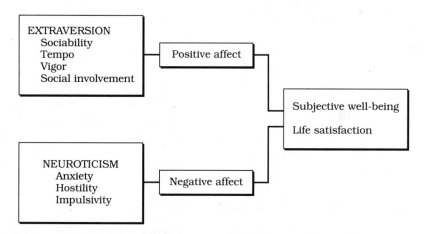

Figure 11.1 A model defining the independence of positive and negative affect.
Source: Adapted from "Influence of Extraversion and Neuroticism on Subjective Well-Being: Happy and Unhappy People" by P. T. Costa, Jr., and R. R. McCrae, 1980, *Journal of Personality and Social Psychology, 38,* 668–678. Adapted with permission of the authors.

their subjective well-being by increasing their positive experiences and by decreasing their negative experiences. What is worth recognizing is that these are two separate endeavors. Positive affect is enhanced by developing one's skills and activities in the area of *extraversion* (forming satisfactory social bonds, engaging in gratifying activities, developing appropriate assertiveness skills). Negative affect is decreased not by increasing one's positive affect but by overcoming coping styles characterized by *neuroticism* (having an anxious and hostile outlook on life and behaving impulsively).

A Program for Increasing Happiness

Fordyce (1977; 1981; 1983) developed a program for helping people increase their happiness. The program consists of practicing the following fundamental tenets.

1. Be more active and keep busy.
2. Spend more time socializing.
3. Be productive at meaningful work.
4. Be better organized and plan things out.
5. Stop worrying.
6. Lower your expectations and aspirations.
7. Develop positive, optimistic thinking.
8. Get present-oriented.
9. Work on a healthy personality: accept yourself, like yourself, know yourself, help yourself.
10. Develop an outgoing, social personality.
11. Be yourself.
12. Eliminate negative feelings and problems.
13. Close relationships are number 1.
14. Value happiness.

A series of research studies demonstrated that people who were taught to practice these fundamental tenets reported being more happy than did people in a control group who did not receive this training. It appears that people can increase their happiness by learning and practicing strategies that work best for them.

Some Conclusions about Happiness

The following conclusions can be reached from research on happiness.

1. Life events that bring joy and elation can be savored and appreciated as long as they don't undermine the value of everyday pleasures. However, it is better to devote one's energies toward achieving a satisfying life than it is to get sidetracked by seeking momentary gratifications.

2. A satisfying life comes from learning to increase one's satisfactions as well as learning to cope with one's dissatisfactions.
3. Everyone needs close relationships with other people and a good support system.
4. The healthiest route is to set goals that are reasonable and that will provide satisfaction over the course of one's life.
5. Life satisfaction comes more from appreciating the process of working through a challenge (being mastery-oriented, see Chapter 2) than from achieving a particular outcome (being performance-oriented).

POSITIVE ILLUSIONS

The traditional view of mental health is that mentally healthy individuals are in touch with reality. As Jahoda (1958) explains, "The perception of reality is called mentally healthy when what the individual sees corresponds to what is *actually there*" (p. 6, emphasis added).

Jourard and Landsman (1980) made a similar point: "The ability to see reality as it *really is* is fundamental to effective functioning" (p. 75, emphasis added).

These definitions of mental health assume that there is one reality and that the goal of psychotherapy is to help clients discover what is *real*. In fact, if we think about it, we can appreciate that this definition of mental health makes little sense, because reality is necessarily in the eye of the beholder. In other words, every person creates his or her own reality (Kelly, 1955). Alfred Adler believed that people construct their own realities through what he called the *creative self* (Bednar, Wells, & Peterson, 1989, p. 21). Nicholas Hobbs (1962) refers to this process as adopting or inventing a *personal cosmology.* Two requirements for a person's cosmology to be effective are (1) that it is convincing to the person who owns it and (2) that it overlaps reasonably with the cosmologies of the people with whom the person associates (otherwise, he or she might be labeled abnormal or mentally ill). The goal of psychotherapy, then, is not to help clients find reality as it *really is* but to help clients construct a reality for themselves that allows them to get along satisfactorily in their world (McNamee & Gergen, 1992). For Paul Watzlawick (1990b), "Successful therapy consists in changing the reality that somebody has constructed for him/herself—a reality that is painful—to a reality that is less painful" (p. xxx).

If we accept the notion of a subjective reality, we can appreciate why it is useful for people to create what Shelley Taylor (1989) calls *positive illusions.* Positive illusions generally fall into three categories (Taylor, 1989; Taylor & Brown, 1988): (1) unrealistically positive views of oneself, (2) illusions of control, and (3) unrealistic optimism.

Unrealistically positive views of oneself A large body of research indicates that people tend to give themselves the benefit of doubt when judging their personal assets and qualities, accomplishments, and potentialities. Most people see themselves as better than average and as better than others see them (Taylor & Brown, 1988).

Illusions of control A sense of personal control is an important ingredient in one's sense of self-esteem and confidence. However, most people tend to believe they have greater control over events in their life than they actually do (Langer, 1975).

Unrealistic optimism An optimistic attitude toward life is a desirable value that will be discussed later in this chapter. Research studies indicate that most people are optimistic and hold unrealistically positive views of the future (Taylor & Brown, 1988).

The significance of people constructing their own realities was also recognized by Greenwald (1980), who points out that people's views of themselves and their environments are influenced by three cognitive biases.

1. *Egocentricity:* The egocentricity bias refers to the tendency to perceive oneself as more central to life events than one really is. People place themselves at the focus of happenings in the world. They interpret events in terms of their own self-interest. People also overestimate their own importance and influence over things that occur in their life.

2. *Positive self-bias:* People engage in a positive self-bias because they are more willing to admit responsibility for positive actions than they are to recognize their negative actions. Generally speaking, people (1) give themselves more credit than they give to others for desirable behaviors, and (2) blame others more than they blame themselves for undesirable behaviors.

3. *Confirmation bias:* People confirm their egocentricity and positive self-bias by perceiving and interpreting their world in a selective manner. In other words, they use information that comes to them in a way that will create the kind of self-image they want to achieve.

What is important about positive illusions and cognitive biases is that they are developed to their fullest extent by people who are generally well-adjusted and satisfied with their lives. The construction of positive illusions appears to be an adaptive coping style. People who are depressed, anxious, and otherwise unsatisfied with their life seem preoccupied with negative thinking. They have a tendency to exaggerate what is bad about their life. These maladjusted individuals also lack the ability to protect themselves from the harsh experiences of life by creating satisfactory positive illusions (Taylor, 1989; Taylor &

Brown, 1988). For this reason, it is reasonable to suggest that it may be helpful and adaptive for people to engage in a certain amount of creative self-deception (Taylor, 1989).

Creative self-deception is accomplished in several ways (Taylor, 1989; Taylor & Brown, 1988). People maximize positive feedback by selecting friends and acquaintances who reinforce their beliefs. People seek out situations and challenges that emphasize their positive qualities and show themselves in a good light. People manage negative feedback with a variety of cognitive maneuvers. They selectively "tune in" what they want to see and hear and "tune out" information that does not please them. People's belief systems are also reinforced by selectively remembering life events in a way that is congruent with their beliefs. If necessary, people can modify their beliefs to fit harsh realities in a way that maintains the continuity of their worldview. People can also deal with indisputable negative information about themselves by acknowledging particular areas of incompetence as real but not of major importance.

To appreciate the value of positive illusions, one must distinguish them from the defenses of denial and repression. *Denial* refers to the blocking out of a fact or event as if it never happened. Denial and positive illusions are different; denial alters life events, whereas positive illusions accept life events but interpret them in a positive light (Taylor, 1989, p. 126). In other words, denial distorts facts, whereas positive illusions allow people to make the best of bad situations by viewing them from a favorable perspective. *Repression* is the inhibition or blocking of negative feelings. Repression is a rigid defensive style because it involves taking a careful and cautious approach toward life in which one's creativity is greatly inhibited. Positive illusions, on the other hand, are built by acknowledging and then creatively making sense of positive and negative events in one's life.

Whereas denial and repression are characterized by inflexibility, the creation of positive illusions is characterized by flexibility. Repression and denial are defense mechanisms that are invoked in response to anxiety and threat. Positive illusions, on the other hand, can be viewed as offensive mechanisms that enhance people's views of themselves, the world, and life's possibilities (Sackeim, 1983). Positive illusions don't inhibit growth and change the way that repression and denial do (Taylor & Brown, 1988, p. 204). Positive illusions inspire perseverance and help people organize the complexity of positive and negative events in their life in a way that provides a sense of security and organization (Greenwald, 1980). The last thing therapists would want to do is encourage their clients to solve their problems with repression and denial. However, assisting clients to develop positive illusions that are compatible with their desire to find meaning in their lives and to develop a satisfactory assumptive world (see Chapter 1) is a viable therapeutic enterprise.

OPTIMISM

Research demonstrating the power of positive illusions reinforces the value of having an optimistic outlook on life. Optimism is an expectation that one can achieve success. This may require persistence, flexibility, development of skills, and even redefinition or modification of goals. Given their willingness to expend these efforts, optimists anticipate that the outcome of their endeavors will be favorable. Scheier and Carver (1985) developed the Life Orientation Test to measure optimism. This test contains the following items.

1. In uncertain times, I usually expect the best.
2. If something can go wrong for me, it will.
3. I always look on the bright side of things.
4. I'm always optimistic about my future.
5. I hardly ever expect things to go my way.
6. Things never work out the way I want them to.
7. I'm a believer in the idea that "every cloud has a silver lining."
8. I rarely count on good things happening to me.

Optimists tend to agree with items 1, 3, 4, and 7 and to disagree with items 2, 5, 6, and 8.

Research has shown that optimists know how to use effective coping strategies such as problem solving, seeking social support, and emphasizing the positive aspects of a stressful situation (Scheier, Weintraub, & Carver, 1986). Optimists are extraverted and their moods are positive (Marshall et al., 1992). Pessimists, in contrast, confront life challenges with denial, avoidance, and an undue amount of emotional distress. Pessimists are characterized by what can be called neuroticism or negative affectivity (Marshall et al., 1992; Smith et al., 1989; Watson & Clark, 1984). They are chronically distressed and worried, they have a negative view of their capabilities, and they dwell on their failures and shortcomings. Optimists have learned to overcome negative affectivity. They know how to find contentment in life by making judicious use of positive illusions. As a result of their effective coping strategies, optimists have fewer health problems than pessimists do, and they adjust more effectively than pessimists do to stressful life situations (Scheier & Carver, 1985; 1987).

Another way to understand optimism is in terms of people's styles of explaining negative events in their life according to the factors of internality, stability, and globality (Peterson & Villanova, 1988; Peterson et al., 1982).

Internality refers to the degree to which people take personal responsibility for negative life events. Pessimists tend to attribute the cause of negative events to themselves. They find a way to blame themselves when things go wrong. Optimists are able to attain a more judicious blend of dividing responsibility for negative events between their own responsibilities and external factors beyond their control. They don't make the kinds of premature cognitive commitments that were described earlier in the section on mindfulness.

Stability is the belief that negative events experienced today will always be present. Pessimists believe their sources of unhappiness and discontent will never go away. They see no light at the end of the tunnel. Optimists interpret negative life events as unpleasant challenges that must be dealt with but that are not permanent. They know how to avoid using words such as *always* and *never.*

Globality is the tendency to overgeneralize negative events to all aspects of one's life. For example, pessimists view a personal loss as something that will affect all aspects of their life. Optimists are more able to place a loss into perspective by viewing it as an unhappy experience but not one that will prevent them from reaching goals and accomplishments independent of what was lost.

People's use of stability, internality, and globality for explaining negative events appears to be a relatively stable characteristic (Burns & Seligman, 1989)—unless it is challenged in psychotherapy. Compared with optimists, people with pessimistic explanatory styles are less likely to accomplish satisfactory achievements and are more likely to be depressed, have low self-esteem, and suffer from health problems (Peterson, 1988; Peterson & Barrett, 1987; Peterson & Seligman, 1987; Peterson, Seligman, & Vaillant, 1988; Pillow, West, & Reich, 1991; Seligman, 1991).

POSSIBLE SELVES

Most people would agree on the value of having a positive self-image and high self-esteem. Research on positive illusions demonstrates that human beings strive to maintain a sense of personal value in the face of threats, challenges, and other negative experiences that confront them during their life. Although the literature on self-esteem is too vast to summarize in this section, several points can be made that are particularly relevant to psychotherapy.

To begin, people need to appreciate the fact that their self-concepts are not bestowed upon them; they are created. "People often say that this or that person has not yet found himself. But the self is not something one finds; it is something one creates" (Szasz, 1973, p. 49). A person's self-image is certainly affected by past experiences, and it may be of value to explore the process of how one has developed into her or his present self. What is more important, however, is to realize that one's self is not fixed and immutable. First, we have a variety of possible selves we can choose to emphasize to fit particular situations. Second, we are not bound to our perceptions of who we are in the present. The future offers the opportunity for our selves to evolve in whatever directions we choose to follow. Carl Rogers (1951) recognized the goal of growing toward one's ideal self. Higgins (1987) developed a theory explaining the need to reconcile one's actual self, ideal self, and ought self. Stanley Graham (1980, p. 371) described the ultimate goal of psychotherapy as reconciling the client's "who I am" with "who I wish to be."

Markus and Nurius (1986) use the term *possible selves* to make the point that people's selves are fluid and dynamic. Their research shows that people's feelings of self-esteem, positive affect, and hope are related to their self-perceptions in the present. However, these feelings are also strongly tied to people's views about what is possible in the future. In other words, although our feelings about ourselves and our lives are certainly influenced by our present situation, they are also affected to a substantial degree by our expectations of what we can achieve. The notion of possible selves is relevant to psychotherapy because it implies that learning to view oneself as fluid and ever-developing rather than as fixed and immutable can provide a strong sense of hope (see Chapter 2). Psychotherapists are not limited to helping clients define their problems in the present. They can also assist clients in outlining possibilities for the future. Psychotherapists can encourage their clients to realize that they are not shackled by their past experiences or limited to their present situation. Clients need to develop possible selves that provide hope and encouragement and inspire achievements rather than possible selves characterized by negativism and pessimism that result in fear and avoidance.

How can therapists help clients achieve possible selves that will inspire them to use their full potentialities? Research studies have made it quite clear that it is not helpful to persuade people to look at themselves in a different light (Markus & Nurius, 1986, p. 964). People tend to believe that, if only they had higher self-esteem, they would be able to reach higher achievements. They lose sight of the fact that self-esteem does not result in achievements; rather, it is achievements that boost self-esteem (Kleinke, 1978). Instead of appealing to clients on an intellectual level, therapists need to approach them behaviorally. If clients could find themselves acting *as if* they were their ideal selves, increased self-esteem would be sure to follow (see Chapter 1).

SOCIAL INTEREST

People generally will be most content if they can find a comfortable balance between their self-interests and their interest in others. Baumeister (1991) provides an historical account of how people have become more preoccupied with themselves during the past century. In earlier times, a person's sense of value and purpose came largely from religion, tradition, and allegiance to one's family. Concern with oneself was discouraged and viewed with disdain. More recently, religion, tradition, and the extended family have diminished as sources of value, and individualism has been promoted through the emergence of capitalism and populist governments. The self has taken on the role of providing value and purpose in life and of determining right from wrong. Rather than being a vice, concern with oneself is now a virtue.

Given the nature of our present world, an adaptive pattern is to develop a sense of self and to pursue one's interests. Assertiveness is a useful coping skill, and people are often required to rely on themselves for direction. However, it is a mistake to focus on oneself to the exclusion of other people. The self is an important resource for value and fulfillment, but it needs reinforcement and support from others. People who expect too much from themselves often end up anxious and depressed (Seligman, 1988). The "Me" ethic of the 1970s and 1980s gave people the false impression that they could become their own source of gratification. The overemphasis on individualism encouraged unrealistic expectations, which resulted in alienation, or what Cushman (1990) called an *empty self*. Upon finding that a self-centered approach toward life did not provide sufficient meaning, people attempted to fill their personal voids by involving themselves with fads, cults, and drugs (Bugental & Bracke, 1992; Lasch, 1978).

Since we live in a world in which our life is affected so much by others, we need to learn how to get along with others. Harry Stack Sullivan (1940, p. 32) points out that a person's self "can never be isolated from the complex of interpersonal relations in which the person lives." For this reason, Markus and Cross (1990) view the self as an *interpersonal self* because other people contribute to its construction as well as to its evaluation and maintenance. Alfred Adler (1964) regarded an interest in other people as a prerequisite for personal adjustment. Research studies indicate that social interest can provide many of the benefits that Adler suggested (Crandall, 1980, 1984; Crandall & Putman, 1980): (1) social interest is associated with an active and effective approach toward confronting life problems, (2) social interest provides an opportunity to develop and benefit from support systems, (3) social interest provides an enhanced sense of meaning in life, (4) social interest broadens one's activities and opportunities for achieving accomplishments and satisfaction, and (5) social interest is a useful distraction from negative events and daily hassles.

FORGIVENESS

The concept of forgiveness is conspicuously absent from most textbooks on psychotherapy. This is interesting given the power of forgiveness in helping people reconcile themselves with harmful events in their lives. Organized religions recognize the value of teaching people the virtues of forgiveness (Szasz, 1985b). Perhaps psychotherapists shy away from the word *forgiveness* because of its religious connotations. Forgiveness, however, is quite relevant to psychotherapy, not for religious or moralistic reasons, but because it provides a sense of empowerment and meaning during times of suffering.

Forgiving Others

Forgiving another person for a transgression does not mean accepting that person's actions as legitimate or relieving the person of responsibility. Forgiving also does not necessarily mean forgetting (Flanigan, 1992). Forgiveness is a method of coping with experiences of harm. It reflects a life philosophy that says:

- Even though a person's behavior is harmful, that does not make him or her a bad person.
- Even though bad things happen in this world, it does not mean that the world is bad.

When people are harmed by others, they need to consider their possible responses and the consequences of these responses. Forgiveness is often a viable option.

Forgiving Oneself

When people harm themselves or others, they will cope better if they accept their behaviors as undesirable but refrain from branding themselves as bad or undesirable people (Ellis, 1962). Self-blame is not a beneficial coping strategy (Kleinke, 1991). People need to take responsibility for their actions, but, to feel good about themselves, they need to forgive themselves for their shortcomings.

Forgiving Clients

It is unlikely that a therapist would say to a client "I forgive you." However, by establishing a relationship characterized by acceptance, empathy, and trust, therapists communicate an attitude of accreditation (Schwartz, 1979) and of forgiving their clients for being fallible human beings (Ellis, 1962).

THE SEARCH FOR MEANING

Thomas Szasz (1985a) makes the analogy between psychotherapy and religion by suggesting that both psychotherapy and religion provide answers to the questions "What are we here for?" and "What are we good for?" As Szasz puts it, "The making, explaining, teaching, and debunking of meaning is as old as mankind." Nicholas Hobbs (1962) explains the value of searching for meaning in psychotherapy.

> The individual has got to have a cognitive house to live in to protect himself from the incomprehensibilities of existence as well as to provide some architecture for daily experiencing. He has to build defenses against the absurd in the human condition and at the same time find a scheme that will make possible reasonably accurate predictions of his own behavior and the behavior of his wife, his boss, his professor, his physician, his neighbor, and of the policeman on the corner. He must adopt or invent a personal cosmology. (p. 746)

In his book *Meanings of Life*, Roy Baumeister (1991) outlines four things people seek to make their lives meaningful: purpose, value, efficacy, and self-worth.

Purpose

Purpose answers the question "Why should I exist unless I'm going to accomplish something or make some kind of contribution?" Baumeister (1991) points out that there can be purposes that people intend to reach during their lifetime and purposes to which people contribute for the sake of future generations. Purpose gives meaning to life by orienting people toward goals and fulfillments.

Goals   Goals are generally defined as something tangible the person wishes to accomplish. Finding meaning in the achievement of goals requires a number of skills that clients might need to work on in therapy. First, goals must be challenging enough to provide a sense of pride but at the same time must be realistic. Second, goals must be planned in small steps. Usually the most effective technique is to set up a series of small goals leading toward the final goal rather than withholding all self-satisfaction until a long-term goal is achieved (Bandura & Schunk, 1981). A third requirement for achieving goals is to ensure that one has the necessary skills and knowledge. If not, some time and effort must be given for these to be mastered. Finally, it is important that one learn how to cope with failure (Kleinke, 1991). Knowing how to cope with failure helps people avoid becoming underachievers and adopting maladaptive self-handicapping strategies.

Fulfillments   Whereas goals are usually defined by their outcome, fulfillments are the pleasures that occur during the process of working toward goals. Fulfillments are based less on tangible outcomes and more on the intrinsic satisfaction of having a purpose to work toward in life.

Baumeister (1991) makes two points about the concept of purpose, which have implications for working with clients in psychotherapy.

First, a client's sense of purpose is related to his or her stage of development (see Chapter 9). Important life events, such as marriage, having children, reaching a plateau in one's job, divorcing, or having one's children grow up and move away often create crises for one's sense of purpose that necessitate some careful planning about where a person wishes to direct his or her energies. Second, since the concept of purpose is highly subjective, it is, in some sense, a myth. People need to learn to avoid the pitfall of assuming that, if only a particular goal could be achieved, everything would be fine and they would have no problems. In addition, people must be disabused of the beliefs that they *should* have a purpose in life and that their personal value depends on it. A life purpose is not something hidden that people have to discover in order to be happy. A purpose in life is something people create to suit themselves, and it is modified to accommodate whatever situation a person happens to find herself or himself in at a given time.

Value

Values provide people with a sense of stability and predictability in life. Value can be defined in terms of two concepts: justification and morality.

Justification   People want to feel that their actions are justified, and they devote a great deal of energy toward presenting themselves in a socially acceptable manner, both to themselves (Greenwald, 1980; Taylor, 1989) and to others (Goffman, 1959; Schlenker, 1980). To put it another way, people have a need to view what they do as *legitimate.*

Morality   Morality is a necessary concept in civilized societies for preserving order and safety for citizens. A moral principle outlined in the U.S. Constitution, for example, is the sanctity of life, liberty, and personal property.

The search for value has a number of implications for working with clients in psychotherapy. First is the goal of helping clients identify values that give their lives meaning. As Viktor Frankl (1963) so eloquently explained, one's life has meaning only to the extent that one has values. And the ultimate definition of one's life meaning are the values for which one is willing to die. People need to feel they are living and striving "for the sake of something" and this "something" can be the topic of fruitful exploration in a therapeutic relationship. Another challenge for psychotherapists is to help clients create a sense of value when they have engaged in socially unacceptable behaviors. The goal is to find the appropriate balance between restitution, atonement, forgiveness, and self-responsibility.

Efficacy

Efficacy refers to people's need to feel that they have some control over events in their life. It is the desire to make a difference and to feel capable and strong. A person's sense of efficacy is developed by pursuing goals that are sufficiently difficult to be challenging but not so difficult as to result in failure. The concept of self-efficacy was defined in Chapter 2 as a common goal in psychotherapy, and many suggestions were given about how a client's self-efficacy can be enhanced through the process of psychotherapy.

Self-Worth

People need to feel that they have value and that their existence is of some worth. The need for value is somewhat more easily satisfied in cultures in which a person's status is clearly defined. People in these cultures have a sense of where they fit by the nature of their social status. In societies such as the United States, status hierarchies are vague, and people face ambiguity when seeking the answer to their value. This ambiguity causes many people to be in a state of perpetual insecurity about their self-worth (Derber, 1979, p. 90). Three criteria for self-worth commonly used in the United States are wealth, beauty, and power. People who possess these attributes may find satisfaction in their quest for personal value. Unfortunately, wealth, beauty, and power are often not permanent, and basing one's self-worth on these criteria poses some risk. Those who adopt these standards for valuing themselves but don't possess them are doomed to a considerable amount of stress, frustration, and dissatisfaction.

One solution to the dilemma of defining one's value is to follow Albert Ellis' advice about avoiding the temptation to rate oneself in the first place (Ellis, 1962; Ellis & Dryden, 1987). Ellis urges people to accept themselves unconditionally as "fallible human beings who do not have to act other than they do and as too complex and fluid to be given any legitimate or global rating" (Ellis & Dryden, 1987, p. 18). In Ellis' view, people engage in behaviors that can be judged as good or bad, but people themselves are unratable. Unfortunately, Ellis' philosophy is in one sense too simple and in another sense too elegant for many people to adopt. We are bombarded daily with advertisements that are based on the philosophy that people *are* ratable and that if they smoke a certain kind of cigarette, drink a particular brand of beer, wear the latest fashions, or drive a special car, they can increase their value. It seems almost impossible in our society to overcome the notion that people are ratable and that they should devote considerable effort toward enhancing their personal value.

If therapists can't convince their clients to refuse to rate themselves, they can hopefully teach them that a sense of self is developed not by capitulating to social pressures but through one's personal creativity (Szasz, 1973, p. 49). A good place to start is by developing a multidimensional image of oneself (Linville, 1985; 1987). This image is created by acquiring a wide range of skills and interests so that one's self-image is not dependent on only one or two factors. One must also avoid making the mistake of basing one's self-value on other people's opinions or actions. Another strategy for placing one's self-worth into perspective, and one that has been used throughout the ages, is *downward comparision*—comparing oneself with less fortunate others (Wills, 1981; 1987a).

FUTURE DIRECTIONS FOR PSYCHOTHERAPY

The Spring 1992 issue of the journal *Psychotherapy* was dedicated to the 100th anniversary of psychotherapy and was devoted toward looking at psychotherapy's future. A survey of 75 leading psychotherapists concluded that psychotherapy will become more directive, psychoeducational, present-centered, problem-focused, and briefer during the next decade (Norcross, Alford, & DeMichele, 1992). Specific areas that were predicted to increase in emphasis were self-change and problem-solving techniques, audio and video feedback, homework assignments, communication skills, cognitive restructuring, in vivo exposure, and training in assertiveness, social skills, and self-control. Respondents to the survey predicted that, during the next decade, psychotherapists will place less emphasis on aversive techniques and will rely less on approaches that are long term, unstructured, historically oriented, and preoccupied with the use of interpretations. Two other points were also emphasized by authors writing in this journal. First, it will become more important to match therapists and clients so they can work effectively in a collaborative relationship. Second, there will be increased attention given to development and implementation of specific methods for helping clients with specific problems (Lazarus, Beutler, & Norcross, 1992).

SUMMARY

Psychotherapy is a value-laden enterprise, and therapists must ask how they can help (and not harm) people through psychotherapy. Perry London outlines the importance of values in psychotherapy by pointing out that psychotherapists have both a scientific and a moralistic function. Thomas Szasz emphasizes therapists' moralistic function by defining psychotherapy as applied secular ethics. A national survey indicated that psychotherapists have high agreement on the following values: (1) sensitivity to feelings; (2) freedom, autonomy, and responsibility; (3) development of successful coping strategies; (4) self-awareness and growth; (5) human relatedness and interpersonal and family commitment; (6) self-maintenance and physical fitness; and (7) having principles, ideals, and a purpose for living. Hans Strupp proposes the following values for psychotherapy: (1) personal freedom and independence; (2) rights and privileges as well as responsibilities; (3) avoidance of undue dependence on others; (4) respect for people's individuality and avoidance of control, domination, and coercion; (5) the right to learn from one's mistakes and experiences; and (6) the value of solving one's own problems. Twelve values suggested for consideration in this chapter include: autonomy, learned resourcefulness, sense of coherence, mindfulness, flexibility, taking a salutogenic approach, happiness, positive illusions, optimism, possible selves, social interest, and forgiveness.

Thomas Szasz made the analogy between psychotherapy and religion by pointing out that they are both oriented toward helping people find meaning in their life. To make their lives meaningful, people seek purpose, value, efficacy, and self-worth.

A survey of leading psychotherapists concluded that psychotherapy will become more directive, psychoeducational, present-centered, problem-focused, and briefer during the next decade. Respondents to the survey predicted that, during the next decade, psychotherapists will place less emphasis on aversive techniques and will rely less on approaches that are long term, unstructured, historically oriented, and preoccupied with the use of interpretations. In the future it will become more important to match therapists and clients so that they can work effectively in a collaborative relationship. There will also be increased attention given to development and implementation of specific methods for helping clients with specific problems.

SUGGESTIONS FOR FURTHER READING

Baumeister, R. F. (1991). *Meanings of life.* New York: Guilford.

Friedman, H. S. (1991). *The self-healing personality.* New York: Henry Holt.

Langer, E. J. (1989). *Mindfulness.* Reading, MA: Addison-Wesley.

Seligman, M. E. P. (1991). *Learned optimism.* New York: Knopf.

Szasz, T. S. (1973). *The second sin.* Garden City, NY: Anchor Press. (Republished as *The untamed tongue* by Open Court Publishing Company, La Salle, IL, 1990.)

Taylor, S. E. (1989). *Positive illusions: Creative self-deception and the healthy mind.* New York: Basic Books.

References

Achenbach, T. M. (1986). The developmental study of psychopathology: Implications for psychotherapy and behavior change. In S. L. Garfield and A. E. Bergin (Eds.), *Handbook of psychotherapy and behavior change* (pp. 117–154). New York: Wiley.

Ackerley, G. D., Burnell, J., Holder, D. C., & Kurdek, L. A. (1988). Burnout among licensed psychologists. *Professional Psychology: Research and Practice, 19,* 624–631.

Adler, A. (1964). *Social interest: A challenge to mankind.* New York: Capricorn Books. (Originally published 1938.)

Aichorn, A. (1943). *Wayward youth.* New York: Viking Press. (Original work published in German 1925.)

Albee, G. W. (1990). The futility of psychotherapy. *The Journal of Mind and Behavior, 11,* 369–384.

Alexander, F., & French, T. M. (1946). *Psychoanalytic therapy: Principles and application.* New York: Ronald Press

Alexander, L. B., & Luborsky, L. (1986). The Penn Helping Alliance Scales. In L. S. Greenberg and W. M. Pinsof (Eds.), *The psychotherapeutic process: A research handbook* (pp. 325–366). New York: Guilford.

Allport, G. W. (1958). *The individual and his religion.* New York: Macmillan.

American Counseling Association. (1988). Ethical standards. *Journal of Counseling and Development, 67,* 4–8.

American Medical Association. (1988). *House of Delegates resolution regarding AIDS.* Chicago: Author.

American Psychiatric Association. (1980). *Diagnostic and statistical manual of mental disorders* (3rd ed.). Washington, DC: American Psychiatric Association.

American Psychiatric Association. (1987). *Diagnostic and statistical manual of mental disorders* (3rd ed., Revised). Washington, DC: American Psychiatric Association.

American Psychological Association. (1992). Ethical principles of psychologists and code of conduct. *American Psychologist, 47,* 1597–1611.

Andersen, B., & Anderson, W. (1985). Client perceptions of counselors using positive and negative self-involving statements. *Journal of Counseling Psychology, 32,* 462–465.

Anderson, C. M., & Stewart, S., (1983). *Mastering resistance: A practical guide to family therapy.* New York: Guilford.

Anderson, H., & Goolishian, H. (1992). The client is the expert: A not-knowing approach to therapy. In S. McNamee and K. J. Gergen (Eds.), *Therapy as social construction* (pp. 25–53). Newbury Park, CA: Sage.

Anderson, M. P. (1980). Imaginal processes: Therapeutic applications and theoretical models. In M. J. Mahoney (Ed.), *Psychotherapy processes: Current issues and future directions* (pp. 211–248). New York: Plenum.

Angus, L. E., & Rennie, D. L. (1988). Therapist participation in metaphor generation: Collaborative and noncollaborative styles. *Psychotherapy, 25,* 552–560.

Annas, G. (1987). Medicolegal dilemma: The HIV-positive patient who won't tell the spouse. *Medical Aspects of Human Sexuality, 2,* 16.

Ansbacher, H. L., & Ansbacher, R. R. (Eds.). (1956). *The individual psychology of Alfred Adler.* New York: Basic Books.

Ansbacher, H. L., & Ansbacher, R. R. (1967). *The individual psychology of Alfred Adler.* New York: Harper & Row.

Antonovsky, A. (1979). *Health, stress, and coping: New perspectives on mental and physical well-being.* San Francisco: Jossey-Bass.

Antonovsky, A. (1990). Pathways leading to successful coping and health. In M. Rosenbaum (Ed.), *Learned resourcefulness: On coping skills, self-control, and adaptive behavior* (pp. 31–63). New York: Springer.

Appelbaum, S. A. (1988). Psychoanalytic therapy: A subset of healing. *Psychotherapy, 25,* 201–208.

Arkowitz, H. (1992). Integrative theories of therapy. In D. K. Freedheim (Ed.), *History of psychotherapy: A century of change* (pp. 261–303). Washington, DC: American Psychological Association.

Arkowitz, H., & Hannah, M. T. (1989). Cognitive, behavioral, and psychodynamic therapies: Converging or diverging pathways to change? In A. Freeman, K. Simon, L. E. Beutler, and H. Arkowitz (Eds.), *Comprehensive handbook of cognitive therapy* (pp. 143–168). New York: Plenum.

Atkinson, D. R., Morten, G., & Sue, D. W. (1989). *Counseling American minorities* (3rd ed.). Dubuque, IA: William C. Brown.

Auld, F., & Hyman, M. (1991). *Resolution of inner conflict: An introduction to psychoanalytic therapy.* Washington, DC: American Psychological Association.

Baker, S. B., Johnson, E., Strout, N. J., Kopala, M., & Pricken, P. A. (1986). Effects of separate and combined overt and covert practice modes on counseling trainee competence and motivation. *Journal of Counseling Psychology, 33,* 469–470.

Baker, S. B., Scofield, M. E., Clayton, L. T., & Munson, W. W. (1984). Microskills practice versus mental practice training for competence in decision-making counseling. *Journal of Counseling Psychology, 31,* 104–107.

Bandura, A. (1969). *Principles of behavior modification.* New York: Holt, Rinehart & Winston.

Bandura, A. (1977). Self-efficacy: Toward a unifying theory of behavioral change. *Psychological Review, 84,* 191–215.

Bandura, A. (1982). Self-efficacy mechanism in human agency. *American Psychologist, 37,* 122–147.

Bandura, A. (1989). Human agency in social cognitive theory. *American Psychologist, 44,* 1175–1184.

Bandura, A., & Cervone, D. (1983). Self-evaluative and self-efficacy mechanisms governing the motivational effects of global systems. *Journal of Personality and Social Psychology, 45,* 1017–1028.

Bandura, A., & Schunk, D. H. (1981). Cultivating competence, self-efficacy, and intrinsic interest through proximal self-motivation. *Journal of Personality and Social Psychology, 41,* 586–598.

Barak, A., Patkin, J., & Dell, D. M. (1982). Effects of certain counselor behaviors on perceived expertness and attractiveness. *Journal of Counseling Psychology, 29,* 261–267.

Barker, P. (1985). *Using metaphors in psychotherapy.* New York: Brunner/Mazel.

Barkham, M., & Shapiro, D. A. (1986). Counselor verbal response modes and experienced empathy. *Journal of Counseling Psychology, 33,* 3–10.

Basch, M. F. (1992). *Practicing psychotherapy.* New York: Basic Books.

Basescu, S. (1990). Show and tell: Reflections on the analyst's self-disclosure. In G. Stricker and M. Fisher (Eds.), *Self-disclosure in the therapeutic relationship* (pp. 48–59). New York: Plenum.

Batchelor, A. (1988). How clients perceive therapist empathy: A content analysis of "received" empathy. *Psychotherapy, 25,* 227–240.

Bauer, G. P., & Kobos, J. C. (1984). Short-term psychodynamic psychotherapy: Reflections on the past and current practice. *Psychotherapy, 21,* 153–170.

Bauer, G. P., & Mills, J. A. (1989). Use of transference in the here and now: Patient and therapist resistance. *Psychotherapy, 26,* 112–119.

Baumeister, R. F. (1991). *Escaping the self.* New York: Basic Books.

Baumeister, R. F. (1991). *Meanings of life.* New York: Guilford.

Beck, A. T. (1967). *Depression: Clinical, experimental, and theoretical aspects.* New York: Harper & Row. (Republished as *Depression: Causes and treatment.* Philadelphia: University of Pennsylvania Press, 1972.)

Beck, A. T. (1976). *Cognitive therapy and the emotional disorders.* New York: International Universities Press.

Beck, A. T. (1985). *Conversation hour with Aaron T. Beck.* Audiotape (L330-CH1) from the Evolution of Psychotherapy Conference, Phoenix, AZ. Phoenix, AZ: Milton Erickson Foundation.

Beck, A. T., Freeman, A., & Associates. (1990). *Cognitive therapy of personality disorders.* New York: Guilford.

Beck, J. (1987). The psychotherapists' duty to protect third parties from harm. *Mental Disability Law Reporter, 11,* 141–148.

Beck, J. T., & Strong, S. R. (1982). Stimulating therapeutic change with interpretations: A comparison of positive and negative connotation. *Journal of Counseling Psychology, 29,* 551–559.

Bednar, R. L., Wells, M. G., & Peterson, S. R. (1989). *Self-esteem: Paradoxes and implications in clinical theory and practice.* Washington, DC: American Psychological Association.

Bedrosian, R. C., & Beck, A. T. (1980). Principles of cognitive therapy. In M. J.

Mahoney (Ed.), *Psychotherapy process: Current issues and future directions* (pp. 127–152). New York: Plenum.

Bennett, M. J., & Wisneski, M. J. (1979). Continuous psychotherapy within an HMO. *American Journal of Psychiatry, 136,* 1283–1287.

Berg, J. H. (1987). Responsiveness and self-disclosure. In V. J. Derlega and J. H. Berg (Eds.), *Self-disclosure: Theory, research, and therapy* (pp. 101–130). New York: Plenum.

Berg, J. H., & Archer, R. L. (1980). Disclosure or concern: A second look at liking for the norm-breaker. *Journal of Personality, 48,* 245–257.

Bergin, A. E. (1980). Psychotherapy and religious values. *Journal of Consulting and Clinical Psychology, 48,* 95–105.

Berglas, S. (1989). Self-handicapping behavior and the self-defeating personality disorder: Toward a refined clinical perspective. In R. L. Curtis (Ed.), *Self-defeating behaviors: Experimental research, clinical impressions, and practical implications* (pp. 261–288).

Berlin, R. M., Olson, M. E., Cano, C. E., & Engel, S. (1991). Metaphor and psychotherapy. *American Journal of Psychotherapy, 45,* 359–367.

Bernstein, H. A. (1981). Survey of threats and assaults directed toward psychotherapists. *American Journal of Psychotherapy, 35,* 542–549.

Beutler, L. E. (1979). Toward specific psychological therapies for specific conditions. *Journal of Consulting and Clinical Psychology, 47,* 882–897.

Beutler, L. E. (1990). Systematic eclectic psychotherapy. In J. K. Zeig and W. M. Munion (Eds.), *What is psychotherapy? Contemporary perspectives* (pp. 225–233). San Francisco: Jossey-Bass.

Beutler, L. E., & Clarkin, J. (1990). *Systematic treatment selection: Toward targeted therapeutic interventions.* New York: Brunner/Mazel.

Beutler, L. E., Clarkin, J., Crago, M., & Bergen, J. (1991). Client-therapist matching. In C. R. Snyder and D. R. Forsyth (Eds.), *Handbook of social and clinical psychology* (pp. 699–716). New York: Pergamon.

Beutler, L. E., Crago, M., & Arizmendi, T. G. (1986). Therapist variables in psychotherapy process and outcome. In S. L. Garfield & A. E. Bergin (Eds.), *Handbook of psychotherapy and behavior change* (pp. 257–310). New York: Wiley.

Blau, T. J. (1988). *Psychotherapy tradecraft: The technique and style of doing therapy.* New York: Brunner/Mazel.

Bolter, K., Levenson, H., & Alvarez, W. (1990). Differences in values between short-term and long-term therapists. *Professional Psychology: Research and Practice, 21,* 285–290.

Bongar, B., Markey, L. A., & Peterson, L. G. (1991). Views on the difficult and dreaded patient: A preliminary investigation. *Medical Psychotherapy, 4,* 9–16.

Bordin, E. S. (1979). The generalizability of the psychoanalytic concept of the working alliance. *Psychotherapy: Research and Practice, 16,* 252–260.

Borys, D. S., & Pope, K. S. (1989). Dual relationships between therapist and client: A national study of psychologists, psychiatrists, and social workers. *Professional Psychology: Research and Practice, 20,* 283–293.

Botkin, D. J., & Nietzel, M. T. (1987). How therapists manage potentially dangerous clients: Toward a standard of care for psychotherapists. *Professional Psychology: Research and Practice, 18,* 84–86.

Bouhoutsos, J., Holroyd, J., Lerman, H., Forer, B. R., & Greenberg, M. (1983). Sexual intimacy between psychotherapists and patients. *Professional Psychology: Research and Practice, 14*, 185–196.

Brady, J. P., Davison, G. C., Dewald, P. A., Egan, G., Fadiman, J., Frank, J. D., Gil, M. M., Hoffman, I., Kempler, W., Lazarus, A. A., Raimy, V., Rotter, J. B., & Strupp, H. H. (1980). Some views on effective principles of psychotherapy. *Cognitive Therapy and Research, 4*, 271–306.

Brajinsky, B. M., & Brajinsky, D. D. (1974). *Mainstream psychology: A critique.* New York: Holt, Rinehart & Winston.

Bray, J. H., Shepard, J. N., & Hays, J. R. (1985). Legal and ethical issues in informed consent to psychotherapy. *The American Journal of Family Therapy, 13*, 50–60.

Breggin, P. R. (1991). *Toxic psychiatry.* New York: St. Martin's Press.

Brehm, J. W. (1966). *A theory of psychological reactance.* New York: Academic Press.

Brehm, S. S., & Brehm, J. W. (1981). *Psychological Reactance: A theory of freedom and control.* New York: Academic Press.

Brehm, S. S., & Smith, T. W. (1986). Social psychological approaches to psychotherapy and behavior change. In S. L. Garfield & A. E. Bergin (Eds.), *Handbook of psychotherapy and behavior change* (pp. 69–115). New York: Wiley.

Brickman, P., Coates, D., & Janoff-Bulman, R. (1978). Lottery winners and accident victims: Is happiness relative? *Journal of Personality and Social Psychology, 36*, 917–927.

Brickman, P., Rabinowitz, V. C., Karuza, J., Coates, D., Cohn, E., & Kidder, Ł. (1982). Models of helping and coping. *American Psychologist, 37*, 368–384.

Brown, L. S. (1985). Harmful effects of posttermination sexual and romantic relationships between therapists and their former clients. *Psychotherapy, 25*, 249–255.

Brown, L. S. (1986). Gender-role analysis: A neglected component of psychological assessment. *Psychotherapy: Theory, Research, Practice, Training, 23*, 243–248.

Brown, L. S. (1990). Taking account of gender in the clinical assessment interview. *Professional Psychology: Research and Practice, 21*, 12–17.

Brown, P. (1990). The name game: Toward a sociology of diagnosis. *The Journal of Mind and Behavior, 11*, 385–406.

Buckley, P., Karasu, T. B., & Charles, E. (1979). Common mistakes in therapy. *American Journal of Psychiatry, 136*, 1578–1580.

Budman, S. H., & Gurman, A. S. (1988). *Theory and practice of brief therapy.* New York: Guilford.

Bugental, J. F. T. (1964). The person who is the psychotherapist. *Journal of Consulting Psychology, 28*, 272–277.

Bugental, J. F. T. (1965). *The search for authenticity.* New York: Holt, Rinehart & Winston.

Bugental, J. F. T. (1978). *Psychotherapy and process.* Reading, MA: Addison-Wesley.

Bugental, J. F. T. (1988). What is "failure" in psychotherapy? *Psychotherapy, 25*, 532–535.

Bugental, J. F. T., & Bracke, P. E. (1992). The future of existential-humanistic psychotherapy. *Psychotherapy, 29*, 28–33.

Burgoon, J. K., Buller, D. B., Hale, J. L., & deTurck, M. A. (1984). Relational messages associated with nonverbal behaviors. *Human Communication Research, 10*, 351–378.

Burlingame, G. M., & Behrman, J. A. (1987). Clinician attitudes toward time-limited and time-unlimited therapy. *Professional Psychology: Research and Practice, 18*, 61–65.

Burns, M. O., & Seligman, M. E. P. (1989). Explanatory style across the life span: Evidence of stability over 52 years. *Journal of Personality and Social Psychology, 56*, 471–477.

Cacioppo, J.T., & Petty, R.E. (1982). The need for cognition. *Journal of Personality and Social Psychology, 42*, 116–131.

Cantor, N., & Harlow, R. (1992). Social intelligence and personality: Flexible life task pursuit. In R. J. Sternberg & P. Ruzgis (Eds.), *Personality and intelligence.* Cambridge: Cambridge University Press.

Cantor, N., & Kihlstrom, J. F. (1987). *Personality and social intelligence.* Englewood Cliffs, NJ: Prentice-Hall.

Cantor, N., & Langston, C. A. (1989). "Ups and downs" of life tasks in a life transition. In L. Pervin (Ed.), *The goals concept in personality and social psychology* (pp. 127–167). Hillsdale, NJ: Erlbaum.

Carkhuff, R. R., & Pierce, R. M. (1975). *Trainer's guide: The art of helping.* Amherst, MA: Human Resource Development Press.

Cautela, J. R., & Upper, D. (1975). The process of individual behavior therapy. In M. Hersen, R. Eisler, & P. Miller (Eds.), *Progress in behavior modification I* (pp. 275–305). New York: Academic Press.

Cautela, J. R., & Upper, D. (1976). The behavioral inventory battery: The use of self-report measures in behavioral analysis and therapy. In M. Hersen & A. S. Bellack (Eds.), *Behavioral assessment: A practical handbook* (pp. 77–109). New York: Pergamon.

Chapman, A. H. (1978). *The treatment techniques of Harry Stack Sullivan.* New York: Brunner/Mazel.

Chelune, G. J. (1977). Disclosure flexibility and social-situational perceptions. *Journal of Consulting and Clinical Psychology, 45*, 1139–1143.

Chemtob, C. M., Hamada, R. S., Bauer, G., & Torigoe, R. Y. (1988). Patient suicide: Frequency and impact on psychologists. *Professional Psychology: Research and Practice, 19*, 416–420.

Ciminero, A. R., Calhoun, K. A., & Adams, H. E. (Eds.). (1977). *Handbook of behavioral assessment.* New York: Wiley.

Claiborn, C. D., (1982). Interpretation and change in counseling. *Journal of Counseling Psychology, 29*, 439–453.

Cohen, R. J. (1983). Professional liability of behavioral scientists. *Behavioral Science and the Law, 1*, 90–122.

Cohen, R. J., & Mariano, W. E. (1982). *Legal guidebook in mental health.* New York: Free Press.

Colby, K. M. (1964). Psychotherapeutic processes. *Annual Review of Psychology, 15*, 347–370.

Combs, A. W. (1989). *A theory of therapy.* Newbury Park, CA: Sage.

Committee on Women in Psychology. (1989). If sex enters into the psychotherapy relationship. *Professional Psychology: Research and Practice,* *20,* 112–115.

Cooley, E. J., & LaJoy, R. (1980). Therapeutic relationship and improvement as perceived by clients and therapists. *Journal of Clinical Psychology, 36,* 562–570.

Corey, G., (1991). *Theory and practice of counseling and psychotherapy.* Pacific Grove, CA: Brooks/Cole.

Corey, G., Corey, M. S., & Callanan, P. (1993). *Issues and ethics in the helping professions.* Pacific Grove, CA: Brooks/Cole.

Cormier, W. H., & Cormier, L. S. (1991). *Interviewing strategies for helpers.* Pacific Grove, CA: Brooks/Cole.

Corsini, R. J. (1981). *Handbook of innovative psychotherapies.* New York: Wiley.

Corsini, R. J. (1989). Introduction. In R. J. Corsini and D. Wedding (Eds.), *Current psychotherapies* (4th ed., pp. 1–6). Itasca, IL: Peacock.

Costa, P. T., Jr., & McCrea, R. R. (1980). Influence of extraversion and neuroticism on subjective well-being: Happy and unhappy people. *Journal of Personality and Social Psychology, 38,* 668–678.

Crandall, J. E. (1980). Adler's concept of social interest: Theory, measurement, and implications for adjustment. *Journal of Personality and Social Psychology, 39,* 481–495.

Crandall, J. E. (1984). Social interest as a moderator of life stress. *Journal of Personality and Social Psychology, 47,* 164–174.

Crandall, J. E., & Putman, E. L. (1980). Social interest and psychological well-being. *Journal of Individual Psychology, 36,* 151–168.

Cummings, N. A., & VandenBos, G. R. (1979). The general practice of psychology. *Professional Psychology, 10,* 430–440.

Cushman, P. (1990). Why the self is empty: Toward a historically situated psychology. *American Psychologist, 45,* 599–611.

Davis, D. (1982). Determinants of responsiveness in dyadic interactions. In W. Ickes and E. G. Knowles (Eds.), *Personality, roles, and social behavior* (pp. 85–140). New York: Springer-Verlag.

Davis, D., & Holtgraves, T. (1984). Perceptions of unresponsive others: Attributions, attraction, understandability, memory of their utterances. *Journal of Experimental Social Psychology, 20,* 383–408.

Davis, D., & Perkowitz, W. T. (1979). Consequences of responsiveness in dyadic interactions: Effects of probability of response and proportion of content related responses. *Journal of Personality and Social Psychology, 37,* 534–550.

Day, R. W., & Sparacio, R. T. (1980). Structuring in the counseling process. *Personnel and Guidance Journal, 59,* 246–250.

DeNelsky, G. Y., & Boat, B. W. (1986). A coping skills model of psychological diagnosis and treatment. *Professional Psychology: Research and Practice, 17,* 322–330.

Derber, C. (1979). *The pursuit of attention: Power and individualism in everyday life.* New York: Oxford University Press.

Derlega, V. J., Lovell, R., & Chaikin, A. L. (1976). Effects of therapist disclosure and its perceived appropriateness on client self-disclosure. *Journal of Consulting and Clinical Psychology, 44,* 866.

Deutsch, C. J. (1984). Self-reported sources of stress among psychotherapists. *Professional Psychology: Research and Practice, 15,* 833–845.

Dewald, P. A. (1965). Reactions to forced termination of therapy. *Psychiatric Quarterly, 39,* 102–126.

Diener, E. (1984). Subjective well-being. *Psychological Bulletin, 95,* 542–575.

Diener, E., Colvin, C. R., Pavot, W. G., & Allman, A. (1991). The psychic costs of intense positive affect. *Journal of Personality and Social Psychology, 61,* 492–503.

Diener, E., Emmons, R. A., Larsen, R. J., & Griffin, S. (1985). The Satisfaction with Life Scale. *Journal of Personality Assessment, 49,* 71–75.

Diener, E., Sandvik, E., & Pavot, W. (1989). Happiness is the frequency, not intensity, of positive versus negative affect. In F. Strack, M. Argyle, and N. Schwarz (Eds.), *The social psychology of subjective well-being.* New York: Pergamon.

Dinkmeyer, D. C., Dinkmeyer, D. C., Jr., & Sperry, L. (1987). *Adlerian counseling and psychotherapy.* Columbus, OH: Merrill.

Dixon, D. N., & Glover, J. A. (1984). *Counseling: A problem-solving approach.* New York: Wiley.

Doster, J. A., & Nesbitt, J. G. (1979). Psychotherapy and self-disclosure. In G. J. Chelune and Associates (Eds.), *Self-disclosure: Origins, patterns, and implications of openness in interpersonal relationships* (pp. 177–242). San Francisco: Jossey-Bass.

Dowd, E. T., & Boroto, D. R. (1982). Differential effects of counselor self-disclosure, self-involving statements, and interpretation. *Journal of Counseling Psychology, 29,* 8–13.

Drane, J. F. (1982). Ethics and psychotherapy: A philosophical perspective. In M. Rosenbaum (Ed.), *Ethics and values in psychotherapy: A guidebook* (pp. 15–50). New York: The Free Press.

Dubin, S. (1972). Obsolescence or lifelong education: A choice for the professional. *American Psychologist, 27,* 486–498.

Duncan, B. L. (1989). Paradoxical procedures in family therapy. In L. M. Ascher (Ed.), *Therapeutic paradox* (pp. 310–348). New York: Guilford.

Duncan, B. L., Parks, M. B., & Rusk, G. S. (1990). Strategic eclecticism: A technical alternative for eclectic psychotherapy. *Psychotherapy, 27,* 568–577.

Dweck, C. S., & Leggett, E. L. (1988). A social-cognitive approach to motivation and personality. *Psychological Review, 95,* 256–273.

Edelson, M. (1975). *Language and interpretation in psychoanalysis.* New Haven: Yale University Press.

Ehrlich, R. P., D'Angelli, A. R., & Danish, S. J. (1979). Comparative effectiveness of six counselor verbal responses. *Journal of Counseling Psychology, 26,* 390–398.

Ekstein, R. (1965). Working through and termination of analysis. *Journal of the American Psychoanalytic Association, 13,* 57–78.

Elliott, E. S., & Dweck, C. S. (1988). Goals: An approach to motivation and achievement. *Journal of Personality and Social Psychology, 54,* 5–12.

Elliott, R. (1985). Helpful and nonhelpful events in brief counseling interviews: An empirical taxonomy. *Journal of Counseling Psychology, 32,* 307–322.

Elliott, R., & James E. (1989). Varieties of client experience in psychotherapy: An analysis of the literature. *Clinical Psychology Review, 9,* 443–467.

Ellis, A. (1962). *Reason and emotion in psychotherapy.* Secaucus, NJ: Lyle Stuart.

Ellis, A. (1980). The value of efficiency in psychotherapy. *Psychotherapy: Theory, Research and Practice, 17,* 414–419.

Ellis, A. (1985). *Overcoming resistance: Rational-emotive therapy with difficult clients.* New York: Springer.

Ellis, A. (1987). The impossibility of achieving consistently good mental health. *American Psychologist, 42,* 364–375.

Ellis, A., & Dryden, W. (1987). *The practice of rational-emotive therapy (RET).* New York: Springer.

Ellis, A., & Harper, R. A. (1975). *A new guide to rational living.* Englewood Cliffs, NJ: Prentice-Hall.

Emmelkamp, P. (1986). Behavior therapy with adults. In S. L. Garfield and A. E. Bergin (Eds.), *Handbook of psychotherapy and behavior change* (pp. 385–442). New York: Wiley.

Epperson, D. L., Bushway, D. J., & Warman, R. E. (1983). Client self-terminations after one counseling session: Effects of problem recognition, counselor gender, and counselor experience. *Journal of Counseling Psychology, 30,* 307–315.

Epstein, S., & Meier, P. (1989). Constructive thinking: A broad coping variable with specific components. *Journal of Personality and Social Psychology, 57,* 332–350.

Erickson, M. H., & Rossi, E. L. (1975). Varieties of double bind. *American Journal of Clinical Hypnosis, 17,* 143–157.

Erickson, M. H., & Rossi, E. L. (1976/1980). Two-level communication and the microdynamics of trance and suggestion. In E. Rossi (Ed.), *The collected papers of Milton H. Erickson on hypnosis. Vol. I. The nature of hypnosis and suggestion* (pp. 108–132). New York: Irvington.

Erikson, E. H. (1963). *Childhood and society* (2nd ed.). New York: Norton.

Evans, M. B. (1988). The role of metaphor in psychotherapy and personality change: A theoretical reformulation. *Psychotherapy, 25,* 543–551.

Everstine, L., Everstine, D. S., Heymann, G. M., True, R. H., Frey, D. H., Johnson, H. G., & Seiden, R. H. (1980). Privacy and confidentiality in psychotherapy. *American Psychologist, 35,* 828–840.

Eysenck, H. J. (1970). A mish-mash of theories. *International Journal of Psychiatry, 9,* 140–146.

Falk, D. R., & Hill, C. E. (1992). Counselor interventions preceding client laughter in brief therapy. *Journal of Counseling Psychology, 39,* 39–45.

Farber, B. A. (1983a). Dysfunctional aspects of the psychotherapeutic role. In B. A. Farber (Ed.), *Stress and burnout in the human service professions* (pp. 97–118). New York: Pergamon.

Farber, B. A. (1983b). The effects of psychotherapeutic practice upon psychotherapists. *Psychotherapy: Theory, Research, and Practice, 20,* 174–182.

Farber, B. A. (1983c). Psychotherapists' perceptions of stressful patient behavior. *Professional Psychology: Research and Practice, 14,* 697–705.

Farber, B. A., & Heifetz, L. J. (1982). The process and dimensions of burnout in psychotherapists. *Professional Psychology, 13,* 293–301.

Faulkner, W. (1964). *As I lay dying.* New York: Random House.

Finkel, N. J. (1988). *Insanity on trial.* New York: Plenum.

Fisch, R. (1990). Problem-solving psychotherapy. In J. K. Zeig and W. M. Munion (Eds.), *What is psychotherapy? Contemporary perspectives* (pp. 269–273). San Francisco: Jossey-Bass.

Fisher, J. D., & Farina, A. (1979). Consequences of beliefs about the nature of mental disorders. *Journal of Abnormal Psychology, 88,* 320–327.

Fisher, M. (1990). The shared experience and self-disclosure. In G. Stricker and M. Fisher (Eds.), *Self-disclosure in the therapeutic relationship* (pp. 3–15). New York: Plenum.

Flanigan, B. (1992). *Forgiving the unforgivable.* New York: Macmillan.

Fletcher, G., Danilovics, P., Fernandez, G., Peterson, D., & Reeder, G. D. (1986). Attributional complexity: An individual differences measure. *Journal of Personality and Social Psychology, 51,* 875–884.

Fordyce, M. W. (1977). Development of a program to increase personal happiness. *Journal of Counseling Psychology, 24,* 511–521.

Fordyce, M. W. (1981). *The psychology of happiness: Fourteen fundamentals.* Fort Myers, FL: Cypress Lake Media.

Fordyce, M. W. (1983). A program to increase happiness: Further studies. *Journal of Counseling Psychology, 30,* 483–498.

Fox, R. E., Barclay, A. G., & Rodgers, D. A. (1982). The foundations of professional psychology. *American Psychologist, 37,* 306–312.

Frances, A., Clarkin, J. F., & Perry, S. (1984). Differential therapeutics in psychotherapy. New York: Brunner/Mazel.

Francis, D., & Chin, J. (1987). The prevention of acquired immunodeficiency syndrome in the United States. *Journal of the American Medical Association, 257,* 1357–1366.

Frank, J. D. (1961). *Persuasion and healing.* Baltimore: Johns Hopkins University Press.

Frank, J. D. (1971). Therapeutic factors in psychotherapy. *American Journal of Psychotherapy, 25,* 350–361.

Frank, J. D. (1978). Expectation and therapeutic outcome—the placebo effect and the role induction interview. In J. D. Frank, R. Hoehn-Saric, S. D. Imber, B. L. Liberman, and A. R. Stone (Eds.), *Effective ingredients of successful psychotherapy* (pp. 1–34). New York: Brunner/Mazel.

Frank, J. D. (1982). Therapeutic components shared by all psychotherapies. In J. H. Harvey and M. M. Parks (Eds.), *The master lecture series: Psychotherapy research and behavior change* (Vol. 1, pp. 7–37). Washington, DC: American Psychological Association.

Frank, J. D. (1986). Forward. In I. L. Kutash and A. Wolf (Eds.), *Psychotherapist's casebook: Theory and techniques in the practice of modern therapies* (pp. ix–xi). San Francisco: Jossey-Bass.

Frank, J. D. (1987). Psychotherapy, rhetoric, and hermeneutics: Implications for practice and research. *Psychotherapy, 24,* 293–302.

Frankl, V. E. (1963). *Man's search for meaning.* New York: Washington Square Press.

Frankl, V. E. (1967a). Logotherapy. *Israel Annals of Psychiatry and Related Disciplines, 5,* 142–155.

Frankl, V. E. (1967b). *Psychotherapy and existentialism: Selected papers on logotherapy.* New York: Washington Square Press.

Frankl, V. E. (1969). *The will to meaning: Foundations and applications of logotherapy.* New York: World.

Frankl, V. E. (1975). Paradoxical intention and dereflection. *Psychotherapy: Theory, Research, and Practice, 12*, 226–237.

Fremont, S. K., & Anderson, W. (1988). Investigation of factors involved in therapists' annoyance with clients. *Professional Psychology: Research and Practice, 19*, 330–335.

Freud, S. (1928). Humor. *International Journal of Psychoanalysis, 9*, 1–6.

Freud, S. (1930). *Civilization and its discontents.* London: Hogarth.

Freud, S. (1937). Analysis terminable and interminable. *International Journal of Psychoanalysis, 18*, 373–405.

Freud, S. (1949). *An outline of psychoanalysis.* New York: Norton.

Freudenberger, H. J. (1975). The staff burn-out syndrome in alternative institutions. *Psychotherapy: Research and Practice, 12*, 73–82.

Friedlander, M. L., Thibodeau, J. R., & Ward, L. G. (1985). Discriminating the "good" from the "bad" therapy hour: A study of dyadic interaction. *Psychotherapy, 22*, 631–642.

Friedman, H. S. (1991). *The self-healing personality.* New York: Henry Holt.

Fromm-Reichmann, F. (1950). *Principles of intensive psychotherapy.* Chicago: University of Chicago Press.

Fujimura, L. E., Weis, D. M., & Cochran, J. R. (1985). Suicide: Dynamics and implications for counseling. *Journal of Counseling and Development, 63*(10), 612–615.

Fulero, S. M. (1988). *Tarasoff:* 10 years later. *Professional Psychology: Research and Practice, 19*, 184–190.

Furrow, B. R. (1980). *Malpractice in psychotherapy.* Toronto, Canada: D. C. Heath.

Garfield, S. L. (1980). *Psychotherapy: An eclectic approach.* New York: Wiley-Interscience.

Garfield, S. L. (1986). Research on client variables in psychotherapy. In S. L. Garfield and A. E. Bergin (Eds.), *Handbook of psychotherapy and behavior change* (pp. 213–256). New York: Wiley.

Garfield, S. L. (1990). Multivariant eclectic psychotherapy. In J. K. Zeig & W. M. Munion (Eds.), *What is psychotherapy? Contemporary perspectives* (pp. 239–243). San Francisco: Jossey-Bass.

Garfield, S. L., & Wolpin, M. (1963). Expectations regarding psychotherapy. *Journal of Nervous and Mental Disease, 137*, 353–362.

Gaston, L. (1990). The concept of the alliance and its role in psychotherapy: Theoretical and empirical considerations. *Psychotherapy, 27*, 143–153.

Gay, P. (1988). *Freud: A life for our time.* New York: Norton.

Gelb, P. G. (1982). The experience of nonerotic physical contact in traditional psychotherapy. A critical investigation of the taboo against touch. *Dissertation Abstracts International, 43*, 1–13.

Gelso, C. J. (1979). Gratification: A pivotal point in psychotherapy. *Psychotherapy: Theory, Research, and Practice, 16*, 276–281.

Gelso, C. J., & Carter, J. A. (1985). The relationship in counseling and psychotherapy: Components, consequences, and theoretical antecedents. *The Counseling Psychologist, 13*, 155–243.

Gendlin, E. T. (1981). *Focusing.* New York: Bantam.

Gergen, K. J. (1990). Therapeutic professions and the diffusion of deficit. *The Journal of Mind and Behavior, 11*, 353–368.

Gilbert, L. A. (1987). Female and male emotional dependency and its implications for the therapist-client relationship. *Professional Psychology: Research and Practice, 18*, 535–561.

Gill, M. M. (1982). *Analysis of transference* (Vol. 1). New York: International Universities Press.

Gilligan, C. (1982). *In a different voice.* Cambridge, MA: Harvard University Press.

Gladstein, G. A. (1983). Understanding empathy: Integrating counseling, developmental, and social psychology perspectives. *Journal of Counseling Psychology, 30*, 467–482.

Glaser, S. R. (1980). Rhetoric and psychotherapy. In M. J. Mahoney (Ed.), *Psychotherapy process: Current issues and future directions* (pp. 313–333). New York: Plenum.

Glass, G., & Kliegl, R. (1983). An apology for research integration in the study of psychotherapy. *Journal of Consulting and Clinical Psychology, 51*, 28–41.

Glasser, W. (1965). *Reality therapy: A new approach to psychiatry.* New York: Harper & Row.

Glenn, M. L. (1971). Separation anxiety: When the therapist leaves the patient. *American Journal of Psychotherapy, 25*, 437–446.

Goffman, E. (1959). *The presentation of self in everyday life.* New York: Doubleday.

Goffman, E. (1961). *Asylums: Essays on the social situation of mental patients and other inmates.* Garden City, NJ: Doubleday.

Goldberg, A. (Ed.). (1978). *The psychology of the self.* New York: International Universities Press.

Goldberg, C. (1975). Termination—A meaningful pseudodilemma in psychotherapy. *Psychotherapy: Theory, Research, and Practice, 12*, 341–343.

Goldfried, M. R. (1980a). Psychotherapy as coping skills training. In M. J. Mahoney (Ed.), *Psychotherapy process: Current issues and future directions.* New York: Plenum.

Goldfried, M. R. (1980b). Toward the delineation of therapeutic change principles. *American Psychologist, 35*, 991–999.

Goldfried, M. R. (Ed.). (1982). *Converging themes in psychotherapy: Trends in psychodynamic, humanistic, and behavioral practice.* New York: Springer.

Goldfried, M. R., & Newman, C. (1986). Psychotherapy integration: An historical perspective. In J. C. Norcross (Ed.), *Handbook of eclectic psychotherapy* (pp. 25–61). New York: Brunner/Mazel.

Goldfried, M. R., & Robbins, C. (1982). On the facilitation of self-efficacy. *Cognitive Therapy and Research, 6*, 361–380.

Goldfried, M. R., & Safran, J. D. (1986). Future directions in psychotherapy integration. In J. C. Norcross (Ed.), *Handbook of eclectic psychotherapy* (pp. 463–483). New York: Brunner/Mazel.

Gomes-Schwartz, B. (1978). Effective ingredients in psychotherapy: Prediction of outcome from process variables. *Journal of Consulting and Clinical Psychology, 47*, 310–316.

Good, G. E., Gilbert, L. A., & Scher, M. (1990). Gender aware therapy: A synthesis of feminist therapy and knowledge about gender. *Journal of Counseling and Development, 68*, 376–380.

Goodman, M., & Teicher, A. (1988). To touch or not to touch. *Psychotherapy, 25,* 492–500.

Goodyear, R. K. (1981). Termination as a loss experience for the counselor. *Personnel and Guidance Journal, 59,* 347–350.

Gordon, D. (1978). *Therapeutic metaphors.* Cupertino, CA: Meta Publications.

Gottlieb, M. C. (1990). Accusation of sexual misconduct: Assisting in the complaint process. *Professional Psychology: Research and Practice, 21,* 455–461.

Gottlieb, M. C., Sell, J. M., & Schoenfeld, L. S. (1988). Social/romantic relationships with present and former clients: State licensing board actions. *Professional Psychology: Research and Practice, 19,* 459–462.

Graham, S. R. (1980). Desire, belief and grace: A psychotherapeutic paradigm. *Psychotherapy: Theory, Research and Practice, 17,* 370–371.

Gray, L., & Harding A. (1988). Confidentiality limits with clients who have the AIDS virus. *Journal of Counseling and Development, 65,* 219–226.

Greben, S. E. (1981). Unresponsiveness: The demon artefact of psychotherapy. *American Journal of Psychotherapy, 35,* 244–250.

Greenberg, L. S., & Pinsof, W. B. (Eds.). (1986). *The psychotherapeutic process: A research handbook.* New York: Guilford.

Greenberg, L. S., & Safran, J. D. (1981). Encoding and cognitive therapy: Changing what clients attend to. *Psychotherapy: Theory, Research, and Practice, 18,* 163–169.

Greenberg, L. S., & Safran, J. D. (1987). *Emotion in psychotherapy: Affect, cognition, and the process of change.* New York: Guilford.

Greene, L. R. (1980). On terminating psychotherapy: More evidence of sex-role related countertransference. *Psychology of Women Quarterly, 4,* 548–557.

Greene, W. (1985, January). Ethical dilemmas faced by physicians treating AIDS patients. *Infections in Surgery,* pp. 12–13.

Greenson, R. R. (1965). The working alliance and the transference neurosis. *Psychoanalytic Quarterly, 34,* 155–181.

Greenwald, A. G. (1980). The totalitarian ego: Fabrication and revision of personal history. *American Psychologist, 35,* 603–618.

Grencavage, L. M., & Norcross, J. C. (1990). Where are the commonalties among the therapeutic common factors? *Professional Psychology: Research and Practice, 21,* 372–378.

Grunebaum, H., & Chasin, R. (1978). Relabeling and reframing reconsidered: The beneficial effects of a pathological label. *Family Process, 17,* 449–456.

Guy, J. D. (1987). *The personal life of the psychotherapist.* New York: Wiley.

Guy, J. D., Poelstra, P. L., & Stark, M. J. (1989). Personal distress and therapeutic effectiveness: National survey of psychologists practicing psychotherapy. *Professional Psychology: Research and Practice, 20,* 48–50.

Haas, L. J., Malouf, J. L., & Mayerson, N. H. (1986). Ethical dilemmas in psychological practice: Results of a national survey. *Professional Psychology: Research and Practice, 17,* 316–321.

Haley, J. (1963). *Strategies of psychotherapy.* New York: Grune & Stratton.

Haley, J. (Ed.). (1967). *Advanced techniques of hypnosis and therapy: Selected papers of Milton H. Erickson, M.D.* New York: Grune & Stratton.

Haley, J. (1973). *Uncommon therapy: The psychiatric techniques of Milton Erickson, M.D.* New York: Grune & Stratton.

Haley, J. (1984). *Ordeal therapy*. San Francisco: Jossey-Bass.

Haley, J. (Ed.). (1985). *Conversations with Milton H. Erickson, M.D.* (Vol. I). New York: Triangle Press.

Hamilton, D. L. (1979). A cognitive-attributional analysis of stereotyping. In L. Berkowitz (Ed.), *Advances in experimental social psychology* (Vol. 12). New York: Academic Press.

Handelsman, M. M. (1990). Do written consent forms influence clients' first impressions of therapists? *Professional Psychology: Research and Practice, 21,* 451–454.

Handelsman, M. M., Kemper, M. B., Kesson-Craig, P., McLain, J., & Johnsrud, C. (1986). Use, content, and readability of written consent forms for treatment. *Professional Psychology: Research and Practice, 17,* 514–518.

Harcum E. R. (1989). Commitment to collaboration as a prerequisite for existential commonalty in psychotherapy. *Psychotherapy, 26,* 200–209.

Harper, R. G., Wiens, A. N., & Matarazzo, J. D. (1978). *Nonverbal communication: The state of the art.* New York: Wiley.

Hayes, S. C., & Melancon, S. M. (1989). Comprehensive distancing, paradox, and the treatment of emotional avoidance. In L. M. Ascher (Ed.), *Therapeutic paradox* (pp. 184–218). New York: Guilford.

Hendrick, S. S. (1988). Counselor self-disclosure. *Journal of Counseling and Development, 66,* 419–424.

Henry, W. P., Schacht, T. E., & Strupp, H. H. (1986). Structural analysis of social behavior: Application to a study of interpersonal process in differential psychotherapeutic outcome. *Journal of Consulting and Clinical Psychology, 54,* 27–31.

Herbert, D. L., Nelson, R. O., & Herbert, J. D. (1988). Effects of psychodiagnostic labels, depression severity, and instructions on assessment. *Professional Psychology: Research and Practice, 19,* 496–502.

Herink, R. (1980). *The psychotherapy handbook: The A–Z guide to more than 250 different therapies in use today.* New York: New American Library.

Hersen, M., & Bellack, A. S. (Eds.). (1981). *Behavioral assessment: A practical handbook* (2nd ed.). New York: Pergamon.

Heuscher, J. (1980). Psychotherapy as uncovering of freedom. *Psychotherapy: Theory, Research and Practice, 17,* 467–471.

Higginbotham, H. N., West, S. G., & Forsyth, D. R. (1988). *Psychotherapy and behavior change.* New York: Pergamon.

Higgins, E. T. (1987). Self-discrepancy: A theory relating self and affect. *Psychological Review, 94,* 319–340.

Higgins, R. L., & Berglas, S. (1990). The maintenance and treatment of self-handicapping: From risk-taking to face-saving—and back. In R. L. Higgins, C. R. Snyder, and S. Berglas (Eds.), *Self-handicapping: The paradox that isn't* (pp. 187–238). New York: Plenum.

Higgins, R. L., Snyder, C. R., & Berglas, S. (Eds.). (1990). *Self-handicapping: The paradox that isn't.* New York: Plenum.

Hill, C. E., Helms, J. E., Tichenor, V., Spiegel, S. B., O'Grady, K. E., & Perry, E. S. (1988). Effects of therapist response modes in brief psychotherapy. *Journal of Counseling Psychology, 35,* 222–233.

Hill, C. E., Mahalik, J. R., & Thompson, B. J. (1989). Therapist self-disclosure. *Psychotherapy, 26,* 290–295.

Hill, C. E., Siegelman, L., Gronsky, B. R., Sturniolo, F., & Fretz, B. R. (1981). Nonverbal communication and counseling outcome. *Journal of Counseling Psychology, 28,* 203–212.

Hills, H. I., & Strozier, A. L. (1992). Multicultural training in APA-approved counseling psychology programs: A survey. *Professional Psychology: Research and Practice, 23,* 1–9.

Hobbs, N. (1962). Sources of gain in psychotherapy. *American Psychologist, 17,* 741–747.

Holroyd, J. C., & Brodsky, A. M. (1977). Psychologists' attitudes and practices regarding erotic and nonerotic physical contact with patients. *American Psychologist, 32,* 843–849.

Holroyd, J. C., & Brodsky, A. (1980). Does touching patients lead to sexual intercourse? *Professional Psychology, 11,* 807–811.

Holub, E. A., & Lee, S. S. (1990). Therapists' use of nonerotic physical contact: Ethical concerns. *Professional Psychology: Research and Practice, 21,* 115–117.

Horowitz, M. J. (1988). *Introduction to psychodynamics: A new synthesis.* New York: Basic Books.

Horowitz, M., Marmar, C., Krupnick, J., Wilner, N., Kaltreider, N., & Wallerstein, R. (1984). *Personality styles and brief psychotherapy.* New York: Basic Books.

Horvath, A. O., & Greenberg, L. S. (1986). The development of the Working Alliance Inventory. In L. S. Greenberg and W. M. Pinsof (Eds.), *The psychotherapeutic process: A research handbook* (pp. 529–556). New York: Guilford.

Horvath, A. O., & Greenberg, L. S. (1989). Development and validation of the Working Alliance Inventory. *Journal of Counseling Psychology, 36,* 223–233.

Horvath, A. O., & Symonds, B. D. (1991). Relation between working alliance and outcome in psychotherapy: A meta-analysis. *Journal of Counseling Psychology, 38,* 139–149.

Howard, K. I., Kopta, S. M., Krause, M.S., & Orlinsky, D.E. (1986). The dose-effect relationship in psychotherapy. *American Psychologist, 41,* 159–164.

Hoyt, M. F., Xenakis, S. N., Marmar, C. R., & Horowitz, M. J. (1983). Therapist's actions that influence their perceptions of "good" psychotherapy sessions. *Journal of Nervous and Mental Disease, 171,* 400–404.

Hugo, V. (1938). *Les Miserables* (L. Wraxall, Trans.). New York: Heritage Press. (Original work published 1862.)

Ivey, A. E. (1986). *Developmental therapy.* San Francisco: Jossey-Bass.

Ivey, A. E. (1988). *Intentional interviewing and counseling.* Pacific Grove, CA: Brooks/Cole.

Ivey, A. E. (1991). *Developmental strategies for helpers.* Pacific Grove, CA: Brooks/Cole.

Ivey, A. E., & Authier, J. (1978). *Microcounseling: Innovations in interviewing, counseling, psychotherapy and psychoeducation* (2nd ed.). Springfield, IL: Charles C Thomas.

Jahoda, M. (1958). *Current concepts of positive mental health.* New York: Basic Books.

Jenkins, A. H. (1991). Self-disclosure and the nonwhite ethnic minority patient. In G. Stricker and M. Fisher (Eds.), *Self-disclosure in the therapeutic relationship* (pp. 117–134). New York: Plenum.

Jensen, J. P., & Bergin, A. E. (1988). Mental health values of professional therapists: A national interdisciplinary survey. *Professional Psychology: Research and Practice, 19,* 290–297.

Jensen, J. P., Bergin, A. E., & Greaves, D. W. (1990). The meaning of eclecticism: New survey and analysis of components. *Professional Psychology: Research and Practice, 21,* 124–130.

Johnson, D. H., & Gelso, C. J. (1980). The effectiveness of time limits in counseling and psychotherapy: A critical review. *The Counseling Psychologist, 9,* 70–83.

Jones, A., & Seagull, A. A. (1977). Dimensions of the relationship between the black client and the white therapist. *American Psychologist, 32,* 850–855.

Jones, A. S., & Gelso, C. J. (1988). Differential effects of style of interpretation: Another look. *Journal of Counseling Psychology, 35,* 363–369.

Jourard, S. M., & Landsman, T. (1980). *Healthy personality: An approach from the viewpoint of humanistic psychology* (4th ed.). New York: Macmillan.

Kahn, M. (1991). *Between therapist and client: The new relationship.* New York: W. H. Freeman.

Kain, C. (1988). To breach or not to breach: Is that the question? *Journal of Counseling and Development, 66,* 224–225.

Kaiser, H. (1965). *Effective psychotherapy: The contribution of Hellmuth Kaiser.* New York: Free Press.

Kanfer, F. H., & Gaelick-Buys, L. (1991). Self-management methods. In F. H. Kanfer and A. P. Goldstein (Eds.), *Helping people change* (pp. 305–360). New York: Pergamon.

Kanfer, F. H., & Goldstein, A. P. (Eds.). (1991). *Helping people change.* New York: Pergamon.

Kanfer, F. H., & Schefft, B. K. (1988). *Guiding the process of therapeutic change.* New York: Pergamon.

Kaplan, H., & Sager, C., & Schiavi, R. (1985). AIDS and the sex therapist. *Journal of Sex and Marital Therapy, 11,* 210–214.

Kaplan, M. (1983). A woman's view of DSM-III. *American Psychologist, 38,* 786–792.

Karasu, T. B. (1986). The specificity versus nonspecificity dilemma: Toward identifying therapeutic change agents. *American Journal of Psychiatry, 143,* 687–695.

Karasu, T. B. (1992). *Wisdom in the practice of psychotherapy.* New York: Basic Books.

Kelly, G. A. (1955). *The psychology of personal constructs* (Vols. 1 & 2). New York: Norton.

Kercher, G., & Smith, D. (1985). Reframing paradoxical psychotherapy. *Psychotherapy, 22,* 786–792.

Kiesler, D. J. (1988). *Therapeutic metacommunication: Therapist impact disclosure as feedback in psychotherapy.* Palo Alto, CA: Consulting Psychologists Press.

Kirsch, I. (1986). Early research on self-efficacy: What we already know without knowing we knew. *Journal of Social and Clinical Psychology, 4,* 339–358.

Kirsch, I. (1990). *Changing expectations: A key to effective psychotherapy.* Pacific Grove, CA: Brooks/Cole.

Kirschenbaum, D. S., & Flaner, R. C. (1984). Toward a psychology of behavioral contracting. *Clinical Psychology Review, 4,* 597–618.

Kisch, J., & Kroll, J. (1980). Meaningfulness versus effectiveness: Paradoxical implications in the evaluation of psychotherapy. *Psychotherapy: Theory, Research and Practice, 17,* 401–413.

Klein, M. H., Mathieu-Coughlan, P., & Kiesler, D. J. (1986). The experiencing scales. In L. S. Greenberg and W. M. Pinsof (Eds.), *The psychotherapeutic process: A research handbook* (pp. 21–71). New York: Guilford.

Kleinke, C. L. (1978). *Self-perception: The psychology of personal awareness.* New York: W. H. Freeman.

Kleinke, C. L. (1984). Two models for conceptualizing the attitude-behavior relationship. *Human Relations, 37,* 333–350.

Kleinke, C. L. (1986). *Meeting and understanding people.* New York: W. H. Freeman.

Kleinke, C. L. (1991). *Coping with life challenges.* Pacific Grove, CA: Brooks/Cole.

Kleinke, C. L., & Taylor, C. (1991). Evaluation of opposite-sex person as a function of gazing, smiling, and forward lean. *Journal of Social Psychology, 131,* 451–453.

Kleinke, C. L., & Tully, T. B. (1979). Influence of talking level on perception of counselors. *Journal of Counseling Psychology, 26,* 23–29.

Knapp, S., Vandecreek, L., & Shapiro, D. (1990). Statutory remedies to the *duty to protect:* A reconsideration. *Psychotherapy, 27,* 291–296.

Kohut, H. (1977). *The restoration of the self.* New York: International Universities Press.

Kohut, H. (1984). *How does analysis cure?* Chicago: University of Chicago Press.

Korb, M. P., Gorrell, J., & Van De Riet, V. (1989). *Gestalt therapy: Practice and theory.* New York: Pergamon Press.

Koss, M. P. (1979). Length of psychotherapy for clients seen in private practice. *Journal of Consulting and Clinical Psychology, 47,* 210–212.

Koss, M. P., & Butcher, J. N. (1986). Research on brief psychotherapy. In S. L. Garfield and A. E. Bergin (Eds.), *Handbook of psychotherapy and behavior change* (pp. 627–670). New York: Wiley.

Kottler, J. A. (1986). *On being a therapist.* San Francisco: Jossey-Bass.

Kottler, J. A. (1991). *The compleat therapist.* San Francisco: Jossey-Bass.

Kramer, S. A. (1986). The termination process in open-ended psychotherapy: Guidelines for clinical practice. *Psychotherapy, 23,* 526–531.

Kramer, S. A. (1990). *Positive endings in psychotherapy.* San Francisco: Jossey-Bass.

Kroll, J. E. (1988). *The challenge of the borderline patient.* New York: Norton.

Kuhn, T. (1970). *The structure of scientific revolutions.* Chicago: University of Chicago Press.

Kupers, T. A. (1988). *Ending therapy: The meaning of termination.* New York: New York University Press.

Kupst, M. J., & Schulman, J. L. (1979). Comparing professional and lay expectations of psychotherapy. *Psychotherapy: Research and Practice, 16,* 237–243.

Kutchins, H., & Kirk, S. A. (1988). The business of diagnosis: DSM-III and clinical social work. *Social Work, 33*, 215–220.

Lakin, M. (1991). *Coping with ethical dilemmas in psychotherapy.* New York: Pergamon.

Laliotis, D. A., & Grayson, J. H. (1985). Psychologist heal thyself: What is available for the impaired psychologist? *American Psychologist, 40*, 84–96.

Lamb, D. H. (1985). A time-frame model of termination in psychotherapy. *Psychotherapy, 22*, 604–609.

Lamb, D. H., Clark, C., Drumheller, P., Frizzell, K., & Surrey, L. (1989). Applying *Tarasoff* to AIDS-related psychotherapy issues. *Professional Psychology: Research and Practice, 20*, 37–43.

Lambert, M. J. (1989). The individual therapist's contribution to psychotherapy process and outcome. *Clinical Psychology Review, 9*, 469–485.

Lane, R. C., & Hull, J. W. (1990). Self-disclosure and classical psychoanalysis. In G. Stricker and M. Fisher (Eds.), *Self-disclosure in the therapeutic relationship* (pp. 31–46). New York: Plenum.

Langer, E. J. (1975). The illusion of control. *Journal of Personality and Social Psychology, 32*, 311–328.

Langer, E. J. (1989). *Mindfulness.* Reading, MA: Addison-Wesley.

Langer, E. J., & Abelson, R. P. (1974). A patient by any other name . . .: Clinical group differences in labeling bias. *Journal of Consulting and Clinical Psychology, 42*, 4–9.

Lankton, S. R. (1990). Ericksonian strategic therapy. In J. K. Zeig and W. M. Munion (Eds.), *What is psychotherapy? Contemporary perspectives* (pp. 363–371). San Francisco: Jossey-Bass.

Larson, D. G., & Chastain, R. L. (1990). Self-Concealment: Conceptualization, measurement, and health implications. *Journal of Social and Clinical Psychology, 9*, 439–455.

Larson, L. M., Suzuki, L. A., Gillespie, K. N., Potenza, M. T., Bechtel, M. A., & Toulouse, A. L. (1992). Development and validation of the counseling self-estimate inventory. *Journal of Counseling Psychology, 39*, 105–120.

Larson, V. A. (1987). An exploration of psychotherapeutic resonance. *Psychotherapy, 24*, 321–324.

Lasch, C. (1978). *The culture of narcissism: American life in an age of diminishing expectations.* New York: Norton.

Lazarus, A. A. (1976). *Multimodal behavior therapy.* New York: Springer.

Lazarus, A. A. (1981). *The practice of multimodal therapy.* New York: McGraw-Hill.

Lazarus, A. A. (1985). *Conversation hour with Arnold A. Lazarus.* Audiotape (L330-CH11) from the Evolution of Psychotherapy Conference, Phoenix, AZ. Phoenix, AZ: Milton Erickson Foundation.

Lazarus, A. A. (1986). Multimodal therapy. In J. C. Norcross (Ed.), *Handbook of eclectic psychotherapy* (pp. 65–93). New York: Brunner/Mazel.

Lazarus, A. A. (1990a). Can psychotherapists transcend the shackles of their training and superstitions? *Journal of Clinical Psychology, 46*, 351–358.

Lazarus, A. A. (1990b). *Clinical/therapeutic effectiveness: Banning the Procrustean bed.* Audiotape (C289-9) from the Evolution of Psychotherapy Conference, Ahaheim, CA. Phoenix, AZ: Milton Erickson Foundation.

Lazarus, A. A., Beutler, L. E., & Norcross, J. C. (1992). The future of technical eclecticism. *Psychotherapy, 29,* 11–20.

Lazarus, R. S., & Launier, R. (1978). Stress-related transactions between persons and environment. In L. A. Pervin and M. Lewis (Eds.), *Perspectives in interactional psychology* (pp. 291–327). New York: Plenum.

Lee, D. Y., & Hallberg, E. T. (1982). Nonverbal behaviors of "good" and "poor" counselors. *Journal of Counseling Psychology, 29,* 414–417.

Lee, D. Y., Uhlemann, M. R., & Haase, R. F. (1985). Counselor verbal and nonverbal responses and perceived expertness, trustworthiness, and attractiveness. *Journal of Counseling Psychology, 32,* 181–187.

Lefcourt, H. M., & Davidson-Katz, K. (1991). The role of humor and the self. In C. R. Snyder and D. R. Forsyth, *Handbook of social and clinical psychology* (pp. 41–56). New York: Pergamon.

Lehman, A. K., & Salovey, P. (1990). Psychotherapist orientation and expectations for liked and disliked patients. *Professional Psychology: Research and Practice, 21,* 385–391.

Leo, J. (1985). Battling over masochism. *Time,* December 2.

Levenson, E. A. (1976). Problems in terminating psychoanalysis (a symposium): The aesthetics of termination. *Contemporary Psychoanalysis, 12(3),* 338–342.

Levinson, D. J. (1978). *The seasons of a man's life.* New York: Knopf.

Levinson, D. J. (1986). A conception of adult development. *American Psychologist, 41,* 3–13.

Lewis, W. A., & Evans, J. W. (1986). Resistance: A reconceptualization. *Psychotherapy, 23,* 426–433.

Liberman, B. L. (1978). The role of mastery in psychotherapy: Maintenance of improvement and prescriptive change. In J. D. Frank, R. Hoehn-Saric, S. D. Imber, B. L. Liberman, and A. R. Stone (Eds.), *Effective ingredients of successful psychotherapy.* New York: Brunner/Mazel.

Linville, P. W. (1985). Self-complexity and affective extremity: Don't put all your eggs in one cognitive basket. *Social Cognition, 3,* 94–120.

Linville, P. W. (1987). Self-complexity as a cognitive buffer against stress-related illness and depression. *Journal of Personality and Social Psychology, 52,* 663–676.

Lloyd, M. E. (1983). Selecting systems to measure client outcome in human service agencies. *Behavioral Assessment, 5,* 55–70.

London, P. (1986). *The modes and morals of psychotherapy* (2nd ed.). Washington, DC: McGraw-Hill.

Lopez, S. R., Grover, K. P., Holland, D., Johnson, M. J., Kain, C. D., Kanel, K., Mellins, C. A., & Rhyne, M. C. (1989). Development of culturally sensitive psychotherapists. *Professional Psychology: Research and Practice, 20,* 369–376.

Luborsky, L. (1984). *Principles of psychoanalytic psychotherapy: A manual for supportive/expressive treatment.* New York: Basic Books.

Luborsky, L., Barber, J. P., & Crits-Christoph, P. (1990). Theory-based research for understanding the process of dynamic psychotherapy. *Journal of Consulting and Clinical Psychology, 58,* 281–287.

Luborsky, L., Crits-Christoph, P., McLellan, A., Woody, G., Piper, W., and Associates. (1986). Do therapists vary much in their success? *American Journal of Orthopsychiatry, 56,* 501–512.

Luborsky, L., McLellan, T., Woody, G. F., O'Brien, C. P., & Auerbach, A. (1985). Therapist success and its determinants. *Archives of General Psychiatry, 42,* 602–611.

Ludgate, J., & Beck, J. (1990). *Staying well: Cognitive-behavioral strategies for maintenance and relapse prevention in depression and other disorders.* Workshop presented at the Association for the Advancement of Behavior Therapy convention, San Francisco, November.

Lunbeck, E. (1987). A new generation of women: Progressive psychiatrists and the hypersexual female. *Feminist Studies, 13,* 513–543.

Maddux, J. E. (1991). Self-efficacy. In C. R. Snyder and D. R. Forsyth (Eds.), *Handbook of social and clinical psychology* (pp. 57–78). New York: Pergamon.

Maher, B. A. (1982). Mandatory insurance coverage for psychotherapy: A tax on the subscriber and a subsidy to the practitioner. *The Clinical Psychologist, 35,* 9–12.

Maholick, L. T., & Turner, D. W. (1979). Termination: That difficult farewell. *American Journal of Psychotherapy, 33,* 583–591.

Mahoney, M. J. (1991). *Human change processes: The scientific foundations of psychotherapy.* New York: Basic Books.

Mahrer, A. R., & Gervaize, P. A. (1984). An integrative review of strong laughter in psychotherapy: What it is and how it works. *Psychotherapy, 21,* 510–516.

Mahrer, A. R., Lawson, K. C., Stalikas, A., & Schachter, H. M. (1990). Relationships between strength of feeling, type of therapy, and occurrence of in-session good moments. *Psychotherapy, 27,* 531–541.

Mahrer, A. R., & Nadler, W. P. (1986). Good moments in psychotherapy: A preliminary review, a list, and some promising research avenues. *Journal of Consulting and Clinical Psychology, 54,* 10–15.

Malett, S. D., Spokane, A. R., & Vance, F. L. (1978). Effects of vocationally relevant information on the expressed and measured interests of freshman males. *Journal of Counseling Psychology, 25,* 292–298.

Mann, J. (1973). *Time-limited psychotherapy.* Cambridge, MA: Harvard University Press.

Markus, H. (1977). Self-schemas and processing information about the self. *Journal of Personality and Social Psychology, 35,* 63–78.

Markus, H., & Cross, S. (1990). The interpersonal self. In L. A. Pervin (Ed.), *Handbook of personality: Theory and research* (pp. 576–608). New York: Guilford.

Markus, H., & Nurius, P. (1986). Possible selves. *American Psychologist, 41,* 954–969.

Marlatt, G. A., & Gordon, J. R. (1985). *Relapse prevention: Maintenance strategies in the treatment of addictive behaviors.* New York: Guilford.

Marmor, J. (1985). *The nature of the psychotherapeutic process.* Audiotape (L330-19) from The Evolution of Psychotherapy Conference, Phoenix, AZ. Phoenix, AZ: Milton Erickson Foundation.

Marmor, J. (1990). *The essence of dynamic psychotherapy: What makes it work?* Audiotape (C289-27) from The Evolution of Psychotherapy Conference, Anaheim, CA. Phoenix, AZ: Milton Erickson Foundation.

Marshall, G. N., Wortman, C. B., Kusulas, J. W., Hervig, L. K., & Vickers, R. R. (1992). Distinguishing optimism from pessimism: Relations to fundamental dimensions of mood and personality. *Journal of Personality and Social Psychology, 62,* 1067–1074.

Martin, E. S., & Schurtman, R. (1985). Termination anxiety as it affects the therapist. *Psychotherapy, 22,* 92–96.

Martin, J., & Stelmaczonek, K. (1988). Participants' identification and recall of important events in counseling. *Journal of Counseling Psychology, 35,* 385–390.

Martin, J., Cummings, A., & Hallberg, E. T. (1992). Therapists' intentional use of metaphor: Memorability, clinical impact, and possible epistemic/ motivational functions. *Journal of Consulting and Clinical Psychology, 60,* 143–145.

Marx, J. A., & Gelso, C. J. (1987). Termination of individual counseling in a university counseling center. *Journal of Counseling Psychology, 34,* 3–9.

Maslach, C., & Jackson, S. E. (1986). *Maslach Burnout Inventory Manual* (2nd ed.). Palo Alto, CA: Consulting Psychologists Press.

Masson, J. M. (1988). *Against therapy: Emotional tyranny and the myth of psychological healing.* New York: Atheneum.

Masters, W. H., & Johnson, V. E. (1975, May). *Principles of the new sex therapy.* Paper presented at the annual meeting of the American Psychiatric Association, Anaheim, CA.

Matarazzo, J. D. (1984). Behavioral immunogens. In B. L. Hammonds and C. J. Scheirer (Eds.), *Psychology and health* (pp. 9–43). Washington, DC: American Psychological Association.

Matarazzo, R. G., & Patterson, D. R. (1986). Methods of teaching therapeutic skill. In S. L. Garfield and A. E. Bergin (Eds.), *Handbook of psychotherapy and behavior change* (pp. 821–843). New York: Wiley.

Maultsby, R. C. (1984). *Rational behavior therapy.* Englewood Cliffs, NJ: Prentice-Hall.

McCarthy, P. R. (1982). Differential effects of counselor self-referent responses and counselor status. *Journal of Counseling Psychology, 29,* 125–131.

McCrae, R. R. (1984). Situational determinants of coping responses: Loss, threat, and challenge. *Journal of Personality and Social Psychology, 46,* 919–928.

McGuire, J. M., Toal, P., & Blau, B. (1985). The adult client's conception of confidentiality in the therapeutic relationship. *Professional Psychology: Research and Practice, 16,* 375–384.

McNamee, S., & Gergen, K. J. (Eds.). (1992). *Therapy as social construction.* Newbury Park, CA: Sage.

Medeiros, M. E., & Prochaska, J. O. (1988). Coping strategies that psychotherapists use in working with stressful clients. *Professional Psychology: Research and Practice, 19,* 112–114.

Megdell, J. I. (1984). Relationship between counselor-initiated humor and client's self-perceived attraction in the counseling interview. *Psychotherapy, 21,* 517–523.

Meichenbaum, D. (1986). Cognitive-behavior modification. *Three approaches to psychotherapy III.* Corona Del Mar, CA: Psychological and Educational Films.

Meichenbaum, D. (1990). *Cognitive-behavior modification*. Audiotape (C289-8) from the Evolution of Psychotherapy Conference, Anaheim, CA. Phoenix, AZ: The Milton Erickson Foundation.

Meichenbaum, D., & Turk, D. C. (1987). *Facilitating treatment adherence: A practitioner's guidebook*. New York: Plenum.

Menaker, E. (1990). Transference, countertransference, and therapeutic efficacy in relation to self-disclosure by the analyst. In G. Stricker and M. Fisher (Eds.), *Self-disclosure in the therapeutic relationship* (pp. 103–115). New York: Plenum.

Michels, R. (1983). Contemporary views of interpretation in psychoanalysis. In L. Grinspoon (Ed.), *Psychiatry update, VII*. Washington, DC: American Psychiatric Press.

Mikkelson, E. J., & Gutheil, T. G. (1979). Stages of forced termination: Uses of the death metaphor. *Psychiatric Quarterly, 51*, 15–27.

Miller, D. J., & Thelen, M. H. (1986). Knowledge and beliefs about confidentiality in psychotherapy. *Professional Psychology: Research and Practice, 17*, 15–19.

Miller, D. J., & Thelen, M. H. (1987). Confidentiality in psychotherapy: History, issues, and research. *Psychotherapy, 24*, 704–711.

Miller, L., & Berg, J. H. (1984). Selectivity and urgency in interpersonal exchange. In V. J. Derlega (Ed.), *Communication, intimacy, and close relationships* (pp. 161–205). Orlando, FL: Academic Press.

Miller, L., Berg, J. H., & Archer, R. L. (1983). Openers: Individuals who elicit intimate self-disclosure. *Journal of Personality and Social Psychology, 44*, 1234–1244.

Millon, T. (1975). Reflections on Rosenhan's "On Being Sane in Insane Places." *Journal of Abnormal Psychology, 84*, 456–461.

Millon, T. (1981). *Disorders of personality: DSM-III: Axis II*. New York: Wiley.

Minuchin, S. (1974). *Families and family therapy*. Cambridge, MA: Harvard University Press.

Mio, J. S., & Morris, D. R. (1990). Cross-cultural issues in psychology training programs: An invitation for discussion. *Professional Psychology: Research and Practice, 21*, 434–441.

Mirowsky, J. (1990). Subjective boundaries and combinations in psychiatric diagnoses. *The Journal of Mind and Behavior, 11*, 407–424.

Morrison, J. K. (1979). A consumer-oriented approach to psychotherapy. *Psychotherapy: Theory, Research and Practice, 16*, 381–384.

Moustakas, C. (1986). Being in, being for, and being with. *Humanistic Psychologist, 14*, 100–104.

Muehleman, T., Pickens, B. K., & Robinson, R. (1985). Informing clients about the limits to confidentiality, risks, and their rights: Is self-disclosure inhibited? *Professional Psychology: Research and Practice, 16*, 385–397.

Muran, J. C., & DiGiuseppe, R. A. (1990). Towards a cognitive formulation of metaphor use in psychotherapy. *Clinical Psychology Review, 10*, 69–85.

Murdock, N. L., & Altmaier, E. M. (1991). Attribution-based treatments. In C. R. Snyder and D. R. Forsyth (Eds.), *Handbook of social and clinical psychology* (pp. 563–578). New York: Pergamon.

Neimeyer, G. J., Banikiotes, P. G., & Winum, P. C. (1979). Self-disclosure flexibility and counseling-relevant perceptions. *Journal of Counseling Psychology, 26*, 546–548.

Neimeyer, G. J., & Fong, M. L. (1983). Self-disclosure flexibility and counselor effectiveness. *Journal of Counseling Psychology, 30,* 258–261.

Nietzel, M. T., Guthrie, P. R., & Susman, D. T. (1991). Utilization of community and social support resources. In F. H. Kanfer and A. P. Goldstein (Eds.), *Helping people change: A textbook of methods* (pp. 396–421). New York: Pergamon.

Nilsson, D. E., Strassberg, D. S., & Bannon, J. (1979). Perceptions of counselor self-disclosure: An analogue study. *Journal of Counseling Psychology, 26,* 399–404.

Norcross, J. C. (Ed.). (1986a). *Handbook of eclectic psychotherapy.* New York: Brunner/Mazel.

Norcross, J. C. (1986b). Eclectic psychotherapy: An introduction and overview. In J. C. Norcross (Ed.), *Handbook of eclectic psychotherapy* (pp. 3–24). New York: Brunner/Mazel.

Norcross, J. C., Alford, B. A., & DeMichele, J. T. (1992). The future of psychotherapy: Delphi data and concluding observations. *Psychotherapy, 29,* 150–158.

Norcross, J. C., & Prochaska, J. O. (1986a). Psychotherapist heal thyself—I. The psychological distress and self-change of psychologists, counselors, and laypersons. *Psychotherapy, 23,* 102–114.

Norcross, J. C., & Prochaska, J. O. (1986b). Psychotherapist heal thyself—II. The self-initiated and therapy-facilitated change of psychological distress. *Psychotherapy, 23,* 345–356.

O'Connell, D. S. (1984). Promise-of-treatment as an opening strategy for psychotherapy. *Psychotherapy, 21,* 473–478.

Okum, B. F. (1990). *Seeking connections in psychotherapy.* San Francisco: Jossey-Bass.

Omer, H. (1985). Fulfillment of therapeutic tasks as a precondition for acceptance in therapy. *American Journal of Psychotherapy, 39,* 175–186.

Omer, H. (1987). Therapeutic impact: A nonspecific major factor in directive psychotherapies. *Psychotherapy, 24,* 52–57.

Omer, H., & Alon, N. (1989). Principles of psychotherapeutic strategy. *Psychotherapy, 26,* 282–289.

Omer, H., & London, P. (1988). Metamorphosis in psychotherapy: End of the systems era. *Psychotherapy, 25,* 171–182.

Orlinsky, D. E., & Howard, K. I. (1977). The therapists' experience of psychotherapy. In A. S. Gurman and A. M. Razin (Eds.), *Effective psychotherapy: A handbook of research.* Oxford, England: Pergamon Press.

Orlinsky, D. E., & Howard, K. I. (1986). Process and outcome in psychotherapy. In S. L. Garfield and A. E. Bergin (Eds.), *Handbook of psychotherapy and behavior change* (3rd ed., pp. 311–381). New York: Wiley.

Orne, M. T., & Wender, P. H. (1968). Anticipatory socialization for psychotherapy. *American Psychologist, 124,* 1202–1211.

Otani, A. (1989). Client resistance in counseling: Its theoretical rationale and taxonomic classification. *Journal of Counseling and Development, 67,* 458–461.

Overholser, J. C., & Fine, M. A. (1990). Defining the boundaries of professional competence: Managing subtle cases of clinical incompetence. *Professional Psychology: Research and Practice, 21,* 462–469.

Parish, T. S., & Kappes, B. M. (1979). Affective implications of seeking psychological counseling. *Journal of Counseling Psychology, 26,* 164–165.

Patterson, C. H. (1984). Empathy, warmth, and genuineness in psychotherapy: A review of reviews. *Psychotherapy, 21,* 431–438.

Patterson, G. R., & Forgatch, M. S. (1985). Therapist behavior as a determinant for client noncompliance: A paradox for the behavior modifier. *Journal of Consulting and Clinical Psychology, 53,* 846–851.

Paulhus, D. L., & Martin, C. L. (1988). Functional flexibility: A new conception of interpersonal flexibility. *Journal of Personality and Social Psychology, 55,* 88–101.

Pedersen, P. (1978). Four dimensions of cross-cultural skill in counselor training. *Personnel and Guidance Journal, 57,* 480–484.

Penn, L. S. (1990). When the therapist must leave: Forced termination of psychodynamic therapy. *Professional Psychology: Research and Practice, 21,* 379–384.

Pennebaker, J. W. (1989). Confession, inhibition, and disease. In L. Berkowitz (Ed.), *Advances in experimental social psychology* (Vol. 22, pp. 211–214). New York: Academic Press.

Pennebaker, J. W., Colder, M., & Sharp, L. K. (1990). Accelerating the coping process. *Journal of Personality and Social Psychology, 58,* 528–537.

Pennebaker, J. W., Hughes, C. F., & O'Heeron, C. (1987). The psychophysiology of confession: Linking inhibitory and psychosomatic processes. *Journal of Personality and Social Psychology, 52,* 781–793.

Pennebaker, J. W., Kiecolt-Glaser, J. K., & Glaser, R. (1988). Disclosure of traumas and immune function: Health implications for psychotherapy. *Journal of Personality and Social Psychology, 56,* 239–245.

Pennebaker, J. W., & O'Heeron, R. C. (1984). Confiding in others and illness rate among spouses of suicide and accidental death victims. *Journal of Abnormal Psychology, 93,* 473–476.

Pennebaker, J. W., & Susman, J. R. (1988). Disclosure of traumas and psychosomatic processes. *Social Science and Medicine, 26,* 327–332.

Persons, J. B. (1986). The advantages of studying psychological phenomena rather than psychiatric diagnoses. *American Psychologist, 41,* 1252–1260.

Peterson, C. (1988). Explanatory style as a risk factor for illness. *Cognitive Therapy and Research, 12,* 119–132.

Peterson, C., & Barrett, L. C. (1987). Explanatory style and academic performance among university freshmen. *Journal of Personality and Social Psychology, 53,* 603–607.

Peterson, C., & Seligman, M. E. P. (1987). Explanatory style and illness. *Journal of Personality, 55,* 237–265.

Peterson, C., Seligman, M. E. P., & Vaillant, G. E. (1988). Pessimistic explanatory style is a risk factor for physical illness: A thirty-five-year longitudinal study. *Journal of Personality and Social Psychology, 55,* 23–27.

Peterson, C., Semmel, A., Baeyer, C., Abramson, L. Y., Metalsky, G. I., & Seligman, M. E. P. (1982). The attributional style questionnaire. *Cognitive Therapy and Research, 6,* 287–300.

Peterson, C., & Villanova, P. (1988). An expanded attributional style questionnaire. *Journal of Abnormal Psychology, 97,* 87–89.

Pillow, D. R., West, S. G., & Reich, J. W. (1991). Attributional style in relation to self-esteem and depression: Mediational and interactive models. *Journal of Research in Personality, 25,* 57–69.

Pipes, R. B., & Davenport, D. S. (1990). *Introduction to psychotherapy: Common clinical wisdom.* Englewood Cliffs, NJ: Prentice-Hall.

Polster, M. (1990). *Therapeutic uses of humor.* Audiotape (C289-P10) from the Evolution of Psychotherapy Conference, Anaheim, CA. Phoenix, AZ: Milton Erickson Foundation.

Pope, K. S. (1985). The suicidal client: Guidelines for assessment and treatment. *California State Psychologist, 20(2),* 3–5.

Pope, K. S. (1988). How clients are harmed by sexual contact with mental health professionals. *Journal of Counseling and Development, 67,* 222–226.

Pope, K. S. (1990a). Therapist-patient sex and sex abuse: Six scientific, professional, and practical dilemmas in addressing victimization and rehabilitation. *Professional Psychology: Research and Practice, 21,* 227–239.

Pope, K. S. (1990b). Therapist-patients sexual involvement: A review of the research. *Clinical Psychology Review, 10,* 477–490.

Pope, K. S., & Bouhoutsos, J. C. (1986). *Sexual intimacies between therapists and patients.* New York: Praeger.

Pope, K. S., Keith-Spiegel, P. C., & Tabachnick, B. (1986). Sexual attraction to clients: The human therapist and the (sometimes) inhuman training system. *American Psychologist, 41,* 147–158.

Pope, K. S., Tabachnick, B., & Keith-Spiegel, P. (1987). Ethics of practice: The beliefs and behaviors of psychologists as therapists. *American Psychologist, 42,* 993–1006.

Pope, K. S., Tabachnick, B., & Keith-Spiegel, P. (1988). Good and poor practice in psychotherapy: National survey of beliefs of psychologists. *Professional Psychology: Research and Practice, 19,* 547–552.

Pope, K. S., & Vetter, V. A. (1991). Prior therapist-patient sexual involvement among patients seen by psychologists. *Psychotherapy, 28,* 429–438.

Posey, C. (1988). Confidentiality in an AIDS support group. *Journal of Counseling and Development, 66,* 226–227.

Purvis, J. A., Dabbs, J. M., & Hopper, C. (1984). The "Opener": Skilled user of facial expression and speech pattern. *Personality and Social Psychology Bulletin, 10,* 60–66.

Raimy, V. C. (1975). *Misunderstandings of the self.* San Francisco: Jossey-Bass.

Rapee, R. (1987). The psychological treatment of panic attacks: Theoretical conceptualization and review of evidence. *Clinical Psychology Review, 7,* 427–438.

Raskin, D., & Klein, Z. (1976). Losing a symptom through keeping it: A review of paradoxical treatment techniques. *Archives of General Psychiatry, 33,* 548–555.

Raskin, N., & Rogers, C. R. (1989). Person-centered therapy. In R. Corsini and D. Wedding (Eds.), *Current psychotherapies* (4th ed.). Itasca, IL: Peacock.

Riebel, L. (1984). Paradoxical intention strategies: A review of rationales. *Psychotherapy, 21,* 260–272.

Robinson, D. N. (1984). Ethics and advocacy. *American Psychologist, 39,* 787–793.

Rogers, C. R. (1951). *Client-centered therapy.* Boston: Houghton Mifflin.

Rogers, C. R. (1957). The necessary and sufficient conditions of therapeutic change. *Journal of Consulting Psychology, 21,* 95–103.

Rogers, C. R. (1961). *On becoming a person.* Boston: Houghton Mifflin.

Rogers, C. R. (1962). The interpersonal relationship: The core of guidance. In C. R. Rogers and B. Stevens (Eds.), *Person to person* (pp. 91–92). Lafayette, CA: Real People Press.

Rogers, C. R. (1977). *Carl Rogers on personal power: Inner strength and its revolutionary impact.* New York: Delacorte Press.

Rohrbaugh, M., Tennen, H., Press, S., & White, L. (1981). Compliance, defiance and therapeutic paradox: Guidelines for strategic use of paradoxical interventions. *American Journal of Orthopsychiatry, 51,* 454–467.

Rosenbaum, M. (1990). The role of learned resourcefulness in the self-control of health behavior. In M. Rosenbaum (Ed.), *Learned resourcefulness: On coping skills, self-control, and adaptive behavior* (pp. 3–30). New York: Springer.

Rosenbaum, R. L., & Horowitz, M. J. (1983). Motivation for psychotherapy: A factorial and conceptual analysis. *Psychotherapy: Theory, Research and Practice, 20,* 346–354.

Rosenhan, D. L. (1973). On being sane in insane places. *Science, 179,* 250–258.

Rosenhan, D. L. (1975). The contextual nature of psychiatric diagnosis. *Journal of Abnormal Psychology, 84,* 462–474.

Rosenthal, T. L., & Steffek, B. D. (1991). Modeling methods. In F. H. Kanfer and A. P. Goldstein (Eds.), *Helping people change* (pp. 70–121). New York: Pergamon.

Ross, R. R., Altmaier, E. M., & Russell, D. W. (1989). Job stress, social support, and burnout among counseling center staff. *Journal of Counseling Psychology, 36,* 464–470.

Roth, S. R. (1987). *Psychotherapy: The art of wooing nature.* Northvale, NJ: Aronson.

Sackeim, H. A. (1983). Self-deception, self-esteem, and depression: The adaptive value of lying to oneself. In J. Masling (Ed.), *Empirical studies of psychoanalytic theory* (pp. 101–157). Hillsdale, NJ: Erlbaum.

Saenger, C. (1987). Sexologists in quandary over AIDS confidentiality issues. *Sexuality Today, 10(42),* 1–2.

Safran, J. D. (1990a). Towards a refinement of cognitive therapy in light of interpersonal theory: I. Theory. *Clinical Psychology Review, 10,* 87–105.

Safran, J. D. (1990b). Towards a refinement of cognitive therapy in light of interpersonal theory: II. Practice. *Clinical Psychology Review, 10,* 107–121.

Safran, J. D., & Segal, Z. V. (1990). *Interpersonal processes in cognitive therapy.* New York: Basic Books.

Salovey, P., & Turk, D. C. (1991). Clinical judgment and decision-making. In C. R. Snyder and D. R. Forsyth (Eds.), *Handbook of social and clinical psychology* (pp. 416–437). New York: Pergamon.

Saltzman, C., Luetgert, M. J., Roth, C. H., Creaser, J., & Howard, L. (1976). Formation of a therapeutic relationship: Experiences during the initial phase of psychotherapy as predictors of treatment duration and outcome. *Journal of Consulting and Clinical Psychology, 44,* 546–555.

Satir, V., Stachowiak, J., & Taschman, H. A. (1976). *Helping families to change.* New York: Jason Aronson.

Schafer, R. (1973). The termination of brief psychoanalytic therapy. *International Journal of Psychoanalytic Psychotherapy, 12,* 135–148.

Scheier, M. F., & Carver, C. S. (1985). Optimism, coping, and health: Assessment and implications of generalized outcome expectancies. *Health Psychology, 4,* 219–247.

Scheier, M. F., & Carver, C. S. (1987). Dispositional optimism and physical well-being: The influence of generalized outcome expectancies on health. *Journal of Personality, 55,* 169–210.

Scheier, M. F., Weintraub, J. K., & Carver, C. S. (1986). Coping with stress: Divergent strategies of optimists and pessimists. *Journal of Personality and Social Psychology, 51,* 1257–1264.

Schlenker, B. R. (1980). *Impression management: The self-concept, social identity, and interpersonal relations.* Pacific Grove, CA: Brooks/Cole.

Schlenker, B. R., Weigold, M. F., & Doherty, K. (1991). Coping with accountability: Self-identification and evaluative reckonings. In C. R. Snyder and D. R. Forsyth (Eds.), *Handbook of Social and Clinical Psychology* (pp. 96–115). New York: Pergamon.

Schofield, W. (1964). *Psychotherapy: The purchase of friendship.* Englewood Cliffs, NJ: Prentice-Hall.

Schwartz, W. (1979). Degradation, accreditation, and rites of passage. *Psychiatry, 42,* 138–146.

Schwebel, M., Skornia, J., & Schoener, G. (1987). *Development of programs to assist impaired psychologists: A manual for state psychological associations.* Washington, DC: American Psychological Association, Board of Professional Affairs Advisory Committee on Distressed Psychologists.

Scott, N. E., Borodovsky, L. G. (1990). Effective use of cultural role-taking. *Professional Psychology: Research and Practice, 21,* 167–170.

Seligman, L. (1990). *Selecting effective treatments.* San Francisco: Jossey-Bass.

Seligman, M. E. P. (1988, April). Boomer blues. *Psychology Today, 22,* 50–55.

Seligman, M. E. P. (1991). *Learned optimism.* New York: Alfred A. Knopf.

Sell, J. M., Gottlieb, M. C., & Schoenfeld, L. (1986). Ethical considerations of social/romantic relationships with present and former clients. *Professional Psychology: Research and Practice, 17,* 504–508.

Seltzer, L. F. (1986). *Paradoxical strategies in psychotherapy: A comprehensive overview and guidebook.* New York: Wiley.

Sesan, R. (1988). Sex bias and sex-role stereotyping in psychotherapy with women: Survey results. *Psychotherapy, 25,* 107–116.

Sharkin, B. S., & Birky, I. (1992). Incidental encounters between therapists and their clients. *Professional Psychology: Research and Practice, 23,* 326–328.

Sibicky, M., & Dovidio, J. F. (1986). Stigma of psychological therapy: Stereotypes, interpersonal reactions, and the self-fulfilling prophecy. *Journal of Counseling Psychology, 33,* 148–154.

Siegel, M. (1976). Confidentiality. *Clinical Psychologist* (Newsletter of Division 12 of the American Psychological Association), Fall, pp. 1–23.

Simonson, N. R., & Bahr, S. (1974). Self-disclosure by the professional and paraprofessional therapist. *Journal of Consulting and Clinical Psychology, 42,* 359–363.

Singer, E. (1970). *Key concepts in psychotherapy* (2nd ed.). New York: Basic Books.

Singer, J. L. (1974). *Imagery and daydream methods in psychotherapy and behavior modification.* New York: Academic Press.

Singer, J. L. (1980). The scientific basis of psychotherapeutic practice: A question of values and ethics. *Psychotherapy: Theory, Research and Practice, 17,* 372–383.

Singer, J. L., & Pope, K. S. (Eds.). (1978). *The power of human imagination.* New York: Plenum.

Slavney, P. R., & McHugh, P. R. (1987). *Psychiatric polarities: Methodology and practice.* Baltimore: Johns Hopkins University Press.

Smith, D. (1982). Trends in counseling and psychotherapy. *American Psychologist, 37,* 802–809.

Smith, D., & Kraft, W. A. (1983). DSM-III: Do psychologists really want an alternative? *American Psychologist, 38,* 777–785.

Smith, T. W., Pope, M. K., Rhodewalt, F., & Poulton, J. L. (1989). Optimism, neuroticism, coping, and symptom reports: An alternative interpretation of the Life Orientation Test. *Journal of Personality and Social Psychology, 56,* 640–648.

Snyder, C. R. (1977). "A patient by any other name" revisited: Maladjustment or attributional locus of problem? *Journal of Consulting and Clinical Psychology, 45,* 101–103.

Snyder, C. R. (1989). Reality negotiation: From excuses to hope and beyond. *Journal of Social and Clinical Psychology, 8,* 130–157.

Snyder, C. R. (1990). Self-handicapping processes and sequelae: On the taking of a psychological dive. In R. L. Higgins, C. R. Snyder, and S. Berglas (Eds.), *Self-handicapping: The paradox that isn't* (pp. 107–150). New York: Plenum.

Snyder, C. R., Irving, L. M., & Anderson, J. R. (1991). Hope and health. In C. R. Snyder & D. R. Forsyth (Eds.), *Handbook of social and clinical psychology* (pp. 285–305). New York: Pergamon.

Snyder, C. R., Shenkel, R. J., & Schmidt, A. (1976). Effects of role perspective and client psychiatric history on locus of problem. *Journal of Consulting and Clinical Psychology, 44,* 467–472.

Soisson, E. L., VandeCreek, L., & Knapp, S. (1987). Thorough record keeping: A good defense in a litigious era. *Professional Psychology: Research and Practice, 18,* 498–502.

Spitzer, R. L. (1975). On pseudoscience in science, logic in remission, and psychiatric diagnosis: A critique of Rosenhan's "On being sane in insane places." *Journal of Abnormal Psychology, 84,* 442–452.

Spitzer, R. L. (1976). More on pseudoscience in science and the case for psychiatric diagnosis. *Archives of General Psychiatry, 33,* 459–470.

Stake, J. E., & Oliver, J. (1991). Sexual contact and touching between therapist and client: A survey of psychologists' attitudes and behavior. *Professional Psychology: Research and Practice, 22,* 297–307.

Stiles, W. B. (1980). Measurement of the impact of psychotherapy sessions. *Journal of Consulting and Clinical Psychology, 48,* 176–185.

Stiles, W. B., Shapiro, D. A., & Elliott, R. (1986). "Are all psychotherapies equivalent?" *American Psychologist, 41,* 165–180.

Stricker, G. (1990). Self-disclosure and psychotherapy. In G. Stricker and M. Fisher (Eds.), *Self-disclosure in the therapeutic relationship* (pp. 277–289). New York: Plenum.

Strupp, H. H. (1970). Specific vs. nonspecific factors in psychotherapy and the problem of control. *Archives of General Psychiatry, 23,* 393–401.

Strupp, H. H. (1973). *Psychotherapy: Clinical, research, and theoretical issues.* New York: Aronson.

Strupp, H. H. (1980a). Humanism and psychotherapy: A personal statement of the therapist's essential values. *Psychotherapy: Research, Theory and Practice, 17,* 396–400.

Strupp, H. H. (1980b). Success and failure in time-limited psychotherapy: A systematic comparison of two cases. *Archives of General Psychiatry, 37,* 595–603.

Strupp, H. H. (1982). The outcome problem in psychotherapy: Contemporary perspectives. In J. H. Harvey and M. M. Parks (Eds.), *The master lecture series: Psychotherapy research and behavior change* (Vol. 1, pp. 43–71). Washington, DC: American Psychological Association.

Strupp, H. H. (1986). Psychotherapy: Research, practice, and public policy (how to avoid dead ends). *American Psychologist, 41,* 120–130.

Strupp, H. H. (1989). Psychotherapy: Can the practitioner learn from the researcher? *American Psychologist, 44,* 717–724.

Strupp, H. H. (1990). Time-limited psychotherapy. In J. K. Zeig and W. M. Munion (Eds.), *What is psychotherapy? Contemporary perspectives* (pp. 64–67). San Francisco: Jossey-Bass.

Strupp, H. H. (1992). The future of psychodynamic psychotherapy. *Psychotherapy, 29,* 21–27.

Strupp, H. H., & Binder, J. L. (1984). *Psychotherapy in a new key: A guide to time-limited dynamic psychotherapy.* New York: Basic Books.

Strupp, H. H., & Bloxom, A. L. (1973). Preparing lower class patients for group psychotherapy: Development and evaluation of a role-induction film. *Journal of Consulting and Clinical Psychology, 41,* 373–384.

Strupp, H. H., Hadley, S. W., & Gomes-Schwartz, B. (1977). *Psychotherapy for better or worse: The problem of negative effects.* New York: Jason Aronson.

Sue, D. W. (1990). Culture-specific strategies in counseling: A conceptual framework. *Professional Psychology: Research and Practice, 21,* 424–433.

Sue, D. W., Bernier, J. E., Durran, A., Feinberg, L., Pedersen, P., Smith, E. J., & Vasquez-Nuttall, E. (1982). Position paper: Cross-cultural counseling competence. *The Counseling Psychologist, 10,* 45–52.

Sue, S., & Zane, N. (1987). The role of culture and cultural techniques in psychotherapy. *American Psychologist, 42,* 37–45.

Suh, C. S., Strupp, H. H., & O'Malley, S. S. (1986). The Vanderbilt Process Measures: The Psychotherapy Process Scale (VPPS) and the Negative Indicators Scale (VNIS). In L. S. Greenberg and W. M. Pinsof (Eds.), *The psychotherapeutic process: A research handbook* (pp. 285–323). New York: Guilford.

Sullivan, H. S. (1940). *Conceptions of modern psychiatry.* New York: Norton.

Sullivan, H. S. (1953). *The interpersonal theory of psychiatry.* New York: Norton.

Sullivan, H. S. (1970). *The psychiatric interview.* New York: Norton.

Suls, J., & Fletcher, B. (1985). The relative efficacy of avoidant and nonavoidant coping strategies: A meta-analysis. *Health Psychology, 4,* 249–288.

Szasz, T. S. (1961). *The myth of mental illness: Foundations of a theory of personal conduct.* New York: Hoeber-Harper. (Rev. ed. New York: Harper & Row, 1974.)

Szasz, T. S. (1965). *The ethics of psychoanalysis.* New York: Basic Books.

Szasz, T. S. (1970). *The manufacture of madness: A comparative study of the Inquisition and the mental health movement.* New York: Delta.

Szasz, T. S. (1973). *The second sin.* Garden City, NY: Anchor Press.

Szasz, T. S. (1985a). *The myth of psychotherapy.* Audiotape (L330-W12AB) from the Evolution of Psychotherapy Conference, Phoenix, AZ. Phoenix, AZ: Milton Erickson Foundation.

Szasz, T. S. (1985b). *The role of the therapist/the role of the client.* Audiotape (L330-P12) from the Evolution of Psychotherapy Conference, Phoenix, AZ. Phoenix, AZ: Milton Erickson Foundation.

Szasz, T. S. (1986). The case against suicide prevention. *American Psychologist, 41,* 806–812.

Szasz, T. S. (1987). *Insanity: The idea and its consequences.* New York: Wiley.

Szasz, T. S. (1988). *The myth of psychotherapy: Mental health as religion, rhetoric, and repression.* Syracuse, NY: Syracuse University Press.

Szasz, T. S. (1990a). *Conversation hour.* Audiotape (C289-CH13) from the Evolution of Psychotherapy Conference, Anaheim, CA. Phoenix, AZ: Milton Erickson Foundation.

Szasz, T. S. (1990b). *Conversation with an officially denominated "schizophrenic" patient.* Audiotape (C289-W9B) from the Evolution of Psychotherapy Conference, Anaheim, CA. Phoenix, AZ: Milton Erickson Foundation.

Tarasoff v. Regents of the University of California, 17 Cal. 3d 425, 551 P.2d 334. (1976).

Taylor, S. E. (1989). *Positive illusions: Creative self-deception and the healthy mind.* New York: Basic Books.

Taylor, S. E., & Brown, J. D. (1988). Illusion and well-being: A social psychological perspective on mental health. *Psychological Bulletin, 103,* 193–210.

Temerlin, M. K. (1968). Suggestion effects in psychiatric diagnosis. *Journal of Nervous and Mental Disease, 147,* 349–353.

Tennen, H., Rohrbaugh, M., Press, S., & White, L. (1981). Reactance theory and therapeutic paradox: A compliance-defiance model. *Journal of Counseling Psychology, 18,* 14–22.

Teyber, E. (1992). *Interpersonal process in psychotherapy: A guide for clinical training.* Pacific Grove, CA: Brooks/Cole.

Thomas, A., & Sillen, S. (1972). *Racism and psychiatry.* New York: Brunner/Mazel.

Thomason, T. C. (1991). Counseling Native Americans: An introduction for non-Native American counselors. *Journal of Counseling and Development, 69,* 321–327.

Thompson, S. C. (1991). Intervening to enhance perceptions of control. In C. R. Snyder and D. R. Forysth (Eds.), *Handbook of social and clinical psychology* (pp. 607–623). New York: Pergamon.

Tichenor, V., & Hill, C. E. (1989). A comparison of six measures of working alliance. *Psychotherapy, 26,* 195–199.

Tomm, K. (1988). Interventive interviewing: Part III. Intending to ask lineal, circular, strategic, or reflexive questions? *Family Process, 27,* 1–15.

Tracey, T. J., & Dundon, M. (1988). Role anticipation and preferences over the course of counseling. *Journal of Counseling Psychology, 35,* 3–14.

Truax, C. B. (1966). Reinforcement and nonreinforcement in Rogerian psychotherapy. *Journal of Abnormal Psychology, 71,* 1–9.

Truax, C. B., & Carkhuff, R. R. (1967). *Toward effective counseling and psychotherapy.* Chicago: Aldine.

Truax, C. B., & Wargo, D. G. (1969). Effects of vicarious therapy pre-training and alternate sessions on outcome in group psychotherapy with outpatients. *Journal of Consulting and Clinical Psychology, 33,* 440–447.

Tryon, G. S. (1983). The pleasures and displeasures of full-time private practice. *Clinical Psychologist, 36,* 45–48.

Tryon, G. S. (1986). Abuse of therapists by patients: A national survey. *Professional Psychology: Research and Practice, 17,* 357–363.

Turkat, D., & Meyer, V. (1982). The behavior-analytic approach. In P. L. Wachtel (Ed.), *Resistance* (pp. 157–184). New York: Plenum.

Ventis, W. L. (1987). Humor and laughter in behavior therapy. In W. F. Fry and W. A. Salameh (Eds.), *Handbook of humor and psychotherapy* (pp. 149–169). Sarasota, FL: Professional Resource Exchange.

Wachtel, P. L. (1977). *Psychoanalysis and behavior therapy: Toward an integration.* New York: Basic Books.

Wade, P., & Bernstein, B. L. (1991). Culture sensitivity training and counselor's race: Effects on black female clients' perceptions and attrition. *Journal of Counseling Psychology, 38,* 9–15.

Walfish, S., Moritz, J. L., & Stenmark, D. E. (1991). A longitudinal study of the career satisfaction of clinical psychologists. *Professional Psychology: Research and Practice, 21,* 253–255.

Walfish, S., Polifka, J. A., & Stenmark, D. E. (1985). Career satisfaction in clinical psychology: A survey of recent graduates. *Professional Psychology: Research and Practice, 16,* 576–580.

Ward, D. E. (1984). Termination of individual counseling: Concepts and strategies. *Journal of Counseling and Development, 63,* 21–25.

Warren, R. C., & Rice, L. N. (1972). Structuring and stabilizing of psychotherapy for low-prognosis clients. *Journal of Consulting and Clinical Psychology, 39,* 173–181.

Waterhouse, G. J., & Strupp, H. H. (1984). The patient-therapist relationship: Research from the psychodynamic perspective. *Clinical Psychology Review, 4,* 77–92.

Watson, D., & Clark, L. A. (1984). Negative affectivity: The disposition to experience aversive emotional states. *Psychological Bulletin, 96,* 465–490.

Watson, D., & Tellegen, A. (1985). Toward a consensual structure of mood. *Psychological Bulletin, 98,* 219–235.

Watzlawick, P. (1978). *The language of change: Elements of therapeutic interaction.* New York: Basic Books.

Watzlawick, P. (1985). *If you desire to see, learn how to act.* Audiotape (L330-7) from the Evolution of Psychotherapy Conference, Phoenix, AZ. Phoenix, AZ: Milton Erickson Foundation.

Watzlawick, P. (1988). *Ultra-solutions.* New York: Norton.

Watzlawick, P. (1990a). *Conversation hour.* Audiotape (C289-CH9) from the Evolution of Psychotherapy Conference, Anaheim, CA. Phoenix, AZ: Milton Erickson Foundation.

Watzlawick, P. (1990b). *Psychotherapy of "as if."* Audiotape (C289-W2AB) from the Evolution of Psychotherapy Conference, Anaheim, CA. Phoenix, AZ: Milton Erickson Foundation.

Watzlawick, P. (1990c). *The construction of therapeutic realities.* Audiotape (C289-12) from the Evolution of Psychotherapy Conference, Anaheim, CA. Phoenix, AZ: Milton Erickson Foundation.

Watzlawick, P., Weakland, J. H., & Fisch, R. (1974). *Change: Principles of problem formation and problem resolution.* New York: Norton.

Weddington, W. W., & Cavenar, J. O. (1979). Termination initiated by the therapist: A countertransference storm. *American Journal of Psychiatry, 136,* 1302–1305.

Weeks, G. R. (1977). Toward a dialectical approach to intervention. *Human Development, 20,* 277–292.

Weeks, G. R., & L'Abate, L. (1982). *Paradoxical psychotherapy: Theory and practice with individuals, couples, and families.* New York: Brunner/Mazel.

Weigert, E. (1952). Contributions to the problem of terminating psychoanalysis. *Psychoanalytic Quarterly, 21,* 465–480.

Weinberger, D. A., Schwartz, G. E., & Davidson, R. J. (1979). Low-anxious, high-anxious, and repressive coping styles: Psychometric patterns and behavioral and physiological responses to stress. *Journal of Abnormal Psychology, 88,* 369–380.

Weiner, I. B. (1975). *Principles of psychotherapy.* New York: Wiley.

Weisskopf-Joelson, E. (1980). Values: The *enfant terrible* of psychotherapy. *Psychotherapy: Theory, Research and Practice, 17,* 459–466.

Whitaker, C. A., & Keith, D. V. (1981). Symbolic-experiential family therapy. In A. S. Gurman & D. P. Kniskern (Eds.), *Handbook of family therapy* (pp. 187–225). New York: Brunner/Mazel.

Whitman, R. M., Armao, B. B., & Dent, O. B. (1976). Assaults on the therapist. *American Journal of Psychiatry, 133,* 426–429.

Widiger, T. A., & Rinaldi, M. (1983). An acceptance of suicide. *Psychotherapy: Theory, Research, and Practice, 20,* 263–273.

Wiedenfeld, S. A., O'Leary, A., Bandura, A., Brown, S., Levine, S., & Raska, K. (1990). Impact of perceived self-efficacy in coping with stressors on components of the immune system. *Journal of Personality and Social Psychology, 59,* 1082–1094.

Wiener, M., Budney, S., Wood, L., & Russell, R. L. (1989). Nonverbal events in psychotherapy. *Clinical Psychology Review, 9,* 487–504.

Wiener, M., & Mehrabian, A. (1968). *Language within language: Immediacy, a channel in verbal communication.* New York: Appleton-Century-Crofts.

Willison, B. G., & Masson, R. L. (1986). The role of touch in therapy: An adjunct to communication. *Journal of Counseling and Development, 64,* 497–500.

Wills, T. A. (1981). Downward comparison principles in social psychology. *Psychological Bulletin, 90,* 245–271.

Wills, T. A. (1987a). Downward comparison as a coping mechanism. In C. R. Snyder and C. E. Ford (Eds.), *Coping with negative life events* (pp. 234–268). New York: Plenum.

Wills, T. A. (1987b). Help-seeking as a coping mechanism. In C. R. Snyder and C. E. Ford (Eds.), *Coping with negative life events* (pp. 19–50). New York: Plenum.

Wills, T. A., & DePaulo, B. M. (1991). Interpersonal analysis of the help-seeking process. In C. R. Snyder and D. R. Forysth (Eds.), *Handbook of social and clinical psychology* (pp. 350–375). New York: Pergamon.

Wilson, D. O. (1985). The effects of systematic client preparation, severity, and treatment setting on dropout rate in short-term psychotherapy. *Journal of Social and Clinical Psychology, 3,* 62–70.

Wilson, M. N., & Rappaport, J. (1974). Personal self-disclosure: Expectancy and situational effects. *Journal of Consulting and Clinical Psychology, 42,* 901–908.

Windholz, M. J., & Silberschatz, G. (1988). Vanderbilt Psychotherapy Process Scale: A replication with adult outpatients. *Journal of Consulting and Clinical Psychology, 56,* 56–60.

Wood, B. J., Klein, S., Cross, H. J., Lammers, C. J., & Elliott, J. K. (1985). Impaired practitioners: Psychologists' opinions about prevalence, and proposals for intervention. *Professional Psychology: Research and Practice, 16,* 843–850.

Wright, B. A. (1991). Labeling: The need for greater person-environment individuation. In C. R. Snyder and D. R. Forysth (Eds.), *Handbook of social and clinical psychology* (pp. 469–487). New York: Pergamon.

Wubbolding, R. E. (1988). Signs and myths surrounding suiciding behaviors. *Journal of Reality Therapy, 8,* 18–21.

Yalom, I. D. (1980). *Existential psychotherapy.* New York: Basic Books.

Yalom, I. D. (1985). *The theory and practice of group psychotherapy* (3rd ed.). New York: Basic Books.

Young, J. E. (1989). *Schema-focused cognitive therapy for personality disorders and difficult patients.* Sarasota, FL: Professional Resource Exchange.

Zeig, J. (1985). *Resistance.* Audiotape (L330-P10) from the Evolution of Psychotherapy Conference, Phoenix, AZ. Phoenix, AZ: Milton Erickson Foundation.

Index

TO THE OWNER OF THIS BOOK:

We hope that you have found *Common Principles of Psychotherapy* useful. So that this book can be improved in a future edition, would you take the time to complete this sheet and return it? Thank you.

School and address: _____

Department: _____

Instructor's name: _____

1. What I like most about this book is: _____

_____

2. What I like least about this book is: _____

_____

3. My general reaction to this book is: _____

_____

4. The name of the course in which I used this book is: _____

_____

5. Were all of the chapters of the book assigned for you to read? _____

   If not, which ones weren't? _____

_____

6. In the space below, or on a separate sheet of paper, please write specific suggestions for improving this book and anything else you'd care to share about your experience in using the book.

_____

_____

_____

_____

_____

_____

Optional:

Your name: _____ Date: _____

May Brooks/Cole quote you either in promotion for *Common Principles of Psychotherapy* or in future publishing ventures?

Yes: _____ No: _____

Sincerely,

Chris L. Kleinke

FOLD HERE

FOLD HERE

Brooks/Cole is dedicated to publishing quality publications for education in the human services fields. If you are interested in learning more about our publications, please fill in your name and address and request our latest catalogue.

Name: _____

Street Address: _____

City, State, and Zip: _____

FOLD HERE

NO POSTAGE
NECESSARY
IF MAILED
IN THE
UNITED STATES

BUSINESS REPLY MAIL
FIRST CLASS   PERMIT NO. 358   PACIFIC GROVE, CA

POSTAGE WILL BE PAID BY ADDRESSEE

ATT: *Human Services Catalogue*

Brooks/Cole Publishing Company
511 Forest Lodge Road
Pacific Grove, California 93950-9968

FOLD HERE